HULA

HISTORICAL PERSPECTIVES

Dorothy B. Barrère, Mary Kawena Pukui, and Marion Kelly

An exposition of the hula as described and depicted from the period of first European contact to modern times, including: the hula in myths and legends, with particular attention to Hi'iaka; records of performances in the 18th and 19th centuries, with contemporary illustrations; essays by Mary Kawena Pukui, with texts of ancient chants and descriptions of early 20th century performances; an assessment of the Kē'ē sites, traditionally associated with hula, and of their use by present-day performing groups on Kaua'i, the island that receives considerable emphasis in this volume.

January 1980

Pacific Anthropological Records Number 30

Department of Anthropology
Bernice Pauahi Bishop Museum
Honolulu, Hawai'i

Library of Congress Catalog Card No. 79-56806
ISBN 0-930897-89-7
ISSN 0078-740X

6 7 8 98 99 00 01

TABLE OF CONTENTS

	Page
PREFACE	v
ACKNOWLEDGEMENTS	vii
PART I. THE *HULA* IN RETROSPECT by Dorothy B. Barrère	1
Introduction	1
The *Hula* in Hawaiian Legends	4
Pele and Hi'iaka	4
The Legend of Kapo-'ula-kīnau	8
The Legend of La'a-mai-kahiki	11
The *Hula* and *Oli* in Legends	12
Notes on *Hula* in Prehistoric Times	13
Historical Accounts of the 18th Century	15
Historical Accounts of the 19th Century	22
1800-1820: Early *Hula* Accounts	22
1820-1830: *Hula* for the *Ali'i*	26
1830-1850: The Decline Begins	36
1850-1870: The Regulation of Public Display	41
1860-1880: Expression of Disapprobation by Hawaiians	43
1875-1900 The *Hula* Revival	49
The "Unwritten Literature of Hawaii"	56
Goddesses of the *Hula*	56
The *Kuahu* Altar	57
Training	58
Graduation	60
Costumes	61
Mele and Types of *Hula*	61
Religious Aspects of *Hula*	63
1910-1930: The *Hula* "Goes Modern"	64
PART II. NOTES FROM A *KUMU HULA*. Selected Articles by Mary Kawena Pukui	69
Introduction	69
"The Hula, Hawaii's Own Dance" (1942)	70
"Ancient Hulas of Kauai" (1936)	74
"The Hula" (1943)	90
PART III. *HĀLAU HULA* AND ADJACENT SITES AT KĒ'Ē, KAUA'I by Marion Kelly	95
Introduction	95
Traditions Collected in 1845	96
Site Names Recorded	99
The Sites	101
Kilioe, *Pōhaku Piko*	101
The House Terrace of Lohi'au	103
Ka-ulu-a-Pā'oa Heiau	106
Ke-ahu-a-Laka, *Hālau Hula*	111
Firebrands (*'Ōahi*) of Makana	115
The *Hālau Hula* Today	117
General Condition	117
Hula Students Visit the *Hālau Hula* at Kē'ē	117
Students Dance at the *Hālau Hula*	118
An Advisory Council on the Kē'ē Sites	121
APPENDIX A. Extracts from "THE GODDESS PELE" by William Hyde Rice	123
B. "HIIAKA AND LOHIAU" by Thomas G. Thrum	127

TABLE OF CONTENTS (Cont'd.)

		Page
APPENDIX C.	Extracts from VANCOUVER'S JOURNAL, 1801	131
D.	LIST OF *HULA* AT THE CORONATION OF KING KALĀKAUA	133
E.	"THE RUINS AT KĒ'Ē, HĀ'ENA" by Kenneth P. Emory	141
GLOSSARY OF HAWAIIAN WORDS		149
LITERATURE CITED		153

LIST OF ILLUSTRATIONS

Figure		Page
1	Onaona (courtesy of Boone Morrison)	3
2	"The Descent from the Cliffs" (illustration by J. M. Fraser for *Pele and Hiiaka*)	7
3	Hawaiian Man Dancing, Three Views (sketch by John Webber)	16
4	Male Dancers of the Sandwich Islands (Louis Choris, 1822)	24
5	Female Dancers of the Sandwich Islands (Louis Choris, 1822)	25
6	A *Hula* Performance at Kailua, Hawai'i, in 1823 (William Ellis)	32
7	"Scène de Danse aux Îles Sandwich" (Lauvergne)	37
8	*Hula* Dancers, c. 1858 (ambrotype; unknown photographer)	42
9	"Scène pris dans l'île d'Oahu (Îles Sandwich)" (J. Masselot)	44
10	Ioane, "Dandy Jim," with Performing Girls	51
11	*Hula* Dancing at Jubilee, 1886	53
12	*Hula* Dancing on the Grounds of 'Iolani Palace, 1886	54
13	*Hula* Puppets, Probably with Their Donor	55
14	*Hula* Dancers, c. 1897-1901 (Frank Davey, photographer)	65
15	*Hula* Dancer, c. 1925 (postcard)	67
16	Map of the Hawaiian Islands, with Location of Kē'ē Area on Kaua'i	95
17	Map Showing Approximate Relative Positions of Kē'ē Sites	96
18	Kilioe, *Pōhaku Piko* at Kē'ē	102
19	Retaining Wall of House Platform of Lohi'au (1927)	104
20	Ka-ulu-a-Pā'oa Heiau (1927)	107
21	Looking *Makai* at the Lower Terrace of Ka-ulu-a-Pā'oa Heiau (1952)	108
22	Ka-ulu-a-Pā'oa Heiau (1927)	109
23	Main Terrace of Ka-ulu-a-Pā'oa Heiau (1927)	109
24	Ka-ulu-a-Pā'oa Heiau and *Hālau Hula* (drawing by Henry K. Kekahuna, 1959)	110
25	Cairn on Ka-ulu-a-Pā'oa Heiau (1977)	112
26	Offerings in Crevices of Cliff Above Ke-ahu-a-Laka (1927)	113
27	Offerings Placed in Crevices in Cliff Behind Structure Identified with Laka (1977)	113
28	Dancers from the Hālau Hula Kahiko Halapa'i Hula Alapa'i Perform on the *Hālau Hula* Platform at Kē'ē (1978)	119
29	Dancers from the Hālau Hula Kahiko Halapa'i Hula Alapa'i Place Their Offerings to Laka at the *Hālau Hula* (1978)	120

PREFACE

The basis for this volume of Pacific Anthropological Records is a report prepared for the Division of State Parks, Department of Land and Natural Resources, State of Hawai'i, in connection with the planning for the Hā'ena State Park. The primary objectives of this report were to provide information relating to:

(1) *hula* rituals, including, but not limited to those connected with structures located in the Hā'ena State Park, and

(2) legends and myths connected with the Park area, particularly the Pele-Hi'iaka epic having to do with the Hā'ena area.

The three papers by Dr. Mary Kawena Pukui, yielding much of the information regarding the *hula* as it relates to Kaua'i, were included in the original report as appendixes. Here, they have been transferred to a central position in the volume. The historical review by Dorothy Barrère has been revised and expanded. Marion Kelly's work on the Kē'ē structures now includes an account of their modern use by serious students of the *hula*; this new material stems from field trips, additional to visits that produced the original description of the physical environment, and the results of interviews with persons familiar with the structures.

Obviously, the geographic emphasis of this volume is on Kaua'i, although there are references to the other Hawaiian Islands. It is hoped, however, that this will encourage the proliferation of such research, to fill out our knowledge of other sites with traditional connections with the dance of ancient Hawai'i. Perhaps as important, the wider circulation of this publication may help to further increase the general, non-specialist awareness of the significance of the *hula*--certainly beyond the interpretations usually available to the casual visitor.

Editorial Note: Diacritical marks (glottal stops and macrons) are used in Hawaiian words and names of persons and places in the text, e.g., Hi'iaka , Kē'ē, except in direct quotations, where the respective authors' word forms are preserved.

ACKNOWLEDGEMENTS

We wish to thank Eleanor Williamson for her assistance in reviewing the *hula* materials in Bishop Museum collections. Kenneth Emory freely made available his early field notes, correspondence, and published reports. Staff of the Hawaiian Historical Society Library, the Hawaiian Mission Children's Society Library, the Bishop Museum Photo Archives, and the Bishop Museum Library rendered much assistance with texts and illustrations.

For permission to republish the articles of Mary Kawena Pukui and others, we gratefully acknowledge: S B Printers, Inc., Honolulu, publishers of *All About Hawaii*, the present-day successor to Thrum's *The Hawaiian Annual*; the California Folklore Society, Los Angeles, and the University of California Press at Berkeley; and *The Garden Island* newspaper on Kaua'i. Specific references may be found in the text.

Special thanks must go to Catherine Stauder, Curator of the Kaua'i Museum, who was kind enough to check the records of the Kaua'i Historical Society for references to the sites at Kē'ē, and who furnished copies of Dr. Emory's report to the Society on his field trip to the area in 1927, as well as her unpublished historical sketch of the Hā'ena area and notes on historical references researched by her.

Appreciation is given to Roselle Bailey of Ka 'Imi Na'auao o Hawai'i Nei, Ku'ulei Punua of Hula Hālau o Ku'ulei Punua, Ivy Nishimoto of Hanalei, and Juliet Rice Wichman of Līhu'e and Hā'ena, for generously providing the time to share their experiences and thoughts on the subject of the *hula*, the Kē'ē sites, and the modern use and management of these vestiges of Hawaiian culture. Without their contributions this account would not have been complete. In addition, thanks go to the members of the Hālau Hula Kahiko Halapa'i Hula Alapa'i for permission to use two photographs of them taken at the Kē'ē site by Boone Morrison of Volcano, Hawai'i. We also thank Mr. Morrison for providing the photograph that appears at the beginning of the volume.

Mary Kawena Pukui is justifiedly named as an author of this volume for the reprinting of her articles on *hula* that are to become--if they are not already--classics in their field. We view this publication as a further tribute to her incalculable contributions to knowledge of Hawaiian culture.

We acknowledge with gratitude the generous gift of Dr. E. Alison Kay toward the cost of publication of this volume.

Dorothy B. Barrère
Marion Kelly

December 1979

PART I

THE HULA IN RETROSPECT

by
Dorothy B. Barrère

Introduction

This article is primarily a collection of descriptions and comments made on the *hula* over a span of 200 years. It is aimed at providing a historical perspective from which to view the role of the *hula* in the Hawaiian society, and does not describe the dances themselves, nor the chants that inspired them.

An attempt to document any rituals associated with the *hula* in ancient--that is to say prehistoric, or pre-1778--Hawai'i is impossible. What may remain today of any older rituals is based on late-19th century training practices, and on chants and dances that survived the attempted extinction of the *hula* as an entertainment form in the earlier part of that century.

Calvinist missionaries from America arrived in Hawai'i in 1820, and as soon as they had secured the interest of the chiefs in their newly introduced *palapala*--reading, writing, and Scripture lessons--they attacked the *hula* as "heathen" and "lascivious," and made strong efforts to drive it out of the culture. At first these efforts were successful only to the extent that public performances of the *hula* became rare and finally disappeared in localities near mission stations and the domiciles of truly converted chiefs.

In 1830, the queen regent Ka'ahumanu, who had been accepted into the church in December of 1825, issued an edict forbidding public performances of the *hula*. After her death in 1832, some chiefs ignored this edict, and for the period of 1833-34, when moral constraints were openly flouted by the young king Kamehameha III and his companions, many of the common people followed suit. Early in 1835 the king conceded that his ways were wrong, and the kingdom returned to domination by Calvinist beliefs and concepts, at least outwardly. But away from the mission stations and the pious chiefs, the *hula* continued to be taught and practiced.

In 1851 public *hula* performances were finally brought under a measure of control through the requirement of licensing and payment of a fairly heavy fee for each performance, but private performances were not controlled so easily. Clandestine *hula* schools operated throughout the islands in the 1860s, much to the displeasure of many a Calvinist Hawaiian, as shown by letters to the newspapers of the period. While these letters imply that there were laws prohibiting such schools, no such laws have been found in the civil code of the period.

Also in the 1860s the rulers and chiefs of the kingdom openly reverted to the old custom of having *hula* people, *po'e hula*, available to provide entertainment, both at home and during their travels about the islands. There was thus a nucleus of *po'e hula* who kept the art alive, and from them have come the traditional 19th-century *hula* that some call "ancient" today.

Full re-acceptance of the *hula* as public entertainment came about in the reign of Kalākaua. For his coronation ceremonies in 1883, there had been months of training and keen excitement among the *hula* people in preparation for the public performance of all manner of *hula*--from those recalled from the past to those expressly created for that great day. Again in 1886, at the King's Jubilee celebrating Kalākaua's fiftieth birthday, there were numerous large public performances. Many of the *hula* danced today are revivals or revisions of those composed and performed during the Kalākaua years. They are sometimes included with the earlier 19th-century *hula* as "ancient *hula*."

It was during the Kalākaua years that Nathaniel B. Emerson, island-born and Hawaiian-speaking son of the Rev. John Emerson of Waialua, O'ahu, began his serious study of the Hawaiian *hula*. His work, *The Unwritten Literature of Hawaii: The Sacred Songs of the Hula*, was published by the Smithsonian Institution in 1909 and soon became the standard reference of authority on all *hula* matters. Emerson's viewpoint was overly idealistic, and he made such unqualified statements as, "The hula was a religious service" (1909:11), and "The ancient Hawaiians did not personally and informally indulge in this dance for their own amusement.... [They] left it to be done for them by a body of trained and paid performers" (Ibid.:13). Neither of these statements is borne out by the historical records, as we shall see. The descriptions of dances and instruments, *hula* training, and costuming gathered by Emerson during the Kalākaua period surely reflected traditional practices, however, as the training and preparations were carried on then in accordance with older ways. Thus, his work is invaluable to the present-day student of the *hula* and is a common source of material used extensively by the *hula* masters of today.

After the end of the monarchy, public performances of the *hula* again declined, and the few attempts early in the 20th century to revive it as public entertainment met with varying degrees of opposition, depending on viewpoints and arguments as to the "innocence" or "licentiousness" of the *hula* being performed. But the popularity of the *hula* as an entertainment form would not be denied, and by mid-century it was flourishing. To appeal to audience taste, many innovations were made both in song and dance forms. Originally danced to chants, now the *hula* were in the main performed to melodic songs. The lyrics of the songs, at best, followed the traditional pattern of containing inner meanings (*kaona*), a characteristic mark of excellence in Hawaiian poetry. At worst, they were merely vapid love songs, many with English words interspersed. Because most audiences did not understand Hawaiian, the words of the song became secondary to the motions of the dancers, a reversal of the traditional relative importance of song and movement.

As in the past, a few chanters, dancers, and teachers among the *po'e hula* kept alive the more traditional forms, and with the flowering of the "Hawaiian Renaissance in the 1970s their knowledge and dedication became a foundation for revitalizing the older forms. Today there are many *hula* masters reproducing the old dances as nearly as possible, or creating chants and dances after the traditional manner (Fig. 1). Sometimes their attempts result in extravagant and spectacular displays that are only reminiscent of the early descriptions. Some have introduced their own conceptions of the ancient *hula*.

Fig. 1. ONAONA. Photograph courtesy of Boone Morrison.

The Hula in Hawaiian Legends

PELE AND HI'IAKA

The Pele and Hi'iaka cycle of legends was published in more than one Hawaiian newspaper in the 19th century. The story was recited among the *hula* people, and chants taken from it became traditional in the observances of *hula* schools. From published sources and from informants among the *po'e hula*, N. B. Emerson translated and compiled what is probably the fullest and most often referred-to version of the story: *Pele and Hiiaka: A Myth from Hawaii* (1915). Martha Warren Beckwith included a lengthy synopsis of this book in *Hawaiian Mythology* (1940:173-177). The story as told by William Hyde Rice seems to reflect a Kaua'i version (see Appendix A). Two other short versions were collected and published in English early in the 20th century by Gorham Gilman (1908: 53-54; see Part III, p. 97) and Thomas Thrum (see Appendix B). In the main, the latter both follow the Emerson version, but Thrum's ending is quite different. Professor Rubellite Johnson of the University of Hawai'i has in preparation translations and a comparative study of two versions from early Hawaiian newspapers.

Katharine Luomala, foremost of our present-day folklorists, included a literary discussion of the Pele and Hi'iaka cycle in her *Voices on the Wind* (1955:34-40); the following passage is extracted from this work.

> The most outstanding Polynesian journey of song through an archipelago is that of the girl goddess, Hiiaka, who went on a mission for her older sister, the volcano goddess, Pele, and traveled from the southernmost to the northernmost of the Hawaiian Islands.
>
> ...Hiiaka's journey gives Hawaiian composers an unparalleled opportunity to pour into song their love of the islands and their keen observation of the changing weather and conditions of the landscape. Here, as everywhere in Polynesia, nature is believed to reflect the mood of the characters in the myths and traditions, as in real life; to communicate with them through omens; and to acknowledge the rank and beauty of highborn characters, male or female. Characters often communicate with each other through chants which outwardly describe the rain or the sun or the ocean but inwardly convey a personal message, usually intelligible only to the composer and the object of his devotion. Other chants carry on the action of the plot and may conveniently refer to geographical places, to the state of the weather, or to the aspect of the sea. But, in addition to these chants which have symbolic meaning, there are many which are intended only to protray nature. All this is true of the songs incorporated into Hiiaka's itinerary [Luomala 1955:34-35].

All versions of the Pele and Hi'iaka story follow a central theme picked up after Pele and her family had come to Hawai'i. They had made their way down the island chain from Kaua'i to Hawai'i while Pele sought a permanent home, and found none suitable until they arrived at Kīlauea Crater on Hawai'i. There they settled, at the volcano that has since been called *ka lua o Pele* or Pele's pit. In the version given by Rice, Pele met the chief Lohi'au when she was first on Kaua'i (see Appendix A, p. 123). In the version that Emerson compiled, during a protracted nap Pele's spirit left Kīlauea, traveled to Hā'ena, Kaua'i, and met Lohi'au at a *hālau hula*, or dance hall. Here her spirit appeared as a woman, and Pele entranced Lohi'au with her beauty and chanting. After spending three nights and days with Lohi'au without allowing him fulfillment of his passion, Pele returned to Hawai'i, promising to send for him. In grief at her departure, Lohi'au hanged himself with his *malo* (Emerson 1915:3-8).

Back on Hawai'i, Hi'iaka-i-ka-poli-o-Pele, the beloved youngest sister of Pele, was summoned when Pele showed no signs of awakening from her long sleep. Hi'iaka gave indication of her healing powers when she called the spirit of Pele back into the sleeping body (Emerson 1915:11-12). Some days later, Pele asked each of her sisters in turn to go to Kaua'i to fetch Lohi'au, whom she called "our lover," promising to give him over after having him to herself for five days and nights. The other sisters refused, but young Hi'iaka, in love and obedience to her older sister, agreed to go.

Exacting a promise from Pele not to destroy her *lehua* groves in Puna nor to harm her friend Hopoe, from whom she had learned the *hula* arts of chant and dance (Ibid.:18), Hi'iaka left to fetch the lover Lohi'au. On her departure from Kīlauea, Hi'iaka pronounced these words, which became the accepted formal Hawaiian expression of leave-taking: "*Ku au e hele; noho 'oe*"--"I rise to go; you remain." (The response, "*O hele*"--"Go," gives consent to the departure.) Emerson gives two versions of the song of Hi'iaka in which these words appear (Ibid.:15-16). Pele assigned Pā'ū-o-Pala'e to Hi'iaka as a travelling companion, and soon after they had started off, she sent her worshipper Wahine'ōma'o to join them (Ibid.:19, 26).* Pā'ū-o-Pala'e left them at Kohala (Ibid.:60), but Wahine'ōma'o continued on with Hi'iaka, completed the journey to Kaua'i, and returned to *ka lua o Pele* with her.

The journey to fetch the lover was long and perilous, but Hi'iaka overcame all difficulties with her powerful magic skirt, *pa'ū-o-palai*, and with the authority bestowed upon her by Pele to call for and receive the aid of the entire family of Pele gods. Her chants of greeting to persons and to personified hills and landmarks she met on the way are called *kau*. They are now called "sacred chants" (Pukui & Elbert 1971:124).

Upon the arrival of Hi'ika and Wahine'ōma'o at Hā'ena, Hi'iaka healed the lame chief Malae-ha'a-koa, who was also a seer and who divined that Hi'iaka was of the Pele family. He ordered a feast to be prepared for the two women, and at its close he and his wife Wailua-nui-a-ho'āno "stood forth and led in the performance of a sacred dance, accompanying their rhythmic motions with a long mele that recited the deeds, the events, the mysteries that had marked Pele's reign since the establishment of her dominion in Hawaii" (Emerson 1915:111-112). This long poem appears in full with Emerson's translation in *Pele and Hiiaka* (Ibid.:112-130), and the same poem, presumably translated by Fornander, is found in the Fornander collection of folklore (1916-20: 6[3]:492-498).

The day after this long *hula* performance, Hi'iaka learned from Malae-ha'a-koa that Lohi'au was dead, and asked to be taken to his body. On the way she saw the spirit of Lohi'au hovering

---

*In the names Pā'ū-o-Pala'e and Wahine'ōma'o are personifications of plant forms. Pā'ū-o-Pala'e is the *pala'ā* or lace fern (*Stenomeris chusana*) (Pukui & Elbert 1971:282, 283, 296). As Hi'iaka became an *'aumakua* or ancestral god of healers, so the *pala'ā* fern became a remedy in their hands, and they used it to treat female disorders (Neal 1965:15). *Wahine'ōma'o* is the vine variously called *mohihihi*, *nanea*, or *pūhilihili* (*Vigna marina*).

In her synopsis of Emerson's book, Beckwith gives the name Pā'ū-o-palai (1940:143). The *palai* fern (*Microlepia setosa*) is a lacy fern similar to the *pala'ā*. The earlier spelling, that of Emerson, reads "Pau-o-pala'e (or Pau-o-palaa)" (1915:19). It also appears as *pala'e* in Thrum's version (see Appendix B). There is no question that in the original it was the *pala'ā* and not the *palai* fern meant in the name. The *palai* fern represented Hi'iaka herself in the *hālau hula*. Her magic skirt, or *pa'ū*, is said to have been made of the *palai* fern.

over a cliff. After an exchange of chants between Hi'iaka and the spirit, Hi'iaka requested Malae-ha'a-koa to keep the *hula* going for the next ten days "as an attraction to draw off the people from playing the spy on her performances" (Emerson 1915:138). She and Wahine'ōma'o then prepared to ascend the cliff to the place where the spirit of Lohi'au lingered, outside the cave in which his body had been secreted by two *mo'o* women, Kilioe and Ka-lana-mai-nu'u (Ibid.:134). The day was ending, and Hi'iaka called upon the sun to pause at the stream of Hea (*E kau i ka muli o Hea*), that they might ascend the cliff in daylight. Reaching the cavern, Hi'iaka caught the spirit and forced it back into the body of Lohi'au--either through the big toe (see Appendix A, p. 125) or through the eye-socket (Emerson 1915:138).* This accomplished, the next task was to strengthen the weakened body. Now all the powers of healing that Hi'iaka possessed or could summon were called upon to restore its vigor. Prayer after prayer followed--prayers used by healing *kahuna* in generations to come--until Lohi'au was able to descend the cliff with her (Fig. 2).

Then began the journey back to Hawai'i with Lohi'au. On the way Hi'iaka saw in the cloud signs that Pele had broken her promise and had consumed not only her *lehua* groves in Puna but also her friend and teacher Hopoe (Ibid.:162-163). Hopoe was changed to stone, a stone that to this day dances in the sea of Nānāhuki at Hā'ena, Hawai'i.

There are several versions of the conclusion of the Pele and Hi'iaka story. In all, however, Hi'iaka takes Lohi'au back to *ka lua o Pele* where, in full sight of her elder sister, she makes love to him. In rage, Pele destroys Lohi'au, covering him with lava. But his spirit escapes, and eventually he and Hi'iaka meet again.

However told, the story of Pele and Hi'iaka is a stirring adventure, and its chants are an inspiration and a foundation for the *hula*, for the healing arts, and for literary composition. In the words of Luomala, "Hiiaka, because of what countless unknown poets have given to her in her name, is the greatest of all artists known in Polynesian oral literature" (1955:35).

Although there are allusions to it, the Pele and Hi'iaka story is never told anywhere in the great collection of folklore made by Abraham Fornander and published by the Bishop Museum in the years 1916-1920. This indicates that the story was a monopoly of the *hula* people, and its recitation with chant and dance was their prerogative, that is, it was *kapu* to them.

We digress here to point out that Fornander regarded Pele as a living person, an actual chiefess who had come to Hawai'i with her family from the "southern groups" (1880:2, 44). His view is not shared by modern scholars, who regard Pele and her family purely as Hawaiian mythological gods of volcanic phenomena. Fornander dates the Pele and Hi'iaka myth by referring to the chant of Mala-ha'a-koa, saying,

> ...If we now turn to the...legend of Pele's sister, Hiiakaikapoliopele, we find that, when she was resting at the house of Malaehaakoa in Haena, Kauai ...Malaehaakoa offered up a prayer or chant, which few Hawaiian meles bear stronger evidences of a comparatively genuine antiquity: and yet this mele,

---

*The big toe was the accepted point of introducing the spirit of a dead person back into his body. Emerson's "eye socket" was actually the tear duct. It was believed that through this passageway the spirit of a living person left and re-entered the body during dreams.

Fig. 2. "THE DESCENT FROM THE CLIFFS." Original illustration for Emerson's *Pele and Hiiaka*. Painting by Juliette M. Fraser; reproduced with permission of the artist.

> prayer or chant, makes special reference to Niheu-kalohe and to Nuakea--an anachronism showing fairly that this mele as well as the legend originated after the time of Maweke's grandchildren [1916-20:6(2)251-252].

Maweke was a traditional migrant chief of the 12th or 13th century whose lines of descent are well documented in Hawaiian genealogies for some thirty generations. If indeed this myth originated in the time of Maweke's grandchildren as Fornander assumes, it had had several hundred years to develop and crystallize into the form recorded in the 19th century.

The notes Fornander gathered on the story of Hi'iaka-i-ka-poli-o-Pele were edited by Thomas G. Thrum, who footnoted: "This is but a brief outline of characters prominent in this story... rather than an outline...of the several plots of this popular myth, its purpose being working notes, likely, for comparison...with other legends or traditions, here and in other parts of the Pacific" (Fornander 1916-20:6[2]343).

THE LEGEND OF KAPO-'ULA-KĪNA'U

In a legend recorded in about the same period as the Pele and Hi'iaka cycle, Kapo-'ula-kīna'u is given as the first goddess of the *hula*. Entitled "A Hawaiian legend of a terrible war between Pele-of-the-eternal fires and Waka-of-the-shadowy waters," the legend was written down by Moses Manu for the Hawaiian newspaper *Ka Loea Kalaiaina*, and was translated by Mary Kawena Pukui (Manu 1899). References cited in this paper refer to the page numbers of the manuscript translation.

In Moses Manu's legend, Kapo-'ula-kīna'u and Pele are sisters, and the two are called the oldest daughters of Haumea, a great goddess of Kahiki-mai-ea. The early incidents in the story tell of the coming of Kapo-'ula-kīna'u to Hawai'i with an older brother, Ka-huila-o-ka-lani, and several younger sisters.

Kapo and her company reached Ni'ihau when the chief Halali'i was having a series of nightly entertainments to which everyone was invited. Kapo and her companions entered the house of amusement and were invited by the chief to sit by him. Kapo possessed the chief by perching upon him in her wind form and chanted through him. The writer Manu says, "Kapo'ulakīna'u began this work of possessing a human being with her spirit in Ni'ihau" (Manu Ms.:9). When the chief ended his chanting, Kapo turned to her youngest sister Kewelani, also called Na-wahine-li'ili'i, and commanded her to dance. This sister was full of fun, and the dance she chose to perform reflected this. Manu describes the scene thus:

> As the crowd quieted, five persons stood holding up a large sleeping tapa which was then held on either side by the strange women as a screen. Two persons sat in front of the screen while the mischievous maiden remained behind it to make preparations for her cue. As she waited for her order to start, Kapo-'ula-kina'u chanted.... When the chant came to an end, the maiden stood up to dance a dance that was never before seen by the people of Ni'ihau.
>
> Her voice rose like the voice of a gentle eyed *lale* bird trying out its song. Her hands were uplifted to gesture to her chanting and began,
>
> It comes, the sun comes, [*Hiki mai, hiki mai ka lā*
> Dearly loved is the rising sun *Aloha wale ka lā e kau nei*
> That appears below Kawaihoa.... *Aia malalo o Kawaihoa....*]*
>
> As the chant ended, she strutted like a bird onto the sleeping tapa and rolled back the dark iris of her eyes till only the white showed, as bright and shiny as a mother-of-pearl shell. This act of Kewe-lani's made everyone shout with excitement. The people there were thrilled with her comical stunt and kept shouting and laughing....
>
> The dance that this maiden danced on the chief's night was the hula-ki'i.** It was first danced on Ni'ihau. The people quickly took to this kind of dance

---

*Given in full as a chant for the *hula pū'ili* by N. B. Emerson (1909:114).

**"Dance of the images in which the dancers are postured stiffly like images" (Pukui & Elbert 1971:83).

> and it became a popular one to all of the generations after the arrival of Kapo'ulakina'u and her company to that land. The people were drawn to this kind of dancing to this day. Perhaps only a few living today are familiar with this dance [Manu Ms.:11-12].

Kapo and her party left Ni'ihau for Kaua'i, and Manu relates several incidents that took place on that island. One concerned a surfing competition at Wailua, in Kapa'a. Here Kapo and her sisters were invited by some men to ride on the surf at Makaīwa. Accepting, they rode the first wave in pairs with the men. But on the second wave, with their supernatural powers they left the men behind while they rode to shore, and on the third wave, which Manu called "not a surf but a mountain," the men were forced beneath the water and pummeled to death. "They were changed into stone in the depths at the mouth of the Wailua river and are known as the *pae ki'i* or row of images. They are there to this day. When a torrent of water scoops up the sand at the beach, the stones resembling men can be seen together" (Manu Ms.:24). A *hula ki'i* of Kaua'i refers to this row of images.*

Continuing their journey, the company moved on to Hanalei where they stayed for several days. Here Kapo had a recurring dream of a handsome man who seemed to call her onward, and with her brother Ka-huila-o-ka-lani she left Kaua'i in search of him. The spirit form of Kapo's dream drew them on to O'ahu, then on to Moloka'i.

Here Manu's story of Kapo suffers a hiatus, for the issue of the newspaper telling of Kapo's early days on Moloka'i (*Ka Loea Kalaiaina*, August 5, 1899) is missing and has not been found in Honolulu libraries. The next issue (Ibid.:August 12) opens with, "Kapo'ula'kina'u became a goddess of the hula and her laws were called Mokulehua (Lehua-grove) and Pi'i-kuahu (Altar-ascending)" (Manu Ms.:33). The story continues with the origin of the *hula* on Moloka'i. Because it comes from the pen of an authoritative Hawaiian writer of the 19th century, the account is given here in Manu's words:

> While Kapo'ulakina'u was with her brother and their friends on Maunaloa [Moloka'i]...her friend asked her to teach her and her family [the art of the *hula*]. Kapo'ulakina'u said to her, "This can easily be taught but it has to be learned by observing my kapus and doing the things that will help my teaching. There are many kapus pertaining to this art and one can only learn by strict adherence until it is learned. If the desire is great it will not take long to graduate." The natives agreed....
>
> ...Kapo'ulakina'u appointed her vivacious sister Na-wahine-li'ili'i, who was also called Kewelani [as instructor]. She was the first one to dance the hula on Ni'ihau, as described earlier. This was the same person. Her older sister Kapo'ulakina'u chose her to instruct and to chant. She placed a conspicuous mark on her right cheek and called her Laea, Ulunui and Laka. By these three names the art of hula was taught.... According to some of this modern age, Laka was a male god. This the author denies. Read the following explanation:
>
> There was only one male Laka in the legends that the author has. He was the son of Wahieloa and Hina-ka-we'o, and belonged to Alae-nui and Alae-iki in Kipahulu, Maui.... Laka-a-Wahieloa was superhuman according to his legend, clever and wise in speech. He went to seek his father and found him in the cave of Kaualehu in Ka-'ū, Hawai'i. But where it concerns the hula, Laka-a-Wahieloa was not the instructor and there was no other but one Laka [in the *hula*]. Kapo'ulakina'u was the goddess of the hula.
>
> When one wished to learn the art of dancing the hula, he first sought a pig and some dark 'awa. These were to be offered to Laka, the woman

---

*Cf. Pukui on *hula ki'i*, Part II, pp. 81-82.

mentioned previously. She taught him the chants to be learned first and when they were learned, the offerings were laid down with this chant.

'O na lehua wale i Ka'ana,	The lehua blossoms of Ka'ana
Ke kui a'e la ua lawa	Are being strung into a complete lei
He lei no ka wahine	A lei for the woman
'O Kapo, ali'i nui o ia moku	Kapo, great chiefess of the forest
Ki'eki'e. Ha'aha'a	Of tall trees. Low,
Ka la o ka 'ike e 'ike ai,	[And] accessible is the day whereby knowledge is obtained,
He 'ike kumu, he 'ike lono,	Knowledge from the source, knowledge by hearing,
He like pū 'awa hiwa ka 'ike a ke akua e---	Like a flourishing *'awa* plant is the knowledge from the gods---
E lo----no.	O hear me.

Here is a prayer for going up to the mountain for greenery with which to build a hula altar.

I uka au e--i uka au,	I go to the upland, to the upland,
I uka ho'i me Laka.	To the upland to be with Laka.
I kela kuahiwi, kualono ho'i,	To that forest, that mountaintop,
E iho e Lauka'ie'ie, e Laukapalai e, &c. &c.	Descend, O Lau-ka-'ie'ie, O Lau-ka-palai, etc. etc.

After this prayer the lehua root was cut, for that was the tree that was the godly symbol of Kapo'ulakina'u and her brothers. Before cutting the tree a chant was uttered thus:

Ku'u ipo mau no me he kane la,	My loved one, dear as a husband,
He ipo na'u ka lehua iluna, lehua ilalo,	A sweetheart to me are the lehuas above and below,
Pupu weuweu e Laka E.	In the leafy bower of Laka.

When the gatherer returned home with these things a hula altar was erected. The placing of all the greenery in the altar was a delightful, creepy, and thrilling experience. That was the time to chant like this:

A kanikaniā'ula ka leo o ka wahine,	Faintly as from a distance comes the voice of the woman,
O Kaniā'ula, O Maheanu,	Of Kaniā'ula, of Maheanu,
O ka wahine e noho ana i ka ulu a ka makani.	Of the woman who dwells where the wind arises.
Noho ana Kapo i ka ulu wehiwehi	Kapo lives in a beautiful grove
Ku aka iluna o Ma'ohelaia,	Standing up on Ma'ohelaia,
'Ōhi'a ku i Maunaloa.	As an 'ōhi'a tree growing on Maunaloa.
Aloha mai Kaulana'ula ia'u,	Have compassion on me, O Kaulana 'ula
Eia ka 'ula la he 'ulāleo.	Here is a sacred thing, a calling appeal.
He mohai na'u ia 'oe e Kapo	Here is my offering to you O Kapo,
'O Kapokulani, O Moehaunaike,	O Kapokulani, O Moe-hāuna-ike [Moehauna-iki*]
E hea au e-o- 'oe.	I call to you....

Manu then resumes his story of Kapo on Moloka'i by alluding to her as one of the originators of sorcery on that island--"When Kapo'ulakina'u and Kahuilaokalani chose to remain on Maunaloa, they had a definite purpose, to establish themselves for endless time. Their 'seed' of the 'Flying-fire-of-Maunaloa' (sorcery) had begun to grow there" (Manu Ms.:36).

Kapo had yet to find the owl spirit form that had led her from Kaua'i, and she went to Maui on her quest. At Hāna the owl changed into a handsome man, and made ready to welcome the goddess.

---

*In Manu's legend Kapo-ku-lani and Moe-hāuna-iki are two names for another sister of Kapo-'ula-kīna'u. Compare the first and fourth chants here with Emerson 1909:33 & 44-45.

There Kapo became the bride of this supernatural man, Ka-pueo-kahi. Later, Kapo took Pua-nui, the younger brother of her husband, as her husband (Manu Ms.:36). These two became the Pua and Kapo sorcery gods of Moloka'i (see p. 56-57).

THE LEGEND OF LA'A-MAI-KAHIKI

The legend of La'a-mai-kahiki is told within a traditional account given of Mo'ikeha, a grandson of the Tahitian chief Maweke (see p. 7). According to the version of the legend in the Fornander collection of folklore (1916-20:4[1] 112-159), after living for some years in Hawai'i, Mo'ikeha sent his son Kila back to Kahiki (Tahiti) to fetch La'a, the son he had left behind when he came to Hawai'i. Kila returned to Hawai'i with La'a-mai-kahiki, who brought with him his priests, his god Lono-i-ka-'ou-ali'i*, and a drum, *pahu*. As their canoes approached Kaua'i, La'a-mai-kahiki signalled his arrival by beating his drum. He was welcomed by his father and lived with him on Kaua'i for a time, then moved to Maui and thence to Kaho'olawe before returning to Tahiti. The waters off western Kaho'olawe were named Ke-ala-i-kahiki, The-Way-to-Tahiti, in commemoration of his departure (Ibid.:128-129).

On a second trip to Hawai'i, La'a-mai-kahiki again brought a drum, and a *hula* instrument called the *'ohe kā'eke*. La'a made landfall at Ka'ū, Hawai'i, then sailed along the Kona coast and on to Kaua'i (Ibid.:154-155). It was on this trip that he introduced the art of *hula* dancing to the accompaniment of a drum. Before returning to Tahiti, La'a is said to have visited all the islands for the purpose of teaching the people the *hula kā'eke* (Ibid.). Emerson refers to La'a and the *hula kā'eke* in his description of the *hula pahu* (1909:103-104).

The "*'ohe kā'eke*" brought by La'a was the bamboo stamping tube, described by Helen Roberts (as "*keeke*") (1926:53) and by N. B. Emerson (1909:122, 143) as being of varying length, sometimes closed at one end by the septum of the bamboo, and sometimes open. Held in pairs and struck upon the ground or other hard surface, these bamboo percussion instruments accompanied *hula* classified by Emerson as *hula kā'eke'eke* (Ibid.:122-125).

The designation of the bamboo stamping tube or *'ohe kā'eke* as *kā'eke'eke* seems to have originated with Emerson. Earlier, the terms *kā'eke* and *kā'eke'eke* were applied to coconut tree drums and to drum beating. The Andrews dictionary, compiled before 1865, gives for *kā'eke*, "to beat the drum...the skill of drumming"(1865:230) and for *kā'eke'eke*, "to beat or play the drum" and "a kind of drum made of the cocoanut tree" (Ibid.). Andrews cites the Hawaiian writer Haleole, author of the legend of Lā'ie-i-ka-wai, as the source for his definition. John 'I'i, writing in 1870, used the terms *kā'eke* and *kā'eke'eke* similarly (1959:137). Malo said the skin of the shark was used in the making of drums (*pahu*) for the worship of the gods and for the "*hula* and the *ka-eke-eke* drum" (Malo 1951:47). Fornander designated the temple drum, usually called *pahu*, as *kā'eke* and *kā'eke'eke* (1880:2, 62-63). He ascribed the use of the temple drum in Hawai'i to La'a-mai-kahiki, and said that the drum that La'a brought with him was deposited at a *heiau* at Wailua, Kaua'i (Ibid.:62).

---

*The god of La'a-mai-kahiki is associated with the *hula* gods of Hawai'i in a chant (*kānaenae*) to Laka uttered while collecting greenery for Laka's altar in the *hālau hula*. Laka is called "sister, wife to Lono-i-ka-'ou-ali'i, O Laka, kaikuahine, wahine a Lono-i-ka-'ou-ali'i" (Emerson 1909:17).

THE *HULA* AND *OLI* IN LEGENDS

A number of persons are mentioned in legends as having attained skill as chanters, and since chanting and dancing often went hand-in-hand, skilled dancers may have been among them as well. However, in the Hawaiian texts of these accounts a distinction is seen in the use of the words *oli* and *hula*. *Oli*, defined as "chant that was not danced to" (Pukui & Elbert 1971:262) were delivered in a variety of voice styles, sometimes with percussion accompaniment, and usually with a minimum of gesture. They were meant to be listened to and appreciated for their beauty of imagery and story. *Hula* implied a chant-and-dance performance, with or without instrumental accompaniment, in either standing or half-kneeling position (*noho*). *Hula* and *oli* were thus two distinct types of performance, each with its own styles of chanting and with songs appropriate to each style. The distinction between the two is sometimes difficult to discern in written accounts.

For all its known importance in the cultural life of the Hawaiian people, the *hula* as a performance in song and dance is seldom found in the legends collected in the late 19th century. In the entire three-volume Fornander collection of folklore (1916-20), *hula* is usually mentioned only in passing, and none are described. Pamano, the hero of one legend, learned "the arts of the hula and the oli (or chanting) of meles" (*a'o i ka hula a me ke oli*) (Fornander 1916-20:5[2] 302-303). He is never mentioned as performing a *hula*, but in the story Pamano displays his skill at chanting. This was at a *kilu* game*, a favorite pastime of chiefs, and a recurring device in legends for bringing together estranged lovers.

The game of *kilu* is described in some detail by Malo (1951:216) and by his translator Emerson (Ibid.:217). Briefly, it consisted of teams of men and women sitting opposite each other at some distance. Each player sat behind a post, which the opposing player tried to hit with a *kilu*, usually a gourd or coconut shell cut lengthwise. If the post was hit, the thrower won a point, and a forfeit was paid either then or at the conclusion of the game of a predetermined number of points.

In the legend of Halemano (Fornander 1916-20:5[2]228-262), the Hawaiian text says that this hero learned the *hula*, and gained fame for his dancing and chanting (*i ka hula, a me ke oli*) (Ibid.:247). The translator rendered this text as "singing and chanting" rather than dancing and chanting (Ibid.:246). Again, a *kilu* game was the scene of a reunion; no dancing is mentioned during the game.

Emerson specifically combined the *hula* with chanting in one game of *kilu*. In their journey back to Hawai'i, Hi'iaka and Lohi'au arrived at Honolulu, where they were invited by the chiefess Pele'ula, a former lover of Lohi'au, to stop awhile and enjoy themselves. Emerson says of Pele'ula, "One of her chief diversions...was the hula, especially that form of the dance which was used in connection with that risqué entertainment, the kilu" (1915:170). There follows in his story a *kilu* game in which Hi'iaka, with her magical powers, continually bested Lohi'au.

---

*The translation given in this instance is misleading--the accompanying Hawaiian text does not say the *kilu* was being held in a "dancing hall" but that the chiefs were playing at *kilu* (*ke kilu ana a na 'lii*) (Fornander 1916-20:5[2]312-313).

Again the main emphasis is on chanting, but Emerson has Lohi'au paying his forfeit for losing in a passionate *hula* by which he hoped to win Hi'iaka as his lover (Emerson 1915:172-184). He gives a quite different version of the *kilu* game at Honolulu in *Unwritten Literature* (1909: 240-241). In this version Hi'iaka and Pele'ula contend for the attentions of Lohi'au, and there is no mention of a *hula* being performed. In a footnote to this passage, Emerson says that his description of the game of *kilu* was based on that of Malo (see Malo 1951:216-217), and that while Malo did not list a *hula kilu*, "this hula was, however, included in the list of hulas announced for performance in the programme of King Kalakaua's coronation ceremonies" (Emerson 1909:240). In the program referred to, the *kilu* are not called *hula*, but are listed as "Na Kilu a Lohiau," and "Na Kilu a Hiiaka" (see Appendix D).

Notes on Hula in Prehistoric Times

In Hawai'i, *hula* groups were not organized in the same way as were the *arioi* societies of Tahiti. Some groups of trained dancers may have been permanently attached to the households of Hawaiian chiefs, receiving their entire sustenance from their patrons, but most late 18th- and early 19th-century *hula* dancers seem to have been mainly self-supporting and to have depended on gifts from their audiences to augment their livelihood. This, at least, is the impression given in the short account of the *hula* written by David Malo:

> The *hula* was a very popular amusement among the Hawaiian people. It was used as a means of conferring distinction upon the *alii* and people of wealth. On the birth of an *alii*, the chiefs and people gave themselves up to the *hula*, and much property was lavished on *hula* dancers.
> The children of the wealthy were ardent devotees of the *hula*.
> It was the custom of *hula* dancers to perform before the rich in order to obtain gifts from them [Malo 1951:231].

It seems reasonable to suppose that some chanters and dancers would become favorites of different chiefs, and that from them would come the *po'e hula*, whose role it became to be "on call" to furnish entertainment for a particular chief. This assumption would account for certain dancers and chanters being known as the "hereditary" *po'e hula* of some chiefs and rulers in the later days of the Hawaiian monarchy.

That the *hula* was performed only by men in ancient times is not confirmed by any documentary evidence. Accounts by the Hawaiian scholars of the 19th century (Malo, Kamakau, 'I'i) make no such statement, nor do the early accounts of the 20th century (Emerson 1909 & 1915, Pukui 1936, 1942, 1943). The first written record of *hula* dancing in Hawai'i, made in 1778 (see p. 15) described women as dancing. Before that date the only records are those of legends, which tell not only of women performing the *hula*, but also as being among the earliest practitioners of the art (Emerson 1915; Manu 1899).

Religious rites associated with the *hula* were carried on in specialized *heiau* or places of worship, such as the *hula heiau* recorded for Kaua'i (see Part III). There is no evidence that the *hula* itself was performed as a religious rite within the precincts of any other type of *heiau*. Any prevailing notion that this was so is probably based upon the descriptions of certain rites in the *luakini heiau*, a paramount chief's "state" *heiau*. One such rite took place when the ridgepole of the *mana* house was overlaid with pieces of tapa. The translation of the passage describing this rite in Malo's *Hawaiian Antiquities* reads: "...two men were at the same time gesturing in pantomime as if performing a hula dance" (1951:171, sec. 87).* The description by John Papa 'I'i of the tying on of coconut fronds to the *anu'u* tower on the *heiau* includes the sentence, "They [two men] stood together up on the *anu'u* to await the response from below, then they moved as though dancing" (1959:38).** Samuel Kamakau's description of this ceremony reads: "Then these two men danced about with bent knees (*kuku mai la ua mau kānaka nei me ka ha'a 'ana*)" (1976:143).*** Kelou Kamakau, in describing a ceremony involving a sacred *'aha* cord, said that two men called with loud voices from the *anu'u* tower and, "While the priests were chanting from below, they (the two men) were dancing above" (Fornander 1916-20:6[1]22).† This is the only documentary evidence we have found that any type of *hula* was performed on a *heiau*. It should be noted that these *hula*, if such they may be called, were performed in enhancement of a rite, and were not themselves rites of worship.

Few *hula heiau* like that recorded for Kē'ē at Hā'ena, Kaua'i, are known. This *heiau* was probably situated in that particular place because it was of great and special significance in the *hula* tradition associated with the Pele and Hi'iaka cycle of legends. On the stone structure called "Lohiau's dancing pavilion and shrine" (Bennett 1931:site 155) perhaps at some time stood a *hālau*, a long building open at both ends, where dancers and chanters were trained or dedicated for the *hula* (see Appendix E). While it is not certain that this was so, it is known that this complex of ruins at Kē'ē was known as Ka-ahu-a-Laka in the late-19th and early-20th century, and was used then as a "*hula heiau*" (see Part II, p. 76; Part III).

For the period just preceding the advent of written records of Hawaiian history, we have two similar accounts by Samuel Kamakau and John 'I'i concerning *hula* performances for the entertainment of a specific chief.

Kamakau wrote that, about 1780

> ...Ka-lani-'opu'u moved to Kainaliu...to Keauhou...and then to Kailua. He delighted in the hula dance. Everyone, young and old, even to the babies just able to walk, was summonded to dance before him. The most popular dances were the *kala'au* [danced to the beating of sticks one against the other]†† and *ala'apapa* [similar to the modern *olapa* but with a different rhythm], and the dance of the marionettes (*hula ki'i*).††† Both chiefs and commoners participated in the dances, Ka-lani-'opu'u, over eighty years old as he was at the time, taking part. As he was dancing to [a] chant...with the gathering of chiefs, lesser chiefs, warriors, notables, and commoners looking on, a chief named Ka-pi'ipi'i-lani, standing among the group of commoners remarked to one of them, "The hula is amusing enough except for that silly old man's dancing." The man addressed answered, "Don't you know who the chief is?" "Who is he?" "That is Ka-lani-'opu'u..." [1961:105].

---

*Malo's original text reads, "*kuhikuhi ko laua mau lima e like me ka hula maoli.*"

**The 'I'i text reads, "*o ka hoolapalapa [ho'ōlapalapa] mai ka laua iluna me he 'ano hula la*" (*Kuokoa*, August 14, 1869).

****Kūkū* means literally "to shake in jerks, bounce, trot, bump" (Pukui & Elbert 1971:163).

†Kelou Kamakau's text reads, for the crucial phrase, "*a hula mai la laua iluna*" (Fornander 1916-20:6[1]23).

††Bracketed material in this quoted paragraph appears in the published text.

†††See pp. 62-63, this paper.

John 'I'i commented on the fondness of Kalaniopu'u for the *hula* in more general terms:

> Kalaniopuu greatly enjoyed the hula in his old age. When a gathering assembled for the hula and the spectators were waiting to see what kind of dance it would be, he would come forth and stand before the dancers to watch them. With his hands outstretched, he would say to the drummers back of the dancers, "More excitement! More excitement!" Those who did not recognize Kalaniopuu grumbled, saying, "The hula is enjoyable except for the interference of that old man" [1959:11].

Historical Accounts of the 18th Century

The ancient or prehistoric period in Hawai'i ended with the arrival of Captain Cook's ships the *Resolution* and the *Discovery* at Kaua'i and Ni'ihau in January of 1778. At that point events and facets of Hawaiian life began to be recorded, with the observations of many of the officers and men aboard Cook's ships. They, as witnesses to what was prehistoric Hawai'i, afford us only a small glimpse of the *hula*. The following extracts from their journals show the limited range of the performances they saw.

The first *hula* performance Cook's people saw was on the island of Kaua'i in January of 1778, although they did not recognize it as a dance but rather as a musical performance. It was the *hula kāla'au*, with the addition of the use of the *papa hehi* or treadle board, described by Cook as follows:

> ...We had no opportunity to see any of their amusements and the only musical instruments that was seen among them was a hollow vessel of wood like a platter and two sticks, on these one of our gentlemen saw a man play: one of the sticks he held as we do a fiddle and struck it with the other, which was smaller and something like a drum stick and at the same time beat with his foot upon the hollow Vessel and produced a tune that was by no means disagreeable.* This Musick was accompanied with a song, sung by some women and had a pleasing and tender effect. Another instrument was seen among them, but it can scarcely be called an instrument of music; this was a small gourd with some pebblestones in it ['ulī'ulī], which they shake in the hand like a child's rattle and are used, as they told us, at their dances [Beaglehole 1967:284-285]. [Fig. 3].

David Samwell, surgeon aboard Cook's ship *Discovery*, recorded another sort of dance on January 10, 1779, off the coast of Kona, Hawai'i:

> The ships continue far from shore, two or 3 Canoes came off to us, many Girls on board. In the afternoon they all assembled upon deck and formed a dance; they strike their Hands on the pit of their Stomack smartly & jump up all together, at the same time repeating the words of a song in responses...[Beaglehole 1967:1157].

The fact that this *hula* was done in unison by a group of women indicates that they had been trained as a group, thus evidencing the existence of *hula* schools of some type in prehistoric Hawai'i. Possibly their *hula* was an honorific one composed for these godlike beings who had appeared off their coast several days previously.

**Hula kāla'au* with *papa hehi*.

Fig. 3. HAWAIIAN MAN DANCING, THREE VIEWS. Original sketch by John Webber in Bishop Mus. Library. (Bishop Mus. Neg. No. CPBM39912)

On January 25, 1779, while anchored at Kealakekua Bay, Surgeon Samwell and some companions saw another *hula* performance, which he described thus:

> ...Two or three of us near the Dusk of the Evening returning from a short walk met on our Way with an Entertainment different from any we had yet seen among these people; it was a woman dancing to the Sound of a Drum. As it was begun just as we arrived on the Spot, & the Scene of it in a place by which they knew we were to return from our Excursion, we concluded that it was prepared for our Entertainment, especially as the Indians behave to us wherever we go with the greatest kindness and good nature & strive to do every thing in their power to oblige us. Within a small Circle sat a pretty little Girl upon a Matt by herself, she seemed of some Consequence & she invited us to sit down by her. An elderly woman advanced into the Ring dressed upon the Occasion. She had a feathered Ruff called Herei [*he lei*] on her Head, a large Piece of Cloth was rolled round her waist with part of it hanging below her knees, round the small of her Legs were tyed some Matting with Dogs Teeth stuck in it in rows which they call Coobe [*kūpe'e*], from the lowest Row the Teeth increased in bigness to the upper, and being loose on shaking her leg they made a rattling Noise. On one side of the Ring sat the Drummer, his Drum [*ipu*] was made of three Gourd Shells inserted into each other, he beat the bottom of it against the Ground & sung a Song in slow time. The Dancer threw her arms about & put her body into various Postures, sometime looking stedfastly toward the sky. Her Step was slow & not unlike a Country man's Hornpipe Step, in this manner she moved about sometimes making a Circle round the ring & every now & then repeating a song in concert with the Drummer. She continued dancing about a quarter of an hour & we thought much superior to any dances we had seen among Indians before [Beaglehole 1967:1167-1168].

As Cook's ships left the islands for the last time, the *Discovery* anchored at Waimea Bay on O'ahu for watering. On board the ship were some girls, and Samwell describes their dancing on this occasion:

> Saturday February 27th.... The Girls we have brought with us buy Cloth here for the iron & other things they have got from their Husbands; soon after our coming to an anchor they performed a dance on the Quarter deck which we had not seen before, it might be perhaps to express their Joy on their safe arrival at this place, it was performed by two at a time--they did not jump up as in the common dance but used a kind of a regular Step & moved their Legs something like our sailors dancing a Hornpipe, they moved their Arms up and down, repeated a Song together, changed their places often, wriggled their backsides and used many lascivious Gestures. Upon the whole we thought it much more agreeable than their common Dance [Beaglehole 1967:1221-1222].

We may be sure that the men of the *Resolution* and the *Discovery* saw many more *hula* than we find described, and probably most of those danced for the entertainment of the sailors were those with sexual themes. Samwell collected the words to two such songs, which were undoubtedly accompanied by what he called "lascivious gestures." Perhaps these were the songs sung by the girls off Waimea Bay (Beaglehole 1967:1221-1222*).

---

*Samwell wrote the words to these songs in his journal purely by phonetic sounds. Mary Kawena Pukui transliterated these syllables into modern Hawaiian spelling, and from her words and translations Beaglehole rendered the songs as published (Beaglehole 1967:1234).

A completely different kind of *hula* performance, if such it may be called, was witnessed by James King of the Cook expedition. It appears to have been performed by a group of professional mourners upon the death of a chief. King described the scene:

> ...a number of People collected together round a square Area fronting the house where he [the dead chief] lay...after a short time a Mat was spread upon the Area, & two men and 13 women came and sat themselves down, in three unequal rows; the two men in front, with three of the Women, their Necks & heads were decorat'd with Feathered ruffs, broad green leaves variously scolloped were thrown with a good deal of taste about the Shoulders, & both Men & Women had a greater quantity of their Cloth wrapt round them, than on Ordinary occasions.... The Company seated on the Mat began by moving their Arms with little infleixion of the body in a very slow but graceful manner, & which was accompanied with a melancholy tune, they afterwards kneeld, or rather half kneeling & sitting* began to move their Arms to a much quicker tune.
>
> We now saw ourselves transport'd to the Friendly Islanders [Tongans], for both the figure & tone of their Voice strongly resembled some of the Ceremonies we saw there...At intervals a single man & woman would repeat something in recitative with slow motions, & at other times their Motions & tunes were so quick & lively, as to destroy its being entirely a grave ceremony. This performance last'd an hour, when some coarse mats & Cloth were brought to the performers...[Beaglehole 1967:622].

In the officially compiled account of Cook's third voyage (Cook & King 1784) are the following general remarks on the *hula*:

> Their dances have a much nearer resemblance to those of the New Zealanders than of the Otaheitians or Friendly Islanders. They are prefaced with a slow, solemn song, in which all the party join, moving their legs, and gently striking their breasts in a manner and with attitudes that are perfectly easy and graceful; and so far they are the same with the dances of the Society Islands. When this has lasted about ten minutes, both the tune and the motions gradually quicken, and end only by their inability to support the fatigue, which part of the performance is the exact counterpart of that of the New Zealanders; and (as it is among them) the person who uses the most violent action and holds out the longest is applauded as the best dancer. It is to be observed that in this dance the women only took part and that the dancing of the men is nearly of the same kind with what we saw at the Friendly Islands; and which may, perhaps, with more propriety, be called the accompaniment of the songs, with corresponding and graceful motions of the whole body.** Yet as we were spectators of boxing exhibitions of the same kind with those we were entertained with at the Friendly Islands, it is probable that they had likewise their grand ceremonious dances, in which numbers of both sexes assisted [Cook & King 1784:3,142-143].

Such "grand ceremonious dances," which King presumed existed, included at least the *hula* concerts staged at the birth of a high chief (Malo 1951:231). A record of such a concert is described as having taken place in Kahalu'u, Kona, on the occasion of the birth of Ka-lua-i-Konahale Kuakini, a brother of Ka'ahumanu. Kamakau dates the performance as occurring in 1791:

> At the birth of the child [Kuakini] there was a great hula at Kahalu'u, and the name hula (*hula inoa*) was being danced for the

---

*The position for the *hula noho*.

**"...small parties of men, sitting, would Sing & move their Arms, something in the manner we describ'd in the burial ceremony" (King, in Beaglehole 1967:627).

> birth of the new son to Na-mahana and Ke'e-au-moku [Kamakau 1961: 388].

The lack of formal *hula* entertainment for the distinguished Captain Cook and his officers during the course of their three and a half months' total stay in the islands may be significant in tracing the development of the function of the *hula* in the social culture of the people. This may even be true of boxing and wrestling exhibitions. The latter were witnessed on two occasions by the Cook people at their own request (Beaglehole 1967:518,627,1173,1174) says King, "and they expected that we should be in part performers; for which purpose on the first time the greatest croud was Collectd we had ever seen on shore" (Ibid.:627).

In the years 1792-1794 Captain George Vancouver made three visits to Hawai'i. While he and his men must have seen the *hula* performed on various occasions, it was not until the 1794 visit that they recorded any descriptions of the dance. In January of 1794 Archibald Menzies, botanist of the expedition, witnessed a professional performance in the uplands of Kona while on a visit to the planting fields above Kealakekua. In February, a grand *hula* concert was staged at Kealakekua for the entertainment of Vancouver and his men, and another was offered for their entertainment when the ships paid their last visit to Waimea, Kaua'i, in March.

Menzies' account of the January performance corroborates two general statements made by Hawaiian writers: that of Malo concerning professional *hula* dancers earning their livelihood from gifts presented to them by their audiences (1951:231) and that of John 'I'i to the effect that there were but two good times for dancing, morning and evening (1959:137).

> After breakfast we were entertained with the performance of a young girl, who danced in a small area before our door. She was ably assisted by her father, who beat on a small drum and joined her in the singing and reciting and sometimes in a brisk dialogue, while she, encumbered as she was with a grotesque dress, traversed the area with such measured paces and fascinating movements, with such graceful attitudes and such agility and animation of acting, so punctually timed and so varied by easy transitions as would have done credit to the most expert attitudinarian in any part of the world, and far exceeded anything of the kind we had before seen at these islands. Every joint of her limbs, every finger of her hand, every muscle of her body, partook unitedly of the varied sympathetic impulses, while the motion of her eyes transferring their transient glances and the harmony of her features were beyond the power of description.
>
> We were given to understand that this actress, who might be termed an opera girl, and her father, belonged to a party who strolled about the country from village to village and gained their livelihood by entertaining the inhabitants with their performances. If we might judge of her merits from the specimen we had just seen of her acting, we think she was possessed of natural powers to entertain even in a more refined country.
>
> After presenting this young actress with suitable presents of beads, looking glasses, scissors, tape and other articles, we descended through the plantations at our leisure...[Menzies 1920:168-169].

The performance staged for Vancouver and his men at Kealakekua in February was a formal *hula* concert, with some of the high chiefesses of the land as the performers. Kamehameha and Ka'ahumanu assisted in preparation for the concert, but could not attend the actual performance. Vancouver explained this by saying they were "prohibited by law from attending such amusements, excepting on the festival of the new year. Indeed, the performance of this day was contrary to the established rules of the island, but being intended as a compliment to us, the innovation was admitted" (1801:5, 70). This may be evidence of a certain formalization of the role of the *hula* in the society in the years following discovery by Cook.

Identifiable performers were Kalaiwohi, a paternal half-brother of Kamehameha; Kalilikauoha, a daughter of Kahekili, who was at this time the wife of Hoapili, in whose yard the performance was held; and Kaheiheimalie, sister of Ka'ahumanu and the wife of Kalaimamahū, another paternal half-brother of Kamehameha. The chiefess in whose honor this *hula* was performed was Kalani-kau-iō-kikilo, also called Kalani-akua, a *pi'o* chiefess of godlike rank, daughter of Kamehameha-nui and his full sister Kalola (Vancouver 1801:5, 71-72).

There are two descriptions of the *hula* concert, one by Vancouver himself (see Appendix C), and the other by Edward Bell, a member of his expedition. We present Bell's description here:

> In the Evening His Majesty gave a grand Hoora (or dance) that had been preparing for our amusement for some time back. About six O'Clock the company began to assemble at the Theater which was a very large space of Clear ground within the walls of Hauripia's [Hoapili's] estate--a chief of considerable rank,--and many of the Chiefs declared that since Captain Cook's time they had never seen such a concourse of Spectators at any one entertainment on the Island, nor such an assembly of their nobility collected at one place. All ranks appear'd in their best, and the Chief's wives were very handsomely dress'd in their finest Cloth, --their heads decorated with ornaments Cut out of Scarlet & yellow Cloth resembling Coronets, and attended by Pages carrying large ornamented Fans and Fly-traps.--The English officers were seated in the Area of a House spread over with matts, and the Spectators in the front were all seated on Matts, whilst thousands stood behind the Audience forming a semicircle--Six men first entered--these were musicians--they had no drums, that instrument being never used in the Royal Entertainments, but they had in their left hands long poles--or Blunt pointed Spears, being very small at one end becoming thicker gradually towards the other end, made of their mahogany--this they strike with a smaller piece of the same kind of Wood, which they accompanied to a song in which they all joined, keeping the most exact time with their right foot beating against the ground. After a short overture the Dancers entered, seven in Number, all women, and came forward on a spot of ground between two Cocoa Nut Trees, opposite to where the English officers were seated,--this spot as well as the whole of the ground having been levelled, clean swept & freed of Stones. All the Women performers were great Chiefesses in their own right, and each wore the order of the Pallowah [*palaoa*].... One of the Ladies was the Queen Dowager (or in other words, one of the Kings former wives) another was a daughter of Titeeree [Kahekili] the King of Waohoo &ca--and a third [Kaheiheimalie] was a sister of the present Queen's [Ka'ahumanu]. They were dress'd up with a profusion of the most esteem'd glazed Cloth made to hang in handsome festoons all round, and reach'd from the middle down to the Knees; Round their heads, middle and Legs were Garlands of green Fern plaited which had a good effect. They commenced their dance slowly and solemnly--and gradually growing quicker and quicker, till at last it required the Dancers most animated and violent exertions at the conclusion of which they were ready to drop with fatigue;--as they approached the quicker part and until it was concluded the dancers join'd in the song with the men, keeping the most exact time--after two or three dances of that kind the entertainment broke up.--

> The movements of the hands and arms, and the feet of the performers are extremely graceful particularly in the slow solemn part, and the extraordinary animated action when it reaches its quickest highest part pleased & surprised us, in this dance, the performers never change nor move from their places, and they all, throughout the dance preserved the same situation as when they commenced--[Bell 1929:2(2)124-125].

Vancouver's description of this performance has a more supercilious tone, and he found the concluding *hula ma'i* an "offensive, libidinous scene" (1801:5,75). These *hula*, composed for the genitals of a chief, were the traditional conclusion of a formal presentation of dances honoring that chief. In the next *hula* performance seen by Vancouver and his men this feature was absent, and the entire performance received Vancouver's praise. The performance was seen in March 1794 at Waimea, Kaua'i, and it was in honor of a yet unborn chiefly child. Vancouver's description of the performance follows:

> On our arrival at the place of exhibition, we found the performers assembled, consisting of a numerous throng, chiefly of women, who were dressed in their various coloured clothes, disposed with good effect. The entertainment consisted of three parts, and was performed by three different parties consisting of about two hundred women in each, who ranged themselves in five or six rows, not standing up, not kneeling, but rather sitting upon their haunches. One man only advanced a few feet before the centre of the front row of the ladies, who seemed to be the hero of the piece, and, like a flugal man, gave tone and action to the entertainment. In this situation and posture they exhibited a variety of gestures, almost incredible for the human body so circumstanced to perform. The whole of this numerous group was in perfect unison of voice and action, that it were impossible, even to the bend of a finger, to have discerned the least variation. Their voices were melodious, and their actions were as innumerable as, by me, they are undescribable; they exhibited great ease and much elegance, and the whole was executed with a degree of correctness not easily to be imagined. This was particularly striking in one part, where the performance instantly changed from a loud full chorus, and vast agitation in the countenances and gestures of the actors, to the most profound silence and composure; and instead of continuing in their previous erect attitude, all fell down as it were lifeless, and in their fall buried themselves under their garments; conveying, in some measure, the idea of a boisterous ocean becoming suddenly tranquillized by an instant calm. The great diversity of their figured dresses on this occasion had a particularly good effect; the several other parts were conducted with the same correctness and uniformity, but were less easy to describe. There appeared to be much variety and little repetition, not only in the acting of the respective sets, but in the whole of the three parts; the performers in which, could not amount to less than six hundred persons. This *hoorah* was completely free from the disgusting obscenity exhibited in the former entertainments, which I have before had occasion to notice. It was conducted through every part with great life and vivacity; and was, without exception, the most pleasing amusement of the kind we had seen performed in the course of the voyage.
>
> The spectators, who were as numerous as at Owhyhee, were in their best apparel, and all retired very peaceably after the close of the performance, about the setting of the sun [Vancouver 1801:5,128-130].

Historical Accounts of the 19th Century

1800-1820: EARLY *HULA* ACCOUNTS

As a pastime, the impromptu *hula* served not only as amusement, but very often as a means of venting emotions. To judge from the following incident of the early 1800s related by John 'I'i, chiefs themselves were quite capable of composing and creating *hula* to match the mood of the moment.

> One evening the king [Kamehameha] was to meet with the gods in the house of Hiiaka.... But after the ceremony there was over, Kamehameha went to spend the night with Kanahoahoa, with the knowledge of the god [Kaneikaulanaula] and the attendant who carried it. The attendant took the god to the king's sleeping house where Kaahumanu and her sister, Kaheiheimalie, were awaiting Kamehameha's return. They asked the attendant of the god where the chief was, and he replied, "They two are at Olo, only at Olo." This reply of his was used in a hula chant the chiefesses composed:
>
> We are sorry for Kaneikaulanaula,
> He flies unattended,
> For they two are at Olo, only at Olo,
> In the presence of Kapo, wife of Puanui,
> Great is your love, it keeps your eyes on her.
>
> When the king returned later that night, the chiefesses were chanting and dancing to the words they had composed.... He asked them at once what they were doing and to explain the underlying meaning of the words they had composed...[1959:18].

This little chant, an improvisation of the moment, nevertheless displays a certain merit in composition in the admired use of words that conveyed an inner meaning, or *kaona*. That this story survived long enough to be recorded later is an example of the preservation of chants by attendants of the high chiefs, their "biographers," if you will.

Archibald Campbell, who lived on O'ahu for most of the year 1809, described the *hula* briefly in his general remarks on the customs of the Hawaiians:

> Dancing, wrestling, and foot races, are also common amusements, particularly at macaheite [Makahiki] time.
>
> The dances are principally performed by women, who form themselves into solid squares, ten or twelve each way, and keep time to the sound of the drum, accompanied by a song, in which they all join. In dancing they seldom move their feet, but throw themselves into a variety of attitudes, sometimes all squatting, and at other times springing up at the same instant. A man in front with strings of shells on his ankles and wrists, with which he marks time, acts as fugel-man. On these occasions the women display all their finery, particularly in European clothes, if they are so fortunate as to possess any. They received great applause from the spectators, who frequently burst into immoderate fits of laughter, at particular parts of the song [1967:146-147].

The chant to which the dance was adapted was always the main focus of a performance. Gesticulation was appreciated for its grace: it was not used or needed to illustrate the meaning of the chant until very modern times. The description by 'I'i of the *hula pā ipu*, as performed by trained dancers for the entertainment of Liholiho and his chiefs about 1815, well illustrates this point:

> In the *hula paipu* [*pā ipu*], gourd hula drums were moved here and there by the dancers. Their hands gestured forward and back, up and down, in unison with the movement of the drums and to the rhythm of the drum-slapping. The left hand of each performer was beautifully tattooed [*kākau pāni'o 'ia*] because that was the hand that held the cord attached to the drum through a hole. The right hand did the gesturing. As this kind of hula was greatly enjoyed, there was much swaying and much chanting of the praises of favorites among the chiefs, favorite children, and native sons. This was kept up from dawn until the sun grew warm. There were but two good times for dancing, morning and evening.
>
> The dancers kept in unison and preserved the pleasing quality of chanting or reciting. Sometimes one would lead and others would join in; but while he was reciting, the others kept their silence and only gestured with their hands and swayed their drums. At the proper place for the rest to join in, they did so with great vigor. Perhaps there would be two or three dances of that kind, followed by the *hula 'aiha'a*, and so on. The dancers received many gifts, and finally a gift was laid at the opening of the head drummer's instrument [Ii 1959:137].

In 1816, while the Russian ship *Rurick* was anchored in Honolulu harbor, the naturalist on board, Adelbert de Chamisso, attended two *hula* performances. His remarks on them, written some years after his visit, follow:

> On the 4th of December, Kareimoku arranged a *hurra-hurra*, or dance performance for us, and another on the 6th. Truly, since I have often seen the ungraceful contortions that we admire in our dances under the name of ballet, it seems to me after observing and viewing the magnificence of the local performances that the former pale in comparison. We barbarians, we call the native who have a love of the beautiful "savages," and we have allowed the ballet of the confounded poets and of the mournful mimics to drive them out of the halls we boast are devoted to art. I have always regretted, and must here repeat my regret, that some good genius should not have brought to these islands a painter, one who was inspired by the art, and not merely a professional draughts-man. Now it is too late. In Tahiti and in Hawaii missionary clothing now covers the splendid bodies, all of the artistic performances have been silenced, and the *tabu* Sunday weighs sadly and drearily upon these pleasure loving children.
>
> I must give you an indication that I am not exaggerating. On the 4th of December three men danced, and on the 6th, a large group of young girls, amongst whom were many of exceeding beauty. But it was not the latter who made a lasting impression upon me, no, it was the men who excelled in their art and whom one could not say that one was better than the other. One may glance at the two horrible drawings which spoil Choris' atlas. The dance does not lend itself to being painted, and for what he has here done, may the Genius of Art forgive him. [Figs. 4 & 5].
>
> Such enthusiasm and joyful intoxication as the Hawaiians showed at this performance, I have never seen in any audience, or at any other performance. They threw presents to the dancers, such as clothing and jewelry [Houston 1940:69-70].*

Among the people the *hula* was performed more informally, but with no less enjoyment, to judge from an 1818 account by Peter Corney, who lived in Honolulu in 1809-1810:

> On moon light nights, the natives collect on the plain to the number of many hundreds, men, women, and children; here they sit

*See Chamisso (1862:15) for his general remarks on the *hula*.

Fig. 4. MALE DANCERS OF THE SANDWICH ISLANDS. Louis Choris, 1822. Plate XII from his *Voyage Pittoresque Autour du Monde*....Paris 1822. (Bishop Mus. Neg. No. CPBM 29145)

Fig. 5. FEMALE DANCERS OF THE SANDWICH ISLANDS. Louis Choris, 1822. Plate XVI from his *Voyage Pittoresque Autour du Monde*....Paris 1822. (Bishop Mus. Neg. No. 873)

> in a ring, where they dance, sing, and play all manner of games, and seldom break up before midnight [Corney 1965:210].

In the foregoing accounts the *hula* has been seen to be primarily for entertainment, whether in celebration of the birth of a chief, as part of the festive celebrations of the Makahiki, or as entertainment for distinguished visitors. It had no place in the formal religious rites of the Hawaiian people, and the abolition of the *kapu* in 1819, which meant the overthrow of the state religious practices, had no effect on the *hula*.

1820-1830: *HULA* FOR THE *ALI'I*

The accounts of the missionaries to Hawai'i in the 1820s contained frequent references to the *hula*. An early one was that of Samuel Ruggles, a missionary stationed at Waimea, Kaua'i. In a letter home dated July 4, 1820, Ruggles said,

> Dancing is another of their common plays, and to the stranger it is a curiosity to behold their performances. Several men and women stand in a row with a wreath of yellow and red feathers on their heads; around their necks, two or three strings of beads made of the teeth of the sperm whale; on their wrists a bunch of smaller ones of the hob [hog], so fixed as to rattle when the arms are moved and on the legs and ankles are strung several hundreds of dogs teeth. All their motions and gestures are the same, dancing sometimes on one foot and sometimes on both. Several drums, made of the gourd are beaten in the meanwhile. There are frequently more than a thousand people attending these dances...[*The Friend* 1913:235].

Samuel Whitney, another missionary at Waimea, Kaua'i, made the earliest mention found of the use of puppets in the *hula*. He called the puppets "idols"--not in the sense that they were objects of worship, but merely as representations or dolls. His journal entry for July 29, 1820, reads:

> The King and Queen [Kaumuali'i and Kapule] this afternoon sent us an invitation to call again. We went, & found them sitting on a mat, surrounded by a numerous train. We soon learned they were going to have a hoory hoory (Idol dance) for amusement. A curtain of tappers [tapa] was fitted across the room, & soon after we entered, an old man began to make a noise by drumming on a hollow instrument with his hands & at the same time singing. After singing & drumming some time, six idols made their appearance above the curtain, & began to dance...[*The Friend* 1925:208].

In the latter part of 1820, in anticipation of the removal of Liholiho and his court to Honolulu, great preparations were made to celebrate the occasion with *hula* performances. Hiram Bingham, leader of the American missionaries, reported on these preparations thus:

> While some of the people who sat in darkness were beginning to turn their eyes to the light, and were disposed to attend our schools and public lectures, others, with greater enthusiasm were wasting their time in learning, practicing, or witnessing the *hula*, or heathen song and dance. This was intended, in part at least, as an honor and gratification to the king, especially at Honolulu, at his expected reception there, on his removal from Kailua.
>
> ...For many weeks in succession, the first sound that fell on the ear in the morning was the loud beating of the drum, summoning the dancers to assemble.... Day after day, several hours in the day, the noisy hula--drumming, singing, and dancing in the open air, constituted the great attraction or annoyance. The principal scene of the *hula*

> at Honolulu was a large yard, contiguous to the house of the governor. The ground was covered with fresh rushes, brought from a neighboring marsh, slung on the backs of the dancers, chiefs, and plebeians, men, women, and children, who, in such cases, walk in single file.... In the *hula*, the dancers are often fantastically decorated with figured or colored *kapa*, green leaves, fresh flowers, braided hair, and sometimes with a gaiter on the ancle, set with hundreds of dog's teeth, so as to be considerably heavy, and to rattle against each other in the motion of the feet. Notwithstanding these decorations, much of the person is uncovered; and the decent covering of a foreign dress was not then permitted to the public dancers. They were arranged in several equidistant ranks of considerable length, and at the sound of numbers, moved together, forward, backward, to the right, and to the left, and vertically, giving extended motions to the hands and feet, arms and legs... without changing their relative position. The musicians who sung without dancing, played on various unharmonious instruments, the drum, the long gourd-shell, or double calabash, and the long hardwood rod. Their wooden drum, with one shark-skin head, is beaten by the fingers of the musician, sitting cross-legged beside it as the uncovered end stands on the ground. The long double calabash standing upright on the ground, is beaten and often raised by the hands of the musician, sitting on his heels, pressing the ground with knees and toes, and resound both by the strokes of the hands on the sides, and by its repeated and forcible thumping on the earth, or the pad laid down for the purpose. The long hardwood rod, used as a most simple drum, is held in the left hand, the fore end pointing obliquely downward, to help keep time, and increase the clatter, is beaten with a small stick held lightly by the thumb and fingers of the right. The numbers heard on these instruments, are sometimes difficult to imitate or describe, and sometimes are more simple and orderly.... All parts of the *hula* are laborious, and under a tropical sun, make the perspiration roll off freely from the performers. Sometimes both musicians and dancers cantilate their heathen songs together. Occasionally a single female voice carries on the song, while the rest are silent, and sometimes hundreds of voices are heard together. Melody and harmony are scarcely known to them, with all their skill and art. The whole arrangement and process of their old *hulas* were designed to promote lasciviousness, and of course the practice of them could not flourish in modest communities. They had been interwoven too with their superstitions, and made subservient to the honor of their gods, and their rulers, either living or departed and deified. Liholiho was fond of witnessing them, and they were managed to gratify his pride and promote his pleasure [1847:123-125].

A similar account, also by the hand of one of the missionaries, was published in the *Missionary Register for 1823*. Sufficient additional details, especially in regard to the god Laka, justify its quotation here, in spite of considerable repetition:

> The scene of the play is a large yard, contiguous to the house of the Governor. The ground is covered with rushes. Those, who danced, were arranged in seven long rows, when one moved, all moved in the same way; and, though they advance and retreat, turn round, incline to the right or left, and employ a great variety of motions of the arms, legs, and body, yet there is no interchange of station, nor material change of relative situation among them. The musicians, or those who sing and violently beat with a small stick upon a larger one, thus measuring the time with great exactness and also by stamping their feet upon the ground, are arranged in two long rows behind the dancers, having their leader in front of them. Those who dance, often sing with the musicians; and, sometimes, one female voice alone carries on the song, while all the rest are silent. One of the musicians, being asked what number of men and women were engaged in the dance, replied, in their method of enumeration, "three forties and three tens of men, and three forties of women;" that is, 270 in the whole.

At the close of the day it was discovered, that, in an enclosure, near the gate of the yard, the Natives had set up a small image, dressed out with beads. On being interrogated as to its nature, they said it was "Akooah hooda-hooda," the "God of the dance."

What is the real design of setting up this lying vanity, it is difficult to tell. It seems the master of the Hoodah-hoodah found it somewhat difficult to preserve perfect order in the play, without resorting to some such expedient as that of setting up an idol, or reviving at least a part of the taboo system. Some were unwilling to acknowledge the authority of such a deity, particularly as it as contrary to the views of the King. Reho-reho expressed his disapprobation of the manner in which this god had been acknowledged, and refused to allow him an image. The senseless and shapeless stick of wood, which had stood in the place of the "God of the Dance," was removed, his little court laid waste, and the visible offerings suspended. But the King, as we are informed, told the Governor of the island, that, if the dancers pleased to acknowledge the Laka in sport, they might do it. We are informed by our pupils, some of whom are obliged to join in the dance, that all the dancers, except those, who belong to our School, acknowledge the Akooah hoodah-hoodah, in order to keep up their attention, and not lose, but acquire skill in dancing; that they eat to the Laka--they smoke to the Laka--they dance to the Laka*--they call their ornaments the Laka's; saying, that, if they do this, the Laka will bye and bye give them good knowledge and expertness to dance well, and those, who refuse to do this, will not become accomplished in the art [*Missionary Register* 1823:558-559].

Kamakau also mentioned the prolonged celebration on the occasion of the arrival of Liholiho and his court at Honolulu in February of 1821:

...On the king's arrival a great reception was given him at which the chief attraction was dancing of which the young king, then almost twenty-four, was very fond. A chiefess named Ke-ana had prepared a special performance of the stick hula (*hula ka-la'au*) in which several hundred took part [1961:250].

The journal of the Spaniard Don Francisco de Paula Marín also notes these *hula* festivities on the occasion of Liholiho's arrival in Honolulu (Gast & Conrad 1973:245-246 *passim*). His journal also notes days of feasts, games, and dancing in commemoration of the death of Kamehameha. These were not strictly annual events, but were proclaimed at will by Kamehameha's son and successor, Liholiho. The commemorative festivities extended over several days** and are noted in Marín's journal for May 1821, May 1822, and March 1823 (Ibid.).

Some of the activities of the 1823 commemorative celebration were seen by Charles Stewart, an American missionary who had recently arrived in Honolulu. After describing the pageantry of a great procession of chiefs in beautiful finery, Stewart commented on the part the *po'e hula* played in the festivities:

Companies of singing and dancing girls and men, consisting of many hundreds, met the processions in different places, encircling the highest chiefs, and shouting their praise in enthusiastic

*The phrase "to the Laka" was introduced by the missionary writer of this passage; it implies that the representation of Laka was more than an image--that it was an idol and was being worshipped as such. There is no such phraseology in Hawaiian accounts--in all chants Laka was addressed as "*E Laka*," that is, "*O Laka*," as a deity. The essence of the deity was represented in concrete form, usually a tapa-covered block of *lama* wood (*Diospyras*, syn. *Maba*, sp.).

**The main day of observance was the Hawaiian lunar month-day of Hoku, the day that Kamehameha had died, which in May of 1819 fell on the ninth.

> adulations. The dull and monotonous sounds of the native drum and calabash, the wild notes of their songs in the loud choruses and responses of the various parties, and the pulsations, on the ground, of the tread of thousands in the dance, reached us even at the missionary enclosure.
>
> I can never forget the impressions made upon my mind, the first few nights after coming to anchor in the harbor, while these songs and dances were in preparation by rehearsal and practice. With the gathering darkness of every evening, thousands of the natives assembled in a grove of cocoanut trees near the ship; and the fires round which they danced, were scarce ever extinguished till the break of day...[1839:94-95].

In May Charles Stewart accompanied the Queen Mother Keōpūolani to Lahaina, Maui, where he witnessed many *hula* performances. He described in detail only the first that he saw there:

> Wednesday, 18 [June, 1823]...towards sunset, we observed an immense crowd of people in the grove, near the establishment of Keopuolani; and hundreds of others hastening from every direction to the same spot. A *hula-hula*, or native dance, was performing in honor of the arrival of the queen and princess.
>
> The dancers were two interesting girls, ten years of age. Their dresses were of beautiful yellow native cloth, arranged in thick folds and festoons from the waist to the knee; with wreaths of evergreen and wild flowers on their heads and necks, ornaments of ivory on their wrists, and a kind of buskin round the ancles, formed of dog's teeth, and loosely fastened to network of hemp so as to rattle like the castanet in the motions of the dance. The musicians were six men, seated on the ground with large calabashes before them, which they beat with short sticks. The sound of these, accompanied by that of their voices repeating the song, constituted the rude music. The girls occasionally joined in the song, and often were the only singers, continuing the subject in duet, and at times by a solo. The motions of the dance were slow and graceful, and, in this instance, free from indelicacy of action; and the song, or rather recitative, accompanied by much gesticulation, was dignified and harmonious in its numbers. The theme of the whole, was the character and praises of the queen and princesses, who were compared to everything sublime in nature, and exalted as gods [1839:144-145].

There are other accounts in missionary writings of the period that describe the more commonly seen performances. Among them are the accounts of William Ellis, an English missionary from Tahiti who came to Hawai'i in February of 1823 to assist the American missionaries. He spent over eighteen months here, two of them on the island of Hawai'i. On his way to Hawai'i island to take part in a survey of that island with a view toward expanding the mission stations, Ellis stopped at Lahaina, Maui, where the American missionaries Charles Stewart and William Richards were then attached to the household of the Queen Mother Keōpūolani. On the day of his arrival, July 4th, Ellis witnessed a *hula*:

> ...a party of musicians and dancers arrived before the house of Keopuolani, and commenced a hura ka raau, (dance to the beating of a stick). Five musicians advanced first, each with a staff in his left hand, five or six feet long, about three or four inches in diameter at one end, and tapering off to a point at the other.
>
> In his right hand he held a small stick of hard wood, six or nine inches long, with which he commenced his music, by striking the small stick on the larger one, beating time all the while with his right foot on a stone, placed on the ground beside him for that purpose.

> Six women, fantastically dressed in yellow tapas, crowned with garlands of flowers, having also wreaths of the sweet-scented flowers of the gardenia on their necks, and branches of the fragrant mairi [*maile*], (another native plant), bound round their ancles, now made their way by couples through the crowd, and, arriving at the area, on one side of which the musicians stood, began their dance.
>
> Their movements were slow, and though not always graceful, exhibited nothing offensive to modest propriety.
>
> Both musicians and dancers alternately chanted songs in honor of former gods and chiefs of the islands, apparently much to the gratification of the numerous spectators.
>
> After they had continued their hura, (song and dance), for about half an hour, the queen, Keopuolani, requested them to leave off, as the time had arrived for evening worship. The music ceased; the dancers sat down; ...I preached to the surrounding multitude with special reference to their former idolatrous dance, and the vicious customs connected therewith...[Ellis 1917:59].

On the 14th of July Ellis arrived at Kailua, Kona, where he met the other missionaries of the survey party and Kalua-i-Konahale Kuakini, then governor of the island of Hawai'i. His description of a *hula 'āla'apapa* there reads:

> In the afternoon, a party of strolling musicians and dancers arrived at Kairua. About four o'clock they came, followed by crowds of people, and arranged themselves on a fine sandy beach, in front of one of the governor's houses, where they exhibited a native dance, called hura araapapa.
>
> The five musicians first seated themselves in a line on the ground, and spread a piece of folded cloth on the sandy beach before them. Their instrument was a large calabash, or rather two, one of an oval shape about three feet high, the other perfectly round, very neatly fastened to it, having also an aperture about three inches in diameter at the top.
>
> Each musician held his instrument before him with both hands, and produced his music by striking it on the ground, where he had laid the piece of cloth, and beating it with his fingers, or the palms of his hands. As soon as they began to sound their calabashes, the dancer, a young man, about the middle stature, advanced through the opening crowd. His jet-black hair hung in loose and flowing ringlets down his naked shoulders; his necklace was made of a vast number of strings of nicely braided human hair, tied together behind, while a paraoa (an ornament made of a whale's tooth) hung pendant from it on his breast; his wrists were ornamented with bracelets, formed of polished tusks of the hog, and his ancles with loose buskins, thickly set with dog's teeth, the rattle of which, during the dance, kept time with the music of the calabash drum. A beautiful yellow tapa was tastefully fastened round his loins, reaching to his knees. He began his dance in front of the musicians, and moved forwards and backwards, across the area, occasionally chanting the achievements of former kings of Hawaii. The governor sat at the end of the ring, opposite to the musicians, and appeared gratified with the performance, which continued until the evening [1917:74].

On the following day Ellis witnessed another *hula* performance. His description of this day's performance follows.

> About four o'clock in the afternoon, another party of musicians and dancers, followed by multitudes of people, took their station nearly on the spot occupied yesterday by those from Kau. The musicians, seven in number, seated themselves on the sand; a curiously

> carved drum, made by hollowing out a solid piece of wood, and covering the top with shark's skin, was placed before each, which they beat with the palm or fingers of their right hand. A neat little drum, made of the shell of a large cocoa-nut, was also fixed on the knee, by the side of the large drum, and beat with a small stick held in the left hand.
>
> When the musicians had arranged themselves in a line, across the beach, and a bustling man, who appeared to be master of the ceremonies, had, with a large branch of a cocoa-nut tree, cleared a circle of considerable extent, two interesting little children, (a boy and a girl,) apparently about nine years of age, came forward, habited in the dancing costume of the country, with garlands of flowers on their heads, wreaths around their necks, bracelets on their wrists, and buskins on their ankles.
>
> When they had reached the centre of the ring, they commenced their dance to the music of the drums; cantilating, alternately with the musicians, a song in honor of some ancient of Hawaii.
>
> The governor of the island was present, accompanied, as it is customary for every chieftain of distinction to be on public occasions, by a retinue of favourite chiefs and attendants.
>
> ...he appeared on this occasion in a light European dress, and sat on a Canton-made arm chair, opposite the dancers, during the whole exhibition.
>
> The beach was crowded with spectators, and the exhibition kept up with great spirit, till the overspreading shades of evening put an end to their mirth, and afforded a respite for the poor children, whose little limbs must have been very much fatigued by two hours of constant exercise.
>
> We were anxious to address the multitude on the subject of religion before they should disperse; but so intent were they on their amusement, that they could not have been diverted from it. I succeeded, however, in taking a sketch of the novel assemblage, in which, a youth, who had climbed a high pole, (that, looking over the heads of the throng who surrounded the dancers, he might witness the scene,) formed a conspicuous object [Fig. 6].
>
> A messenger now invited us to sup with the governor, and we soon after joined him and his friends around his hospitable board.
>
> Our repast...was enlivened by an interesting youthful board, twelve or fourteen years of age, who was seated on the ground in the large room in which we were assembled, and who, during the supper, sung, in a monotonous but pleasing strain, the deeds of former chiefs, ancestors of our host. His fingers...beat, in a manner responsive to his song, a rustic little drum, formed of a calabash, beautifully stained, and covered at the head with a piece of shark skin [1917:78-80].

The episode that Ellis described illustrates the sometimes fine distinction between a *hula* and an *oli* performance. The content of the song, a *ko'ihonua*, or genealogical eulogy, belonged properly to the *oli*, as did the chanter's style of rendition, while the small drum was commonly used for the *hula*. No gesturing with the drum or hand is recorded, however, and the performance is deemed to have been an *oli*.

On the following day, the 16th of July, Ellis finally had an opportunity to preach to the people, as he reported.

> At four p.m. the musicians from Kau again collected on the beach, and the dancer commenced a hura, similar to that exhibited on Monday evening. We had previously appointed a religious meeting for

Fig. 6. A *HULA* PERFORMANCE AT KAILUA, HAWAI'I, IN 1823. William Ellis. Published in Ellis' *A Narrative of a Tour through Hawaii*. London, 1826. (Bishop Mus. Neg. No. 39061)

> this evening, and, about an hour before sun-set, proposed to the governor to hold it on the beach, where the people were already assembled. He approved, and followed us to the edge of the circle, where we took our station, opposite the musicians.
>
> At the governor's request the music ceased, and the dancer came and sat down just in front of us. We sang a hymn; I then offered up a short prayer, and afterwards addressed the people from Acts xiv.15: "And preach unto you, that ye should turn from these vanities unto the living God..." [Ellis 1917:81].

In 1824, missionary Elisha Loomis returning from a journey to the summit of Mauna Loa, passed through the fishing village of Kā'iliki'i in Kā'ū. There he found about 200 people gathered, waiting for a dance concert to begin. The dance was "performed by three or four females fancifully dressed with 20 or 30 folds of elegant tapa around the waist--a string of dog's [pigs'] tusks on each wrist, and a bandage to which was affixed loosely a great number of dog's teeth around the ankles. There were five or six musicians, who sang with all their might, beating at the same time upon calabashes..." (Loomis Ms.:13).

These early 19th century descriptions of the *hula* seen performed as entertainment for the chiefs and their people corroborate what both Malo and Kamakau had to say, and surely reflect what had been customary in the music and dance of pre-contact Hawai'i. Interestingly, young children were often the dancers, as in Kamakau's seemingly highly exaggerated account (1961:105), and even more interestingly, the musicians often outnumbered the dancers in such "everyday" performances.

These were days of transition into a new religious experience and viewpoint for many of the Hawaiian chiefs. For a time old and new customs marched side by side, and *hula* performances occurred almost daily near the residences of chiefs, with great crowds attending. Soon, however, under the pressure of missionary sermonizing against the *hula* and because of the desire to embrace Christianity, the *hula* fell into disfavor among many of the high chiefs. Stewart recorded a few instances of their disapprobation in 1823 and 1824 (1839:153, 241-42, 261-62). There were other chiefs, however, who clung to the old ways. In January of 1824 Stewart reported from Lahaina:

> For a year past, except in one or two instances, we have scarce heard the sounds of the native songs and dances. But an expected heir, in a high branch of the Pitt family, has filled the minds of some of the chiefs and people, not particularly interested in the palapala and the pule--learning and religion--with a desire for the renewal of former expressions of joy on such occasions: among which songs and dances, in honor of the young chief at his birth, were some of the most favorite. These persons have for some time had pieces in preparation for the event. The rehearsal of such...disturb the peacefulness and quietude of our nights; and the groves around us, especially since an unclouded moon has been on the increase, are filled till daybreak, with the dull and monotonous drumming of the calabash and musical sticks, accompanied by the more piercing and equally rude and inharmonious intonations of the voice.
>
> Our governess, Wahine Pio, sister of Mr. Pitt--Kalaimoku--is the grandmother of the expected chief. She has never been distinguished for her attachment to the new system of things, and is supposed to have ordered the practicings of the hula. The common people, desirous of having the dances, have sedulously encouraged a report in circulation, that Kalaimoku, still at Kauai, has sent orders to the

> windward islands, to have all attention to the palapala and pule, except the observance of the Sabbath, suspended for the present, and to have all the people engage in the dances, as was formerly the case, when thousands joined at one time in the same performance [Stewart 1839:260-261].

The pious chiefs prevailed, and the *hula* concert was not performed. Stewart concluded his account by saying, "We are satisfied that the report in reference to Kalaimoku is false, and that he has not commanded, or even countenanced, the spirit of dissipation existing in some" [1839:262].

The missionaries had, of course, been appalled by what they insisted was the "licentiousness" of the *hula*. Additionally, they disliked the amount of time the people "wasted" in attending performances, or in preparation for *hula* concerts--time much better spent, in their opinion, in learning the *palapala* and the *pule*. Their exhortations had their cumulative effect. By September of 1825 the Rev. Stewart could say:

> Incidents of a most interesting character, in reference to the success of the mission and the state of the people, were [in the previous three months] daily taking place--incidents which testified to a change, in the intellectual and moral prospects of the nation, of the most gratifying character.
>
> ...In the region of every missionary establishment, the songs, and dances, and games, and dissipation, once so universal, had ceased [1839:319].

While this may have been true in areas near to mission stations, in country areas where there were no missionary establishments, and in the households of unconverted chiefs, for whom the new religious teachings had little appeal, however, the old ways continued. One such chief was Boki, brother of the Kalanimokū and Wahinepi'o mentioned above. A *hula* troupe seems to have been in residence at or near Boki's place at Wai'anae, O'ahu, through the 1820s. Boki accompanied Liholiho on his ill-fated trip to England; after the death of the king and his queen, Kamāmalu, in July of 1824, Boki returned to Hawai'i on the ship bearing the bodies. This was the *Blonde*, under command of Capt. Lord Byron, which arrived in Honolulu in May of 1825. After the funeral observances were over, Byron stayed on for a visit in the islands. On June 1, he went to Wai'anae, where Boki's *po'e hula* entertained his party with a *hula* composed in celebration of the return of their chief.

> We were seated on mats in front of the dancers, who were twenty-five young girls disposed in five rows. Their dresses consisted each of two pieces of fine tapa; the under piece, dyed yellow, fell only to the knee in full and graceful folds; the upper tapa was green, arranged in festoons, and confined to the waist by a broad band of the same. The heads of the dancers were adorned with chaplets of flowers, and their arms and legs with network, to which dogs' teeth were loosely attached, so as to rattle and produce an effect not unlike that of the castanet in the dance.
>
> On either side of us sat two old men holding large calabashes, on which they beat time with the palms of their hands to the dance and to a slow song which accompanied it. The dance itself consisted of various and ever-changing motions of the limbs and body, without moving farther from the spot than a single step forwards, backwards, to the right or to the left. The song was monotonous, and sung, sometimes by a single voice, sometimes by two, and then the whole chorus would join. It was in praise of Boki, and congratulation of his happy return

> to Oahu. They tell us the dance may consist of any number of persons, from one to a thousand. The songs are frequently composed for the occasion; they are sometimes in dialogue, and usually in praise of some chief. They are of all descriptions: religious, heroic, and amatory [Byron 1826:143-144].

Later in the month the *Blonde* sailed to Hilo, Hawai'i, and Lord Byron and a party made a visit to Kīlauea crater. On the way they stopped for refreshments at some temporary huts that Ka'ahumanu had ordered built for their comfort, and while there were entertained again with a *hula* performance. This one was composed as a lament for the death of Liholiho. It was described by Andrew Bloxam, naturalist aboard the *Blonde:*

> While we were here we were treated with a native dance. A girl of sixteen or seventeen years of age, ornamented with bracelets of hog's tusks on each arm, with greaves of dog's teeth set in parallel rows and reaching on the forepart from the knees to the ankles while two different colored tapas were arranged gracefully around her middle was introduced thus ornamented before the huts. A circle was immediately formed by the kanakas into which two old men entered, each with a large ornamented calabash and sat themselves on the ground. The men commenced, both performing exactly the same motions, beating the calabashes with the palms of their hands and sometimes striking them on the ground, accompanying the motion with a song in a long monotonous tone. The damsel now commenced her part keeping time and gracefully moving her arms and legs to the sound of the drums, while she very now and then relieved the two men by uttering a few words herself. We found that they were lamenting the death of Riho Riho but we could not understand anything that was said [Bloxam 1925:60].

In Honolulu the presentation of a formal *hula* concert remained the customary court entertainment for visiting dignitaries for some years to come. In January of 1827 Captain Beechey of the British royal navy came to anchor in Honolulu Harbor. The king, young Kamehameha III, gave a feast or *lū'au* in his honor, and at its close a grand *hula* performance was offered for his entertainment. Beechey's description of the affair follows.

> ...The performance opened with a song in honour of Tamehameha, to which succeeded an account of the visit of Rio Rio and his queen to England; their motives for undertaking the voyage were explained; their parting with their friends at Woahoo [O'ahu], their sea-sickness; their landing in England; the king's attempts to speak English; the beautiful women of this country; and the sickness and death of the youthful royal pair, were described with much humour, good nature, and feeling.
>
> The natives were delighted with this performance, especially with that part which exhibited the sea-sickness, and the efforts of the king to speak English; but our slight acquaintance with the language did not enable us fully to appreciate the allusions. In the next performance, however, this defect was less felt. The song was executed by three celebrated bards, whose gray beards hung down upon their breasts: they were clothed in their rude native costume, and each had the under part of his right arm tatooed in straight lines from the wrist to the armpit. They accompanied themselves upon drums made of two gourds neatly joined together, and ornamented with black devices. Each bard had one of these instruments attached to his left wrist by a cord; the instrument was placed upon a cushion, and the performer throughout measured time by beating with his right hand upon the aperture of the gourd. The subject related to the illustrious Tamehameha, whose warlike exploits are the constant theme of these people. Occasionally the bards seemed to be inspired; they

> struck their left breasts violently with the palms of their hands, and performed a number of evolutions with their drums, all of which were executed simultaneously, and with ease, decision, and grace. On the whole it was an exhibition very creditable to the talents of the performers. To this succeeded several dances: the first, performed by a native of Atooi [Kaua'i], was recommended principally by a display of muscular energy; the next was executed by a man who was esteemed the most accomplished actor of his time in Woahoo, and the son of the most celebrated dancer the islands ever had. He wore an abundance of native cloth, variously stained, wrapped about his waist, and grass ornaments fixed upon his legs above the ancles. A garland of green leaves passed over his right shoulder and under his left arm, and a wreath of yellow blossoms, very commonly worn in the Sandwich Islands, was wound twice round his head. Unlike the former dance, the merit of this consisted in an exhibition of graceful action, and a repetition of elegant and unconstrained movements.
>
> The dance of the females was spoiled by a mistaken refinement, which prevented their appearing, as formerly, with no other dress than a covering to the hips, and a simple garland of flowers upon the head; instead of this they were provided with frilled chemises, which so far from taking away the appearance of indecency, produced an opposite effect, and at once gave the performance a stamp of indelicacy. In this dance, which by the way is the only one the females of these islands have, they ranged themselves in a line, and began swinging the arms carelessly, but not ungracefully, from side to side; they then proceeded to the more active part of the dance, the principal art of which consisted in twisting the loins without moving the feet or the bust. After fatiguing themselves in accomplishing this to the satisfaction of the spectators, they jumped sideways, still twisting their bodies, and accompanying their actions with a chorus, the words of which we supposed bore some allusion to the performance [1831:2:105-107].

From Beechey's description, it appears that the musical narrative of Liholiho's trip to England may have been performed as an *oli*, since there is no mention of instrument or movement. The second performance, although not recognized as a dance by Beechey, was a *hula noho*, performed in half-kneeling position. The instrumental accompaniment of the gourd drums, the brandishing of the instruments, and gesturing of hands all clearly mark this performance as a *hula*.

1830-1850: THE DECLINE BEGINS

The converted queen regent Ka'ahumanu had been baptized in December of 1825, and in reaction to missionary teaching had begun to look upon the *hula* as a "heathen practice." In 1830, according to Kamakau (1961:299), she forbade its performance in public. However effective her edict may have been, it was short-lived; after her death in June of 1832 the edict was ignored by chiefs and commoners alike, mainly because of the "fall from grace" of the young king Kauikeaouli in 1833. While the edict does not seem to have been reinstated when the king returned to more moralistic ways, the tone of missionary-oriented accounts imply that it had never been rescinded. At any rate, in 1836 the formal *hula* concert was again recorded as "state entertainment" in the account by Théodore-Adolphe Barrot, French consul for Manila, who was aboard the *Bonite* when it stopped at Honolulu (Barrot 1978). The visitors were given an entertainment by the king at Luakaha, his country place in Nu'uanu Valley (Fig. 7). It will be noted that Barrot considered as dance only the performance by the female dancer in standing position. In fact,

Fig. 7. "Scène de Danse aux Îles Sandwich." Lauvergne. Plate 42 in *Album Historique* accompanying Vaillant's *Voyage autour du monde*....Paris 1866. (Bishop Mus. Neg. No. 29192)

the two performances by men that Barrot described first were *hula noho*, and were illustrative of the types of honorific *hula* that opened the formal *hula* concerts of the chiefs of old. Barrot's account takes note of the changes that had come to the *hula*.

> After dinner we all mounted our horses again and started for the King's country house, where we were to hear Hawaiian songs and to see Hawaiian dancing. On our way to the Pali we had left this house on the right. Everything had been previously arranged: mats were spread in front of the cottage, and chairs were placed in a circle, and first, five singers appeared and kneeled down. Each of them was armed with a large calabash, which was made thin towards the middle; this calabash, held in the left hand by a string, aided the expression of their gestures in a singular manner. They were naked to the waist; their arms and breast were tattooed, and loose folds of tapa of various colors covered the lower part of their bodies. Their songs were a sort of recitative, or of modulated conversation, animated or slow, as the subject required.
>
> The theme they had chosen, or which had been suggested to them, was a eulogy of the king. They spoke at first of the love which his people had for him. "A flower," said they, "grows upon the mountain height.--When the stars hide themselves and the sun comes out from the sea, it turns of itself and holds out its cup for the morning dew. We climb to the mountain's summit and pluck the flower that we may bear this health-giving dew to Kauikeaouli."
>
> Then they extolled his prowess in war.--"His horse turns his head to look at him, for he knows that he does not bear a common man. His lance is always red with the heart's blood of his enemies, and his battle-axe bristles with the teeth of warriors, who have fallen under his blows. When he speaks, his voice is heard beyond the mountains, and all the warriors of Oahu hasten to range themselves around him, for they know that under such a chief their feet will speedily tread in blood."
>
> It may be perceived that Hawaiian poets also indulge in some license, and that court flatterers are everywhere the same. Kauikeaouli listened to it all with the greatest indifference.
>
> But what was admirable in this song, which however had a compress of only two or three notes, was the perfect accordance with which the five singers spoke and gesticulated. They must have rehearsed many times to attain to this degree of perfection. Each one of the five pronounced at the same time, the same note, the same word, made the same gesture, and moved his calabash in the most perfect time, either to the right or to the left, or striking it against the ground he caused it to give forth sounds somewhat similar to those of a bass drum.--It might be said that they were all moved by the same impulse of thought and will. Sometimes the gestures varied and became inconceivably rapid, yet I was never able to discover a mistake. The voice, the hands, the fingers, the calabashes, the bodies of the five singers were always extended, moved, regulated by a spontaneous movement.
>
> These singers were succeeded by three others, who were clad like the former, but garlands of leaves encircled their foreheads, while strings of the yellow fruit of the *pandanus odorantissimus* ornamented their necks and arms. All three were of admirable proportions, and of a beauty of countenance seldom seen on these islands. They sung of love and pleasure;--of love, Hawaiian, in its characteristics, a little too material, perhaps, and which was expressed by gestures none too modest. Pleasure the most sensual was indicated by the looks, the gestures, the words, and even the tones of these young men. At one time their countenances became dark, they waved with violence the feather fans which they held in the left hand, and the base which, formed

> of a small calabash filled with shells [*'ulī'ulī*] and struck by the right at regular intervals, performed the office of castanets. Thus they sung the frenzy of jealousy.
>
> The dancing was, at length, announced. But the time is past when the swarms of male and female dancers assembled on the green grass, and there, in their graceful dances accompanied by songs, recounted the glorious achievements of warriors. Singers and dancers were the historiographers of the country. In their memory the ancient traditions were preserved. The details of a war formed the subject of a song, and from the songs of the ancient Hawaiian bards have navigators drawn materials for their descriptions. It is then with regret that I have seen these national songs prohibited, under the pretext of their being profane. As well almost, might Homer and Virgil be prohibited! Dancing has also fallen into great disfavor in consequence of missionary influence. The dance which we witnessed felt the effects of this disposition.
>
> Only one female dancer appeared. Formerly, graceful and easy, the upper part of the body of these dancers was entirely naked. Pieces of cloth, suspended from the hips, and hanging in graceful folds, imparted a sort of originality to their movements.--Necklaces composed of the fruit of the pandanus, garlands of leaves or of feathers, bracelets of teeth either of the dog or whale encircling the arms and legs, and shaking in regular time, composed their apparel. The one who presented herself before us, wore a calico shirt. Her dancing appeared monotonous. She sung at the same time, and a singer behind her, lent the assistance of his song and marked the time, by striking a calabash against the ground. Only one thing appeared remarkable in this dance; and that is, that the dancer regulated the measure, and, from time to time, gave to the musician the subject of his song. The musician endeavored to make his time accord with the movements of her feet, and he succeeded with remarkable precision. Yet, at the end of half an hour, the dance began to seem long. The king perceived that we were becoming weary, and, as it had not been possible to procure other female dancers, we listened to a few more songs, after which we mounted our horses to return to Honolulu.
>
> Formerly the women were passionately fond of these sports and these public dances. Many females even of the royal family had the reputation of being finished actresses; for this people had once had plays, and the members only of distinguished families appeared on the stage. Now, this taste has yielded to the counsels of the missionaries. Perhaps also the fear of their reprobation alone prevents the women from giving themselves up to their old practices; at any rate, we were completely excluded from the society of the ladies of the King's family [Barrot 1978:50-55].

It is clear from this account that the *hula* was by no means completely stamped out in the 1830s. However, no account of the period other than Barrot's speaks of the *hula* as the art form that it once was, and his remarks in this regard bear repeating: "It is with regret that I have seen these national songs prohibited under the pretext of their being profane.... Dancing has also fallen into great disfavor in consequence of missionary influence. The dance which we witnessed felt the effects of this disposition" [Ibid.].

The next visitor who wrote of the *hula* was not as sympathetic as Barrot. This was Charles Wilkes, commander of the United States Exploring Expedition of 1838-1842. A great deal of the information that Wilkes incorporated in the narrative of the Hawai'i expedition (1845) was received from the missionaries, principally William Richards. On the subject of the *hula* Wilkes said,

> Since the introduction of Christianity, these amusements [songs and dances] have been interdicted; for, although the missionaries were somewhat averse to destroying those of an innocent character, yet, such was the proneness of all to indulge in lascivious thoughts and actions, that it was deemed by them necessary to put a stop to the whole, in order to root out the licentiousness that pervaded the land. They therefore discourage any kind of nocturnal assemblies, as they are well satisfied that it would take but little to revive these immoral propensities with more force than ever. The watchfulness of the government, police, and missionaries, is constantly required to enforce the due observance of the laws [Wilkes 1845:4,47].

Although Wilkes' account indicates that at the time of his visits to Hawai'i there were laws in existence that prohibited the performance of the *hula* in public, none such have been found. It may be that there were edicts directed against the *hula* circulated by proclamation or hand bills, none of which seem to have survived.

Throughout the 1840s the *hula* continued to be taught and performed, at least in the country districts. Missionaries on Kaua'i reported that the *hula* was frequently performed for the enjoyment of the chiefess-governor of the island, Miriam Kekau'onohi, daughter of the Wahine-pi'o who had once been the governess of Maui (see p. 33). In a letter written to Levi Chamberlain on October 2, 1844, Samuel Whitney wrote,

> We hear that a good deal of wickedness is going on at Hanalei these days. Our Governess has been there ever since her return from Oahu. It is said she has been drunk on brandy, moe-kolohe, huluhulu [sic; read hulahula], &c. I saw her there last week and talked with her about it. She stoutly denied it all, except the hula....

The missionary-teacher at Wai'oli wrote in January of 1845:

> "Kekauonohi has taken up her residence at Kealia, about half way between Waioli & Koloa, where she can take her fill of hula with none to molest" [Stauder 1979].

Emerson recorded several occasions in this decade when Kamehameha III was entertained by the *po'e hula*. One such occasion is recorded for Waimanalo, O'ahu, in the year 1846 or '47, when a *hula kōlani* was performed for the king's pleasure. Emerson described this *hula* as being of "gentle, gracious action, acted and sung while the performers kept a sitting position, and was without instrumental accompaniment" (1909:216). On another occasion in 1847 the king was entertained with a *hula manō* ("shark hula") while at Waimea, O'ahu (Ibid.:221). This, too, was a *hula noho*, "sitting *hula*," performed without instrument. At Kahuku, O'ahu, in 1849 the king was again entertained with a *hula*. The chant of this *hula* is given by Emerson, but he did not learn what kind of *hula* was danced to it (Ibid.:129-130). Emerson also recorded the performance of the *hula kā'eke'eke* at the royal palace about 1850 (Ibid.:144).

The "marionettes" that Emerson described as used in the *hula ki'i** (1909:91-92) date to about this time. Six of these puppets came into the possession of Emerson through the brother of a *hula* master in the court of Kamehameha III. Emerson says, "These ki'i have therefore figured in performances that have been graced by the presence of King Kauikeaouli (Kamehameha III) and his queen, Kalama, and by his successors since then down to the times of Kalākaua. At the

---

*Emerson gives chant texts for six *hula ki'i*, which he described as dances of "marionettes," and which he accepted as ancient (1909:91-102). See pp. 26,55.

so-called Jubilee, the anniversary of Kalākaua's fiftieth birthday, these marionettes were very much in evidence" (Ibid.:91). Three of these marionettes are now in the Bishop Museum ethnological collection (B221, B222, B223) (see Fig. 13, p. 55).

1850-1870: THE REGULATION OF PUBLIC DISPLAY

Missionary influence, while strong, never wiped out the *hula* as a functional part of the Hawaiian society. Faced with this undeniable fact, the authorities sought to curb performances by regulation. The first published law regulating public performances of the *hula* was an Act passed in May of 1851. It empowered the Minister of the Interior to license all "public shows... to which admission is obtainable on payment of money...and the chief of police in any town or district where the same shall be exhibited may regulate such show or exhibition in such manner as he shall think necessary for the preservation of order and the public peace" (Laws...Section 1-2, 1851). Failure to obtain a license was punishable by a fine of $500. In 1859 the Minister was further empowered to issue annual licenses for shows, including Hawaiian *hula*, "not of an immoral character, to which admission is obtainable by the payment of money," subject to payment of a fee of ten dollars for each performance (Civil Code, 1859, Ch. 7, Art. 2, Sec. 96). Furthermore, no license was to be granted for any place other than Honolulu or Lahaina (Ibid.:Sec. 99).

Failure to comply carried a penalty of a $500 fine or imprisonment at hard labor for six months (Ibid.:Sec. 98). In its session of 1864-65 the legislative assembly amended Section 98 of the Civil Code to reduce the above penalties to $100 or three months at labor (Laws...1865, p. 4). In 1870 the assembly amended Section 96, which reduced the fee for each performance to $5.00, and repealed Section 99, which had restricted performances to Honolulu and Lahaina (Laws... 1870, p. 25).

The reduction in fees, fines, and penalties, and the lifting of the restriction on permissable localities for public performances opened the way for a wide participation in *hula* performances. In addition, the open indulgence of the rulers and chiefs in the pleasures of the *hula* were common knowledge and were aped by the people (Fig. 8).

Nevertheless, during this period--roughly 1850 to 1875--disapprobation of the *hula* was often voiced, not only among the self-styled moral leaders of the *haole* community, but among the more moralistic of the Hawaiians themselves. In some extenuation of their severe disapproval it may be noted that the *hula* exhibited by paid performers were for the most part attuned to the taste and expectation of audiences considerably more uncouth than those we have so far read of as being present at chiefly *hula* entertainments. Many, if not most, of these dances were far from being the stately, or dignified, or graceful *hula* performed for visiting dignitaries, and some were lascivious by any standards. There can be no doubt that sexually exciting dances were a large part of the repertoire of those dancers who performed for transient sailors, especially during the visits of the whaling fleets. Not surprisingly, such dances are not found described. G. W. Bates, a visitor who travelled on his own throughout the islands in 1853, came nearest to such a description (1854:284-285). That such dances were not an innovation, but had been commonly performed from ancient times, must be admitted (see p. 17).

Fig. 8. *HULA* DANCERS, c. 1858. (Ambrotype, Bishop Mus.; photographer unknown)

1860-1880: EXPRESSION OF DISAPPROBATION BY HAWAIIANS

Among themselves, the *hula* continued to be a major source of pleasure to the Hawaiians. We have no expressed opinions of those who indulged in this pastime, but the very fact that clandestine *hula* schools operated on all the islands and that people were irresistibly drawn to *hula* performances argues that the majority of the people never gave up this facet of their lifestyle (Fig. 9).

We do, however, have written evidence of the disapprobation of some of the Hawaiians of the period. The following extracts of letters to the Hawaiian newspaper *Kuokoa* in the 1860s and '70s present the views of some of these Hawaiian Calvinists (*Nupepa Kuokoa*, 1864-1880). The extracts are presented in some detail here, both as an expression of their viewpoint and because the descriptions and comments give us a glimpse of what was actually happening among the *po'e hula* in the mid-century.*

The first letter presented here may be the earliest written description of the rituals accompanying the graduation of a *hula* class:

> To the *Ku'oko'a*, Greetings. There is much hula dancing at Halehaku [Maui]. Much of it is being done at the house of a man named Ka-ma'i-ka'a-loa. There hula is danced daily and this is what he does. When a pupil applies at his school, he asks, "Will you remain permanently in my troupe?" When the pupil answers "Yes," the teacher prays....
>
> On the 5th of August, the class graduated. It meant a procuring of a pig and roasting it. The house was bedecked with greenery and inside was an altar. The altar was decorated with all kinds of flowers. Should you ask, "What is the altar for?" the teacher would answer, "For Laka to occupy. This is true; I know it, not just heard it. I know that Laka dwells on the altar for she is the goddess of the dance." This is what they say. At the door of the house two long sticks were set up, entwined with *maile* and greenery of all kinds. When all of these things just described were ready, the pupils took their places within the house. All within was quiet, not a sound was uttered. A man stood up and uttered a strange prayer to the god. Everyone joined him in praying.
>
> After praying, the dancing began. Their silly behavior was most unbecoming. There were nine dancers in all and their names are Hu, Kekila, Kahikina, Kahea, Lino, Kapahi, Kaleiopu, Kaniho and Keakealani. Two of the girls are under eight years of age. Oh how sad for these young girls to be permitted by their parents to dance. If it is true that their parents have sent them to learn to dance the hula, leading them to a worthless practice, then the misbehaving parents should be arrested.
>
> Here is another thing, perhaps the Constitution does not permit these people to dance at Halehaku or elsewhere. The kind of dance they are doing is with the feathered rattles [*'ulī'ulī*] and if the Constitution allows them to dance with a feathered rattle then they are in the right in persisting in this worthless practice. If the Constitution does not, then the police should watch at the place mentioned above, because these people are doing it all the time [S.K.K., Makawao, Maui, Aug. 9, 1864, in *Kuokoa*, September 10, 1864].

* * *

---

*The letters from which these extracts are taken were translated by Mary Kawena Pukui.

Fig. 9. "Scène pris dans l'île d'Oahu (Îles Sandwich)." J. Masselot. Published as Plate 22 in *Atlas Pittoresque*, accompanying Du Petit-Thouars' *Voyage autour du monde*....Paris 1840-1864.

...Up at Kawananakoa in Nu'uanu Valley [O'ahu] is a house where hula dancing is accompanied with a gourd drum. There the drum is playing daily, often nightly, throughout the year...Have those people paid for a permit allowing them to dance the hula? If not, why aren't they arrested by the police? A police should guard that area, spy on and arrest those who encourage the cultivation of idle minds [*Kuokoa*, April 16, 1864].

* * *

My mind is stirred to write to the newspaper about this evil thing, pleasure loving in Hanapepe [Kaua'i]...In the two years I've resided here...I have noticed how it has increased.

These are the kinds of dances that they are indulging in: those with shark skin drums, with gourd drums, the *ki'elei,** the *ka-la'au* and so forth. Many go to watch the dancers, including women and children. They enjoy them and are learning to do them. All of the church members are participating in this worthless pastime with the exception of two.

If there is a hula at the residence of Wahine-'ae'a, all of the men and women go there...This is their kind of conversation: "So-and so is a good dancer; she is so attractive; her gesture, the movement of her feet and of her hips are good." All of the young people who are employed under yearly contracts at Koloa, have attended the hula and have given money to Wahine-'ae'a's girls. They were punished for it by the district judge of Kauai [S. Papiohuli, in *Kuokoa*, Aug. 27, 1864].

* * *

News of East Maui...The ku'i** dance. The people are spending much time in this occupation, just as they do in drinking sweet potato brew. This activity was started at Mu'olea by Kapu, and his pupils taught others all over east Maui. If a joint feast is held at Kipahulu, those of Ko'olau and Hana attend. If at Hana, those of Kipahulu and Ko'olau come there. Men, women, boys and girls are being taught.

This is very much like the 'ōlapa of olden times and is done with the idea of preventing aches. Here in Hana they are singing songs like those for the hula, and drinking songs. They also chant old familiar ones and compose others themselves. They do this all the time [*Kuokoa*, Dec. 9, 1865].

* * *

The hula is increasing in our district and men and women go to watch. I, too, went. When I arrived at the place where the dancers danced, I saw many others there laughing till the tears ran. The names of the dancers were Keawe, Luahiwa, 'Ike'ole and 'Iwakiani. The instructors were Kanahele and his wife. They are the couple who are lighting these people with the lamps of Satan. One hula troupe was brought before the judge and was punished [D.W. Golia, Nawiliwili, Kauai, in *Kuokoa*, March 31, 1866].

* * *

---

*Described by Emerson as a dance "marked by strenuous body action, gestures with feet and hands, and that vigorous exercise of the pelvis and body termed *ami*, the chief feature of which was a rotation of the pelvis in circles and ellipses, which is not to be regarded as an effort to portray sexual attitudes. It was a performance in which the whole company stood and chanted the mele without instrumental accompaniment" [1909:210]. Cf. Pukui & Elbert: "Type of hula in which the dancer danced in a squatting position" [1971:136]. (For more on the *ami* see Part II, p. 73).

**Emerson describes a *hula ku'i* that he designates as "hula ku'i Molokai" (1909:207). He says the dancers "were arranged in pairs who faced each other and went through motions similar to those of boxing" [Ibid.]. The Pukui & Elbert dictionary expands on this description; it reads "an ancient, fast dance with stamping, heel twisting, thigh slapping, dipping of the knees, doubling of fists as in boxing, vigorous gestures...and unaccompanied by instruments" [1971:83].

News of Waikiki-waena [O'ahu]...The sound of the hula drums of the daughters of Ke'ino-ho'omanawa-nui (Persistent Evil One) are heard no more. This was the constant occupation of Kaluahine and others...[*Kuokoa* April 21, 1866].

News of Waikiki-waena...It was thought that the hula was extinguished but the drums are still sounding. This continues because people attend to watch and if we remain at home instead, they can go on until they find Pale-ke'auka* and wear themselves out [*Kuokoa*, May 5, 1866].

* * *

J. N. Petero of Moanalua [O'ahu] has reported to us that hula dancing has been resumed there a few days ago. From his letter we have taken this: "Since the month of March I have seen the silvery backs of the sword fishes swaying with the youth of this locality. Our ancestors did the same and we have no proof that they profited thereby. So here others are following their example in a work that brings no good. Shouldn't we desert the old ways?" [*Kuokoa*, April 28, 1866].

* * *

In May of 1866, Victoria Kamāmalu Ka'ahumanu, sister of Kamehamehas IV and V, died at Honolulu. For over a month her body lay in state in 'Iolani Palace and hordes of Hawaiians came from all the islands to mourn her in the time-honored way--with wailing and with chanting and dancing the name songs (*mele inoa*) that had been composed for their *ali'i* in her lifetime.** No foreigners were allowed within the Palace gates until the night before the funeral procession. Mark Twain happened to be in Honolulu at that time and he wrote a fairly detailed and more or less sympathetic account of this chanting and dancing (Day 1975:126-128, 162-168 *passim*). He pointed out that the exclusion of foreigners and the license allowed the common people to mourn in the old way was by the express command of the king, Kamehameha V. Many Hawaiians disapproved of this type of display of grief, and their feelings were expressed editorially in the *Kuokoa*:

Old doings here in Hawaii are not ended. Some may ask, what kind of doings? The hula. Hula belongs to pleasure and is not for the sober-minded who regret the passing of a beloved one. If so, then why was this done in the yard of Hawaii's palace in the days of mourning for the Princess, V. K. Kaahumanu? That wasn't the right thing to do because it was done with real joy as though a great good would be derived therefrom. It was the mourning of a pagan people, not of a people who believe Jehovah to be the true God.

Are we truly pagans? No indeed; the light of learning of this little kingdom has reached out to the great kingdoms of the world. Why then this heartless deed to the dead? Isn't it so that when a high chief dies that we know we shall see him no more, and mourn him for a proper length of time. It isn't wrong to lament, to chant his name *mele* (*kahea inoa*) if done as a regret for the separation, but to dance to and fro, that is not affectionate mourning [*Kuokoa*, July 7, 1866].

The *hula ku'i*, first mentioned in 1865 (see p. 45), was the subject of disapproval in the following letter from Moloka'i:

A ku'i dancing group has been organized at Kawela [Moloka'i].... Some girls who are well behaved and religious are being trained, as well as some boys who are capable of preaching in the meeting houses....

*Translator's note: A play on words in both names; the latter carries an insult. M.K.P.

**For more on this mourning custom see Handy & Pukui 1958:156.

One Saturday evening, while I was riding on horseback, I came to a certain place. I drew near to the house where the ku'i dancing was being held and heard thumping noises inside. I dismounted and went to the window. As I looked in I saw two women and two men standing up. While I watched, I was reminded of cocks who are being made to fight, with tail feathers jerking. The people gathered inside were absorbed in listening. Their gathering inside of K's house was like the congregating of hinalea fish around the basket traps of those who fish thus. The ears of these religious people were not offended at listening to them. Such benightedness!

These people's instructor is Kua'ino from Honolulu. His residence is in Kaunakahakai [sic] and his ku'i dancing house is at Kawela. I looked at this instructor's face when he stood up and uttered a ku'i chant before his pupils. His lips trembled and he spoke with effort, as though stammering. This is one of the ku'i chants I heard:

The smoke of Hamakua rises	Kū ka uwahi o Hamakua
In back of the forest of 'O'opu-ola.	Ma kua i ka nahele o 'O'opu-ola.
The *'ohiki* crabs of long eye-stalks--	'O ka 'ohiki-makaloa--
Your eyes, like those of the *'ohiki*,	Ko maka i 'ohiki 'ia,
Are cut off by the bamboo--	A moku i ka 'ohe la*--
You are drawn to me!	Ho'opa'a mai!

This preceded another ku'i chant which I heard them doing, the one that is constantly uttered by the mouths of the pupils and others:

There at Maunahina	Aia i Maunahina
The chilling Kīpu'upu'u rain	A ka ua Kīpu'upu'u
Drawing up the skin**	Kō mai 'ana i ka 'ili
[Brings you] to the bosom of the ardent lover.	I ka poli o ka ipo ahi.
You can barely see	'A'ohe 'ike wale iho
The heel of my shoe,	I ka hila o ku'u kama'a,
Cut off as it is by the bamboo--	A moku i ka 'ohe la--
You are drawn to me!	Ho'opa'a mai!

This district was once the strongest in religion; the men and women stood fast, but now I see that half of them have gone into the work of the Devil. How sad for them!

I am making a request to the police of this district to be watchful and remove this evil tare that is growing with the wheat [P. Kawelaakawai, in *Kuokoa*, March 21, 1868].

* * *

The Mormons, who first came to Hawai'i in the 1850s, took a more liberal view of human nature than did the Calvinists who had preceded them. They became subject to censure for their allowing of pleasures. Said one indignant writer,

> There is no righteousness in that sect for one of the chief activities of the Mormons at Salt Lake City and in La'ie is dancing. In dancing mischief can develop between certain persons...In the month of August they had a feast which was attended by a multitude and the main occupation all through the night was hula dancing. Great indeed are the mistakes and errors of the Mormons! Do they not know that the hula belongs to the Devil's choir? Hula is improper among the religious because all leanings within the chants are unfit for the hearts of the righteous to rejoice in. Chants are composed with thoughts of love making or ridiculing [D. Onaona, in *Kuokoa*, Oct. 21, 1871].

*An allusion to the method of catching sand crabs by means of a bamboo snare, which catches and holds fast the eye-stalks. Figuratively, an ensnarement.

**The Kīpu'u'pu'u rain of Waimea, Hawai'i, is chilly, causing the skin to rise in goose pimples.

Disapproval of the *hula* on moral grounds continued through the 1870s as indicated in the following excerpts:

> Although the hula is a customary and familiar thing from ancient times, it does not belong in this progressive enlightened era. It is an ancient thing. Because I have seen the young people, the physically perfect, the aged, and whoever else in whom the urge has entered, to behave as children and indulge in this pastime, I think of the hula as the Devil's nest...
>
> Not very many people would attend a hula gathering unless something they call "mynah bird" (piha-'ekelo, fig., "full of chatter") is obtainable. This is fermented sweet potato juice mixed with *mo'o 'awa*.* The word usually applied to "mynah bird" was unsuitable, so they changed it. If they hear of "mynah bird" somewhere, many will walk, and there will be a company on horseback heading to where they can tilt a glass of it...The eyes look strange, the conversation becomes confused, and from their mouths come the silliest words--like this,
>
> | | |
> |---|---|
> | Where *kē* are you *kē* going | 'Auhea *kē* wale ke 'oe *kē* ho'i |
> | O companion *kē* of mine | E ku'u *kē* wale ke hoa ke nei? |
> | Let us *kē* be on our way | Hō'ae kaua *kē* wale *kē* ho'i |
> | To tilt *kē* a cup of juice *kē*. | I ka wala kiaha *kē* wale *kē* nei. |
>
> These lines are accompanied by a wink, the swaying this way and that, with the hands making improper gestures. Therefore I declare a second time that the hula is the Devil's nest, in which he looks about, rears himself up, and sniffs for the person he wishes to swallow....
>
> These words are not on the decent types of hula, a pleasant entertainment, but on the hulas that produce lust. While the Book is before you, look up this reference, "Beloved, do not follow after sin but do good works."
>
> Who are to place a restraint on your young girls and boys from being led into this dark benighted practice of your parents?... Hearken, you who cherish righteousness and the peace of the land. Have you gone to extinguish it? Have you prohibited it?...O people who hate sin, you whose hands handle the work of the government, arise! Take up the sword of the spirit with a brave heart...throw this ball of 'auhuhu (intoxicants) into the deep ocean...[J.W. Ielelehilika, North Kohala, Hawai'i, in *Kuokoa*, Nov. 1, 1873].

* * *

> Here in Honoka'upu, Honolulu, a hula teacher is training his pupils. He works during the afternoon hours. Isn't he a vagrant? Is there no law for such people? If the police go to arrest him they will find him an idler, a vagrant. There is such noise with rattling of feather rattles! Arrest and fine the property owner too for permitting this wrongdoing [*Kuokoa*, June 5, 1875].

* * *

> We have heard of a Hawaiian minister without a parsonage who requested that name chants be composed for his grandchild. The hula dancers did compose them on the day of the hula graduation he paid them twenty dollars for their work of chanting them. This minister has not been tried in court to this day [*Kuokoa*, May 8, 1875].

* * *

> In some districts of Kohala [Hawai'i] there are many people of our race who flow like running water to this worthless occupation,

---

*Translated as "soured snake;" figurative meaning not known. Possibly *mo'o 'awa* was a piece of *'awa* root.

> the hula, from boys and girls of ten to adults of fifty or more. Hearken, O parents, do not allow your children to indulge in such a worthless practice lest it become a nest of prostitution [Z.M. Kauhi, in *Kuokoa*, March 27, 1880].

1875-1900: THE *HULA* REVIVAL

The lifting of restrictive laws on public performances of the *hula* in the 1870s opened the way for more public display, but did not end criticism directed against such display. One critic was Thomas G. Thrum, who as early as 1875 took a stand against the hula *per se*, and maintained that position throughout his long writing career. Thrum was a *kama'āina* of the land--he arrived in the islands in 1853 as a boy of eleven, and made Hawai'i his home until his death in 1932. He is perhaps best remembered as the originator and main contributor to the *Hawaiian Annual and Almanac*, which he began in 1875. Thrum acquired an extensive knowledge of the Hawaiian language, both the written and the spoken, and published innumerable articles dealing with the history and legends of his adopted land. Ever a defender of the essential worth of the old Hawaiian culture, and yet committed to the "civilizing" of the Hawaiians, he wrote the following article on the *hula* in 1875, offering a novel suggestion for its suppression.

> The Hawaiian Hula
>
> In the warfare against evil, the influence of fashion is not to be overlooked as one of the legitimate weapons. Most especially it is to be valued in certain reforms because it has greater utility and power than other influences of higher character. The Hawaiians of forty years ago were induced to dress decently according to civilized standards, not so much from arguments of propriety from a moral standpoint, as from the demands of propriety, from a dress or fashionable standpoint, and so under the new regime, the sense of shame naturally gradually occupied the domain which competitive display had first seized.
>
> If public opinion among the Hawaiians can be so modified in regard to the Hula, that they shall gradually come to view it as something low and inferior, as something ridiculous and ungraceful even, then will the power and influence of their national dance be destroyed. But how shall this result be attained;--how shall the Hula be made to seem undesirable to the Hawaiian mind? This brings up the great question of amusements, which has so long been the bugbear of the majority of religious teachers. The missionaries on beginning their work at these islands, found the Hawaiians with a large variety of games and amusements, many of which were utterly objectionable. A large proportion of them however, were admirable in themselves... but were generally associated with betting and gambling, which at that time were national vices among the Hawaiians. For these reasons the missionaries opposed all the national games, including those which were intrinsically innocent, making the very common judgement of condemnation on account of accidental evil associations. With their great influence and authority they were successful in rooting out these sports, good, bad, and indifferent; as vestiges of heathenism, they were all condemned to extinction. It is difficult to imagine a more exposed and defenceless national condition than that of a people who had thrown aside their old religious faith, who were excited beyond description by their glimpses of the ouside world, who were thirsting for the new, and deprived in this transition state of all their ancient and renowned amusements and games; there is little wonder that when nothing was left to them, they should have shown in the revival of the Hula, a reaching back for their lost national customs, and there is as little cause for surprise that as no discrimination was shown in the sweeping condemnation of their amusements, they should have shown no creditable taste in their return to the objectional [sic] national dance....

> Amusements may be made a means of grace, and no moral teacher can safely neglect the aid and opportunities they afford. No one can pretend that any nation, and especially a people so child-like as the Hawaiians, can get along without sports of some kind; but what have they? Is there a single game of any dignity, respectability and manliness which they possess or which they may indulge in as Hawaiians, away from foreign association and influence? There is little hope of extinguishing the Hula, until something is provided to take its place. To refer again to our former illustration, as going nearly naked in old times was successfully broken up by the greater attractions of dress and display which rendered the former custom unfashionable and then disreputable, so we may hope successfully to oppose the Hula when we can offer something so much better as amusements and recreations that that will seem unfashionable and disreputable by way of contrast, and undesirable from its inferior attractions [Thrum 1875:146].

The "power and influence" of the national dance was never threatened, nor did it ever become "undesirable from its inferior attractions." Quite the contrary; the *hula* remained the favorite entertainment of the Hawaiians of all classes.

During the reign of King Kalākaua (1874-1891) the *hula* gained its widest acceptance in over fifty years and the *po'e hula* flourished. For the coronation of King Kalākaua and Queen Kapi'olani in 1883, nine years after ascending the throne, the *po'e hula* outdid themselves in reviving and creating chants and dances that were presented at official and unofficial functions. Many of these have come down to the present day as reflections of the more ancient forms of the dance. Unfortunately, no detailed descriptions of the coronation performances seem to be available. A list of *mele*, *oli*, and *hula* staged by seven *hula* masters was printed, however (Papa Kuhikuhi, 1883), and is appended here (Appendix D). This official program is dated February 12th, the date of the coronation, but the performance was actually held in the afternoon and evening of the 24th, as entertainment following the grand *lū'au* at 'Iolani Palace.

Little was said about the dancing itself in the *Advertiser* account in English, other than that it was "interesting and varied," but much space was given to the director of the *hula*, who was known as the "Honolulu Dandy," or "Dandy Jim" (Fig. 10). An extract from the newspaper reads,

> After the feasting was over and the preparations for the ancient songs and games were commenced the assemblage of people greatly increased in number.... In the Coronation Pavilion were seated Her Majesty the Queen with members of the Royal family and Ministers. The seats of the amphitheatre in front of the Palace were densely crowded, and the whole spacious floor beneath the mammoth tent canopy was packed with people, almost all natives, seated on the floor and leaving only a small space for the native performers of the occasion. Prominent among these was our inimitable "Dandy Ioane," our Beau Brummel.... With tall plug hat tipped to a rakish angle, well dressed with a perfumed head of hair and a dress coat...a satin vest of dandy cut, fancy colored pants fitting like tights, and terminating in patent leather boots.... But our dandy is an artist, and the hands that can pack the coal or handle the sugar bags can handle most deftly the common jewsharp, which is equal to the Jewsharp of David, that moved the heart of a king. So has he moved with the tremulous, vibrating tongue of his harp the sympathies and dollars of Royalty. Dandy Ioane was in his glory on this occasion; he was floor-manager, and the master of the situation. He marshalled the performing girls in their short skirts and hula buskins, and accompanied their gyrations with his tremulous-toned instrument. The programme of the songs "Hula Kui" and "Mele inoa,"

Fig. 10. IOANE, "DANDY JIM," WITH PERFORMING GIRLS. (Bishop Mus. Neg. No. 44723)

> and other native performances were very interesting and varied--commencing about 4 o'clock and continuing with scarcely any intermission, except on the occasion of the performance of the band until half-past 11 o'clock, when the gates were closed by order of His Majesty [*Advertiser*, Feb. 27, 1883].

A picture of the scene in the amphitheatre was painted by the artist Charles Furneaux and was described in the newspaper thus:

> The view is taken from the verandah of the Palace, on which is seated His Majesty and near him a group of ladies. In the center of the amphitheatre are a couple of the female dancers, and near them their director, the Honolulu Dandy. A throng of spectators fill all the space except that immediately around the dancers, and the scene is lit up by innumerable lamps and torches [*Advertiser*, Feb. 28, 1883].

The Hawaiian newspaper *Kuokoa* did not report on the *hula* entertainment in its account of the *lū'au*, but the following week the editor, then Thomas Thrum, expressed a viewpoint quite opposite that of the *Advertiser* reporter:

> If it had just been a *lu'au*, we would have said nothing; that would have been fine. But here is the evil: when the feasting was over there were displayed ancient pagan hulas of the time of deepest darkness of this people. It seems that this was preplanned for [the program of the] *mele inoa* sung by the *po'e hula* was printed and bound. The songs were worthless, the words so shameful they cannot be uttered by good people, the thoughts obscene. It is impossible to tell how evil and polluting were the things done last Friday at the Royal Palace [*Kuokoa*, Mar. 3, 1883].

There were great festivities again in Honolulu in 1886 for the King's Jubilee celebrating Kalākaua's 50th birthday on November 16th. The celebration occupied a fortnight and included a torchlight procession, fireworks display, dinners and balls, a parade, and a *lū'au*. The *hula* is mentioned only in passing in the *Advertiser* accounts of the festivities. In the description of the floats in the parade on November 20th is, "The next car carried the hula o healani, or Queen's dancing girls, who performed the native step dance to the tune of the ancient instruments of music" [*Advertiser*, Nov. 22, 1886]. The *Kuokoa* account was somewhat more specific: "The hula dancers (*po'e hula 'ōlapa*) with their gourd drums (*ipu*) came next, on a long float decorated with greenery" [*Kuokoa*, Nov. 27, 1886].

In the account of the November 23 *lū'au* on the Palace grounds, where 1,500 or more people were served, the *Advertiser* reported, "On rising...visitors strolled through the grounds and halls of the Palace, and in the evening a number of hula-dancers were called into requisition for their amusement" (Nov. 24, 1886). Again, the *Kuokoa* account was more explicit:

> Hawaiian hula was the entertainment, and there were throngs of *po'e hula*, men, women and children of seven or eight with their parents of forty or more. They were beautifully adorned, and the women wore short dresses and *pa'ū* skirts which swirled as they danced up and down in unison, and their hands gestured here and there as their feet moved swiftly. The hula kept up from evening until dawn. There were some songs (*himeni*) sung, but it was the grand hula that made the people shout...[Nov. 27, 1886].

Although not reported in the newspapers, there were *hula* performances going on all over the city during the celebration week, and there are several photographs of the *hula* troupes that performed (Figs. 11 & 12).

Fig. 11. *HULA* DANCING AT JUBILEE, 1886. (Bishop Mus. Neg. No. 380)

Fig. 12. *HULA* DANCING ON THE GROUNDS OF 'IOLANI PALACE, 1886. (Bishop Mus. Neg. No. 382)

In the evening of November 27th a tableau of Hawaiian scenes was presented. Among the scenes was one featuring *hula* puppets (Fig. 13), described in *Kuokoa*:

> Six hula puppets (*po'e hula ki'i*) next appeared, and one woman, who beat the *ipu* sang while they were made to dance (*ha'a*). There were shouts of laughter and great commotion at this [Dec. 4, 1886].*

The great stimulus given to the revival of the *hula* in the Kalākaua years carried through to the 20th century. Little is heard of the *hula*, however, for the years following the death of the king and the subsequent period of political turmoil. It certainly ceased as a form of official entertainment after the overthrow of the monarchy in 1893, and remained largely unknown to the outside world as an indigenous art form of the Hawaiian people, until the publication of N.B. Emerson's *Unwritten Literature of Hawaii* in 1909.

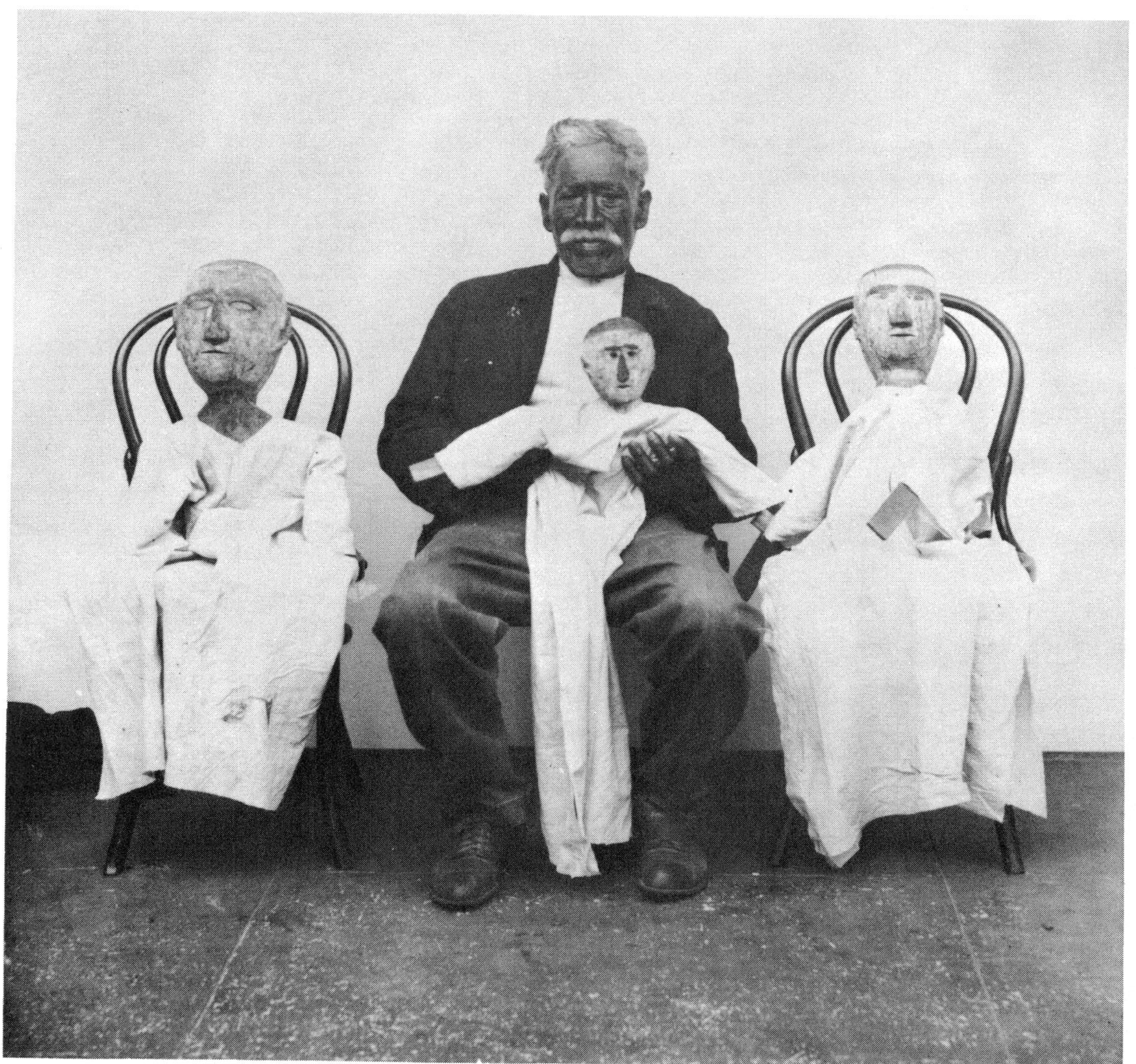

Fig. 13. *HULA* PUPPETS, MAKAALEI, HI'ILANI, KA-WEHI-O-KA-NAHELE, PROBABLY WITH THEIR DONOR, E. PA'AKAULA. (Bishop Mus. Neg. No. 952)

---

*See Emerson on these puppets, pp. 40-41 this paper.

The "Unwritten Literature of Hawaii"

The most detailed account written to date on the rituals and practices of the *hālau hula* of the late 19th and early 20th century is N.B. Emerson's *Unwritten Literature of Hawaii* (1909). Emerson's work was based on personal knowledge gained from years of contact and research among Hawaiian informants whose memories stretched back at least into the Kalākaua days, some of whom had been participants in the *hula* performance of the 1883 and 1886 celebrations. Emerson says in his opening remarks on the *hula*:

> The hula was a religious service, in which poetry, music, pantomime, and the dance lent themselves, under the forms of dramatic art, to the refreshment of men's minds. Its view of life was idyllic, and it gave itself to the celebration of those mythical times when gods and goddesses moved on the earth as men and women and when men and women were as gods. As to subject-matter, its warp was spun largely from the bowels of the old-time mythology into cords through which the race maintained vital connection with its mysterious past. Interwoven with these, forming the woof, were threads of a thousand hues and of many fabrics, representing the imaginations of the poet, the speculations of the philosopher, the aspirations of many a thirsty soul, as well as the ravings and flame-colored pictures of the sensualist, the mutterings and incantations of the *kahuna*, the mysteries and paraphernalia of Polynesian mythology, the annals of the nation's history--the material, in fact, which in another nation and under different circumstances would have gone to the making of its poetry, its drama, its opera, its literature [1909:11-12].

In much the same hyperbolic style Emerson proceeds with descriptions of the building of the *hālau hula*, its *kuahu* altar, its gods, the organization of a *hula* school, the ceremonies of graduation, and the debut of its dancers. Following this, Emerson presents a unique collection of *hula* chants and descriptions of the dances to which they pertained. Flowery in style as it may be, Emerson's work is a firm foundation upon which to build a simpler structure to house the components of the *hālau hula* of the times. In the following passages we present a condensation of Emerson's descriptions.

GODDESSES OF THE *HULA*

The principal goddess in most *hālau hula* was Laka, although some schools had Kapo in this role. Emerson comments at length on the identity of these two goddesses, seeking to reconcile the two (1909:24-25, 47-48). He says of Kapo,

> Like Laka she was at times a sylvan deity, and it was in the garb of woodland representations that she was worshiped by hula folk. Her forms of activity, corresponding to her different metamorphoses, were numerous, in one of which she was at times employed by the kahuna as a messenger in their black arts.... Kapo seems to have lived a double life...now an angel of grace and beauty, now a demon of darkness and lust [Ibid.:25].

Tracing the name Kapo as recorded chronologically, we find that in 1870 S.M. Kamakau named Kapo as the goddess who with Kāne-i-kaulana-'ula and Ka-huila-o-ka-lani* entered certain trees on Maunaloa, Moloka'i, and became a *kālaipāhoa* or poison god used in sorcery (Kamakau 1964:129-130). She was called, in Kamakau's account, Kapo Ka-ulu-i-Maunaloa (the grove at Maunaloa)

---

*Her brother, according to Manu (Ms.:2-3; p. 8 this paper).

(Ibid.:132-133). Also in 1870 Kamakau recorded Kapo as the wife of Pua, and said that together they became another kind of sorcery god. Kamakau's account of these two gods explains that their first keeper, or *kahu*, "just took care" of them but did not send them on errands of death or destruction through sorcery; however, after his death, through different incantations, they were used as such, "although the gods were the same kind (*ma ke 'ano ua like*). The two sides, *'ao'ao* [that is, the side that sent the spirits to do harm and the side that counteracted their harm] would conflict; one or the other of the *kahu* of the gods would be defeated, or victorious, and the contesting (*ku'e*) goes on between them to this day" [Ibid.:132]. This statement by Kamakau offers a basis of Hawaiian thought for the combining of opposing qualities or characteristics within one god.

In 1899, Moses Manu said that Kapo-'ula-kīna'u, sister of Pele, was the only chiefess named Kapo mentioned in his legend (Manu Ms.:3) and that she was goddess of the *hula* (Ibid.:33). He also called her the wife of Pua, and alluded to her as a sorcery goddess (Ibid.:36). He gave the name Laka as an alternate name for Kapo's sister, to whom she relegated the duty of instruction in the *hula* (Ibid.:33-34; see this paper, p. 9).

One of Emerson's informants told him that Kapo and Laka were "one in spirit, though their names were two" (1909:47), and that Laka was the daughter of Kapo (Ibid.:48). According to this informant Laka was worshipped at an earlier date than Kapo, "but they are really one" (Ibid.).

In 1958, an explanation of Kapo's dual nature appeared thus:

> Her nature [Kapo's] was dual. As Kapo'ula-kina'u (Kapo-red-spotted) she was the Kapo invoked by *kahuna* when sending evil back upon a witch. This Kapo was a goddess whose temper was violent and vengeful. But when worshipped by dancers and chanters, this same person was the gentle Laka, the spirit of the wild wood. Yet when the *kapu* of seclusion was disregarded by a student or teacher during the period of devotion to *hula* training in the *halau*, the loving Laka quickly changed into vengeful Kapo and smote the culprit [Handy & Pukui 1958:124].

A case might be made for a distinction having been made between the two goddesses at sometime or in some localities by reference to the chants beginning *Noho ana Laka i ka ulu wehiwehi* (Emerson 1909:33, lines 1-7) and *Noho ana Kapo i ka ulu wehiwehi* (Ibid.:44-45, lines 9-14). The former seems to be a portion of the latter chant; both allude to Kāne-i-kaulana-'ula, the poison god with whom Kapo is associated. In the latter chant Moe-hāuna-iki,* a younger sister of Kapo-'ula-kīna'u in Moses Manu's legend (Ms.:1, 15) is named. Manu also gives the shortened version of this chant, naming Kapo as the goddess (Ibid.: 35; see p. 10, this paper).

THE *KUAHU* ALTAR

The *hālau hula*, according to Emerson, was built on purified ground, and each stage of its building was accompanied by prayers. Within the *hālau* was built a *kuahu* altar to Laka, the principal goddess of the *hula*. (The *kuahu* was usually a shelf or rack attached to the siding between wall posts.) Greenery from the forests was ritually gathered and the altar decorated, all with appropriate *pule* (literally, prayer chants), which Emerson happily defines as "song offerings" (1909:22).

---

*This name appears in the Emerson rendition in line 16, "E moe hauna-ike".

Five plant forms were commonly used to decorate the *kuahu* altar, and in most *hālau hula* these five were considered essential.* They are: (1) *Maile*, a straggling or twining shrub with fragrant stem, bark, and leaves. Several forms of *maile* are found in the lower and middle forest regions of the islands--one with wide, blunt, oval leaves, another with narrower leaves, another with rounder leaves, etc. (2) *'Ie'ie*, a woody climber with aerial roots and clusters of slender, shiny, green leaves, found in woods between 1,000 and 2,000-ft elevation. In summer the *'ie'ie* develops fragrant bracts of bright orange-red leaves within which are three brilliant cones. These cones are borne on separate plants, male and female. (3) *Halapepe*, a much-branched tree with long narrow leaves in tufts at branch ends and with clustered, round, golden fruits. (4) *Lehua* (*'ōhi'a-lehua*), a forest tree growing in a wide range of elevations, from 1,000 to 9,000 ft. Young leaves are reddish, and are called *liko*. Flowers are composed of many bright stamens forming tufts at branch ends, usually bright red, but also found in salmon, pink, yellow, or white. (5) *Palai* (*palapalai*), a fern bearing lacy, slightly hairy fronds, 2 or 3 ft long, borne on foot-long stems. Emerson adds to this list a number of others: *'ōhi'a-'ai*, the mountain apple; *'ekaha*, the bird's-nest fern; *hau*; and breadfruit, banana, ti, and *'ilima* (1909: 19-20).

Gods and demi-gods were represented by the five main plant forms on the altar. Kū-ka-'ōhi'a-laka, a form of Kū in the *'ōhi'a-lehua*, was one such god.** Hi'iaka was there in the *palai* fern, and Kapo was represented by the *halapepe*. Lau-ka-'ie'ie was a beautiful demi-goddess whose brother obtained for her a chiefly husband from Kaua'i. She was transformed into the *'ie'ie* vine (Westervelt 1915:36-48) and was so represented on the altar. From legend also came the four Maile sisters, Maile-ha'i-wale, Maile-kaluhea, Maile-lau-li'i, and Maile-pākaha, who were represented by one or more varieties of the *maile*. Other gods and demi-gods were no doubt invoked in the *hālau hula* of the past, depending upon their association with the locality and with the *po'e hula* of the place.

In the midst of the greenery on the *kuahu* altar was set a small block of *lama* wood, representing the goddess Laka. *Lama* is a hard, red-brown wood, and it was chosen to represent Laka because its name means "light" or "enlightenment." This block was wrapped in yellow tapa, a color most suitable for female gods, and a color conveying the appearance and the feeling of light.

TRAINING

In his discussion on the organization of a *hālau hula* Emerson touches upon the composition of the *mele* that were to become the stock repertoire of a teacher of the *hula*, a *kumu hula*. Whether composed in company with others, or by a single person, the *kumu hula* himself or another,

*Plant identifications and descriptions are taken from Neal (1965) and Degener (1945). See Glossary for scientific identifications of plants and animals mentioned in this work.

**Kū-ka-'ōhi'a-laka is given by Malo as one of the gods propitiated by those who took timber in the forest (Malo 1951:82). N.B. Emerson's note on this name explains *laka* (*rata*) as a widespread Polynesian name for the *Metrosideros* (*'ōhi'a lehua*) (1909:84, n. 5), confirmed by Neal (1965:637). It is probably because of this similarity in name that a male *Laka* was regarded by some as a god of the *hula* (Pukui 1942, p. 70, this work. See also Manu Ms.:34; see p. 9).

the words of every *mele*, *hula* and otherwise, had to be of only propitious meaning, or calamity would result. This careful attention to the literal as well as figurative or alternative meanings of words in a composition was vital (Emerson 1909:27). It has endured among Hawaiian composers to this day both as a mark of excellence in composition and as a remnant of the old belief in "word magic."

Having a stock of *mele*, and himself an accomplished dancer or chanter, the *kumu hula* was ready to organize a dancing school. Emerson thus describes the organization of such schools formed in the late days of the Hawaiian monarchy, which were perhaps truly representative of those of the early 19th century, at least.

> The organization of a hula company was largely democratic. The kumu--in modern sense, the teacher--was the leader and conductor, responsible for the training and discipline of the company. He was the business manager of the enterprise; the priest, *kahuna*, the leader in the religious exercises....
>
> The *po'o-puaa* [*po'opua'a*] was an officer chosen by the pupils to be their special agent and mouthpiece. He saw to the execution of the kumu's judgments and commands, collected the fines, and exacted the penalties imposed by the kumu. It fell to him to convey to the altar the presents of garlands, awa, and the like that were contributed to the halau.
>
> The *paepae*, also chosen by the pupils, subject to confirmation by the kumu, acted as an assistant of the po'opuaa.
>
> The *ho'o-ulu* was the guard stationed at the door. He sprinkled with sea-water mixed with tumeric [*'ōlena*] everyone who entered the halau. He also acted as sergeant-at-arms to keep order and remove anyone who made a disturbance. It was his duty each day to place a fresh bowl of awa on the altar of the goddess (*hanai kuahu*), literally to feed the altar [Emerson 1909:29].
>
> * * *
>
> The performers in the hula were divided into two classes, the *olapa* [*'ōlapa*]--agile ones--and the ho'opaa [*ho'opa'a*]--steadfast ones. The role of *olapa*...was assigned to the young men and women.... It was theirs, sometimes while singing, to move and pose and gesture in the dance; sometimes also to punctuate their song and action with the lighter instruments of music. The role of ho'o-paa [*ho'opa'a*], on the other hand, was given to men and women of greater experience and of more maturity. They handled the heavier instruments and played their parts mostly while sitting or kneeling.... They also lent their voices to swell the chorus or utter the refrain of certain songs, sometimes taking the lead in the song or bearing its whole burden, while the...*olapa* gave themselves entirely to the dance.
>
> Such was the personnel of a hula troupe when first gathered by the hula-master for training and drill in the halau, now become a school for the hula [Emerson 1909:28].

In a brief discussion of the rules and regulations observed during the course of training in the *hālau*, Emerson stressed the attached *kapu* as being the main disciplinary force that upheld the authority of the *kumu hula* (1909:30). In the Hawaiian society the breaking of any *kapu*, intentionally or unintentionally, brought severe retribution, spiritual and secular, and fear of this retribution maintained order everywhere. In the *hālau*, fear perhaps did contribute to discipline, but on the positive side, total observance of the *kapu* brought favorable responses from the gods, and strengthened and increased proficiency in the arts of the *hula*.

Different *hālau* had differing *kapu*, but all presumably observed the basic three *kapu* that Emerson mentions: total abstinence from sexual indulgence, personal cleanliness, and avoidance of contact with dead bodies (Ibid.). He cites one example of a food restriction, that against the eating of sugarcane:

> ...The reason assigned was that if one indulged in it his work... would amount to nothing...*aohe e ko ana kana mau hana*....The argument turned on the double meaning of the word *ko*, the first meaning being sugar cane, the second, accomplishment. The Hawaiians were much impressed by...nominalism. Yet there is a backing of good sense to the rule. Anyone who has chewed the sweet stalk can testify that for some time thereafter his voice is rough [Ibid.].

For similar reasons of double entendre, usually based on equally practical reasons, other foods were banned.

Emerson reveals the historic context of his work when he says:

> The ordinary penalty for a breach of ceremony or an offence against sexual morality was the offering of a baked porkling with awa. Since the introduction of money the penalty has generally been reckoned on a commercial basis; a money fine is imposed. The offering of pork and awa is retained as a concession to tradition [Ibid.].

GRADUATION

Ceremonies of graduation (*'ūniki*) from the *hālau hula* followed training. For several days beforehand, the pupils had to remain in the *hālau*, leaving it only for "the most stringent necessity," as Emerson puts it (1909:31). Most of the night before actual graduation was spent in chant and dance--in dress rehearsal, one might say. At one point the company went to the sea for ceremonial bathing to purify themselves, and re-entered the *hālau* after being sprinkled (*pī kai*) with "holy water" by the *kumu hula*, who then went himself to his purifying bath (Ibid.). At daybreak, after a short rest, a tabu-removing prayer was chanted to Laka before the *kuahu*, then the company sat down to eat, joined by friends, relatives, and other *po'e hula*. The pig that was to be consecrated for eating later at the ceremonial *'ailolo* feast marking the end of training was then brought in for ritual killing by the *kumu hula*. The *kuahu* altar was then dismantled, and a new one set up; the pupils retired to groom and adorn themselves. Upon their return they resumed their *pule* to the goddess Laka, and then, divesting themselves of their *lei*, offered them on the altar.

At the final religious rite, the *'ailolo* feast marking the end of training, each pupil received a portion of snout, ear-tips, tail, feet, spleen and brain (*lolo*) of the consecrated pig. The *kumu hula* now lifted the tabu from the *'ailolo* ceremony.

> ...The pupils have been graduated from the school of the halau; they are now members of the great guild of hula dancers....The time has come for them to make their bow to the waiting public outside.
>
> The kumu with his big drum, and the musicians, the ho'o-paa, pass through the door and take their places outside in the lanai, where sit the waiting multitude. At the tap of the drum the group of waiting olapa...pass out the halau door and [as they] present themselves to the breathless audience, into every pose and motion of their gliding, swaying figures they pour a full tide of emotion in studied and unstudied effort to captivate the public [Emerson 1909:35].

COSTUMES

The costumes of the dancers, according to Emerson, consisted of *lei* for head and shoulders, *pā'ū* (for both men and women), and *kūpe'e*. He confines the term *kūpe'e* to anklets, fashioned he says of "whale teeth, bone, shell-work, dog-teeth, fiber-stuffs, and what not" (Emerson 1909:49). *Kūpe'e* was a term applied also to bracelets, such as those worn by the dancers described by Ellis and Stewart (see pp. 29-31; 33). The *lei* were of indigenous plants, says Emerson, "...the ilima, the lehua, the maile, the ie-ie, and the like" (Ibid.:56). Emerson's description of the *hula pā'ū* and the methods of wrapping it reads:

> In the costuming of the hula girl the same variety obtained as in the dress of a woman of rank. Sometimes her pa'ú would be only a close-set fringe of ribbons stripped from the bark of the hibiscus (*hau*), the ti leaf or banana fiber, or a fine rush, strung upon a thong to encircle the waist.* In its most elaborate and formal style the pa-ú consisted of a strip of fine tapa several yards long and of width to reach nearly to the knees. It was often delicately tinted or printed, as to its outer part, with stamped figures. The part of the tapa skirt thus printed, like the outer, decorative one in a set of tapa bed-sheets, was termed the *kilohana*.
>
> The pa-ú of the women was worn in addition to that of daily life; the hula pa-ú of the men, a less pretentious affair, was worn outside the malo, and in addition to it.
>
> The method of girding on the pa-ú was peculiar. Beginning at the right hip--some say the left--a free end was allowed to hang quite to the knee; then, passing across the back, rounding the left hip, and returning by way of the abdomen to the starting point, another circuit of the waist was accomplished; and, a reverse being made, the garment was secured by passing the bight of the tapa beneath the hanging folds of the pa-ú from below upward until it slightly protruded above the border of the garment at the waist. This second end was thus brought to hang down the hip alongside the first free end; an arrangement that produced a most decorative effect.
>
> The Hawaiians, in their fondness for giving personal names to intimate objects, named the two free ends (*apua*) of the pa-ú respectively *Ku-kapu-'ula-ka-lani* and *Lele-a-mahu'i*.
>
> According to another method, which was simpler and more commonly employed, the piece was folded sidewise and, being gathered into pleats, a cord was inserted the length of the fold. The cord was passed about the waist, knotted at the hip, and thus held the garment secure [Ibid.:50].

MELE AND TYPES OF *HULA*

Throughout the pages from which the above passages have been taken, Emerson interspersed *mele* appropriate to each occasion. These *mele* are used today by modern *hula* masters at comparable occasions within their own *hālau*, and many are taken from the story of Pele and Hi'iaka. One such is the chant which begins "*Ke lei mai la o Ka'ula i ke kai*," the "wreath song" given by Emerson as the chant uttered as the dancers adorned themselves with head and neck *lei* for their graduation performance (1909:56). He gives the origin of this song as that uttered by the ghost of the lame girl Mana-mana-ia-kalu-ea at Kahakuloa, Maui (Ibid.:212). He treats the

---

*Such fibrous skirts date from the Kalākaua period; earlier *hula pā'ū* were invariably of tapa or foreign cloth.

incident of the lame girl quite differently in his version of *Pele and Hi'iaka*, and the chant does not appear at all in that version (1915:68-72). The first two lines of this chant are found again in his *Pele and Hi'iaka* as opening a chant uttered by Lohi'au at a *kilu* game in Honolulu (Ibid.:177).

This is but one instance of the repeated use in different versions and situations of the same or similar chants that formed the common stock of "free" (*noa*) material used over and over again by the *po'e hula* in their various *hālau*. Chants taken from various versions of the Pele and Hi'iaka story are most frequently found as free material. Such material contrasts with the repertoire of the individual *hula* masters who receive material from their own former teachers, and who compose for themselves. The latter materials are *kapu*, meaning restricted to the use or performance of their own *hālau*. Such *kapu* or restricted material is sometimes called "sacred."

Before beginning his chapters on individual *hula*, Emerson dwelt upon the differences in the "whole body of mele, pule, and oli that makes up the songs and liturgy of the hula as well as to the traditions that guided the...kumu-hula in the training of his company." He concluded that "jealousy had much to do with the slight differences now manifest, that one version is as authoritative as another, and that it would be well for each *kumu hula* to have kept in mind the wise adage that shines among the sayings of his nation: *'Aohe pau ka ike i kau halau'*--'Think not that all of wisdom resides in your *halau*'"(Emerson 1909:38-39).

In the *Unwritten Literature of Hawaii* Emerson discusses no less than 29 *hula*, classified, apparently by him, as to type, and gives at least one *hula mele* to which the particular dance was performed. The earlier Hawaiian writers--Malo, 'I'i, and Kamakau--by no means mentioned as many kinds of *hula* as did Emerson, nor did they describe them in such detail. Malo said:

> ...The *hula* most frequently performed by the chiefs was the *Ko-laau* [*kā-la'au*] (in which one stick was struck against another).*
>
> ...Among the varieties of the *hula* were the *pai umauma* (beating the chest), *hula pahu* (with a drum accompaniment), and the *hula pahua*; others were the *alaa-papa*, the *paipai*, the *pa-ipu*, the *ulili*, the *kolani*, and the *kielei* [1951:231].

The *hula paipai* is not described in Emerson, nor is the *'ūlili*. The *hula pā ipu* is a synonym of the *hula kuolo*, according to Emerson (1909:73).

John 'I'i mentioned the *hula 'aiha'a* as a type of *hula* (1959:137). Emerson applied the term to a style of chanting for the *hula 'āla'apapa* (1909:58). The term has come to mean a style of dancing (Pukui & Elbert 1971:9). Perhaps to 'I'i it was synonymous with the *hula 'āla'apapa*. The description of the *hula pā ipu* by 'I'i is quoted here on page 23. He mentions the *hula kāla'au* in passing, saying that it was popular at the time of Kamāmalu's birth, about 1802 (1959:70), and that the Spaniard Paula Marín was an expert at it (Ibid.:94).

In Kamakau's account of the pleasure that Kalani'ōpu'u took in the *hula*, quoted here on page 14, he mentions the *'āla'apapa* and the *hula ki'i* (1961:105). This passage in the published work was edited so as to define the *hula ki'i* as "the dance of the marionettes," a definition taken from Emerson (1909:91-102) that is at odds with the period of which Kamakau was speaking.

---

*Parenthetical remarks are by Emerson, translator of Malo.

The dictionary defines this *hula* as "dance of the images in which the dancers postured stiffly like images" (Pukui & Elbert 1971:83); this is without doubt the proper description of the truly old *hula ki'i*. In the Moses Manu legend the dance originated on Ni'ihau (Manu Ms.:11; see pp. 8-9, this paper. See also pp. 14, 40-41, this paper).

Elsewhere Kamakau listed the *hula* "Hawaiian chiefs danced" as the *'ōlapa, pahu, kuolo, 'alalā, pihi (pihe?)*, ki'i, pa'iumauma,* "and innumerable others" (1961:350). The *'ōlapa* appears to have comprised those dances accompanied by gourd drums (Pukui & Elbert 1971:260). Emerson specifies these gourd dances as the *hula 'āla'apapa, ipu, pā-ipu* (or *kuolo*)*, ho'o-nānā,* and *ki'i* in one grouping of *hula* types (1909:102), but reserves the term *'ōlapa* for the dancers. The *'alalā* is typed by style of chanting, rather than by kind of dance (Pukui & Elbert 1971:17).

Of all the *hula* mentioned by name, the *hula kāla'au* was the first described and the one that endured longest in popularity. It was first described by Captain Cook as it was seen on Ni'ihau in January of 1778 (see p. 15). Kamakau named it as one of the two "most popular dances" of the period of about 1780 (the other being the *'āla'apapa*) (see p. 14); Malo called the *kāla'au* the *hula* "most frequently performed by the chiefs" (see p. 62); it was mentioned by 'I'i as being popular in the period 1802-1810 (see p. 62); and it was again described in 1823, by Ellis (see p. 29). Emerson gives two *mele* for the *hula kāla'au* (1909:117-118), one the ever-popular "*Kona kai 'ōpua i ka la'i* much performed today.

The other *mele* that Emerson gives for the *hula kāla'au* is that which begins, "*O Kalākaua, he inoa, 'o ka pua mae 'ole i ka lā,*" which is more commonly seen today as a *hula 'ōlapa*. Emerson's remarks on the "naming" of this *mele* to Kalākaua is an oblique rebuke to that monarch for appropriating not only this but other *mele* to himself, or at least in permitting their re-naming to himself (1909:116-117).

RELIGIOUS ASPECTS OF *HULA*

In the *Unwritten Literature of Hawaii* Emerson made repeated reference to the "Sacred" character of the *hula*. His unqualified remarks that the *hula* was "a religious service" (1909:11) and a "sacred and religious performance" (Ibid:57) indicate that he carried over the religious aspects of the *hālau* training into the performance of the dances themselves (Ibid.:13, 103, 187). None of the Hawaiian writers whose remarks on the *hula* have been cited made any such inference, and the eyewitness accounts of *hula* performances reproduced in this paper do not bear out such statements.

There is no question that *hula* dancers formally trained in the *hālau* practiced their art with reference and supplication to the gods of the *hula*. That is not to say, however, that their performances were acts of worship, or "a religious service." A spiritual affinity with the gods of family, of arts and crafts, and of all of nature permeated Hawaiian society in pre-Christian days, and carried over in greater or lesser degree into Christianized times. A pronounced revival of this feeling and attitude is being evidenced today, not the least among the *po'e hula*.

**Pihe*: to mourn or lament. Possibly descriptive of *hula* performed in mourning or lamentation. See pp. 18 and 35, this paper.

The religious aspects of training in the *hālau hula* ended with the final ritual of the graduation exercises when the restrictions (*kapu*) of the gods upon the participants were lifted. Thereafter, their performances were "free" (*noa*), that is, without any religious restriction or ritual other than those they wished to observe. Customarily *hula* troupes maintained a certain religious aspect through ritual prayers preceding formal appearances. These prayers or *pule* were essentially supplications for agility, memory, and grace necessary to present a flawless performance (see p. 28), but the dances were by no means a religious service in the sense of being acts of worship.

Chants and their accompanying dances composed for chiefs or gods were also sacred (*kapu*) in that they were restricted to performances in honor or veneration of the chief or god to whom they were dedicated or "named." Again this sacredness implied a restriction, and not a religious service. The chants and dances associated with any particular *hālau* were also sacred (*kapu*) because they were restricted to that *hālau*, meaning that school, and the troupe representing it. Pupils leaving the *hālau* to form troupes of their own performed such sacred dances only upon the lifting of the *kapu* on them by their former *kumu hula*.

Emerson's work, however, had the weight of authority, and his designation of the *hula* as a sacred dance was followed for many years. *The Unwritten Literature of Hawaii* became the indisputable reference on all *hula* matters, and remains so to a large extent today.

1910-1930: The Hula "Goes Modern"

The *hula* came into public prominence again after the first decade or so of the 20th century, this time under the stimulus of business--the entertainment business. The *hula* became a feature of carnivals and pageants and then became entrenched as standard entertainment fare catering to the growing tourist trade (Fig. 14). But it was a quite different *hula* than that seen through the years when it was performed as Hawaiian entertainment for Hawaiians. It had undergone a radical change, from that of a dance form subordinate to the poetry of the chant to which it was danced, to a style of dancing in which gesture became the important feature. This was understandable in the light of the audience it now attracted--an audience that had little or no knowledge of the Hawaiian language. Its music also was quite different: now most of the *mele hula* were sung to melodic tunes, and were no longer chanted. Again the cries of "lasciviousness" and "indecency" were raised--and again they were voiced by that long-time opponent of the *hula*, Thomas G. Thrum (1917:120-125).

There were others, apart from the businessmen who were doing the actual promoting of this new "tourist attraction," who, while they recognized the appeal of this *hula* to the general public, deplored the "degradation" of the dance. The following extracts from an article by Lorin Tarr Gill in 1923 express their viewpoint:

> ...the Hawaiian hula as known to the world at large is a spectacle of which we who make our homes in these islands can not in any way be proud.
>
> The familiar picture of the lei-bedecked, dusky-skinned beauty, more or less adequately clad in her wreath and anklet of flowers, her bracelet of green, and the inevitable grass skirt expresses all

Fig. 14. *HULA* DANCERS, c. 1897-1901. Photograph by Frank Davey. (Bishop Mus. Neg. No. 1924-203.05, No. 96).

> that the hula means to those citizens of the earth who have never visited our beautiful land, as well as to many others who, as tourists, have done so [Fig. 15].
>
> The truth of the matter is that the real Hawaiian hula has little in common with the coarse imitations frequently served up to sightseers, magazine readers, and the general public [Gill 1923:7].

There follows in Gill's article a long synopsis of Emerson's *Unwritten Literature*, which she accepted as being a true picture of pre-Kamehameha times; then she resumed her remarks on the modern *hula* being presented:

> The fragments of Hawaiian music that have drifted down to us from the early part of the nineteenth century show in their plaintive, unmelodious monotony, the characteristics that stamp all primitive song.
>
> Almost none of the singing that one hears at the so-called hula performance is Hawaiian music of the old sort, "nor" says an authority, "is the modern hula a more fair and true representative of the savage Hawaiian or Polynesian dance than the Parisian cancan is of a refined and civilized dance."
>
> With the arrival of the first whaling vessels, the hula was modernized to suit the jaded palates of the sailors of a hundred years ago. More and more objectionable features were introduced. The natives, ever obliging, were influenced by the effects of gin and the desire for the suggestive dance, and the hula degenerated into the thing it is today.
>
> Under King Kalakaua, less artistic or coarser forms of hula became the court dance.
>
> And this is the commercialized hula as known to the tourist.
>
> The indecent hula is sometimes foisted upon the public as a religious and ceremonial performance of the early Hawaiians and hence, "having the approval of the gods, it should have the approval of mortals."
>
> This is a view, according to the same authority, "that meets with but ridicule from those best qualified to know, the Hawaiians themselves."*
>
> But the hula has been popularized and commercialized; it has been displayed at public gatherings as an ancient religious ceremoney; it has suffered the addition of imported steps from the mainland, and the vulgarities introduced to pander to tourists; yet it has been called the national dance of Hawaii, and its grass skirt, unknown to early Hawaii, has been called the national costume [Gill 1923:7-8].

"Vulgar," "obscene," "lascivious," are relative terms, and there were many who did not view this developing style of *hula* as such. At its best, it was a graceful, eye-appealing dance, and its popularity among visitors and also among the multi-ethnic groups of Hawai'i became as great as that of the traditional *hula* of the Hawaiians of earlier times, and remains so today.

The traditional *hula* forms, however, never died out, although they became less often seen in public. *Hālau hula*, much the same as those described by Emerson, carried on the traditional training in the 20th century; occasionally their *kumu hula* put on a performance in public, usually to a discriminating and appreciative audience of Hawaiians and *kama'āina*. An account of such schools is given by Mary Kawena Pukui in the following chapter.

---

*Quoted from Thrum 1917:120-125, cited above.

Fig. 15. *HULA* DANCER, c. 1925.
(Tinted postcard in Bishop Mus.)

PART II

NOTES FROM A KUMU HULA

Selected Articles by Mary Kawena Pukui

Introduction

Mary Kawena Pukui has been for a great many years a foremost authority on Hawaiian culture, and above all, on matters of the *hula*. Over the course of the years she has often shared her knowledge of the *hula* as an informant for writers, composers, and performers in this field, and has preserved additional material in manuscripts and publications.

This section consists of three articles by Mrs. Pukui. The first, "The Hula, Hawaii's Own Dance," was published in *Thrum's Hawaiian Almanac and Annual...All About Hawaii in 1942* (Pukui 1942: 107-112). It describes the *hula* training and practices of an earlier day and was written for the edification of visitor and *kama'āina* alike.

The second article, "Ancient Hulas of Kauai," was prepared for the occasion of a demonstration of *hula* by Mrs. Keahi Luahine Sylvester Gomes before the Kaua'i Historical Society at Līhu'e, Kaua'i, on January 31, 1936. It was published in the local newspaper, *The Garden Island*, in six installments in February and March of that year (Pukui 1936).

The third article, "The Hula," is extracted and reprinted from a larger article entitled "Games of My Hawaiian Childhood," which appeared in the *California Folklore Quarterly* with footnotes by Martha Warren Beckwith in 1943 (Pukui 1943). It is similar in some aspects to the Emerson account of the training for the *hula* (1909:14-56), and demonstrates the universality of *hula* practices throughout the islands.

The Pukui articles, taken together, contain so much material on the *hula* at the turn of the century and well into the 1920s that they stand as the modern authoritative reference on the subject, replacing Emerson's *Unwritten Literature* to a large extent.

THE HULA, HAWAII'S OWN DANCE

by

Mary Kawena Pukui
Assistant in Hawaiian Linguistics,
B. P. Bishop Museum
1942

The hula is a general name for many types of Hawaiian folk dances. Some originated in one locality and spread to others. Some were peculiar to one island, while others belonged to a whole group but had many versions. A Kauai and a Maui troupe might dance to the same song or mele and yet be different in many ways. Most of the ancient hulas are gone for all time, although many remain.

When every island had its own ruling chiefs, hula dancing was practiced by chiefs and commoners, by old and young. Dancers of one locality vied with those of another and many localities gained a reputation for having excellent dancers. A good hula master was always found in the court of his chief. There were dances for everyone; standing dances for those whose limbs were young and spry and sitting dances for those who preferred to sit, like the aged and over-plump.

Kamakau, a Hawaiian historian, said that Queen Kaahumanu tried to discourage awa drinking and hula dancing when she became converted to Christianity. Yet here and there in remote country places the people kept up with their dancing. Small groups trained under a master, thus preserving many of the old meles which have come down to the present day.

Approved by Emma, Kalakaua

The later Hawaiian rulers did not seem to discourage its practice, for when Queen Emma visited the Big Island the people composed meles in her honor and danced to them for her entertainment. At King Kalakaua's jubilee, dancers and musicians assembled from end to end of the group. Many rare dances were seen then as well as the commoner ones.

Nevertheless, for many years, the hula was looked down upon and no respectable boy or girl was ever permitted to watch one, much less to dance it. As a child I mingled freely among my relatives and learned that the meles and hulas were not entirely bad. Many were in honor of the gods and of chiefs and were just as harmless as the folk songs of America, such as Dixie, Yankee Doodle, or My Old Kentucky Home.

I have not heard of heiaus dedicated to Laka, the patron deity of the hula, outside of Kauai. The two whose sites were pointed out to me by Keahi Lauhine Sylvester were Ka-ulu-o-Lono at Wahiawa and Ke-ahu-a-Laka beyond Haena. The plants used on the kuahu, or altar, the dregs of awa used in daily offerings to Laka, the remains of ceremonial feasts connected with the hula, and the skirts and leis worn at graduation were deposited in these heiaus. The remains of a ceremonial feast to Laka were never thrown carelessly around lest they become defiled by being walked over or eaten by animals. On the other islands these were cast into the sea or into deep streams.

Also Were Other Hula Gods, Goddesses

Some hula experts claim that Laka is a male deity; others say female. One Oahu teacher told me that Laka was a term applied to a male and female deity whose plant forms were the ohia and halapepe. No altar was complete without these two plants. Under Laka were other gods and goddesses of the hula among whom were Lau-kaieie, whose form was the ieie creeper, and the four maile sisters, Maile-lau-nui, Maile-ha'i-wale, Maile-kaluhe-a and Maile-lau-lii.

Prayers to Laka were numerous and varied. They were not like any of our Christian prayers but more like the Psalms or the Song of Solomon. There were prayers for inspiration (pule hooulu), prayers for Laka to come and dwell in the newly built altar (pule hoonoho), prayers for a better voice (pule leo), prayers for the limbering of the body (pule ha'iha'i), prayers for protection against sorcery (pule pale), and many more. Every pupil of the old-time hula schools not only learned the meles for the dances but also a score of more prayer chants before graduating.

The gathering of the greenery for the altar was an important undertaking. The person sent was watchful for any inauspicious sign such as the barking of a dog, chirping of a bird, crowing of a cock or the meeting of a person on the highway. He started at dawn when silence ruled, uttering his prayers on the way and as he reached forth his hand to gather each necessary plant. He must have no fear and under no circumstances should he utter a sound besides the prayers.

Must Never Reply, Nor Look Back

There were times when the invisible woodland spirits protested against the breaking of their plants and demanded to know what he was going to do with them. To these angry voices he must give no reply and must go about his business as though stone-deaf. He went home without a backward glance no matter what he heard.

The kumu or hula master sprinkled the greenery with salt water and a bit of olena root to cleanse them of any chance defilement. Not all plants were used in the kuahu or altar, only those that were the plant forms of the gods or those that were significant like the koa or to make the pupil koa or unafraid of crowds. In southern Hawaii, the plants used in building the kuahu were the ohia lehua, the halapepe, the maile, the palapalai fern and the ieie. To this Kauai added the lama, the ginger, the akolea fern, the lauae fern, the koa, the breadfruit, the kukui and the pili grass and Maui added the lama, the ginger, ti, kupukupu fern, pamoho fern and koa. The breadfruit (ulu) signified growth, which is also called ulu. Pili is not only the name of the grass but it also means to cling and so its use signified the wish of those of that school to have the wisdom and understanding of the hula cling to them all the days of their lives.

The kuahu or altar was built on the wall on the eastern wall of the halau (hula house), and never on the west. The sun rises, flooding the earth with light and bringing forth life and vitality to all nature. The Hawaiians wished for life, health and growth in dancing and expressed it by building the kuahu on the east side, or side toward the sunrise.

Fish Could be Substituted for Hog

A hog was the usual offering for an initiation ceremony but if that were impossible to obtain, then a certain fish called a sea hog (puaa kai) was substituted, such as the kumu or amaama (mullet). With a prayer the teacher nipped off a piece of the head and gave it to each pupil before they partook of the rest of the feast. No part of the feast was shared with an outsider nor was it thrown out to the animals. The remains were carefully gathered and cast into the sea or placed where there was no danger of defilement.

The pupils (who did not leave the halau except to relieve nature) danced and chanted day or night. The kumu taught the dances he knew and waited prayerfully for Laka's instructions. New steps, new meles or old forgotten ones were sometimes taught in dreams. A pupil would dream of a dance and upon waking describe it to the kumu who taught it to the whole class. Sometimes, instead of dreaming, the pupil heard the voice of an invisible chanter and as he listened he memorized the mele. Many of the meles were said to have been composed by the gods and given by them to us through the halau hula or hula school. These meles were called mele kumu and were used in hula dancing before any of the others.

Halau Rules Exceptionally Strict

The rules of the halau were many and strict. A pupil was not permitted to share a portion (hakina) of his food with any one except with members of his own halau. Sugar cane, taro tops, sea weeds of the lipeepee variety and squids were kapu articles of food and must not be eaten until after graduation. The word pee (to hide) occurs twice in the name of the sea weed and the word hee does not only mean a squid, but also to flee. Hence to eat such articles of food would cause the knowledge of the hula to flee and hide away from the pupil.

If the pupil were married he did not sleep with his wife or vice versa. All kissing was prohibited until graduation.

It was kapu to "talk back" to the kumu. It was kapu to come in contact with dead bodies and if a relative of one of the pupils died, the pupil forfeited a pig to Laka before he left the halau. Upon his return he was sprinkled with salt water to cleanse him of defilement. Quarreling was not allowed nor was criticizing the methods of another school permitted. This old but true saying has been handed down, "Aohe i pau ka ike i ka halau hookahi" or "All knowledge was not taught in one school."

Strictest Cleanliness was Required

Although nail paring, hair cutting or shaving was not permitted, strict cleanliness was stressed. The pupils bathed daily and changed the clothing entirely. There must be no uncleanliness in the presence of Laka. Women did not wear the hair coiled or braided but simply combed it free of tangles.

No outsider was allowed to enter the halau without having chanted the password. The password chant or mele kahea was the key by which one entered the halau, whether one was an outsider or one of the pupils who had gone outside for a little while. Some one from within responded with a chant calling him to come in. If after chanting the password several times, he was ignored by those within the halau, he could call to Laka to depart from hence with him and Laka did. The password must not be ignored lest Laka be offended.

From the day of the building of the kuahu to the day of graduation, the greenery remained fresh and green because Laka's spirit was there but should Laka leave, the leaves and blossoms turned brown and fell to the floor.

Prayer Required While Donning Pa-u

Everything was done in an orderly manner in the old hula schools. The pa-u or skirt was girded on only when the kumu chanted the mele of the pa-u, never before or after. Anklets and leis were put on with their appropriate meles. The anklets were made of sea shells in the olden days and in the days of the monarchy were made of worsted.

Men and women dressed alike for the hula with pa-u or skirt and the kikepa. The kikepa was draped under one arm and knotted on the opposite shoulder. Malos were not worn by the men for hula dancing. The pa-u was made up of several layers of tapa, about a yard in width and four in length, sewed together on one side. When worn, the pa-u reached just below the knees.

Hula girls of the olden days did not dance with bared thighs as they do today for they were taught that to leave the thighs uncovered was immodest. Even down to the days of our last rulers hula dancers wore knee-length skirts. Dancing with bared thighs came into fashion ten or fifteen years ago.

When tapa cloths were no longer made, cloth skirts and blousy muumuus came into fashion. These skirts were very wide, about four yards around tied with a draw-string. A handkerchief was tucked in by one corner at the belt and used to wipe the face of the perspiring dancer. There is a great contrast in the appearance of those who danced before our aliis and some of the dancers of today. Today's hula costumes consist of brassieres, abbreviated panties, leis and grass skirts, and almost all of both thighs is glimpsed. Grass skirts were not Hawaiian and were introduced to Hawaii by laborers from the Gilbert islands.

Critics Invited Before Uniki

In southern Hawaii (Puna and Kau) a teacher called in several others to look his pupils over and to watch them dance before they graduated. These teachers made their criticisms and offered suggestions. The graduation ceremony or uniki followed after the pupils had been pronounced perfect.

While a teacher acted as judge in the halau of another he did not attempt to learn any new meles belonging to the other lest he appeal to Laka in this manner, "Oh Laka, so-and-so has taken one of my meles. Make him stutter and stammer when he tries to use it. Make his memory fail him so that he would not remember the words." And Laka would indeed make the one who had taken that which did not belong to him, forgetful and nervous whenever he tried to use it. Laka liked honesty among her devotees.

A hog was the usual offering at the uniki or graduation. The essence or aka of the feast belonged to the gods but the material to pupils and their guests. Everybody was welcome to a uniki feast, the more the merrier. There were no obligations whatever but almost everyone gave a gift to the dancers. Gifts thrown or laid in the area where the dancing was held were divided among the musicians and dancers but gifts tucked into the hand or blouse were personal and not shared with others.

In the days of the monarchy and later, those who came to see the hula tossed money into the area instead of other gifts. It was fun to every one to see the dancers dance in a shower of coins. If a dancer did so well that the spectators surged forward to see better, she was considered a very good dancer. This was called "hui ka aha" or "mix-up among the spectators."

A graduating pupil could voice no objection if she were kissed, even if the person who kissed her was not much to her liking.

Had to Learn Both Meles and Prayers

In the olden days, the musicians or hoopaa were men and never women, but the dancers were both men and women. To become a hoopaa it was necessary to learn not only the meles but also the innumerable prayers. It was the hoopaas who eventually became kumus or teachers of the hula.

The ami or revolving of the hips is one thing much misunderstood. In most of the old hulas it was not meant to be suggestive nor vulgar. During the chanting of a hula prayer in the halau, the dancing pupils gestured softly, revolving the hips all the while with three rotations to the right and three to the left. Care was taken not to roll the abdomen (ami opu) and not to move the shoulders any more than necessary. A dancer who could keep her shoulders steady while moving her hips or legs was said to be "paa o luna" or steady-shouldered. Whether dancing alone or in a group, the old time dancer required very little space to dance in, though she moved forward and backward or from side to side.

Meles for hula dancing were composed for almost every and any occasion and for every emotion, love, hatred, jealousy, admiration or woe. From birth to old age meles were composed for the alii (chiefs). When one came for a visit, meles were composed to commemorate it; if his leis were beautiful, they were sung about; if he were fond of surfing, that was a theme for a mele and if he were a member of a riding club, that, too, was sung about.

The hula olapa accompanied by the ipu or gourd instrument, the uliuli or hula in which the feather rattle is used, and the puili or hula with split bamboo rattles are still fairly common.

Some of the rare dances are danced by a very few such as the canoe hula, pa'i umauma, hula pahu, helo, the treadle board kalaau, the hog hula, the alaapapa and the dog hula. Most of Hawaii's beautiful hulas are gone for all time. Even the old hula ku'i created and danced in the days of the last monarchs have changed greatly. Today's hula ku'i, often called the interpretive hula, is no more like the hula ku'i of Kalakaua's day than a lily is like a rose. Pretty, yes, but not the same.

ANCIENT HULAS OF KAUAI

by

Mary Kawena Pukui

As Demonstrated by Mrs. Keahi Luahine Sylvester Gomes for the Kauai Historical Society at Lihue, January 31, 1936.

The Hula

Every country in the world has its folk dances, and we have ours in Hawaii. These are not of one type only but a large number generally called the hula. Some were peculiar to one island; some originated in one locality and spread to others; and some belong to the whole group, but had many different versions. I should say there were not less than 36 different kinds of hula in Hawaii.

In the days when every island had its own ruling chief or chiefs, hula dancing was much practiced by chiefs and commoners, by the aged as well as by children. Dancers of one locality vied with those of another and a very good hula instructor was usually found in the court of his chief.

Then the islands became united under one king. Even then, dancing was held in deep regard, but a few years after the death of Kamehameha the Great the hula became a dance of ill repute. Kamakau, the historian, in speaking of the beloved Kaahumanu, said that she tried to discourage the growing of awa and the dancing of the hula.

Yet here and there in remote country places the people kept up with their dancing. Small groups trained under a master thus preserving many of the old meles to come down to us today. Except for these people, the hula would have gone the way of other lost arts, such as tapa making, and would have vanished from Hawaii nei.

The latter rulers did not seem to discourage its practice, for at Kalakaua's jubilee, dancers and musicians gathered from end to end of the group.

Hula Looked Down Upon

Nevertheless, for many years, hula dancing was looked down upon and well do I remember the natives dancing freely when among themselves, but sitting still and trying to look dignified when a native minister or a foreigner was in their midst. Thus I learned as a small girl that a hula dance or song was not as bad as it was believed to be. Many were in honor of their rulers and were just as harmless as "Yankee Doodle," "My Old Kentucky Home" or "Mt. Vernon."

Many of our folk dances are gone for all time. A few, due to the courage and interest of some of our people, remain to us today, but are not commonly seen. The olapa, a tune danced to the gourd beat, the uliuli (in which a feathered gourd rattle is used), the puili (with a split bamboo rattle) are still fairly common, but many others are not. Among those seldom seen now are the hula alaapapa, a more dignified gourd dance; the hula pahu, with the big drum; the hula pahu and puniu, with the big drum and small coconut shell drum; the hula ka-laau, or treadle board, peculiar to Kauai; and the iliili, a sitting hula timed to the clapping of two smooth pebbles held adroitly in each hand.

There were likewise the turtle dance of Maui, hula honu; the pueke in which two dancers tossed small gourds back and forth between them like playing ball; the hula kuolo, for musicians with gourds; the hula mano or shark dance; the hula kolea or plover dance; the hula lelekawa, an Oahu dance of diving off from the back of the big whale that came to get the prophet Makuakaumana; the hula pahua, or spear dance; the hula pai umauma, beating the chest; the hula kilu, on Kauai with both pahu and puniu; the hula oniu, top spinning; the hula kielelei and Kolani, two very obscure dances.

Helo is Old Hula

Another old hula, the helo (misnamed ohelo by Dr. Emerson in his "Unwritten Literature of Hawaii") was danced on all the islands of the group. It was a sitting dance in which every now and then the dancer took a reclining position on balancing with one hand and moving one foot in a swaying motion under the other leg. This sawing motion gives it its name, which means "to draw through a loop." Well do I remember my aged grandmother doing the Hawaii version of the helo with a mele in which every other line was "E ni-olo e!" ("Saw away there, saw away!").

When men did not care to learn the old dances any more, it was the women who learned and saved them for us. Innumerable were these dances and meles now lost to us, but for the remaining fragments we are deeply grateful to those who preserved them. To the women who learned the dances that the men were forgetting, I also give my mahalo nui.

My Teachers

Keahi, my teacher and informant, was born May 3, 1877 at a place called Kunu in Pa-a, Koloa, Kauai. Her full given name is Ke-ahi-nui-o-ka-Lua-o-Pele, or Great-fire-in-the-Pit-of-Pele.

Kauai-iki was located near Keahi's childhood home, at Wahiawa, Koloa district. It is a large rock shaped like the island of Kauai which stood in a small taro patch very close to Keahi's home. Even though you might have been around Kauai-nui many times, the saying was that you had not compassed the whole island unless you had also walked around this stone, Kauai-iki. In later years, Mr. Alexander McBryde preserved Kauai-iki by taking it to his old home, Maialoa in Wahiawa. It is said by Hawaiians who were present when McBryde attempted to move the stone that it was so heavy that it proved impossible to budge it by any known means. Mr. McBryde was told that he must find an old chanter who could oli the hula Kauai-iki and talk the rock into a moving mood. An old chanter, Piheleo, was found; and, sure enough, as he chanted its special mele, the stone grew lighter and lighter, and thus allowed itself to be removed to the McBryde's old home at Maialoa. It was taken there on an oxcart. A rainbow arched overhead above it. Upon reaching Kiwaa the stone grew heavy again and more chants were uttered to lighten it.

A riddle was made soon after the coming of the white men in which the name of Keahi's birthplace was used. "Kunu ia Pa-a, noho i Weliweli, ku aku ka moku ia Mahaulepu, he pu aku ka'u, heaha mai kau?" (Kunu is located in Pa-a; the inhabitants dwell in Weliweli; the ships moved on to Mahaulepu. When I say "pu" to you, what is your answer to my riddle?) To one who is not accustomed to the Hawaiians' use of the play on words, the meaning of the riddle is obscure. Kunu (broiling, which signified wrath) was found in Pa-a' (literally, flaming wall). The inhabitants dwell in Weliweli (great fear). The ship moved on to Mahaulepu (Fall-down-together). When I say "pu" (gun) to you, what is your answer to my riddle? Answer: Kiwaipoha, a term used by the natives to designate the gunpowder that exploded (poha) from the guns of the foreigners.

Father Was Native of Maui

Her father, Luahine Na-waa-holo-kulua, was a native of Maui and her mother, Ka-wahine-noho-i-ka-uka-Koaia Kapahu-eleele (The woman-who-dwells-in-the-upland-of-Koaia The-hidden-drum) was a Kauaian. Koaia is a place in the Waimea Canyon, below Puu-ka-pele.

Keahi remembers so well the house in which she was born in Pa-a'. It was a large, grass-thatched, frame house. In it were long shelves, one for the bed clothes and one for the family clothing. The sleeping place was a pile of mats two feet high. Beside the sleeping place was a lower pile of mats for the weary worker to rest on in the day time. The floor was entirely covered by mats. From the beams hung the food calabashes suspended in carrying nets (koko). There was a hala tree directly behind the house at the base of a small hill. Terraces of stone were built all around the house and on these terraces grew onions of the old mahina variety. When returning home from fishing or from farming the horses on which they rode stopped at the lowest terrace where the riders dismounted and unloaded the horses.

Keahi's parents moved to Nupalani, Wahiawa when she was a small child and there they made their home. Her relatives were all hula dancers and all her babyhood and childhood was spent in that environment. Her baby feet learned the steps and her wee hands the gestures, but as she told me, they were meaningless to her until she was eight years of age.

When she was still a little girl, her two sisters, Kapo-ula-Kinau and Ka-lei-hulu-mamo-i-ka-poli-o-Hiiaka (the-mamo-feather-wreath-in-the-bosom-of-Hiiaka) were learning the hula under Naupuaea, an aged Kinsman, great-grandfather of the composer Kaehu. His halau, or hula training school, was close to the ruins of the heiau of Ka-ulu-o-Lono in Wahiawa. This was a heiau in which the plants, awa dregs, and other articles used in hula school were deposited. The dregs of awa and the remains of the ceremonial feasts for hula were never thrown around carelessly lest they become defiled.

Had Ceremonial Bath

Keahi remembers seeing her sisters come out of the halau early every morning to the pool called Poolimu where they had their hiuwai or ceremonial bathing before returning into the halau. They had a complete change of clothing after the bath and the hair was not braided nor coiled up in a knot, but merely combed free of all tangles. One of the rules of the hula schools was strict personal cleanliness, although such things as paring the finger nails, shaving and hair cutting were never permitted until after graduation from the hula school. These pupils returned from Poolimu pool to the halau with prayer chants every step of the way.

Another hula school in the same locality was conducted by Kanupaka, also a relative, at Kamokila. This Kanupaka was noted for his beautiful chanting voice. His children became hula experts, but his grandchildren did not learn. His son, Piheleo, was the last to know his father's old meles and methods of teaching in that particular family. Kanupaka and Piheleo were experts in healing broken bones with the laau kahea or healing by prayers. Not only the Hawaiians but the Chinese and Japanese had great faith in their method of healing.

Keahi was about eight years old when Queen Kapiolani toured Kauai to interest the people there in the welfare of their babies. Queen Kapiolani had organized a society called Ahahui Hooulu Lahui or Society for the Propagation of the Race. It was in accordance with the wish of the Queen that Keahi was brought to Honolulu to be reared by her sister, Kapoula-Kinau, who was then married to John Hili. From that time on Keahi went back and forth between Oahu and Kauai. For many years she lived in the home of Judge and Mrs. Luther Wilcox at Kuloloia, Alakea and Queen Streets, in Honolulu. The lei kukui which Keahi owns is an old one strung on olona fiber. It was formerly the special necklace of Kapiolani and was given recently to Keahi as a close friend of the Queen.

Became Pupil

At the age of twelve, she became a pupil of a hula school on Kauai at the place called Nana in Kauai-iki, Wahiawa. A kuahu or altar to Laka was built in their halau or school, and there Keahi learned not only the meles and dances but the rites, ceremonies and prayers of the hula. Hookano, the teacher from Waimea, was a mahu (a hermaphrodite, having qualities of both sexes). Piheleo, a son of Kanupaka, was the hoopaa or musician, and his wife, Kealaula, was the alakai hula, that is, she danced and the pupils imitated her until they learned. Keahi was the poopuaa or head pupil of the class. Her classmates were five sisters who were all cousins of hers. They were Kahulu, Keluia, Lahilahi, Emma and Kina. At the same time, three boys, Kelii-hele-i-ke-kai, Moe-anu (Keahi's half brothers), Kaliko (her own brother) and Hoopii, a brother of the five girls, were being trained to become hoopaa or musicians.

Keahi's father did not approve of hula dancing, but her mother, who belonged to a family of poets, musicians, dancers and doctors, saw nothing wrong in her daughter's learning the chants and dances of her people. Her great-grandfather, Paele, was a kahuna who knew the uses of herbs for healing and who was also an expert in discerning signs and omens, whether good or bad. He belonged to Nupalani, Wahiawa on this island.

Besides the heiau of Ka-ulu-a-Lono for the hula on Kauai, there was another one called Ke-ahu-a-Laka beyond Haena. This heiau was famed all over Kauai. When a hula school had completed its course, it was customary to take the leis, skirts, anklets, awa cups and the greenery that was used in the construction of the altar to deposit at this heiau. The cups were broken before leaving it. The graduation feast was held here and the pupils danced in honor of Laka. The remains of the feast were left there. An uniki or graduation at this heiau always drew a large crowd of people who enjoyed hearing the meles and seeing the new dancers and musicians who had just completed their course of training.

The heiau of Ka-ulu-o-Lono was also used as a depository for the greenery, the paus, leis, anklets, awa cups, awa dregs and the bones of food that were eaten in the halau.

Sister Was Beautiful Dancer

Keahi's sister Ka-lei-hulu-mamo was a beautiful dancer and it was in her honor that the mele hula, "No Ka-lei-hulu-mamo ke aloha" was composed. She became the wife of a noted Maui composer, Hauola Makekau. They had a son, Manasseh Makekau, who was a representative in the House of the Legislature. Among Manasseh Makekau's daughters is Iolani Luahine, one of Honolulu's charming and popular exponents of the hula, and a pupil of Keahi Luahine, her grand-aunt and foster mother.

Another of my teachers was Kapua of upper Hanapepe valley. He was the son of Kapuanui, a hula master of the same valley. Kapua learned the hula from his early boyhood and his mind is a storehouse of meles, but due to an explosive temper he is not easy to approach. I have not seen any one handle the ipuwai or hula gourd as he does. His use of the instrument is difficult to imitate; he is adept in the art.

Kameahaiku and Makea, two well known dancers of Hanapepe Valley, were trained in the same school as Kapua, whose teachers were his father and grandfather.

His method of teaching is different from Keahi's. Keahi gave the words of the mele to the haumana hoopaa or pupil musician to memorize and then when that was learned, the timing on the instrument. As soon as that was mastered, she concentrated her attention on the dancing pupil, watching each gesture and step carefully, noting the posture and movements and checking a fault at once. With Keahi it was one mele and dance at a time; a more modern method and easier.

Kapua would not give a line of mele to pupils, nor would he instruct them just where this beat or that came in. He played on his instrument and chanted mele after mele for two hours every class night. It was up to the pupils to listen, learn the words and beat, and if they did not catch them, then it was their own fault for lack of concentration. The pupils had to beat on their gourds as long as he did. It was extremely difficult at first, but as time went by order came out of a confusion of words and thumps till the pupils could distinguish one mele from another, and one type of gourd beat from another.

Two Musician Pupils In Class

In our class, there were two musician pupils, a man and myself. Kapua did not like me, as he felt that a woman had no business to learn a man's part in the hula. In the olden days, the musicians were naturally men, but the dancers could be both men and women. To find a silly woman who was determined to be a musician in his class was very trying to poor Kapua's patience and several times he did voice his opinion. When told that I meant to write about it rather then to become a hula teacher, he was positive then that he had an idiot before him. His disgust was freely expressed, but what could he do with a determined woman?

I am a graduate of both schools, not an uniki graduate, but a hu'elepo one. The uniki is a ceremonious graduation requiring a sacrificial hog as well as fish appropriate to the occassion. The hu'elepo (literally "dust scattering") needed but an offering of a fish, ceremoniously called a "sea-hog," such as the kumu or mullet. The aka or essence of the feast belonged to the patron deity of the hula, but the material was ours to eat. The bones and whatever was left of the feast were consigned to the sea. Before partaking of this sacrificial feast, the pupils went outdoors to dance in the sunlight. It did not matter if the neighbors became interested and lined up on the fences to see what was going on. A pupil was not permitted to dance or chant for an audience without having first gone through an uniki or hu'elepo graduation.

An uniki graduation was formerly, and still is, imperative when the pupils are taught with the kuahu or altar in the halau. The rules of such a halau were many and strict. A pupil was not permitted to share a portion of his food (hakina) with any one except a member of the halau. Sugar cane (ko), taro tops (luau), bananas, seaweed of the lipeepee variety and squids were kapu articles of food and must not be eaten until after graduation. If a pupil was married, he did not sleep with his wife, or vice versa. All kissing was prohibited until at the graduation. It was not permissable to urinate in water nor on a stone; nor to come in contact with dead bodies. Quarreling, or criticizing the methods of another school was not allowed. This old, but true, saying had been handed down from antiquity, "Aole i pau ka ike i ka halau hookahi" or "All knowledge was not taught in one school."

Could Not Object to Kissing

At the time of the uniki, every one who wishes to could kiss the graduating pupils and the pupil could not voice her objection, no matter if the person who kissed her was not much to her liking. If a dancer did so well that her spectators pushed and surged forward to see better, she was considered a very good dancer. This was called "hui ka aha" or "mix up among the spectators." Gifts laid or thrown into the area where the dancing was held were divided among the musicians and dancers, but gifts tucked into the hand or clothing of the dancer or musician were personal and not shared with the others.

There were three types of initiation used on Kauai, the ai-holoholo, the hoolulu-lei and the kukulu kuahu. Of these types the second and third were also used on the other islands. I have never heard of the first type outside of Kauai. I was initiated by this particular Kauai method, the ai-holoholo.

A pupil should not be taught alone, but should have one or more companions, Keahi told me, and so my adopted sister, a Japanese girl born in Waimea, Kauai, was initiated with me. This Japanese girl, named Patience Na-maka-uahoa-o-Kawena Wiggin, was adopted by my parents after the death of her own in the influenza epidemic in 1920. She was then two months of age.

It was at my insistence that Keahi showed me the ceremonies and taught me some of the old pules or prayer chants. These prayers are not much like our Christian prayers, but more like the Psalms or the Songs of Solomon.

Describes Ceremony

Let me describe the ai-holoholo initiation ceremony. A pupil who learned to become a hoopaa, or musician, memorized a large number of meles, remembered the various pitch of some of the meles for the olapa dances, concentrated on timing and watched the olapa or dancer to see whether the steps were right. Without the hoopaa many of the dances could not be danced. That is one reason some of our younger people prefer to learn the modern hulas danced to recorded songs on the phonograph. A hoopaa, if he was studious, could and often did become a kumu or instructor. So for an offering, he gave a fish also called kumu. The olapa, or dancer, offered either a mullet (amaama) or moano. The amaama, that the gods may give the dancer grace to please (A-ama) her spectators. Besides these there were the greens to deck the center of the table or eating mat, three ti leaves spread out with the ends of the stems meeting in the center and on these were laid others, lama, koa, palai ferns, maile; and if other significant greens were obtainable, then they too might be added. The food placed on the table was not eaten raw. It was dedicated by prayers before being cooked and when on the table re-dedicated. Following this, the whole was sprinkled with the waters of purification, salt water to which a pinch of tumeric (olena) root and red earth (alaea) had been added. The instructor, after a prayer offering the essence of spirit of the food, took a piece of the head of the fish and gave it to the pupil to eat. The teacher ate nothing himself, but throughout the meal he chanted chant after chant used in the hula service. The pupil had to eat all of his fish; but if he could not do it, then at the end of the meal it was rolled up with the other things and cast into the sea. Beside the fish as an offering, there was awa (the one thing that a Hawaiian ceremony was never complete without). The kapu was removed when all the greenery and remains of the feast were taken to the sea. "Ai ku, ai hele" or "eat standing up or eat walking about," that is, there is no striction or kapu; except, of course, that there must be no demonstration of a dance for one's friends until the hu'elepo. The ai-holoholo ceremony was customarily performed at noon ("kau ka la i ka lolo" or when the sun is directly overhead) and the remains of the feast removed to the depths of the sea before the sun had vanished in the west. Not even the slightest thing was without significance in these ceremonies.

The revolving of the hips or ami is one thing much misunderstood in the hula. In some hulas, perhaps, it meant to be sexually suggestive, but in most of the old hulas it was neither suggestive nor vulgar. During the chanting of a hula prayer in the halau, the dancing pupil gestured softly, with both feet planted firmly on the floor, revolving the hips all the while with three rotations to the right and three to the left. Care must be taken not to roll the abdomen (ami opu), but the hips were revolved backward and never forward. This helped to limber and loosen the tightened abdominal muscles. There were special prayers used to soften the body without the painful handling called hakihaki.

In the hakihaki a pupil was made to kneel with buttocks resting on the heels, then the instructor stepped upon the legs above the knees to keep them on the floor. The pupil bent backward until the back of his head touched the floor while her hands were held by the instructor. Another method was to hug a post and revolve the hips as much as possible.

These methods my own teachers did not use on any of their pupils. It was not necessary. The revolving of the hips while a long prayer chant was recited was sufficient to limber a pupil. Now and then the shoulders were held to steady them, as good dancers are not supposed to move them any more than necessary. I have noticed that a pupil who began a training under Keahi did not hop or have an exaggerated swing of the hips as we term "ami naaupo" or "silly revolving." They danced easily. I do not mean pupils who began elsewhere and then came to Keahi for further instruction, but I do mean those who had never had any other teacher than Keahi.

Program

All these Kauai hulas and meles were given to me freely by Mrs. Keahi Luahine Gomes-Sylvester, my first teacher. The English translations are my own, and very literal.

These eight dances are followed by six special mele inoa, or name songs.

1. Hula Pele (goddess of the volcano)
2. Hula Hoe (paddle)
3. Hula Kii (images)
4. Hula Ilio (dog)
5. Hula Puaa (hog)
6. Hula Kalaau (treadleboard)
7. Hula Pahu (big drum)
8. Hula Kuhi (gesture of honor).

Hulas given for an audience in old Kauai were never hit or miss affairs without care for order and sequence. One part linked into another, whether the dances were of the same type or not. It took careful thought to plan the general scheme or pattern of dances. The program itself had its kaona or special inner meaning. The one represented here is as follows:

Hula Pele followed by the hula hoe or canoe paddling hula. That signifies "The goddess Pele comes on a canoe." The hula kii or dance of the wooden images that follows conveys the idea that the spirits represented by the images shall man Pele's canoe. The dog deity Ku-ilio-loa, welcomes Pele ashore and so the dog dance or hula ilio follows. Then comes a feast in which a hog is served, hence the hog dance or hula puaa. But the hog must be cooked and the house built to receive the royal guest and here we have the hula ka-laau or stick dance, laau meaning stick or wood. After the feast, the entertainment, a royal one befitting her rank, and the pahu or drum is brought forth to entertain her with the hula pahu. The guest is a beloved one, and the dance of all favorite sitting and gesturing hula. This is the pattern or inner meaning of the program itself. This kaona was very important in early Hawaiian life and is so today among the older people.

Color Combinations Important

On Kauai great regard was paid to appropriate combinations even in costume and color. Pele was fond of red, hence her red cloak. Hiiaka, as one of the gods of the hula altar, wore the green of the altar. It is as if the god, or spirit, were veiled by the greenery. Hence, the dancer appears enveloped in green which is dropped as the dance proceeds. In any song pertaining to the sea blue tapa is used for the pa-u, or skirt. For earth, a pa-u of brown tapa. For the drum dance, hula pahu, a kikepa or long garment of tapa wound around the body, tied over the left shoulder and allowing free movement of feet. Any color appropriate to the chief to be honored might be chosen.

When a friend comes to your house you do not keep your mouth shut to greet him. You begin to call out in song or greeting of welcome as soon as he appears. Hence, any hula was introduced by some appropriate song or prayer.

Before the eight dances Keahi introduces the whole with an opening chant called Wailua-iki. Every phase of the hula had its particular chant or in many instances a large number of chants. Among these were some of Hiiaka's chants while on the way to Kauai to seek her sister's lover, King Lohiau. Her call to Kapo, whom she referred to as "Wailua-iki," or lesser Wailua, was used in the halau. It was first uttered by Hiiaka when she visited Kapo's home on Kauai. Finding her gone to gather flowers on the hillside above, she called to her in a chant:

WAILUA-IKI

O oe ka ia e Wailua-iki, E ka la ulu pali o Waioli, I hele ia mai e Li'a wahine, Ka wahine kui pua o Hoakalei e, E lei oe.	It is thou (whom I seek) O Wailua-iki On the sunlit hill of Waioli, Li'a-wahine advances hither, This woman who strings the flowers of Hoakalei to wear.
E lei oe i na hala i pala iloli i ke kai Ua hele wale a maka eleele i ka anu, Hina ia e ke Kina'u Ola ia Mahamoku ka makani ku puni kawalawala.	Wear thou the hala that is speckled by the sea, Speckled black by the cold, And tossed down by the Kinau (breeze). Mahamoku, the blustering wind, renews life.
Kahea i ka luna o Kamae la e hoi	When it calls to you from the top of Kamae to return
He malihini puka ko ka hale nei.	For visitors have come to your home.

1. Pele Dance

When Pele the volcano goddess came to these islands, her first home was on Kauai. Then going from island to island she found a permanent home on Hawaii. Pele herself did not dance, but her sister Hiiaka was numbered among the gods of the dance. Like all great rulers here in Hawaii, Pele had her particular dance. It was one in which no musical instruments were employed. The musicians sat in rows and kept the time by clapping their hands while one or two dancers stood up to dance. Kauai, her first home, had its version of the Pele dance and Hawaii, her present home, had another. Perhaps the other islands also had dances in honor of Pele. I have not heard of any, but the dance used in Honolulu today by some exponents of the hula is a Hawaii version. The one demonstrated this evening is the Kauai version, the older of the two.

For the hula Pele, a big fire was always built because she is the goddess of fire, and its hula was danced around it. Today this ceremonial fire is always to be imagined when not actually practicable. Modern performers use guitar or ukulele for the hula Pele but in Kau, Hawaii, and on Kauai the proper musical accompaniment for her dance was in ancient times furnished by clapping of hands.

Mele for Hula Pele

Lapaku ka wahine o Pele i Puukapele, Owaka i ka lani, noke, noke, Lapaku ka wahine o Pele i Nomilu, Owaka i ka lani, noke, noke, Lapaku ka wahine o Pele i Kakakalua, Owaka i ka lani, noke, noke, Elieli kau mai, elieli kau mai, Owaka i ka lani, noke, noke, Amama ua noa, amama ua noa, Owaka i ka lani, noke, noke.	The woman Pele burst forth at Puukapele, She flashed to the heavens, on and on. The woman Pele burst forth at Nomilu, She flashed to the heavens, on and on. The woman Pele burst forth at Kakakalua, She flashed to the heavens, on and on. It was awe-inspiring, it was awe-inspiring. She flashed to the heavens, on and on. Amama, the kapu is freed, the kapu is freed, She flashed to the heavens, on and on.

2. The Paddle Dance

Most hulas were introduced by a few opening lines as the dancers entered. Some of these were pule (prayers), some were not. These introductory lines for the paddle dance are the Pule Hoe, a prayer for guidance to the right spot in the well known fishing ground. The last persons whom Keahi recalls hearing sing this paddle prayer were her father and other close kinsmen when they went in canoes to a favorite fishing ground called Pohakuloa outside of Nomilu. On moonlight nights they caught uu, aweoweo (small weoweo) and upapalu, such as appeared chiefly on moonlight nights. On dark nights oio and aawa; in the daytime alaihi. Once arrived at the fishing ground the position of the canoe must be sighted absolutely by certain points; otherwise no fish appeared.

When this hula was given by great numbers of dancers these introductory lines took on the quality of a march. Such mass dancing, numbers of men or women, was most impressive, especially accompanied, as here, by the rhythmic swinging of many paddles in unison.

Introductory March or Prayer for the Hula Hoe

Kuu halau waa i Makanoni,	My canoe-shed is at Maka-noni,
Pae i ke ko'a i Pohaku-loa,	(The canoe) goes to the fishing ground at Pohakuloa,
Ka ihu o kuu waa i Iole-au,	The prow of my canoe (must) turn toward Iole-au (a small hill),
I ka hope kai e.	The stern toward the open sea.

One of the hulas danced on Kauai and Oahu was the hula hoe or canoe paddling dance. The dancer either sat or stood up and sometimes alternated in the same dance. A paddle was held in the hand and wielded just as one would on a canoe, rowing, holding the handle of the paddle under the arm for a rest, turning the canoe about, and so on, the motion depending on the context of the chant. This was a group dance and when done in unison, was beautiful to behold.

This is one of the very old meles used in the hula hoe:

Kapae Moku

Ka pae moku nonoho like,	The island groups lie close together
I ka hikina a i ke komohana,	Stretching out from east to west
Pae like ka aina	Lie these island groups.
Lalani i Nuuhiwa,	The Nuuhiwa group lies in a row,
Hui aku hui mai me Holani,	Intermingled with those of Holani
Naha i Nuuhiwa lele i Polapola,	(He) leaves Nuuhiwa and goes to Borabora
Puni na moku,	And circles each island
O Hilauale'a a ke kilo.	Hilauale'a was the astronomer.
Kaawale ka aina,	The islands were separated,
Moku i ke aho lawaia'a Kahai	Each cut off by Kahai's fish line
Puni na moku ia Kukanaloa,	(Thus did) Kukanaloa traverse these islands.
Kaawale na aina, na moku.	The land, the islands were separated,
Moku i ka ohe kaulana a Kanaloa.	Cut apart by Kanaloa
E ola!	Long may he live!

Kukanaloa was a foreign navigator who came to these shores with his sister long before Captain Cook's discovery. He married a Hawaiian chiefess and remained here the rest of his life. Some believed that he was a Spaniard. Whether he was or not, I cannot say.

3. The Dances of the Images

The dance of the wooden images (kii) was originated by the natives of Kalalau on Kauai and did not spread to any of the other islands. In this dance, musicians were unnecessary. The dancer chanted and by stiff posturing told of the small and large wooden images or idols. Keahi told me that small children on Kauai used to dance this on almost all the beaches after returning from a swim. This hula kii of Kauai must not be confused with Dr. Emerson's hula kii or dance in which puppets were used.

The hula kii of Pokii (a place below Kekaha) told of the row (pae) of wooden images (kii) that stood at Wailua, Kauai, near the mouth of the stream. Keahi believes that they are there yet, covered with earth and sand. This row of images was referred to as the "Pae kii mahu o Wailua" or the row of sexless images at Wailua. Kaia'kea, a kinsman (kupuna) of Keahi, was the last keeper of these kiis.

Hula Kii

Pokii ke kii,	The Pokii dance of the images,
Hookiikii ke kii,	The images that tilt,
Hoonaanaa ke kii,	The images with protruding abdomen,

Hooualehe ke kii,	The images with knees spread out and bent,
Kaunalewa ke kii,	The images that sway,
Hi'uwai i Wailua,	Washed by the waters of Wailua,
Ka pae kii mahu.	Is this row of sexless images.
Ua ike a.	They are well known.

4. The Dog Dance

The Kauai version of the hula ilio or dog dance did not need any timing by a musician. The dancer wore dog's teeth buskins fastened one under each knee. The rattling of these teeth was all the music that the dancer needed as he stepped to the words of the mele he chanted. This dance was usually done by men either standing or sitting. The standing form, with long spears, was used as a war dance. Keahi will demonstrate the sitting dog dance.

The introductory pule is a prayer for protecting the way to the forest from evil of every kind.

March for the Hula Ilio

Noho ana ke akua i ka nahelehele.	The gods dwell in the woodlands.
I alai ia e ke kiohuohu, e ka ua koko,	Hidden away in the mist, in the low-hanging rainbow,
O na kino malu i ka lani,	O beings sheltered by the heavens,
Malu e hoe.	Clear our path of all hindrance.
E hooulu aku ana ia ulu kupu,	We call to (the gods of) growth to inspire us,
Ia ulu noho, ia ulu kini o e akua,	To the (woodland) dwellers for inspiration, To the hosts of gods for inspiration.
Ulu i ke kapa kanaka.	To be given to the dwelling place of (us) human beings.
Kahea ke akua kiai pali,	The guardian god of the hills calls
E wikiwiki, e holoholo, e na kaa loa,	To hasten to hurry, to speed along the way,
Maile, ki ke 'kua ke ano mai.	The maile and ki thickets are the dwelling places of these revered ones.
E ulu, e ulu, i ko kahu,	Inspire us, inspire and dwell on your altar,
Ia ka hookapuhi noa.	Give us the lithe freedom of an eel.

Mele for the Hula Ilio

Ka ilio i ka lae-oka-ilio, au	The dog (cried) at the Cape-of-the-Dog, owooh,
I ka pali pohaku i kuala, au, au	To the stony cliff of Kuala, owooh! owooh!
I Ahulua ka ilio,	The dog ran to Ahulua,
I ka lae o Kawahaala,	Then to the cape of Ka-waha-ala,
Aala ka uahi e.	The smoke there smells so fragrant.

The dog of this hula belonged to Leiwi, chief of Lawai, Kalaheo and Nomilu. The residence of this chief retains the name of Leiwi to this day. At this Cape-of-the-Dog stands a high stone from which a long drawn-out howling, as of a dog, is heard at times foretelling death. This hula was danced only on the nights of Kane, Ku, and Lono.

5. The Hog Dance

The hog dance originated on Kauai. Later it spread to Oahu where the hog god Kamapuaa later made his home. Thus arose two versions, the Kauai form (which was older) and the Oahu version.

Mele for Hula Puaa

Nemonemo ka puaa iluna o Haupu	The hairless pig up on Haupu
E ha'i ana he malie, hu! hu! hu!	Announces the calm, hu! hu! hu!
Okala ka puaa i Kalanipu,	The bristling pig on Kalanipu
E ha'i ana he ino, u! u! u!	Announces a storm, u! u! u!
Inu wai i Kemamo,	They drink the water of Kemamo,
He pali iki o Kipu, uhu! uhu! uhu!	Kipu is but a small hill, uhu! uhu! uhu!
I Mahaulepu o a'u mau pu,	At Mahaulepu are my conch shells,
Ami!	I shake my hips!

The amipuaa is not a revolving of the hips as in some of the other dances, but a swinging of the hips from side to side as in imitation of the waddling of a fat hog.

6. The Treadle-Board Dance

The music of the ka-laau was produced by striking two sticks together in time with the chant. The longer stick three or more feet long was held in the left hand, resting on the extended index finger and held by the thumb and the other three fingers. This long stick was struck by a small stick about the length and size of a thick lead pencil held in the right hand. The sticks were never held in a tight grip as that deadened the vibrations of the wood. Different woods gave out different tones in vibration when struck together, and so the hula experts chose the best obtainable for this purpose, such as the ohia, koa, koaie, kauila, ulei, and other hard woods.

William Ellis described as follows a ka-laau dance which he witnessed on Hawaii in 1823:

> ..."A party of musicians arrived before the house of Keopuolani and commenced a hura ka-raau. Five musicians advanced first, each with a staff held in his left hand five or six feet long, about four inches in diameter at one end and tapering off to a point at the other. In his right hand he held a small stick of hard wood six or nine inches long with which he commenced his music by striking the small stick on the larger one, beating time all the while with his right foot on a stone placed on the ground beside him for the purpose. Six women, fantastically dressed in yellow tapas, crowned with garlands of flowers, having also wreaths of scented flowers of the gardenia on their necks and branches of fragrant maire around their ankles, now made their way by couples through the crowd, and arriving at the area on one side of which the musicians stood, began their dance. Their movements were slow and though not always graceful, exhibited nothing offensive to modest propriety"...

The natives of Kauai and Niihau did not stamp on a stone as did those whom Ellis saw on Hawaii, but used instead a board shaped like a rude wooden platter. This was laid on a stick, rounded on one side and flattened on the other. The flat side rested on the ground and the rounded side permitted the board to see-saw back and forth. The right foot was placed on this platter-shaped board and tapped on the ground in time with the sticks, either in front by the ball of the foot or behind by the heel, this rocking giving out a vigorous tapping sound. Although the ka-laau was danced on all the islands, the Kauai manner was very different, in the use of the treadle-board. As the cultures of Kauai and Niihau were practically the same, it was only on these two islands that the treadle boards were ever used. There is but one really old treadle board in the Bishop Museum which we copied in order to revive this Kauai form of the dance in our own little group of pupils.

Mr. Pukui, who went to see the dancers from all the islands who came to celebrate King Kalakaua's jubilee, saw a troupe of Niihau men who danced the ka-laau. There were just the musicians who struck their sticks together and rocked their treadle boards in time to their chanting. It was rather mild and did not rouse such excitement as the livelier dances did. The unity of movement and the rhythm were beautiful, he told me, but lacked what we call today "pep."

The following old Kauai kalaau chant points out an excellent moràl:

Ahuwale Ka Mamane*

Ahuwale e ka mamane kau i ka laau,	The mamane berries in full view on the bush
Ke kaohi ala ka wahine kapu a,	Were plucked by the sacred woman.
Na ka manu e ai	(She was taunted for) eating the food of birds,
Ai lahui....	Food of which the birds are fond.
Lahui aku ia po.	(She) met (her tormentors) there at night.
Hookaawale i ke alo na'u e moe,	(And said) "Turn your faces away and let me sleep.
Moe aku au, paio olua,	While I sleep you may continue your quarrel,
Loaa kauhale ka imu ai ole.	(But) you'll find that it brings no food to your homes and imus.

The sacred woman referred to here was Pele who came to Kauai from Kahiki. Seeing the pretty berries, she went up the hillside to pluck them. There she met two quarrelsome woodland sprites who had come from Kahiki with her and her family some time before. One of them was named Kaumupue. He and his companion not only quarreled continuously themselves, but tried to arouse her ire by taunting her for eating bird's food. She was tired after her climb and so decided to sleep rather than pay attention to their foolish chatter. Before sleeping she said, "Turn your faces away so that I may sleep. Quarrel if you must, but those who spend their time in quarrel often find no food to put into their imus."

The ka-laau dancers of today use neither treadle board nor stone, and only two small sticks about six or more inches in length held one in each hand. The dancers either kneel while beating time with the sticks or use steps that are a cross between the two-step and the olapa. The ka-laau of today is somewhat lively and rather pretty.

Keahi knows also another hula ka-laau of Kauai called Kinau's house, Ka Hale Kinau, a very sacred one danced only on the night of Kane.

7. The Drum Dance

To Kauai from far-off Kahiki came Laa to see his father Moikeha. With him came the first drum ever seen in these islands.

The natives on Oahu heard the sounds of his kaeke or bamboo instruments, his pu-niu (coconut drum) and pahu (big drum) as his canoe passed along, and were delighted with their sounds. A man ran along the shore of Oahu from Hanauma to Waimanalo to keep within earshot of Laa's drums. So at that time (about six hundred years ago) the hula pahu or drum dance came to Kauai. From thence it branched out to the other islands.

Laa-mai-Kahiki landed at a small canoe landing called Ahukini, a little south of Hanamaulu bay and the present Ahukini landing. His drum was taken to the heiau of Ka Lae o Ka Manu at Wailua. This is the heiau restored recently by the Kauai Historical Society.

---

*This particular chant, the animal chants, the drum chant, the image chant, and the name chants to Renown Sylvester and Keahi's great grandmother belong to the family of Keahi Luahine; i.e., they are *kapu* to all others who have not been given permission to use them. The reader is requested by the author to respect this *kapu*, as was done traditionally by Hawaiians.

Opening Prayer for the Hula Pahu

Ke akua uwalo i ka la'i e,	The god who shouts aloud in the calm,
E hea wale ana iluna o Puaa-hulu-nui,	Is calling from the heights of Puaa-hulu-nui,
Ke akua pee i ka lau kiele,	This is the god that conceals himself amidst the kiele leaves,
O'u makua i kui lei,	Who strung the wreaths (of honor) for our forefathers to wear.
E Kui no oe a e lei no makou a.	String us wreaths that we, too, may wear.

Kalani Kamanomano

Eia o Kalani ka-manomano	Here is our chief, our sacred one,
Ka manomano heke o ke kapu,	He of the strictest kapus.
Ka honu peekua wakawaka,	A turtle with a horny shelled back,
Pipii ka unahi ma ke kua,	With scales up the back,
Hiolo ka unahi ma ke alo,	Scales down the front,
Ma ka maha opi o Kalani,	Close to his wrinkled jowl.
Kalani ka hiapo, kama kapu,	The chiefess is his first-born child, a sacred child,
Hanau mua o Hawaii,	First-born chiefess in Hawaii,
Ka ilio nukea ma ka lani,	A white-fanged dog in the heavens,
Eia la ke o nei.	We sing of her always.

This hula chant was said to have been composed by a god. This is the legend to which it belongs:

A beautiful young, kapu chiefess of Kauai was noticed to be continuously drowsy all day and when night fell, she was eager to retire into her private sleeping house and go to sleep.

Her father questioned her, but finding no satisfactory answer, consulted his kahunas. They told him she was in love with a sea god and that if he wished to see him for himself to set guards at intervals from her house to the shore. These guards were to maintain a perfect silence and when the god left just before the break of dawn, to gesture to the next one farther on when he had passed.

The chief and his kahunas were on the shore to see which form he would take before going out to sea.

Just before the dawn, a hand was seen to move to one side the mat that covered the doorway of the chiefess' sleeping house and a handsome youth emerged. He walked quickly to the beach and there he vanished. As he passed, a guard signaled by gesturing to the next guard that he was going that way.

The watching chief saw the youth vanish among the vines that grew over the sand and soon a huge, scaly and thick shelled turtle was seen to move toward the sea and swim away.

The following night the chiefess waited in vain for her lover. He did not come in person but instead he appeard to her in a dream and said, "You will never see me any more for I was seen by many eyes when I left you last night. When our child is born name her Honu (Turtle) for me. Listen, this is the name chant that you must sing for her and for her descendants, for she is both of divine and royal rank." This is how the chant "Kalani kamanomano" came into being.

The hula pahu was and is a hula of dignity and never danced for the pleasure of a ribald crowd.

Kamakau, in his story of Kamehameha I, tells of Kaahumanu's rank and of her descent from the high chiefs of Hawaii, Maui, Oahu, and Kauai and ends it with this phrase, "He honu peekua wakawaka o Kaahumanu," (a thick shelled turtle was Kaahumanu) or in other words, a descendant of this turtle god.

In the olden days the priests scanned the sky for signs and omens, and if the ever-changing clouds assumed the shape of a dog with bared fangs facing the land with tail on the seaward side, it foretold the coming of invaders that would slaughter and abuse the people, but if the dog-shaped cloud faced the sea with fangs bared, then the inhabitants, under the leadership of their chiefs, would be able to repel and defeat any invaders that dared to attempt an invasion. "A white-fanged dog," signified protection and ability to protect one's own land and people.

The Pointing or Special Dance

As a final honor to Goddess Pele in this program Keahi will give the hula kuhi, a sitting dance always performed in the house in the immediate presence of the chief. This one is a kuhi called "Oili pulelo i ke ahi o Kamaile."

The hula kuhi, or pointing out hula, used on Kauai was in the form of a dialogue, a row of seated dancers keeping time with clapping hands behind the first row of dancers seated in front of the chief. The back row would call out the question where? The front row would kuhi, point, and answer.

Mele for Hula Kuhi

Oili pulelo ke ahi o Kamaile

Auhea? Aia!
Lele hoaka ana iluna o Kamaualele.
Auhea? Aia!
Ka alawa iki o ka manu o Kaula i
ke kai,
Auhea? Aia hoi!
He mea okaikai ia loko i ko i
ana mai,
Eia la e, ua ike a.

The fire brand appears over Kamaile
(near Haena).
Where? There!
It sails yonder above Kamaualele.
Where? There!
The birds of Kaula, startled,
glance at the sea.
Where? There they are!
Anger rises within me at the things
you say,
Ah, this is known.

Following this group of eight dances Keahi will give a group of six personal songs, or mele inoa, of Kauai origin and dating from Kaumualii, the last king of Kauai, to the present time.

A. Hula Kauai for Kaumualii

Maikai Kauai, hemolele i ka malie,
Kupu kelakela ke poo o Waialeale.
Kelakela ia Kalanikini, kilakila ia
Kawaikini,
Maloeloe e ka laau, huli e mai e ka
pua.
Ke ike iho oe ia lalo o Maunahina,
He nani, he maikai, hemolele i ke alo
o Hihimanu!
I ana kapuai lima ia i ka loa me ka
laula,
O ka heke ia a o ia kuahiwi,
Aole a'u mea makemake ole o laila.
Makamaka e ke oho o ka palai,

Lipolipo i ka ua, ke hopu aku i ke
konane.
Paheehee i ka limu ka kanaka o
Manuakepa
Pekupeku lua i luna ka ua o Hanalei,
Owaowala na hala o Naue i ka makani.

O mai e ka lani, he alii, no he inoa,

He inoa no Kaumualii!

Beautiful Kauai, majestic in the calm,
Regally rises the summit of Waialeale.
Stately is Kalanikini, royal is Kawaikini,

The tree trunks are straight,
the blossoms flourish.
When you gaze down to the base of Maunahina,
The view before the face of Hihimanu
is beautiful, lovely, majestic!
The length and the breadth of the
greatest of mountains is measured,

There is nothing left to be desired.
The leaves of the ferns are fresh
and green,
Crisp in the rain, easily gathered
in the moonlight.
(There is) the moss of Manuakepa
on which men slide (and fall),
The heavy rains pelt down on Hanalei,
The hala trees of Haena writhe in the
wind.
Answer, O heavenly one, O chief, to
your name chant,
Your name chant, O Kaumualii!

B. From the cliff where stood the heiau Kuhiau above Nawiliwili Bay, the young composer Kaehu once burst into song at sight of one of the first sailing vessels, the Hetty, making her rapid way into the bay. Contrast with small, slow-moving canoes inspired the poetry of this Hawaiian ballad.

Kuhiau

This was a sitting dance in which the dancer swayed and made appropriate gestures. It was composed for one of the very first schooners that came to Kauai. Kuhiau means literally, "I point."

O luna au o Kuhiau,	I stood upon Kuhiau,
Alo ana o Heke i ka moana.	When Heke sailed by on the sea.
Hele a hilala na kia,	Her masts swaying to and fro,
Kikii na pe'a i ka makani,	Her tilted sails filled with the breeze,
Walawala ka pulumi o hope,	Her rudder was revolving behind,
Hulilua ka ale o ka moana.	The billows went this way and that.
Uiui ka papahele o luna,	The floor of the deck was creaking,
Lewa o lalo, oni pono ole,	She rocked violently below,
Kau a ka iwa o Kaula,	The sea birds of Kaula soared above,
Ha'i i ka ino o ka moana.	Telling us of stormy weather.
Ha'i o Heke i ka inoa,	Heke told us her name,
I ka la'i i Kuhiau.	In the calm of Kuhiau.

C. The Alphabet, or Vowel, Mele

The Hawaiians were, and are, very fond of chanting and singing, though it is mostly singing today and very little chanting.

When the teaching of letters came to Hawaii nei, many of the Hawaiians learned to read and write. Kamakau, the historian, tells in his story of Kamehameha the Great, that those who learned first were sent out to teach others. There were not enough books, so the pupils committed the lessons to memory. These lessons were then sung or chanted. Some of the country folks dearly loved to chant and so went to school eagerly in order to learn new material to chant! Thus learning spread far and wide. Some studied in order to learn the Scriptures, others studied so that they could sing the lessons. It was fun to sing a lesson, and much easier than just plain reciting.

This Kauai one was used when the people were learning the letters on that island. Later, it was revised and made into a mele inoa or name song for Kapiolani, the granddaughter of Kaumualii, the hereditary chief of Kauai. Kapiolani was dearly loved, but more so by those of the island of her illustrious ancestors.

Ula Noweo (Vowel Hula)

Ula noweo la,	The sun shines brightly down
E ka la i ka pua ilima.	On the ilima blossoms.
A ka lae o Nohili	At the cape of Nohili
Ka huailana a ka awapuhi.	A brook winds through the ginger plants.
Ike wale aku no oe	You can easily see
I ka ua loku o Hanalei.	The heavy rains of Hanalei.
Lipolipo wale mai la,	The forest of Hoohie,
Ka nahele o Hoohie.	Is brightly green.
Eia he a,	Here is a,
Eia he e,	Here is e,
Eia he i,	Here is i,
Eia he o,	Here is o,
Eia he u, u!	Here is u, u!

D. Waioli (A Rain Mele for Kapiolani)

Auhea wale ana oe,	Where are you,
E ka ua loku o Waioli.	O heavy showers of Waioli?
Ka manawa pehu keia	This is the time to swell
O ka limu o Manuakepa.	The moss of Manuakepa.
Hehi aku i ka wawae,	So when one steps upon it,
He mau ia, he pahee na'e.	It is moist and slippery.
Holu i ka puu mahiki,	(I) slide on the grassy slope,
I ka ehu kai o Makahoa,	Wet by the sea of Makahoa,
A he hoa no oe no'u la,	You are my companion,
I ka welelau o ka ano'i.	Drawn hither by love.
Haina mai ka inoa,	Thy name I will mention,
Kapiolani i ka iu o luna.	Kapiolani, the supreme one.

This mele is sung either to the hula olapa, accompanied by the ipu-wai, or to the hula iliili in which two stones are held in each hand. The stones are clapped together to give a clicking sound. The dancers kneel and sometimes sway or rise to the knees and sink back to a kneeling position again, while they click their stones. Smooth river stones or beach pebbles are essential to this primitive percussion instrument, also hard, smooth, close-grained pebbles which will give out a clear click.

E. Kaulu (for Mr. McBryde and Lawai)

One of the well-loved men of Kauai was the late Alexander McBryde. Makea, a very old Hawaiian lady of Hanapepe, composed for him a mele inoa called Kaulu, the name by which he was affectionately known among Hawaiians. Introductory to this mele inoa Keahi chants the name song of her own great-grandmother whose name was so kapu or sacred that she cannot reveal it even today. Kona in the song refers of course to the Kona or south to southeast side of Kauai. Maialoa, mentioned in the sixth line, became much later the site of Judge McBryde's home in the hills of Wahiawa. In very early days it had been the home of Keahi's family.

Mele for Keahi's Great Grandmother

Hanohano Kauai i ka malie,	Majestically Kauai stands in the calm,
Malino i ke kai o Kona i ka la'i,	The seas of Kona are unruffled,
Hooipoipo a ka ipo ahi	The lover woos his loved one
I ka ua kewai lawe malie.	In the light and gentle showers.
Pulu elo ke oho a loke lau lii,	(Showers) that moisten the dainty rose leaves,
Ka palai moe anu o Maialoa.	(And) the ferns that drop in the cold of Maialoa.
He loa ka imina a ka huapala	Long did (he) seek his sweetheart
A loaa i ke kai o Keawaiki.	And found her by the sea of Keawaiki.
Ka iki kumu ulu ia o Lele,	(She) is small as the breadfruit tree of Lele,
Kepau papala pili a ka manu.	But like the papala gum in holding the bird (lover) fast.
Manuahi mai nei kau ka opua,	A bird lover drawn hither like the clouds
Na kohi kelekele a Kapuukolu.	(That gather) on the moisture-laden summits of Kapuukolu.
Hana pono i ka loa o Mailehuna.	(Together we) shall travel the long trail to Mailehuna.
Piko waena o Waialeale,	Leading to the summit of Waialeale,
Aleale mai nei ko'u manao	My thoughts are filled to overflowing
Ka ai kahela o Makaukiu.	As the Makaukiu, love laden, wafts hither.
He kiu manu au no ka nahele,	I am the bird-watcher of the forest,
No ka po lealea o Halalii.	Mine the gay nights of Halalii.

The Hawaiians of Kauai danced the hula olapa to this mele hula that was composed in honor of Alexander McBryde. Kaihoolale is the islet that stands at the mouth of the stream at Lawai. Halepua is the name of his house which used to have a yellow painted roof. This had been Queen Emma's house upon the hill, but Mr. McBryde brought it down to the Lawai garden which he created there on the beach. The first line recalls the loveliness of that tropical garden.

Kaulu

Ua nani Lawai e waiho nei,	Lawai lies beautifully below,
I ke ala kikee a ka manu.	The winding trail of the birds.
A he manu o kaulu a hoea mai,	Kaulu comes like a bird,
Ke oni e nei i ke ala hao.	Moving on the railroad track.
Aia iluna o Kaihoolale	From the top of Kaihoolale
Au ana o Kaiwa i ke kai.	Kaiwa can be seen out at sea.
Kilohi i ka ani a o Hale pua	I glance at the beauty of Halepua
Kohu lei oo hulu melemele.	It is like the yellow feathered oo.
Haina ia mai ko inoa,	This is your name song,
O Kaulu la e o mai.	Answer our call, O Kaulu.

After his mele inoa was sung to him, it was customary for him to reply, "E o-" ("Here I am!"). Keahi says that Hawaiians always loved to sing this hula olapa whenever Mr. McBryde appeared, both as an affectionate greeting and because he was in the habit of "handing out not less than ten dollars in return!" The Hawaiians were very fond of both the McBryde brothers, who were always ready to go fishing or up into the kuahiwi (mountains) with them.

F. It is perhaps not generally known that these occasional odes or genealogical ballads called name songs are still composed and still sung. When Keahi's only child was born, in 1920 after her skilled fingers had made all the great feather kahilis for the centennial pageant in Honolulu, she named the beloved babe not only Centennial, but also Renown, for the Prince of Wales' battleship that day in port. In a dream a vision bade her name him also for the royal featherworkers of her family. Ka-haku-hulu-lani-alii, names which, with his father's he proudly wears to this day. Her mele inoa for him tells not only the names of the street where he lives, but gives beautiful expression to her love for her only child. It is built on the plan of all Kauai genealogical chants using the names of the Kauai lands of his ancestors. It is a poem set to ancient music, and to hear the composer sing it is to hear the call of old Hawaii.

Mele Inoa for Renown Sylvester

O Ka-haku-hulu-lani-alii,	(This is the name chant for) Ka-haku-hulu-lani-alii,
Ua puka i ke ao Malamalama,	Who is born in this world of light,
He pua nani no Ilaniwai,	A beautiful blossom of Ilaniwai,
He waiwai nui oe na ke kama,	You are a great wealth to the beloved child (your mother),
Like oe me ka onohi	Like a gem
Me ka opuu nani o ka makemake,	A cherished bud, much desired,
I ka uka, i ka uka o Koai'a	You belong to the upland, to the upland, to Koai'a (the secret cave)
I Koaekea, Koaekea lani mama o.	On Koa'e-kea, on Koa'e-kea, that rears itself toward heaven.
Kilakila oe i ka'u ike,	You are majestic to me,
A he ipo honehone,	A sweetheart dearly loved.
e o e.	Answer to your name chant.

THE HULA

by

Mary Kawena Pukui
1943

It was a custom in Kau district, if distinguished strangers came to a village, to give a *hula* dance in honor of the visitor. The performers were trained in schools set up in the district under expert masters who had themselves been graduated from schools of the *hula*. In these schools the pupils were advanced from grade to grade until they had gained a position to set up a school for themselves and become *hula* experts. Few reached this rank; most were satisfied to join a troupe of dancers and make tours through the villages. Not all the prayers of the various dance halls were alike, nor the motions made by the feet and hands. Hence came this saying of old, *Aole i pau ka ike i kau halau* ("Not all knowledge is to be found in your dance hall").

The *hula* of ancient times was not like the modern performance. Very many of the old are passing and will in time be lost. [The prayers today are generally omitted. The general procedure is however the same.]

Before beginning instruction in the *hula*, the master selected one pupil to act as leader, called *po'o-pua'a* [literally "pig's head," whose duty it was also to secure the pig for the offering]. The other pupils made up the *paepae* or "supporters." Upon the *po'opua'a* rested the responsibility for the performance and hers was the honor in case of success.

The first step was the decoration of the dance hall. The master and his attendants went to the mountains to gather ferns, *ieie* vine, *maile* vine, and other sweet-smelling plants, together with the *ohia-wao-akua*, all accompanied by chanting. These were arranged in a corner of the hall with this prayer:

Ku mai iuka i Mo'ohelaia,	It stands on the uplands of Mo'ohelaia,
Ka ohia ku iluna o Maunaloa,	The *ohia* tree stands erect on Maunaloa,
Loa'a e, Laka, e!	Gathered for Laka!
Ho'oulu ai, ho'oulu i'a, ho'oulu aahu,	Cause food plants to grow, fish to increase, give raiment,
Ho'oulu lako, ho'oulu hula,	Give riches, inspire the *hula*,
No kau poe pulapula,e!	For your children!
Amama, ua noa! noa kanawai!	It is free! the taboo is lifted!

Before entering the hall the *po'opua'a* chanted to the master as follows:

Kunihi ka mauna i ka la'i i Waialeale, i Wailua,	The mountain stands out cleary in the calm, at Waialeale, at Wailua,
Huki a'e la ka lani, i ka papa auea a ka nakini,	Lifted up to heaven by the sacred order of the kinship of gods,
Alai ia a'ela la e nounou,	Now obstructed by Nounou (?),
Ha'a ka lau la mauka o Kapaae,	The leaves dance mountainward of Kapaae,
Mai pa'a i ka leo,	Do not withhold the voice,
He ole ka hea mai, a!	Speak the call to come in!

The master answers from within:

E hea i ke kanaka e komo maloko,	Call the man to come within,
E hanai ai, a hewa a'e ka waha.	Feed him lest his mouth err.
Eia no ka uku la, he leo,	Here is the pledge, a voice,
He leo wale no!	Only a voice!

The door was now opened and the *po'opua'a* entered bearing a black pig and a plant of green *'awa*. The pig was released and wandered where it would before the altar, then fell dead. If the hula master was a woman, a prayer was then offered to Hi'iaka, if a man, to Kane. The woman's prayer was as follows:

Ku'u aikane i ka la o lalo, e,
Aloha oe, e Hi'iaka, i ka wai huna i ka palai
Haua ia i ka pu'awa hiwa,
I molia ia i ka ihu o ka pua'a.
Hi'iaka e, e noho ia, ho'i mai iluna o ko kahu.
He mau kanaenae keia na'u ia oe,
Hi'iaka e! ho'oula ia!

My friend in the day of trial,
Love to you, Hi'iaka, in the hidden water of the fern
Given to you in the bundle of green *'awa*
Offered at the snout of the pig.
O Hi'iaka, come and possess your keeper.
This is a prayer from me to you,
O Hi'iaka, grant me inspiration!

This was the man's prayer:

Kane, i ka wai huna, i ka wai ola!
Haua ia ka pu'awa hiwa
I molia ia i ka ihu o ka pua'a.
E Kane, e, e noho ia, ho'i mai iluna o ke kahu.
He mau kanaenae keia na'u, na ke kahu,
Ia oe, e Kane, e! e ho'oulu ia!

Kane of the hidden water, of the living water!
The bundle of green *'awa* is presented,
Offered at the snout of the pig.
O Kane, come and possess your keeper.
This is a prayer from me, the priest,
To you, O Kane! Grant me inspiration.

When the pig expired, although no person was concealed within the greenery, there proceeded from the altar a chanting voice:

Pueueu au, e Laka, e!
Kona weuweu au e ku ana,
Kaumaha aela ia Laka, e,
E Laka, e, ho'oula ia!

From the woodlands am I, O Laka!
In the greenery am I standing,
Offer sacrifices to Laka,
O Laka, possess and inspire!

The pig was then taken out to be made ready for the oven and the *'awa* was prepared; it was softened by chewing, water was added, then it was stirred and strained through the fiber of rushes or the clothlike sheath of the coconut leaf or the hollow roots of the pandanus.

At the entrance of the *po'opua'a* into the dance hall, she was accompanied by the young pupils. They sat quietly until the pig was cooked. All activities were in the hands of the master and the *po'opua'a*. Portions were cut from the nose, ears, feet, side, and tail of the pig and placed on ti leaves. From the sea had been brought *kala* seaweed, shrimps, black crab, the spawn of mullet and of *ahulu* fish (*weke*), marine mollusc (*kuapa'a*), and red and white fish. One of each was selected and placed on a plate of ti leaf with a portion of pork for each dancer. A special portion was set aside for the *po'opua'a*. The master ate the brain (*lolo*) that he might be *ailolo*, "endowed with wisdom," in his art. The feast was spread before the altar for the dancers alone. No outsider was allowed to eat with them. Special *poi* [pounded taro root] was prepared to eat with the meat. It was served to each dancer in her own calabash, not, as was usual, in a common bowl. After a prayer by the master all the pork and fish were consumed, only the bones were left to be carefully cast into the sea or buried.

A portion (*apu*) of *'awa* was given to each dancer. The first portion was poured as an oblation upon the altar while the master chanted:

Eia ka 'awa, e ke akua!
He 'awa lani wale no.
Inu a ke kama iki;
I ka 'awa lau lena,
I ka 'awa Ke-ahi-a-Laka
Halawai akula me Pele,
Ke ako, ala i ka lehua,
Ke ku'i ala i kai o Hopoe, la.
He 'awa no na kane
A me na wahine o ka lani
He 'awa no na kane
Me na wahine o ka lua
Pela aku, pela mai,

Here is the *'awa*, O god!
It is wholly heavenly *'awa*
Drink of the beloved child,
The *'awa* of the yellow leaf,
The *'awa* of The-fire-of-Laka
Meeting with Pele,
Plucking the *lehua*
Stringing it down by Hopoe.
'Awa for the men
And for the women of the heavens,
'Awa for the men
And for the women of the pit,
Thus it was, thus it is,

E mu ka waha, e,	Silence the mouth
E holoi i ka lima.	Wash the hands,
Elieli kapu, elieli noa,	Sacred is the taboo, sacred the freeing,
Noa ke kapu, noa ka hele,	The taboo is lifted and one can go,
Noa kanawai a ke akua.	The law is lifted by the gods.

Should there be no response from the altar, the ceremony could not proceed, but if chanting was heard, all was well. The response from the altar was in these words:

Kulia e Uli, ka pule kanana ola imua o ke kahuna,	Lift, O Uli, the purified prayer before the priest,
Kulia i ke Alohi-lani,	Lifted to Alohi-lani,
Kulia i kupukupu oluna nei,	Lifted here to the gods of the woodland.
Owai kupukupu?	Who are the gods of the woodland?
O Ilio uli, Ilio mea,	The dark dog, sacred dog,
O Kukeao-iki,	Ku of the little cloud,
O Kukeao-loa,	Ku of the long cloud,
O Kukeao-poko,	Ku of the short cloud,
O Kukeao-pihapiha-o-ka-lani	Ku of the fringed cloud of heaven,
O ke kanaka o ka mauna,	The man of the mountain,
O ka hoa o ka ulu laau,	The companion of the forest,
E ku ai o Hina i ka o maka e pule,	Hina may stand among the buds to pray.
Ua kana, ua kahe ka wai,	Till they are filled and the sap flows,
E kahoali'i, moku ka piko, e,	O Kahoali'i, break off the top,
O imi o nalowale i loa'a, e,	Seek that which is to be obtained,
Loa'a ka'u hala, uku i ka oiwi.	Seek out my faults that I may atone.
Na ke aloha e kona, haele maua	It is love that invites us, we will go,
I ike aku i ka uwe ana iko, e,	For we see tears of affection,
Elieli kapu, elieli noa, ua noa!	May the taboo and the freedom be made sacred by the gods!

From this time forth until their graduation, the pupils were laid under strict rules; such as not to visit the dead, not to defile water or stones, not to kiss or indulge in love-making, not to eat from another's portion of food or allow another to eat of their portion. All their dishes were to be kept separate from those used by others. If any one of these commands was broken, the *po'opua'a* was obliged to offer another pig before the altar as at the first.

When the feast was over, instruction in the dance began. The first chant given by the master was a prayer to the gods to draw near and give wisdom to the pupils. The gods were honored in this prayer, then the chiefs of the land. After that, different objects of clothing and adornment were called for, such as the wreath for the head, the garland about the neck, the bracelet for the arm, the anklet, and the skirt (*pau*). As each was mentioned the pupils, in a place partitioned off by themselves, consecrated it by putting it upon their own body. Then the master called them forth and they appeared, gesturing with their hands as they had been taught. The first chant was in celebration of the names of chiefs. Other *hula* chants followed. When the day's lesson was over, the pupil might return to her home, but she must keep the taboos and her head and body were closely covered with a sheet made of a certain kind of tapa cloth called a *pāupāu* that no one might recognize her, and she was forbidden to speak to anyone on the way, whether relative or friend.

New steps and gestures were revealed to the *po'opua'a* at night through the medium of a dream or through the sounding of the drum in the dance hall. Then the pupils followed her dance to the new gestures. This training went on for about a month and as the time for graduation drew near the pupils were given small portions of a strong intoxicant to clear the skin from the effects of the *'awa* drinking. After the chapped skin was healed they bathed in water dyed yellow by dissolving in it a kind of red clay (*alaea*). At midnight they followed their master to the sea for a purification ceremony through ablution. A feast followed at the dance hall consisting again of black crab, shrimp, red and white fish, and a species of seaweed called *kala*, chosen because the word means "forgiveness" or "loosening from obligation," together with pig baked in an underground oven.

At the graduating exercises friends, family, and visiting strangers came to view and pass judgement upon the performance. If the audience became excited and pushed forward to see better or pulled others back to get a nearer view, the occasion was considered a success. The pupils were dismissed to be kissed by anyone who chose in the throng; it was forbidden to repel any such embrace, however unsightly the person who offered his congratulations in this form. Thus in old days the art of the *hula* was encouraged to give pleasure to the chiefs, especially to entertain the guests of a chief. The performers on such occasions received gifts of fish and *poi* and of clothing from the chief.

Among the *hula* of ancient times were the *hula uliuli, hula Pele, puili, kolani, ala'apapa, olapa, pa'iumauma.* This last is much like the game of "Pease porridge, hot!" as played by foreign children. Seated on the floor, the performers strike first the hand of the one opposite them, then their own chest (*umauma*). The *kakalaau* is similar, only that sticks (*laau*) are used and struck (*kaka*), first together,then on the floor. In the *hula iliili* pebbles (*iliili*) are held in the hand and struck together as gestures follow the words of the chant. In the *hula puili* split bamboos are hit one against another. In the *hula uliuli* a gourd filled with pebbles and wreathed with ti leaves is shaken in time to the chant. These last are modern *hula* and are performed seated. Both the *olapa* and the *ala'apapa* are standing dances. The master strikes the gourd and the pupils gesture, slightly bending the knee or making rotary motions.

Chants for the *hula* vary according to class. Some praise the deeds of a chief and recall incidents in his life; these are called name chants (*inoa*). Other *hula* chants describe journeys and point out the beauties of certain places. Chants of reviling are composed to reproach or defame some person in the audience. Today such chants speak out the thought without mincing matters, but in old days the words were couched in a hidden way so that no one not versed in chant language could find anything opprobrious in the meaning. Here is a *mele* composed in ridicule by a man whose wife left him hastily one early morning to meet another lover.

Huhului'i ka hulu o na manu	Tousled are the feathers of the birds
I ka ua kakahiaka,	In the morning rain,
Akaka wale no kau mai ka ohu,	Clearly one can see through the mist,
Ohuohu Punaluu i ka wai hu o Kauila,	Punaluu is decked out in the swelling waters of Kauila,
I ka ho'owali ana pau ia	Completely stirred up
E ke kai o Kamehame,	By the sea of Kamehame, [but]
A ohe wahi hemahema o ka pali o	The cliff of Pohina lacks nothing,
Kahiko ia nei e ka ohu o Waiohinu.	Clothed in the mist of Waiohinu.

All these old *hula* named were decent dances in ancient times. The mixture of indecency in modern times is not the fault of the dancers but of the disreputable persons who have money to spare and bring in this element for their own enjoyment. It is the dollar that has brought low the *hula* of *Hawaii nei.*

PART III

HĀLAU HULA AND ADJACENT SITES AT KĒ'Ē, KAUA'I

by
Marion Kelly

Introduction

The most famous site associated with *hula* instruction (*hālau hula*) in the Hawaiian Islands is at Kē'ē, Kaua'i (Fig. 16). Although other *hālau hula* are reported to exist in the Hawaiian Islands, as far as is known today the Kē'ē *hālau* and related sites have the most extensive recorded traditional history. For this reason the Kē'ē sites will be the primary concern of this chapter.

Kē'ē Bay faces northwest and is located west of Hā'ena Bay at the end of the present highway on the windward (northern) side of Kaua'i (Fig. 17). "In sayings, the word Kē'ē represents great distances and trouble," a place too far away "to bother about," literally, "avoidance" (Pukui, Elbert & Mookini 1974:105). Westward from Kē'ē Bay the cliffs of Nāpali dominate the coastline for about twelve miles to Polihale. When the sea was calm, Hawaiians used to board their canoes at the reef-sheltered sand beach of Kē'ē Bay for trips along the coast to the many

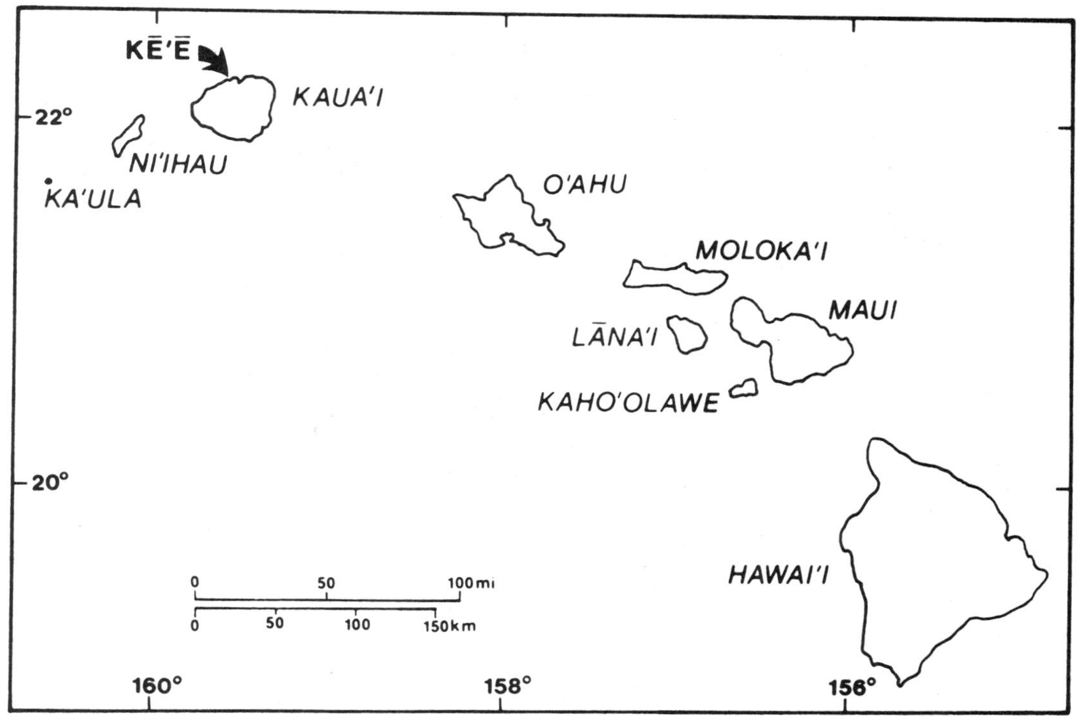

Fig. 16. MAP OF THE HAWAIIAN ISLANDS. The location of the Kē'ē area is indicated on the island of Kaua'i, beyond Hanalei Bay.

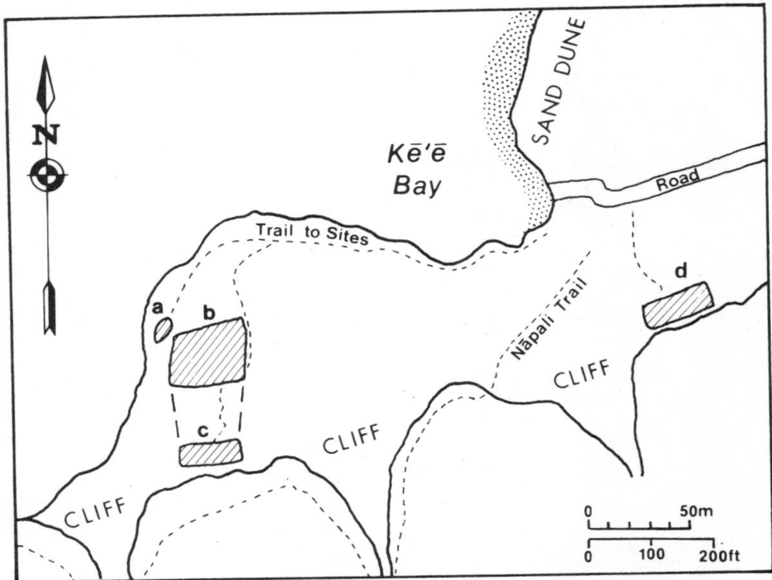

Fig. 17. MAP SHOWING THE APPROXIMATE RELATIVE POSITIONS OF SITES AT KĒ'Ē BAY. a. Kilioe (*pōhaku piko*); b. Ka-ulu-a-Pā'oa Heiau; c. Ke-ahu-a-Laka (*hālau hula*); d. and e. modern houses; f. house platform of Lohi'au. (Drawn by Eric Komori.)

valleys of Nāpali. Or, when the ocean was too rough for canoe voyaging, they walked the foot trail that begins at Kē'ē, rises above the sea, and meanders along the cliffs and valleys.

The most accessible of the traditional sites at Kē'ē today is the large, unpaved platform built at the base of the cliff next to the end of the road. It has been associated with the legendary Kaua'i chief Lohi'au. The well-built stone retaining wall of this platform is visible in the underbrush, a few feet from the road (Fig. 17, f).

On the cliffs above Kē'ē are said to be two curiously shaped natural stones, one resembling the profile of a man, and the second that of a stooping man. In 1845 the name Pōhaku-a-Kāne was recorded for the latter stone. A third stone, located in the sea below, was said to represent Hauwa, the sister of Pōhaku-a-Kāne (Gilman 1908:54-55).

Just beyond the sand beach of Kē'ē Bay a short coastal trail leads to the last rock-strewn stretch of shoreline before the cliffs (*pali*) begin. There, a very large boulder known as Kilioe, the *pōhaku piko* (see p. 101) of the area (Gilman 1908:52), stands against the base of a low cliff (Fig. 17, a).

Directly above Kilioe is the impressive stone structure identified as Ka-ulu-a-Pā'oa Heiau (Fig. 17, b). At the top of the slope above the *heiau* and against the *pali* is the unpaved platform identified as a *hālau hula* and sometimes called Ke-ahu-a-Laka, or Ka-ulu-o-Laka (Fig. 17, c).

Traditions Collected in 1845

Sometimes it is difficult to determine whether a story associated with a particular site is traditional, or of relatively recent origin. Motivation to provide a story for an ancient site can be strong, particularly in times of general cultural revival. In the case of the Kē'ē sites, the earliest known written record telling about these sites and the traditions associated with them was made by Gilman in 1845. Presumably, at that early date, there were still people who had heard the traditions associated with these sites from their *kupuna* (grandparent generation), although 67 years had passed since Europeans first set foot on Kaua'i, and the population of the Island had declined by about two-thirds (Schmitt 1968:42).

In 1845, Gorham D. Gilman, an American who had been living in the Islands for about three or four years, made a trip to Kaua'i. He had been asked to manage the Titcomb coffee plantation at Hanalei, Kaua'i, for a few weeks during the owner's absence (Gilman Ms.:4).* In August of 1845 Gilman made a horseback trip to the famous Hā'ena caves and the Kē'ē sites, accompanied by missionary Edward Johnson and about twenty students from the Hanalei Mission School.

The journal of Gilman's trip to Kē'ē was written in final form in December of the same year and sent as a gift to his parents in Boston (Ms.:1). Thus, the traditions it contains were probably collected at the time of his visit to the sites. Presumably, his friends on this expedition were his primary source of information, although he would have had opportunities for discussing the sites and their traditions with others between August and December.

Gilman's journal contains a synopsis of one version of the famous legend involving Pele, legendary goddess of the volcano, her younger sister, Hi'iaka, and Lohi'au, a legendary Kaua'i chief. Gilman associated this tradition with the Kē'ē *heiau* site, although he failed to record a name for the *heiau*, or to mention the *hālau* platform. In fact, the only names Gilman recorded for the Kē'ē sites were those given for three natural stones: Kilioe, Pōhaku-a-Kāne, and Hauwa.

Gilman's description of this area, the sites, and the traditions he collected about them are given here in his own words as written in 1845 and published in part in 1908.

> As the termination of the sea beach and the commencement of the famous "Pali" or precipice is near the caves, we took a guide and rode on to visit it.... We had not ridden far before we were obliged to dismount, as the ground was so thickly covered with stones. Clambering a short distance over these rocks, we came to a little strip of pretty sand beach, at the farther extremity of which the black cliffs lifted their heads, and presented an unbroken wall as far as we could see the coast. This is the farthest point that can be reached by land, and is a starting place for travelers, who are passing around the Pali, and a landing place for canoes.
>
> Near this beach stands a singular rock, called "Kilioe," which attracted our attention from the numerous perforations like those of a honey comb, which we noticed in it. ... We also observed a little above this singular rock, a rough terrace built of the stones that lay around. We scrambled up to it with some difficulty over the rugged stones, and gained the platform, which was perhaps twelve feet square. With this spot is associated one of the latest, and to an Hawaiian, the most interesting of their legends. It is entirely fictitious, yet such is its fascination for them that they will sit and listen while it is being recited, all day and from sunset to sunrise. In its full detail it is very lengthy, but it can be abridged. The chief characters are Pele, the dread goddess of the Volcano; Hiiaka, Pele's sister, and Lohiau,

*Titcomb had originally started a "silk plantation" in Koloa in 1836, and moved it to Hanalei in 1840. By the time Gilman arrived in 1845, it had been transformed into a coffee plantation. (Wilcox Ms.).

a young man. A brief summary of the story, as I have heard it, is as follows:

The goddess Pele, who held her court in the fiery lake of Kilauea, as she was reclining one day on her fiery couch, was overpowered by the "drowsy god," and fell asleep. While her body was thus enjoying rest, her spirit was awake, and attracted by the sound of sweet music in the distance, it left her court in search of it. She passed around the island of Hawaii, but could not discover where it came from. Next she crossed over to Maui, and sought there for the source of the enticing strains, which still eluded her. In the same way she visited Molokai and Oahu, without success, and at last landed on Kauai, where to her joy she found that she was drawing near to the object of her desire. Thus she was led on to the very spot on which we were standing. Here she saw a company of musicians seated around their leader, whom she soon singled out as the youth whose dulcet strains had so entranced her. Lohiau, the young musician, was entirely unconscious of the presence of the goddess, although he was aware of a pair of beautiful eyes gazing upon him. He soon formed an acquaintance with her, and for a short time enjoyed the happiness of love.

But it was all too brief, for the object of his love disappeared as suddenly and mysteriously as she had made her appearance. To account for this, we must return to the court at Kilauea, where we will discover a group of her attendants in earnest conversation. They are much concerned at the long continued absence of their sovereign lady, who had now been lying for five whole days without waking. Yet none of the group dared to disturb her slumber. At last, it was decided that her younger sister, Hiiaka-i-ka-poli-o-Pele, or Hiiaka, the bosom companion of Pele, should go in and arouse her, which she did, and thus caused the sudden disappearance of Lohiau's lover, for as the body awoke it recalled its animating spirit.

As Pele awoke, she said: "I am sorry you awoke me from my pleasant dream." After this her sister, Hiiaka, went to the sea to bathe, but more in truth to see a friend residing there, who was a mortal and very expert in the dance. During her absence Pele proposed that one of her attendants should proceed to Kauai to bring Lohiau to her court, so that he might enter her service. They all declined, saying that her sister, who was far more powerful than they, was the one best fitted for the task. On Hiiaka's return, she consented, and with two companions started on the expedition. While passing through Hilo, she encountered two hostile inferior deities, whom she overcame and slew. Her various adventures on the several islands on her way to Kauai would take too much time to narrate here.

Arriving in Kauai, she had no difficulty in finding Lohiau, and after a brief sojourn prepared to return with him. Embarking in a canoe, they passed from island to island until they arrived at Hawaii, and repaired to the border of Pele's abode, on the edge of the crater.

Here Hiiaka learned that Pele, contrary to her (Hiiaka's) express injunction, had gone to the sea side, and on seeing her friend there, had taken her or eaten her. This highly incensed Hiiaka. She was very wroth with her sister, and in a rage she dived down deep into the bowels of the earth, causing the rocks and earth to fly out so that none dared to approach.

As for Pele, on seeing Lohiau, she came up out of the crater to meet him, but he who was enamored with her fair young sister, had no inclination to wed the fiery old hag, and as she flowed out to embrace him, and her arms (of lava) clasped his feet, he intoned a prayer or incantation, which proved too strong for Pele, and she had to retire. Again she came and embraced his knees, and again his prayer proved to be effectual, and he was delivered, but he remained fast as high up as he had been embraced.

Still again she advanced and reached his waist, and again was repulsed by his prayer. Each of the several prayers of the victim are duly recited by the story-tellers, but I have not transcribed them. Pele then determined to make one more effort, and this time she was successful, for his prayer went up too late. She overwhelmed him, and he sank overpowered into her arms.

There are two or three other versions of this story, but this is the one most generally received as far as I know, and the above is only a rough outline of it. To write it all out would make an ordinarily sized novel. Towering far above us, rose the mountain peaks, two of which are pointed out to travellers. One of them is very peculiar, and attracts every one's attention. It is a colossal head framed by nature, the proportions being excellent and in good keeping, and the profile very lifelike. The other point with which the tradition is connected, is a rock, somewhat resembling a man stooping, which bears the name of "Pohaku a Kane." It stands on a sharp spar of the mountain, overlooking a little bay. The tradition says that "Pohaku a Kane" and his sister, "Hauwa," were travelling over the sea, (being deities), when they came upon the island of Kauai. It was night when they arrived, and the sister remained in the sea, while her brother landed and commenced the ascent of the mountain. Morning dawned, and found him several hundred feet above his sister, who was detained by some stronger power, and he, not being able to descend, maintained the position of a watchful brother over his sister. She is or was an object of worship to the fishermen, who believed in her ability to help them on the sea [Gilman 1908:52-55].

Site Names Recorded

As mentioned above, Gilman collected three names associated with the sites at Kē'ē. The one most closely connected with the *hālau hula* was Kilioe, the "singular rock" on the coast.

Over half a century later this name was again recorded by historian Thomas G. Thrum, who identified it as the name of the *heiau* site, rather than of the rock described by Gilman. Thrum listed two *heiau* at Hā'ena. He called one "Kilioi" (Kilioe) and commented that it was a "*heiau* consisting of two platforms, highly terraced; very famous, very sacred and an immense structure." The other he associated with the name Lohi'au, and described it as a walled structure on Hā'ena "Point" dedicated to Laka, goddess of *hula*. He named his Kaua'i informants as J. K. Farley, W. H. Rice, Sr., Francis Gay, and A. F. Knudsen (Thrum 1907:43).

In a later article Thrum gave the measurements of the "walled *heiau*" as 77 by 85 feet, and further explained that he had visited neither the *heiau*, nor the Lohi'au "walled structure" (1924:36). In this report he listed a total of 126 *heiau* for Kaua'i, two of them located at Kē'ē (Ibid.:34).

When Kenneth P. Emory, Bishop Museum Anthropologist, visited the Kē'ē sites in 1927, he was informed that Kilioe was the name of the land on which the *heiau* was built, the name of "the great rock on the beach below the heiau, and also of the beach" (Appendix E:145). As a result of his 1927 survey of the Kē'ē sites (see Appendix E), his analysis of Thrum's comments, and informaton he received from Judge Lyle A. Dickey of Kaua'i, Emory concluded that Thrum had listed two *heiau* where there was only one. Emory identified the *makai* (seaward) structure as the *heiau* site (Fig. 17, b) and as the terraced stone structure that had been called "Kilioi" by Thrum (1924:36). He identified the *mauka* (inland) platform (Fig. 17, c) as the dancing pavillion and shrine of

Lohi'au (Bennett 1931:137-138 & fig. 45).* Presumably it was this site that had been called the temple of Lohi'au by Thrum (1924:36), although earlier he had placed it on "Ha'ena Point" (1907:43).

In 1928 Judge Dickey informed Emory that the name of the terraced *heiau* was Ka-ulu-a-Pā'oa [literally, "the inspiration of Pā'oa"] (Emory 1929:89). Dickey had learned this name on May 12, 1928, "from two men and women [living] in a fishing shack on the beach near the heiau" (Dickey Ms.).

In notes on place names collected by Mary Kawena Pukui, the "*heiau* at the end of the road beyond Allerton's [formerly Brown's] property is called Ka-ulu-o-Laka [the inspiration of Laka]" (Pukui Ms.). Elsewhere Ka-ulu-o-Laka is identified as "A heiau for hula dancers not far from Ka-ulu-Paoa *heiau*, both below Kē'ē cliff..." (Pukui, Elbert, & Mookini 1974:94). The term Ka-ahu-a-Laka has also been similarly used (Pukui 1942:107). Names that incorporate the name of Laka, patron of *hula*, probably refer to the *hālau hula*, the *mauka* structure.

Following the tradition collected by Dickey, the name "Ka-ulu-Paoa" is also identified with the "Heiau at the foot of Kē'ē cliff, near Hā'ena, Kaua'i [the inspiration (of) Paoa]," the place where "Lohi'au and his friend Paoa trained in hula" (Pukui, Elbert, & Mookini 1974:94). It can be assumed, also, that the name into which Pā'oa is incorporated probably refers to the *makai* structure, the terraced-stone *heiau*.

Pā'oa is identified as "the great friend of Pele's lover, Lohi'au" (Pukui & Elbert 1971:396). Pā'oa was also the name of Pele's "divining rod with which she tested the suitability of Nihoa, and various places on Oahu and Maui, for her excavations" (Ibid.), although Emerson noted that at least one person said the divining rod should be called *pahoa* (Emerson 1915:xi, footnote, b).

Abraham Fornander gave the name of the friend of Lohi'au as Kahuakaiapaoa [Ka-huaka'i-a-Pa'oa ?]. He also gave the name Mapu as that of the music teacher, whose drum beating at Kē'ē had disturbed Pele's sleep at Kīlauea on Hawai'i. Lohi'au, Pā'oa, and Mapu were all sitting on the *heiau* platform when Pele came to Hā'ena, according to Fornander (Fornander 1916-20:6,343).

Dickey's informants also provided the name "Hula platform of Kilioe" for the *mauka* structure. In one of his notes Dickey comments: "Kilioe, Koe and Milolii were noted dragons on the island of Kauai; they were the dragons of the precipices of the northern coasts of this island, who took the body of the high priest Lohiau and concealed it in a cave far up the steep side of the mountain" (Dickey Ms.).

According to Fornander, Kilioe and Aka "were two women who watched over the cave where Lohiau was interred. They were killed by Hiiaka" (1916-20 :6,343). Storyteller William H. Rice identified Kilioe as the sister of Lohi'au, a celebrated tapa maker of Kalalau Valley, and a "great hula dancer and teacher. No one could hula in public on Kauai unless approved by her and given the *uniki*, the sign which served in place of a diploma" (Appendix A:124).

Juliet Wichman identified Kilioe as "part *mo'o* " the sister of Lohi'au, and patroness of the whole area, that is, everything from the Dry Cave at Hā'ena to Kē'ē. She also thought that she was probably the patroness of *hula* in that area (Interview, 1979).

---

*Bennett's illustration is reproduced in Appendix E, p. 148.

In summary, the names associated with the two structures in the records researched are as follows:

Makai Site (terraced stone structure)	*Mauka* Site (unpaved platform)
Kilioe	Hula platform of Kilioe
Ka-ulu-o-Laka	Lohi'au *heiau*, dedicated to Laka
Ka-ulu-a-Pā'oa	Lohi'au, or Kē'ē
Ka-ulu-a-Pā'oa, Lohi'au *hula* temple	Ke-ahu-a-Laka
Ka-ulu-Pā'oa Heiau	Ka-ulu-o-Laka

All of the incorporated names (Kilioe, Pā'oa, Lohi'au,and Laka) have one thing in common: they are associated with *hula* in one tradition or another. At one time or another both sites have been identified as *heiau*, and the *mauka* site also as a "*hula* platform" or *hālau hula* dedicated to Laka, and the *makai* site as the *hula* temple of Lohi'au.

From the above evidence it would appear that these structures must be considered a site complex associated with *hula*. Regarding the apparent confusion of names for the two main structures in the complex, it is possible that the evidence reflects different periods of time. The two structures may have been built at different times, or their functions may have changed over time. Multiple names associated with the two sites may even indirectly reflect changes in political conditions. It might be possible that with additional research such a theory could be elaborated; however, it is not within the scope of this paper to do so.

The Sites

KILIOE, *PŌHAKU PIKO*

The large stone identified by Gilman as Kilioe is described by him as having the function of a *pōhaku piko*. Although this rock and its location have been described, as far as is known no photograph of it has been published before. However, when one is at the site, there is little doubt that the rock illustrated here (Fig. 18) is the one referred to by Gilman. There are other rocks in the area with more honeycomb-like indentations, but none are as impressively large, nor located as close to the *heiau*. There appears to be a short stone wall that connects this boulder with the cliff directly below the *heiau*.

Gilman wrote the following information about Kilioe in his journal:

> ...many places or cells [in the rock] were plugged up.... [We] were told that when a child was circumcised, ...the portion that was removed was taken and brought to this rock here and deposited. And when the child grew up it was told "A part of your body is in the stone of 'Kilioe'"--very many make a visit to this stone. We found some of the plugs that did not appear to have been long put in--showing that they cling in a measure to their old customs [Gilman Ms.:35].

Gilman further pointed out that because nearly all male children were "circumcised," this accounted for heavy usage of the rock. Today, it is understood that the type of operation done by Hawaiians in pre-contact times was not precisely circumcision, but more nearly approximated subincision, although this is not exactly clear either (Pukui, Haertig, & Lee 1972:182, notes and references 1; Malo 1951:93-95, see note on sect. 9). The early Hawaiian term for the process is *kahe*, which carries the connotation of cutting or slitting longitudinally (Pukui &

Fig. 18. KILIOE, *PŌHAKU PIKO* AT KĒ'Ē. Located directly below the northwestern corner of Ka-ulu-a-Pā'oa Heiau on the rocky shoreline, this stone can be identified by the numerous small indentations about its base. (Photo by M. Kelly, Dec. 3, 1977)

Elbert 1971:104). This operation would presumably not result in a piece of flesh being cut away, and it may be that Gilman made an assumption regarding the source of the piece of flesh that was hidden away. Lacking Gilman's notes on the information he collected, there is no way of knowing today exactly what was described to him. Pukui points out that the genitals as well as umbilical cords ("the stump that later dropped off the infant's body") were considered *piko* (Pukui, Haertig, & Lee 1972:183-185). As the practice of circumcision replaced subincision in the post-contact period, it probably followed that the excised flesh would have been treated in a manner similar to that previously reserved only for the umbilical cord.

Emory was told that the *piko* of children of the neighborhood were deposited in depressions in the rock known as Kilioe (Emory 1929:92). He observed that the rock was "heavily combed on part of the outside by weathering." His informant, Mr. Kapae, who was 68 years old at that time, was one of several local residents who cleared the sites for Emory's 1927 survey (Appendix E:145). The others were James Kanei, Kalei Kelau, David Pā, and Joseph Maheole (Emory Ms.). No mention is made in Kekahuna's notes of the *pōhaku piko* Kilioe, nor does the boulder appear on his ground plan made in 1959 (see p. 107 and Fig. 24).

Thrum considered the custom of depositing *piko* as "a kind of birth registration connecting the child with the land of its birth" (Thrum in Emory 1921:25, note). Emory considered the custom as "the material link with the past, along which was communicated the spiritual power of ancesters" (Appendix E:146).

Ancient chants sometimes mention the place of deposit of the *piko* (Thrum in Emory 1921:25). Hawaiian informants born in the latter half of the 19th century also knew about a few such sites and provided some details to ethnographers. "In every district on every island were places, usually stones, especially reserved for the *piko*" (Pukui, Haertig, & Lee 1972:184). Two places mentioned by Pukui on Hawai'i Island are Wailoa and Mokuola. "*Ola* means 'life' and *loa* means 'long.' Mothers took the cords to stones with names like these so their babies would live long, healthy lives" (Ibid.).

As early as 1914, Martha Beckwith recorded that Pu'uloa, on the Island of Hawai'i, was a "large pahoehoe mound used as a depository for the umbilical cord at the birth of a child" (Beckwith Ms.:393-395). According to her informant, who was born in 1862 and lived in nearby Kamoamoa village,*

> A hole is made in the hard crust, the cord is put in and a stone placed over it. In the morning the cord had disappeared; there is no trace of it. This insures long life to the child [Ibid.].

The name Kilioe at Kē'ē is said to have been the name of one of three "noted dragons" on the Island of Kaua'i. "They were the dragons of the precipices of the northern coasts of this island" (Westervelt 1915:258). In one legend Kilioe was a male god of precipices at Hā'ena (Malo 1951:86-87), while in another Kilioe is identified as one of two "mo'o-witches" (Emerson 1915:134). In a chant sung by Hi'iaka, Kilioe is said to be Kilioe-i-ka-pua (Kilioe-of-the-flower-like-beauty). She and her companion, Aka, were two "women with naked bodies who sometimes flit o'er reef-plates," and sometimes "squat over Hala-aniani," a small lake of fresh water in a cave at Hā'ena (Ibid.:136). Lastly, Rice identified Kilioe as "the sister of Lohi'au, a celebrated kapa maker of Kalalau, and a great hula dancer and teacher" (Appendix A:124).

It may be that Pōhaku-o-Kilioe was used as a *pōhaku piko* because parents wanted their children to become expert *hula* dancers, as Kilioe was said to have been. Or, it may be that Kilioe was the "goddess of the pali" and was able to give the children whose umbilical cords were deposited there a sense of belonging to the coast of Nāpali, their *one hānau*, or birthplace.

THE HOUSE TERRACE OF LOHI'AU

The house terrace associated with the legendary Kaua'i chief, Lohi'au, is located against the cliff approximately 200 meters east of the Ka-ulu-a-Pā'oa Heiau (see Fig. 17, f). Both Emory and Dickey identified this terrace as the structure that had also been called the Heiau of Lohi'au (Dickey Ms.; Emory 1929:94). Judging from its lack of typical *heiau* features, Emory indicated that it may have been a house platform. He described the retaining wall as having an unusually even facing, that is almost perpendicular (1929:94; Fig. 19). Emory reported that this "imposing structure" was said to have been "where Lohiau...dwelt" (Appendix E:141).

---

*See Emory, Ladd, & Soehren 1965:7-8.

a. Middle section, looking west along face of wall.

b. Detail of wall construction, looking east.

Fig. 19. RETAINING WALL OF HOUSE PLATFORM. (Photos by K. P. Emory, 1927; Bishop Mus. Neg. Nos. 13632, 13633)

In his notes dated September 22, 1927, Emory describes this site as "a great earth and stone-filled, unpaved terrace." He noted that the corner stones had been knocked down, so that no corner stone-work technique could be observed. He also observed that no cut stone was used (Emory Ms.).

Emory remarked that he "had not seen this type of work in Hawai'i before [prior to 1927], except an approach to it in some of the house foundations of Nihoa. The work is, however, common in the Society Islands" (Appendix E:147). In a recent conversation with the author, Emory indicated that this technique of wall building may not be as unique in Hawai'i as it seemed to him in 1927.

In Emerson's telling of the legend of Pele and Hi'iaka, after Lohi'au met Pele, presumably at the *hālau hula*, "he [Lohi'au] led her [Pele]...to his house" where they remained for "three days and three nights" (1915:7). In the legend the house of Lohi'au was referred to as "a sleeping house" and also as the house in which Lohi'au hanged himself (Ibid:8).

According to Emerson's version there were other people besides Lohi'au living in the area. When Hi'iaka came to take Lohi'au to Hawai'i, she is said to have first gone "to the house of Malae-ha'a-koa [Malae-ha'a-koano], a man of chiefish rank, and one who had the reputation of being a seer." Malae was also a fisherman, but being "lame and unable to walk," his wife Wailua-nui-a-ho'ano had to carry him down to the seashore. On the day Hi'iaka arrived, Wailua had left him there to fish while she returned "home to her work of tapa-making" (Emerson 1915:109). One of the chants by Hi'iaka comments that Malae-ha'a-koano was fishing beneath "the bluffs of Haena" (*Lawai'a ku pali o Ha'ena*) (Ibid.:110).

The location of either house is not mentioned more precisely, except to say that from where Wailua-nui-a-ho'ano sat beating *kapa* she could see Hi'iaka and her companion "as they turned and faced the path that climbed the pali wall" (Emerson 1915:110). Later, mention is made of a "fence that enclosed the house-lot" (Ibid.:111) of Malae and Wailua-nui.

After the feast given to honor Hi'iaka and her companion upon their arrival at Hā'ena, Malae and his wife "stood forth and led in the performance of a sacred dance, accompanying their rhythmic motions with a long mele that recited the deeds, the events, and mysteries that had marked Pele's reign since the establishment of her dominion in Hawaii" (Emerson 1915:112). No mention appears in the Emerson version of where this dancing took place and one is led to assume that it occurred in the house yard of Malae and Wailua-nui.

Other houses mentioned in the Emerson version were one belonging to Kahua-nui, the sister of Lohi'au, and one that she had built in which she interred the body of her brother (1915:135). Later, the body of Lohi'au was removed to a cave in the cliff of Hā'ena by two *mo'o*, Kili-oe-i-ka-pua and Ka-lana-mai-nu'u (Ibid.:131, note a; 134). After Lohi'au had been restored to life, Hi'iaka, Wahine-oma'o, and Lohi'au descended the cliff on three rainbows. They went to the sea to "perform the rite of cleansing." Lohi'au went with them and then, taking up his surfboard, he left to surf the waves off Hā'ena. Leaving her house, Kahua-nui went to the beach and was happy to see her brother Lohi'au well and surfing again. She returned to her house and instructed her husband Nakoa-ola to go to Ni'ihau and bring Pā'oa back to Hā'ena (Ibid.:152-154). When

Pā'oa returned, he found Lohi'au "quiet and thoughtful, surrounded by a houseful of people, in conversation with his sister and two women [Hi'iaka and her companion] who were strangers" (Emerson 1915:155).

No further mention is made of houses at Hā'ena, and none of the remarks in the legend give any further clues to the precise location of the house site of Lohi'au, nor any of the others. We are, of course, dealing with an elaborate legend and legendary characters--Pele and Hi'iaka are goddesses and, similarly, Lohi'au and Pā'oa are lesser gods (Pukui & Elbert 1971: 392). According to Fornander (1916-20:6,252), the date of the composition of this legend is some time in the late 16th century.* It was probably this belief that prompted Gilman to write that the Pele and Hi'iaka legend is "one of the latest...of their legends" (see p. 97).

In summary, four separate houses were mentioned in the legend, including those of Lohi'au, Malae and Wailua-nui, Kahua-nui, and the house in which the body of Lohi'au was interred. House sites for Pā'oa and Mapu are not mentioned. Following Emory's analysis, the well-built retaining wall and platform could easily be considered a house site for an important person of the area. By 1927, local residents had firmly associated this site with the name of Lohi'au.

KA-ULU-A-PĀ'OA HEIAU

There seems to be no question to the identification of the Ka-ulu-a-Pā'oa Heiau. It has been described as "an immense structure" (Thrum 1907:43; Fig. 20). Located as it is on a prominent headland, it dominates the area immediately above Kē'ē Bay (Fig. 21) "in the manner typical of the *heiau* of high rank" (Appendix E:143).

Looking west from its main platform, the cliffs of Nāpali begin; the *heiau* seemingly guards the beginning of the trail leading westward (Fig. 22). Emory's field notes identify a short trail that leads from Keahualaka, the *hālau hula* terrace, to the waterfall west of the *heiau* as "the ancient trail to Kalalau" (Emory Ms.). The terrace is the last bit of relatively flat land before the *pali* begins, and may have once been the place where the *pali* trail started. Today the trail begins on the *mauka* side of the road near its end, just west of the Lohi'au house terrace.

Although Emory believed this *heiau* was one of considerable significance, he was unable to find anything that documented the class to which it belonged. He postulates that the building of such a structure "must have required the controlling power of the high chief of that region" (Appendix E:145). At least from its name, Ka-ulu-a-Pā'oa, a connection with Pā'oa of the Pele and Hi'iaka legend can be presumed. Pā'oa has been variously described as the "intimate friend" of Lohi'au (Emerson 1915:6), and a "deputy" of Lohi'au who was to rule "over the land" while Lohi'au went with Hi'iaka to Hawai'i to meet Pele (Ibid.:156). In Fornander's notes Pā'oa appears as "Kahuakaipaoa" who was "chief of that part of Kauai and went with all his men to Niihau" (Fornander 1916-20:6,344).

In the "Brief Descriptive Notes" that accompany his 1959 ground plan, Henry Kekahuna

*Fornander uses the 30-year generation count; Stokes (1933:62) uses the 20-year generation count, which would place the legend in the early 17th century.

Fig. 20. KA-ULU-A-PĀ'OA HEIAU AT KĒ'Ē, HĀ'ENA, KAUA'I. Looking westward toward the supporting wall of the lower terrace. (Photo by K. P. Emory, 1927; Bishop Mus. Neg. No. 13627)

identified Pā'oa as a "dearest chiefly friend of Chief Lohi'au," and as the founder of the "ancient, most renowned hula seminary of the island of Kaua'i, Ka-ulu-a-Paoa, institution for the Growth (*ulu*) of knowledge of the Art of Hula Dancing."

Emory identified the two separate structures, the *hālau hula* and the *heiau* in 1927, but he did not mention the distance between them. In his notes, he described the condition of the land between them as having six "little terraces" on the trail from the *heiau* to the dancing platform (Emory Ms.). The distance between the two structures, measuring from the *mauka* edge of the lower structure to the *makai* edge of the upper terraces, is approximately 45 meters. In this area today there are several rock outcroppings and hidden under grass, vines, and bush, is what appears to be the terracing observed by Emory. At the time Emory surveyed the sites, the lower structure, or at least the northeastern corner of the lowest paved terrace of the *heiau* was being used "by native fisherman as an observation station" (Emory 1929:91) (Fig. 23).

Kekahuna (1959) gave the overall measurements of the entire site, including the *heiau*, *hālau*, and terraces between them, as 104 by 260 feet (Fig. 24). Kekahuna recognized three "divisions" in his ground plan: the first included the *makai* structure that has been called the *heiau* proper; the second included a series of terraces leading up to the *mauka* structure; the third (about 25 feet higher in elevation than the *makai* site) included the *mauka* unpaved platform, or

Fig. 21. LOOKING *MAKAI* AT THE LOWER TERRACE OF KA-ULU-A-PĀ'OA HEIAU FROM THE *MAUKA* STRUCTURE, SHOWING OUTCROPPINGS AND TERRACING BETWEEN THE TWO STRUCTURES. (Photo by Mary S. Judd, 1952; Bishop Mus. Neg. No. 56298)

Fig. 22. KA-ULU-A-PĀ'OA HEIAU AT KĒ'Ē, HĀ'ENA, KAUA'I. Looking westward across the pavement of the lower terrace. (Photo by K. P. Emory, 1927; Bishop Mus. Neg. No. 13269)

Fig. 23. MAIN TERRACE OF KA-ULU-A-PĀ'OA HEIAU. Looking down at the northeastern corner, used by local fishermen as an observation post for fish entering the bay. (Photo by K. P. Emory, 1927; Bishop Mus. Neg. No. 13628)

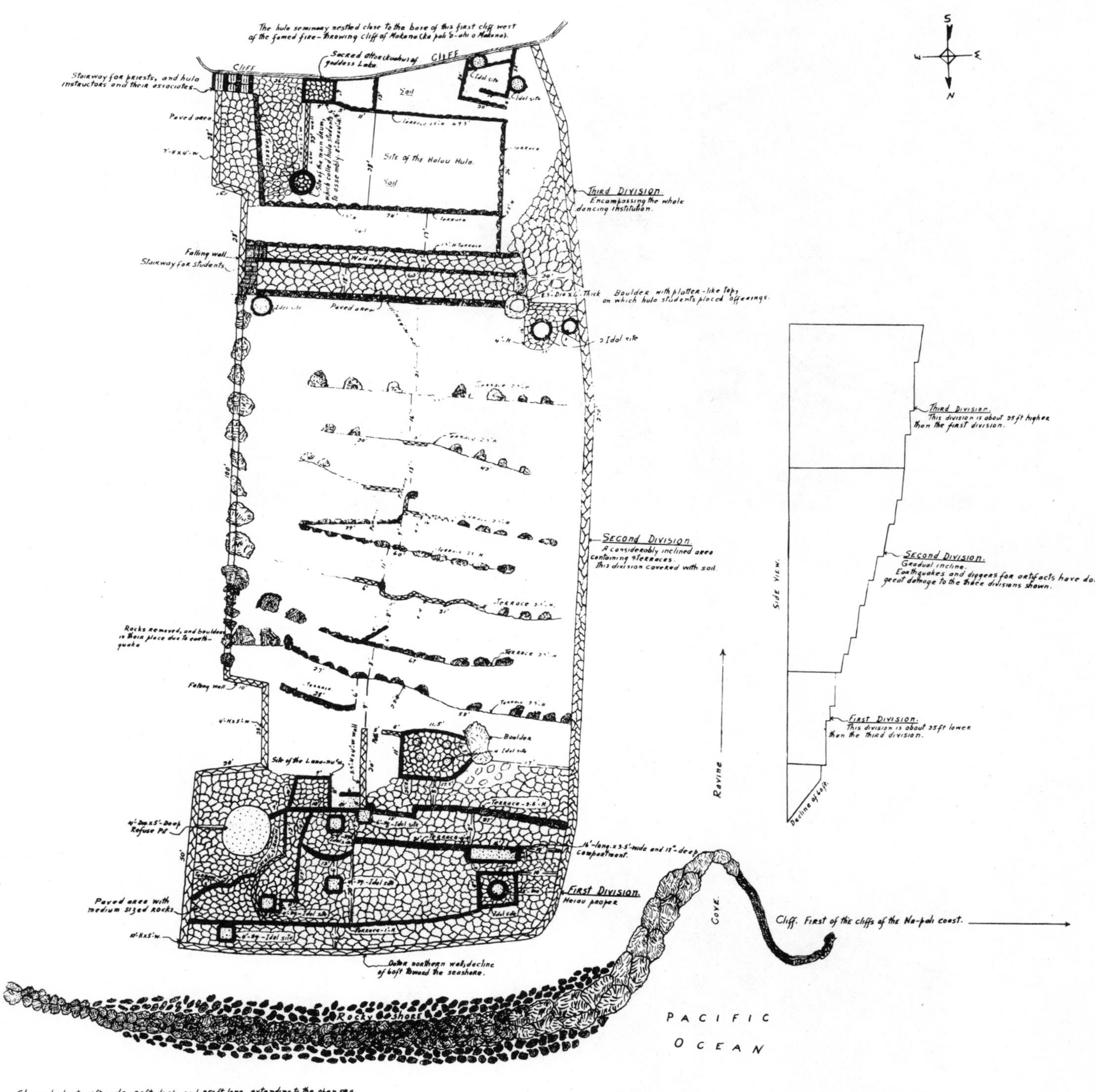

Fig. 24. KA-ULU-A-PĀ'OA HEIAU AND *HĀLAU HULA*. Drawing by Henry K. Kekahuna, Oct. 4, 1959, for the Kaua'i Historical Society.

the *hālau hula* proper. Kekahuna wrote that the third division encompassed "the whole dancing institution" (Fig. 24). However, he entitled the whole (all three divisions) Ka-ulu-a-Pā'oa Heiau, thus linking the *hālau hula* to the *heiau* and thereby suggesting that the *hālau hula* was part of the *heiau*, not a separate entity.

In 1977, the *makai* end of one of the short walls located approximately in the center of the *heiau* site (*makai* structure) appeared to have been heightened so that a cairn was formed (Fig. 25a). Numerous offerings had been placed on the cairn. Each was a stone wrapped in a ti leaf (*Cordyline terminalis*), except for the remains of one head wreath made of *kauna'oa* (*Cuscuta sandwichiana*) (Fig. 25b). On a visit to the *heiau* in 1977 the author witnessed an offering (*mōhai makana*) of cooked taro corms wrapped in a ti-leaf bundle (*pū'olo*) being placed on a large stone at the western side of the *heiau*. This was done to honor an apparition seen--or perhaps sensed--by the donor, on a previous visit to that spot.

KE-AHU-A-LAKA, *HĀLAU HULA*

The *hālau hula*, located directly below the Kē'ē cliff and above Ka-ulu-a-Pā'oa Heiau, is a single unpaved terrace that could qualify as an ideal house site for a priest or chief, if it were not so firmly associated in tradition with a school for *hula*, and with Laka, the patroness of *hula* (see Barrère's discussion, pp. 56-57).

An earth-filled terrace, such as this one at Kē'ē, would probably have had a large house or hall built on it. In such a hall students would have been taught the art of *hula* by the *kumu hula* (*hula* teacher) of that *hālau*. At one time within the *hālau* there was probably an altar (*kuahu*) where students of that *hālau* made offerings to Laka. They may have also placed their offerings on the small ledges in the cliff at the back of the *hālau* terrace, as is done today. Students visiting from other *hālau* may have used the crevices in the *pali* as a repository for their offerings to Laka, or perhaps the ledges were used only after the *hālau* structure and its *kuahu* had disappeared.

In an interview in 1949, John Hanohano Pā said that when he was young "the elders taught the young to hula, and when the students 'graduated' from the school of hula, they went to a small cave at Hā'ena that had a flat floor and left their lei there in a ceremony to the goddess of hula [Laka], then left" (T. Emory Ms.:8). Perhaps Pā was referring to the crevices in the cliff next to the *hālau hula* when he spoke about the "small cave" with a "flat floor."

In 1927 Emory observed "numerous stones placed on bits of grass skirts, and anklets, and on remains of fern and hala wreaths; offerings to Laka" (Appendix E: 146) (Fig. 26). From the evidence observed by the author in October and December 1977 and also in June 1979, these traditions are still being carried on.

Students of *hālau hula* from other parts of Kaua'i still visit the site, sometimes after a graduation performance, but not necessarily only then, to leave their *lei* and other adornments used in *hula* dancing as offerings to Laka (Fig. 27). These visitors treat the site with great respect.

In 1928 Dickey collected the name "hula platform of Kilioe" for the *hālau hula*. Emerson identified Kilioe as "the god of precipices" who lived at Hā'ena (Malo 1951:86-87, footnote 17).

a. The *makai* end of the upper terrace wall of the *heiau* is built up into a cairn.

b. Offerings on the cairn.

Fig. 25. CAIRN ON KA-ULU-A-PĀ'OA HEIAU. (Photos by M. Kelly, Oct. 6, 1977)

Fig. 26. OFFERINGS IN CREVICES OF CLIFF ABOVE KE-AHU-A-LAKA, OBSERVED BY EMORY IN 1927. Note numerous stones placed on offerings. (Photo by K. P. Emory, 1927; Bishop Mus. Neg. No. 13630)

Fig. 27. OFFERINGS OF *PALAPALAI* AND *KAUNA'OA LEI* PLACED IN CREVICES IN CLIFF BEHIND THE *MAUKA* STRUCTURE IDENTIFIED WITH LAKA, GODDESS OF *HULA*. (Photo by M. Kelly, Oct. 6, 1977)

Rice identified Kilioe as a *kumu hula* and as the sister of Lohi'au (see Appendix A, p. 124). Putting all this together, Dickey accepted the name of the dance platform as "Kilioe." He further assumed that the dance platform was the place where Pele met Lohi'au when he and his companions were "playing drum for the hula" (Dickey Ms.).

Emerson relates that when Pele first arrived at Kē'ē, Pā'oa was "sitting at Lohiau's right hand, with a drum between his knees" (Emerson 1915:7). Lohi'au was sitting in the midst of the musicians; on either side of him sat a "fellow drummer" and "flanking these to right and left, sat players with a joint of bamboo in either hand (the kekeeke)[*kā'eke'eke*]" (Ibid.). The site itself was described as "the rustic hall where the hula was in full blast" and "the hall of the hula--the halau--where throbbed the hula drums and where was a concourse of people gathered from the whole island" (Emerson 1915:4-5). Emerson's account gives the impression that the performance in progress when Pele arrived took place on the *mauka* structure, specifically the *hālau hula*, rather than on the *makai* structure, the *heiau* proper. Of course, this is a legend and its charm is enhanced with a lack of concreteness and a generous willingness to leave a lot to the imagination of the audience.

Wichman, when questioned about this, felt that such a performance may have taken place on the terraces between the two structures (Interview, 1979). She also pointed out that the "people on the outskirts of the assembly"--that is, the "multitude" or the "audience" listening to the musicians when Pele arrived--may have been sitting in the terraced area just east of the *heiau* where the present modern structures are located (see Fig. 17 d, e).

One tradition connected with the *'ūniki* (graduation), told to Wichman by Jacob Maka, concerned a guardian shark that was said to live at the entrance to the channel between the reef and the shore of Kē'ē Bay. Before graduating, the *hula* students took a ceremonial swim across the Kē'ē lagoon and through the narrow channel toward Nāpali. They emerged from the sea at a small cove where the *pali* begins, just beyond the *heiau*. The object of the swim was to test all graduation candidates to be sure that they had kept their strict vows. Any who had not, it was assumed, would be caught and consumed by the guardian shark.

David Pā was said to have been in the last graduating class at the *hālau* at Kē'ē. His mother, also, had been a graduate of the Kē'ē *hālau*. Her yellow *kapa* skirt, worn when she danced and kept for many years as a family heirloom, unfortunately was swept out to sea and lost at the time of the 1957 tsunami (Wichman interview, 1979).

In addition to the teaching of *hula* at the Kē'ē *hālau*, there also was chanting, drumming, and *kā'eke'eke*, according to the traditions. And Emerson adds:

> In the ancient regime of Hawaii, the halau, as the home and school of the hula, stood for very much and for many things. It served, after a fashion, as a social exchange or clearing house for the whole nation; the resort of every wandering minstrel, bohemian soul or *beau esprit* whose oestrus kept him in travel; the rallying point of souls dislocated from an old and not yet accommodated to a new environment; a place where the anxious and discouraged, despairing of a new outlook, or seeking balm for bruised hearts, might quaff healing nepenthe [Emerson 1915:235].

Although there were other *hālau hula* on Kaua'i and on other islands, the *hālau* at Kē'ē appears to have had the highest standing of any in the islands. It was considered the "graduate school" of *hālau hula* (Wichman interview 1979).

FIREBRANDS (*'ŌAHI*) OF MAKANA

The cliffs above Hā'ena were famous as the setting for the spectacular "fireworks" of the Hawaiians. These displays evidently were associated with graduation of *ali'i* at the *hālau hula*, as well as with other celebrations. The throwing of firebrands was also a theme included in the text of *hula* chants.

Theo H. Davies was present when Queen Emma, the Queen's mother, the Prince of Hawai'i, and the Governor of Hawai'i all visited Hā'ena in 1860 (Davies n.d.:58). After "tea" they all "wandered down to the seashore to watch the 'fireworks'." Davies described how the tossing of firebrands was done: "Several natives climb to the summit of a stupendous and almost perpendicular peak, and taking light dry stakes about six feet long, ignite them at both ends, and throw them far out and the wind carries them backwards and forwards until they reach the sea" (Ibid.:59).

A page from the Francis Gay list of place names of Kaua'i indicates that the peak associated with firebrands is called Makana (Gay Ms.). After Makana Peak, Gay wrote "*o-ahi*" (*'ōahi*) which is the Hawaiian term for such firebrands.

In an interview with Mr. Simeon Maka on August 13, 1959, the following information was obtained:

> Maka is a *kama'āina* of Hā'ena, Kaua'i. Maka recalled his participation in the hurling of firebrands, *'ōahi*, over the cliffs of Makana. This took place at night to celebrate the Kamehameha Day holiday in 1925. Maka and Hanohano Pā of Wainiha, Kaua'i, were the only ones living then, in 1959, who had gathered bundles of dry *hau* and *pāpala* before ascending the foot-path along the steep *pali*.
>
> A firebrand was lit at one end and hurled when the *Kehau* breeze lifted the firebrand high into the air, until the firebrand burned itself out.
>
> Maka said the *pāpala* wood with a pithy center was very long-lasting. The flame streamed through the wood with a continuous glow [Pukui Ms.].

In his discussion on the uses of the *hau* (*Hibiscus tiliaceus*) botanist Otto Degener includes a description of the Hawaiian practice of hurling firebrands from cliffs. He says:

> *Oahi*, the fireworks of the Hawaiians, was by far the most spectacular of their amusements. This took place on the northern coast of Kauai where the cliffs drop perpendicularly almost 2,000 feet into the ocean. On these heights the performers stationed themselves with oiled, dried sticks of *hau* or some other light wood. At night each performer lit one of these inflammable sticks and cast it into the air to the delight of the spectators gathered in canoes hundreds of feet below. The blazing wood was buoyed up by the strong trade wind and able to drop only very slowly into the ocean. As fast as these sticks were lighted the performers cast them into space until, to the spectator below, the sky appeared to be ablaze with scores of comets and shooting stars rising and falling, darting

> seaward or receding toward the cliffs, crossing and recrossing each other in the most fantastic way. This weird spectacle, sometimes supplemented with glowing *kukui* nuts that quickly reached their goal, continued long into the night. One by one the oiled sticks were consumed and the blazing firebrands flickered and disappeared, or the winds gradually subsided and they glided slowly and gracefully into the ocean where eager hands were outstretched to receive them. With these burning sticks the agile youths branded their arms as proof of having witnessed the *oahi*.
>
> It was customary for those ascending these heights to carry bundles of green sticks and *kukui* nuts to the top and to scatter them about to dry. In this way, the proper fuel would be available for the succeeding performers to cast over the precipice [1945:218].

Firebrands are also the subject of at least two modern chants collected by Helen Roberts (1926:77-81, 260-61), although both chants refer to Kamaile, the cliff above the Nu'alolo Kai landing, rather than to the cliffs that tower over the beach at Kē'ē (Knudsen 1945:144).

According to Knudsen, to prepare for a firebrand display took months of work.

> An *oahi* required months of preparation. Two kinds of wood were used, the *hau* and the *papala*. The *hau* was easy to get and was cut into ten or twenty foot lengths, the bark peeled off, and then dried until it was as light as a feather. The *papala* grew in the high mountains and was hard to get, so it became the king's special fireworks. It had a hollow core when dry, and the flame ran through it as it fell, giving the effect of a shooting star.
>
> These dried sticks were carried up the high cliffs to a ledge a thousand feet or more above the sea. On a dark night the men climbed up to the ledge, built a fire, and lighting the ends of the sticks, hurled them like javelins into space.
>
> The two most famous *oahi* places on Kaua'i were Kamaile peak, rising 2500 feet over Nuuololo landing [sic] on the Na Pali Coast, and the high cliffs that tower over the wet caves at Haena.
>
> The cliffs being concave, the trade winds are forced upwards forming a sort of air cushion from which the blazing *hau* sticks rise and fall. The force of the wind and gravity together fan the burning end into a blazing ball of fire as the stick works up and down in the air and away from the cliff until it reaches the outer edge of the air cushion. There it comes tobogganning down, blazing fiercer and fiercer, until like a great rocket it sails over the flats below and rushes out to sea [Knudsen 1945:144].

Juliet Rice Wichman talked with Simeon Maka many years ago about his participation in *'ōahi* at Hā'ena. He impressed on her that it was a test of bravery as well as of strength and endurance for the men who conducted the firefall. Maka had been one of the young Hawaiians who, with sticks for the firefall strapped to his back, made his way to the top of Makana mountain. At one point on the trail of Pali-o-Makana the carriers had to work their way around a windy cliff by facing it and feeling for grips with their fingers and toes (Wichman interview 1979).

The firefall exhibitions were connected with the *hālau hula* at times when a person of *ali'i* rank was graduated. Whether that person was from Kaua'i or from another island was not the deciding factor. Regardless, a firefall would be put on for the occasion. To view the firefall, some people went out in canoes and others stayed on the sand dunes. A great many omens and signs were read into the courses taken by the firebrands. For example, if two firebrands met over a canoe in which a man and woman sat, it was said to mean that the couple were "fated to be together." The firebrands at times were wrapped with wild *hinahina-kuahiwi* (*Artemesia* sp.) (Wichman interview 1979).

While on a helicopter ride, one informant noticed what she believes to be a man-made platform on one of the ridges above Kē'ē. She thinks it may have been used by the men who threw the firebrands off the cliff at Pu'u Makana.

The Hālau Hula Today

GENERAL CONDITION

The *hālau-heiau* complex of sites today appears neglected. Brush, grass, and vines have taken over, nearly completely covering the terraces between the *heiau* and the *hālau hula*, and hastening the general degeneration of the structures.

At the time of Emory's visit in 1927, the entire *hālau-heiau* complex was cleared. Following Emory's suggestion, the Kaua'i Historical Society, as the result of a donation of funds for the purpose, placed the care of the Kē'ē sites in the hands of David Pā and Thomas Hashimoto, who kept them clear of weeds for many years. Their efforts helped to preserve the sites and to maintain an orderly appearance as late as 1952 (see Fig. 21). Even in 1959, when Henry Kekahuna made his site plan, the area was fairly clear of brush. Since then, however, the condition of the sites has degenerated.

A few recent attempts have been made to clear the *hālau* platform. Members of the Kaua'i Community College Anthropology Club and of Ka 'Imi Na'auao o Hawai'i Nei and friends, under the watchful eye of archaeologist Dr. William K. Kikuchi, cleared the site in 1978. But for one reason or another, subsequent attempts to organize regular clean-up groups, however, have been less successful.

Concerned Kaua'i residents interviewed by the author have all expressed the hope that the sites would be cleared, well kept, and protected now, as well as later when the land they are on becomes public.

HULA STUDENTS VISIT THE *HĀLAU HULA* AT KĒ'Ē

The present resurgence of interest in Hawaiian history and culture, and particularly the strong revival of *hula*, has led to renewed interest in the Kē'ē sites among the students of the various schools of *hula* on Kaua'i and on other islands as well.

Asked how he first became involved with the *hālau hula* at Kē'ē, one Kaua'i *kumu hula* answered, "Through Andy Bushnell, professor of Hawaiian history at Kaua'i Community College." Bushnell took his class on a field trip to the sites at Kē'ē, and this *kumu hula* went along. The Kaua'i Historical Society has also sponsored trips to the sites.

---

*The following sections are based on 1979 interviews with *kumu hula* on Kaua'i.

One *kumu hula* took her students to Kē'ē to acquaint them with the area because, as she said, they were learning dances "concerning the people connected with the site." After that initial visit in 1976, the students returned to the *hālau* platform in order to clear it. The students have to be ready for such selfless devotion to the art of *hula,* the *kumu hula* pointed out. Not all are. It is a long trip to the end of the road, and then to put in several hours of hard physical labor clearing the site by hand, including pulling out guava stumps, takes real dedication. When they visit the site to clear it, someone from the *hālau* usually takes an offering to Laka. They approach the site with an *oli* and a prayer before setting to work.

Because Laka, Lohi'au, Pele and Hi'iaka are all connected with the Kē'ē sites, as one *kumu hula* explained--Laka lives there, Lohi'au danced there, Pele met him there, and Hi'iaka was in the vicinity--these personages and events provide a certain aura to the *hālau* platform. Feelings experienced by the student visitors are sung about in the *mele* that are used in the *hula.* Laka represents *ulu* (growth), the *kumu hula* explained, fruitfulness, truth, a clear mind, and love--love from the *na'au,* not romantic love in the modern sense. These feelings don't end when you leave the site. You carry them with you into your everyday life. Through the experience of a visit to the site one achieves a serenity that the usual outside noises and distractions fail to penetrate. There is a greater ability to concentrate, and as a result the students can dance better.

STUDENTS DANCE AT THE *HĀLAU HULA* AT KĒ'Ē

One *kumu hula* has taken her students to the *hālau hula* to dance and receive inspiration in their dancing through their association with the site and the traditions connected with it. She explained that when they visit the site, they first offer a prayer before entering the *hālau* area. Then, as they approach the site they chant an *oli kāhea,* followed by an *oli komo,* and then an *oli kau.* Examples from Emerson of the first two *oli* are "*Li'u-li'u aloha ia'u, ka uka o Koholā-lele*" and "*E hea i ke kanaka e komo maloko*" (Emerson 1909:39, 41). No example was given for the *oli kau,* except that it was one taught by her *kumu hula.*

Students first do one or more *hula* in the *kahiko* (ancient) style (Fig. 28). Two *mele,* selected by their *kumu hula,* were "*Aloha i ke kai o Kalalau,*" a chant with drum accompaniment, and "*Aia i Kamaile ko lei nani,*" in which the dancers chanted and accompanied themselves on the *kāla'au.* This *kumu hula* believed it was appropriate to first do one or two *hula kahiko* in respect for the traditions connected with the site. Afterwards it was perfectly appropriate for the students to select *hula* in the *'auana* (modern) style, such as "*Nani Lawa'i,*" and they are free to choose whatever they wish to dance as a group.

The *kumu hula* sits at the back of the terrace near the *kuahu,* the crevices in the *pali* where the offerings to Laka are placed (Fig. 29). She chants and accompanies her chanting with a *pahu.* The students dance either facing the ocean (Fig. 28), or facing their *kumu hula.* Students enjoy performing there; they have a warm feeling when they perform and work there, and are very comfortable in this setting.

After leaving the site, a parting prayer is offered.

Fig. 28. DANCERS FROM THE HALAU HULA KAHIKO HALAPA'I HULA ALAPA'I PERFORM ON THE *HĀLAU HULA* PLATFORM AT KĒ'Ē, 1978. (Photograph by Boone Hekili Morrison)

Fig. 29. DANCERS FROM THE HĀLAU HULA KAHIKO HALAPA'I HULA ALAPA'I PLACE OFFERINGS TO LAKA AT THE *HĀLAU HULA* AT KĒ'Ē. (Photograph by Boone Hekili Morrison)

THE FUTURE OF THE KĒ'Ē SITES

The government agency that takes over the Kē'ē sites for a park will assume the burden of setting guidelines for their future care and use, an awesome responsibility for agencies that have had little or no involvement in *hula*, performing, teaching, or history. The author discussed with several *kumu hula* the possible future use of the sites.

One *kumu hula* felt that there was a need for a keeper, much in the same way that there is a keeper at the Royal Mausoleum, for the purpose of making certain that the public respects the sites. At present, curious visitors are climbing the walls of the sites to look at them, not knowing where to go to have proper access to the area, and some of the walls are beginning to deteriorate. Visitors are making their own trails and this is very unfortunate.

Another *kumu hula* felt that the sites should not be open to the public, or to tourists in general; those who have no functional relationship to the sites should not just go there to have a look at them. It would be advisable, she thought, to allow visits to the sites by *hula* groups or members of classes involved in studying Hawaiian traditions, language, and culture. They should visit the sites with a responsible person, perhaps a guardian of the area.

It was expressed to the author that these sites are very precious to the *kumu hula* on Kaua'i and their students, as their *makua* and *kumu hula* of the past and their *'ohana* went there, or were chosen to go there. It was not a place where just anybody went. Whatever remains should be preserved and protected for future generations.

AN ADVISORY COUNCIL ON THE KĒ'Ē SITES

More than one Kaua'i *kumu hula* felt that it would be a good thing to have a community council or committee to advise the county or State on policy for the proper care, use, and maintenance of these sites, providing the advice given would be followed. Otherwise, such a council would be meaningless, and possibly used merely as a facade.

One *kumu hula* pointed out that an organization called Hula Hālau o Kaua'i was formed about 1974. It included all the *kumu hula* who were interested at that time in keeping in touch with each other, but everyone is so busy that there have been few occasions since then to get together. It was thought that perhaps this group, or some of its members, would be willing to be the nucleus of a larger group, which would include other Kaua'i residents interested in the preservation and future use of these sites. The challenge of developing policy in regard to the use and maintenance of the Kē'ē sites might be the spark that would rekindle the interest of the original group of *kumu hula*.

There was enthusiasm expressed generally for participating in planning the future of these sites. As one *kumu hula* put it,

> Whenever I do anything Hawaiian...I was taught...to give it all my attention and to have care and concern. You don't just do things carelessly. You have to do things because there is a reason.... I feel that whatever belongs to us, we should keep it, otherwise we will not have anything to pass on to our children.... They will lose their own culture.

Among all those interviewed, there was sincere interest expressed and a willingness to set aside time to cooperate with Kaua'i County or the State and share the responsibility of preserving that part of Hawaiian culture expressed in the traditions of the Kē'ē site.

APPENDIX A.

Extracts from
THE GODDESS PELE*

by
William Hyde Rice

Pele was the daughter of Moemo and Haumea, both well-known names in the oldest Hawaiian legends. Many other children were born to this couple, seven illustrious sons and six distinguished daughters. The youngest sister of Pele, Hiiaka-ika-poli-o-Pele, was born into the world as an egg. Pele concealed this egg under her arm until the child was hatched, and ever afterwards showed great affection for her.

When Pele had grown to womanhood, she begged her parents' consent to travel. This was granted, and wrapping Hiiaka in her pa-u, or tapa skirt, the adventurous Pele set forth.

* * *

...Pele went to Point Papaa from where she looked across to Kauai. Taking on her spirit body, she quickly passed through Mana and the mountains back of Waimea and came to Haena.

As darkness fell she heard the hula drums beating. Following the call of the music Pele came to a rude enclosure where the people were gathered for sports. In the crowd she saw a very handsome man, Lohiau, the king of Kauai, whom she suddenly resolved to seek for her husband.

The assembly was startled by hearing a beautiful voice chanting a *mele* of the hills, and by seeing at the door a woman of wondrous beauty and charm.

Lohiau ordered the people to stand aside so that the stranger could enter. The chiefs of Kauai crowded around Pele, wondering who she was. Lohiau was surprised when his unknown guest asked him to become her husband. He did not consent until he heard that she was Pele, the mortal.

Then Lohiau bade his servants prepare the tables for a feast, and he invited Pele to sit with him and partake of the food. After the meal was eaten Pele told Lohiau that she could not live with him until she had found a suitable home for them. The king of Kauai was rather ashamed to have his wife prepare the home, but he consented.

Kaleiapaoa, Lohiau's best and truest friend, was summoned to see Pele. But before he looked upon her he hurried to the king's sister, the celebrated tapa maker of Kalalau, and asked for a pa-u. She gave him one she had just made by beating with *lauae* from the cliffs of Honopu. Pele was very much pleased with this pa-u because it was so sweet scented. When she had finished admiring it, she said to Lohiau, "Now I shall go to prepare our house."

At once she began to dig a cave, but striking water she left it. She tried again and, meeting with the same results, left Haena and came to the *kukui* grove near Pilaa. Pleased with this spot she turned to the mountains where she dug as before, but met with unsatisfactory results.

Taking the form of an old woman, Pele hurried to Koloa. There she again struck water. Repeated efforts to dig a dry cave having failed, she decided to leave Kauai and to find on Oahu a suitable place for her home.

* * *

Pele landed at Puna on Hawaii. She decided to call first on the god of the island, Ailaau, the Wood-Eater, who had his dwelling at Kilauea. When Ailaau saw Pele coming towards his home, he disappeared because he was afraid of her.

Pele began to dig. At last success crowned her efforts. Digging day and night, she came to fire and knew that this spot would be suitable for the long-sought home. She decided to make a home large enough for all her many brothers and sisters.

After the fiery pit was dug, Pele changed her egg-like sister, Hiiaka, into human form and the two lived happily in her new home.

* * *

*From Rice, W. H. 1923. *Hawaiian Legends*. Bishop Mus. Bull. 3, pp. 7-17. (Reprinted 1977, Bishop Mus. Bull. 63, with photographs by Boone Morrison.) The material extracted refers to Pele, Hi'iaka, and Lohi'au on the island of Kaua'i.

As Pele worked she heard the voice of her beloved Lohiau calling her, for the wind carried his sad song to her ears. So Pele called her sisters to her and asked each one to go to Kauai to find her husband. All refused. Then Pele commanded Hiiaka, "Go to Kauai and bring my husband to me. Do not dare to kiss him, lest some dire disaster befall you. Be gone no longer than forty days." All agreed that it was wise for Hiiaka to go, as she was the youngest.

Stretching out her right hand to her sister, Pele bestowed upon her all the supernatural powers she possessed, so that the journey could be accomplished in safety.

* * *

[After an eventful journey from Hawai'i to Maui, Hi'iaka and her companion, Wahine-o-ma'o, reach Kalihi, on the island of O'ahu.]

...Nearby two men were preparing a canoe for a trip to Kauai. Hiiaka told them that she had heard many times of Kauai but had no way of going there. The men, noticing that the speaker and her friend were young and beautiful, generously offered them a seat in their canoe.

As the sea was rough Hiiaka wanted to help with the paddling, but the men were strong and never became tired. They landed at Wailua and encountered many difficulties in traveling from there to Haena.

First a certain *kupua*, the demi-god of the locality, guarding the surf, saw them coming and sent messengers to see if they walked over the ti leaf without breaking it, which was a sign that they were supernatural beings--*akua*. Hiiaka deceived them by sending Wahine-omao ahead as she was more human and her feet tore the leaves. The messengers returned and reported that the strangers were human beings.

Next they came upon a *kupua* swollen to twice his natural size, but he was unable to stop them.

Near Kealia they came upon a man cooking his *luau* or young taro leaves to eat with his poi. Hiiaka by her magic power cooked the *luau* in a few minutes.

Looking into the man's house Hiiaka saw a very sick woman whom all the *kahuna* had been unable to help. Hiiaka uttered a prayer and at once health was given back to the woman.

Having done this act of kindness, Hiiaka went on her way to Hanalei. At the valley of Kiaiakua the *akua* were lying in wait to stop them. As one tried to block their way, Hiiaka gave him a blow like a stroke of lightning and he fell back stunned.

At the mouth of the Hanalei River they again met resistance from an angry *akua*, who was struck to earth as the others had been.

Coming to Kealahula they saw Hoohila combing her hair. She, too, tried to delay their journey by making the sea break over the cliff. Wahine-omao threw sand into the eyes of the *akua*, and this difficulty was overcome.

Near Wainiha they were treated more kindly. The great fisherman of the place killed his favorite dog for them and then gave games in their honor.

So the travelers were nearing their journey's end. As they came to the wet caves dug by Pele in her efforts to find a suitable home for herself and Lohiau, Kilioe, the sister of Lohiau, saw them, covered with lehua leis, and knew that they had come for her brother. Kilioe was the great hula dancer and teacher. No one could hula in public on Kauai unless approved by her and given the *uniki*, the sign which served in place of a diploma.

But, alas, the beloved Lohiau was dead and in a *mele* Kilioe made known this sad fact to Hiiaka. Hiiaka was not discouraged, for magic power was in her hands and she set about overcoming this difficulty, apparently the greatest of all.

As luck would have it, she saw the spirit of Lohiau flying over one of the points nearby. He was beckoning to her. Hiiaka gave to Wahine-omao swiftness of flight and together they chased the elusive spirit over many a steep *pali*. When they came to the ladder of Nualolo, the weary Wahine-omao cried, "Indeed you must love this Lohiau greatly."

At last Hiiaka caught the spirit in a flower and hurried back to the *pali* above the wet caves where the body of Lohiau had been laid. Then she began her task of putting the spirit back into the body.

Kaleiapaoa was fishing and grieving over the death of his truest friend. Looking towards the mountains he was startled to see a fire. At first he thought it was only the spirit body of Lohiau, but as it continued to burn he thought that someone must be attempting to steal the body of his chief. Quickly coming ashore he silently climbed up the *pali* and was greatly surprised to see two beautiful women trying to put the spirit back into Lohiau's body. This sight filled him with gladness and he returned to his home, where he told his wife what was being done by the strangers.

In the meantime Hiiaka was patiently accomplishing her task. She put the spirit back into the body through an incision in the great toe, but she found it very difficult to get the spirit past the ankles and the knee joints. However, after she had worked for eight days Lohiau was restored to life. Hiiaka carried him to his home and bathed him in the sea on five successive nights, as was the custom. At the end of that time he was purified, so that he could again mingle with his friends.

Then for the first time in many days Hiiaka and Wahine-omao slept very soundly. Lohiau's sister passed by the house and, seeing the door open, entered. She was surprised to see her brother sleeping soundly. She beat the drum and made known to all the people that Lohiau, their chief, was alive again. Many came, bringing gifts with grateful hearts.

Hiiaka was very anxious to start for Hawaii, as the forty days allotted her had long since expired and she feared that Pele would be angry.

At Kealia the chief entertained the three guests with sports in which Lohiau was very skillful. Reaching Kapaa, they met the king, who gave them a canoe to carry them to Oahu.

After a short stay on this island, where there was much dancing and royal feasting, the travelers left for Hawaii. As they were passing Molokai, Hiiaka saw a chiefess standing near the shore and asked her to give them fish. The chiefess replied, "I have no fish for you, proud slave." These words so angered Hiiaka that she swam ashore and killed her.

After this adventure they went on quietly until they reached Hawaii, where they landed at Puna and then hastened on towards the home of Pele and to a relentless fate.

When they came to the brink of the volcano, Hiiaka sent Wahine-omao ahead to greet Pele while she and Lohiau stayed behind. There in full view of Pele and her other sisters, Hiiaka, suddenly overcome with emotion for the man she had grown to love, threw her arms around him and kissed him.

Pele's anger knew no bounds. She cried, "Why did she not kiss Lohiau while they were on Kauai? She does it before my eyes to laugh at me."

Seeking revenge, Pele sent her sisters to destroy her lover by means of a lava flow. They put on their fire robes and went forth rather unwillingly. When they came near and saw how handsome Lohiau was, pity took hold of them and they cast only a few cinders at his feet and returned to Pele in fear. Hiiaka knew that the falling cinders would be followed by fire, so she told Lohiau to pray.

When Pele saw her people returning from their unaccomplished errand she sent them back, commanding them to put aside their pity for the handsome man. So the fire burst forth again and gradually surrounded Lohiau. At last the rocky lava covered his body.

When Hiiaka saw what her sister had done, she was so angry that she dug a tunnel from the volcano to the sea, through which she poured the fire, leaving only a little in the crater. This small amount was kept by one of her brothers under his arm.

Seeing what Hiiaka was doing, Pele became alarmed and sent Wahine-omao to beg her to spare her sisters. Hiiaka did not heed her friend and Pele cried, "This is a punishment sent upon me because I did not care for Hiiaka's friend, and I allowed her lehua trees to be burned."

Wahine-omao again entreated Hiiaka to spare Pele, recalling to her mind the many days of travel they had spent together. At last Hiiaka promised to spare Pele but refused to see her again.

As soon as possible she returned to Kauai and told the faithful Kaleiapaoa what Pele had done. This true friend of Lohiau made a solemn vow to pull out the eyelashes of Pele and fill her mouth with dirt.

Led by the magic power of Hiiaka, Kaleiapaoa soon reached the outer brink of the crater and began to attack Pele with vile names. Pele answered by urging him to come down and carry out his oath. Attempting many times to descend and punish Pele, he was always forced back. At last Pele allowed him to come before her, but he no longer wished to carry out his threat. Pele had conquered him by her beauty and charm. After he had remained in the crater four days, he was persuaded to return to Kauai with Hiiaka as his wife.

Two brothers of Pele who had come from foreign lands, saw Lohiau's body lying as a stone where the lava flow had overtaken him. Pity welled up in their hearts and they brought Lohiau to life again. One of these brothers made his own body into a canoe and carried the unfortunate Lohiau to Kauai, where he was put ashore at Ahukini.

Coming to Hanamaulu, Lohiau found all the houses but one closed. In that one were two old men, one of whom recognized him and asked him to enter. The men were making tapa which they expected to carry soon to Kapaa, where games were being held in honor of Kaleiapaoa and his bride, Hiiaka.

As soon as the tapa was prepared, the men, joined by Lohiau, started for the sports. At the Wailua River discussion arose. Lohiau wanted to swim across, but the men insisted on carrying him over on the palms of their outstretched hands.

When they reached Waipouli, Lohiau suggested that the men carry the tapa over a stick, so that he could be concealed between its folds. This was done and at last they came close to Hiiaka.

Lohiau told the men to enter the *kilu* game. Lohiau promised to *oli* for them in case they were struck. First the old man was struck, and from his hiding place Lohiau sang a song that he and Hiiaka had sung in their travels. The next night in the game the other old man was struck, and Lohiau sang the song that he and Hiiaka had composed as they neared the volcano.

Hiiaka knew that these were the songs that she and Lohiau had sung together during their days of travel. She lifted up the tapa and saw again Lohiau--the man twice restored to life from death, the lover for whom she had dared the wrath of Pele, the mate whom she now encircled with loving arms.

When Kaleiapaoa saw that his old friend had returned, his shame and sorrow were so great that he hastened to the sea and threw himself into the water to meet his death.

So, at last, Hiiaka and Lohiau were united--and lived happily at Haena for many years.

APPENDIX B.

HIIAKA AND LOHIAU

Condensed Version of Hawaii's Popular Legend*

by
Thomas G. Thrum

Pele, the goddess of volcanoes, was the eldest of nine sisters and five brothers, all of whom migrated from Kahiki, landing first on the island of Kauai. After a short sojourn there they set forth, touching at the various islands till reaching Hawaii, where they located, and made Kilauea their permanent home.

One day, at Pele's behest, her sisters went with her down to the seacoast of Puna, where they wandered away to the beach to fish, excepting the youngest sister, Hiiaka-i-ka-poli-o-Pele. (All of Pele's sisters were Hiiaka's of various characters, but this story has to do only with this favorite sister of Pele. As the name indicates, she becomes the famed Hiiaka of the family.)

When they were alone, Pele prepared to repose, and said to her sister: "Listen; I am going to sleep. Let no one disturb me. Your duty will be to wave the kahili over me until I myself awaken." With that she fell into a deep sleep, and her spirit heard the beating of two drums with chanting, one by Lohiau, the other by Kauakahi.

The sounds lured her spirit along past the windward coast of Hawaii, across the channel, past Maui and Oahu, and on to Haena, Kauai, where she landed in her natural person while a dance entertainment given by Lohiau and Kauakahi was in progress, to which she was invited. Lohiau inquired of her where she was from. She replied: "Why, from Kauai here." "There is not a woman here in Kauai like you," said Lohiau, "because I am the king and have visited all around the island and know."

Pele said: "You have, of course, seen parts of Kauai, but some places you have not seen, and in one of these was I." "No, you are not even a woman of Kauai. Where do you belong?" said Lohiau, and in response to his pressing inquiries she answered, "I am from Puna, where the sun rises."

A feast was therefore made ready, but she declined Lohiau's call to come and partake, saying, "I have eaten." During the feast Lohiau's mind was in commotion through watching Pele, so that at last he gave up eating and asked her to come and stay with him. She arose, and the two went into the house and remained together three days and three nights. Lohiau, becoming very hungry, said to Pele, "Let us go and eat." She replied, "You go." Lohiau then said: "Perhaps if I go for food you will secretly leave me." "No," said Pele, "I will await your return," but as soon as he had gone she took her departure. On returning he found she had vanished; she had returned in spirit to Hawaii.

Upon her spirit reaching Puna, the body of Pele, which Hiiaka was fanning, awakened, and, with her sisters hastened to return to Kilauea, where they rested that night. The next day Pele requested each of her sisters, from the eldest down, to go and bring their husband, but for one reason or another they all refused, except the youngest.

In due time Hiiaka was outfitted for the journey, and Pauopalae, a maid, was assigned as companion, and on setting forth Hiiaka chanted a mele while they disappeared. Many difficulties were encountered in their travels, both by land and by sea, all of which were surmounted by the exercise of Hiiaka's miraculous powers. At length, with Wahineomao, who had joined them on the way, they reached Haena, Kauai, the residence of the lover of Pele. As they glanced around they perceived the spirit of Lohiau beckoning them from within a cave half way up the precipice. They discerned only the hand, the spirit having been taken by two lizards. Thus Lohiau came to dwell half way up the cliff, the domicile of the lizards.

*From Thrum, Thomas G. 1929. *Hawaiian Annual for 1929*. pp. 95-103.

After chanting a short mele, Hiiaka said to Wahineomao, "We have no husband; he is dead; the spirit is up there in the cliffs, beckoning." She then said to her companions, "You two stay here below while I go up to rescue the spirit of our friend. In my attempt, if the lizards have the greater power and I die, you know the way back; but should I conquer them there will be no trouble."

As the day was far spent she called on the sun to stand still until she could climb the pali, and her prayer was heard. Hiiaka climbed the precipice and when the lizards saw her they forthwith sharpened their teeth and prepared the things with which to kill her. The spirit of Lohiau was in the interior of the cave, while the lizards stood guard, one on each side of the entrance. After climbing for some time Hiiaka reached the entrance, whereupon one of the lizards leaped upon her and was soon followed by the other. Just then Hiiaka waved the end of her skirt which reduced the lizards to nothingness. Going into the cave she brought out the spirit of Lohiau and descended with it to Haena, where she joined her companions, and together they wended their way to the house of Lohiau's sister, Kahuanui, and there met Lohiau's friend, Kauakahi.

Hiiaka then applied to Lohiau's sister for his body. The sister remarked: "What benefit will it be to you? The period of usefulness when he was alive is passed, and now he is dead he is not of any use." Hiiaka replied: "I wish to see the body," and as she persisted, the sister acquiesced and all went to the house where the body lay. The sister entered first, followed by Hiiaka and her companions. Going up to where the body lay, the sister undid the wrappings and then said: "There it is."

Hiiaka declared: "I shall have to operate on him to restore his spirit, and may be within two anahulus (twenty days) you shall see him." The sister assenting, Hiiaka straightway began the operation through her supernatural powers for the return of his spirit to the lifeless body. Within one anahulu success crowned her effort so that Lohiau was able to rise and walk, and during the second anahulu he became as his former self. One day Hiiaka sent him out surf-riding, after which he was to come back and bathe in a pool of fresh water within a cave, as the final cleansing ceremony.

The following day Hiiaka said to Lohiau: "There is nothing more to do in your case. You are revived and out of danger. The next thing is to let us go." Lohiau then said to his friend Kauakahi: "Take charge of the kingdom, preserve the land, the people, and protect our sister also. I am going away." To all of which Kauakahi gave assent. When ready they entered a canoe and, sailing, arrived at Waianae, where they sojourned awhile, then moved to Kou (Honolulu).

The night of their arrival, Peleula, the chief of Oahu, had a kilu entertainment, and as the coming of Hiiaka and her party had been made known, a royal edict was proclaimed that all the strangers must come and visit, and share his night of enjoyment. In the evening they came and occupied a place set apart for visitors. Peleula then said: "Say, the visitors should start the game." Hiiaka replied, "No, residents first; this entertainment is not by the visitors but by the residents."

The game was commenced by a chiefess throwing the kilu at the goal nearest Hiiaka and her party, but she missed it through the stranger's influence. At the end of their inning, without scoring, Hiiaka picked up a kilu which she threw, after first chanting a mele, hitting the post and scoring one.

Peleula then called out: "Let the other woman (Wahineomao) make the next throw, but a mele must be chanted before throwing the kilu." Wahineomao replied: "From my birth until now, I have not known how to chant; I am utterly devoid of such knowledge." "That is the law of my house, chant first, then throw the kilu," said Peleula, and because of his insistence she uttered a few words, almost inaudible, and threw the kilu, and scored their second count. The other side, however, remonstrated, saying: "Yours did not sound like a chant; it was simply a talk," but throwing again in their turn, and missing the goal it was again Hiiaka's throw. Chanting her mele she threw the kilu and won as before.

At midnight the entertainment ceased and the audience was dismissed. They then took a short sleep, arising at daylight to set forth on their voyage for Hawaii. In due time they landed at Kohala, then went by way of Waimea and entered the forest of Mahiki where they rested.

While sojourning here a new interest in Hiiaka entered the mind of Lohiau as she sat before him on the ground, a passion which pierced his heart, causing a feeling of uneasiness and shuddering to creep over his body. When Hiiaka noticed the emotions under which he was laboring she chanted a mele to comfort him.

After their rest they again went on till they emerged from the forest at the boundary of Hamakua, where Hiiaka chanted the beauties of the distant Honokane cliffs, then continued their way to Makahanaloa, Hilo, where Hiiaka, after gazing on Puna, noticed that it was scorched with lava flows, and that her friend Hopoe had been consumed by Pele. Hiiaka said within her, "So then I have guarded your lover, while my friend you failed to protect. I am going to win your husband. I will not do so here, but right before your own eyes, that you yourself may see."

They went through Panaewa, emerging on the other side of the forest, then up to Olaa where, upon arrival, Hiiaka said to Pauopalae and Wahineomao, "You two go up ahead, and we two will follow." When they were gone Hiiaka went gathering lehua blossoms with which she braided wreaths for Lohiau and herself. In the meantime Pauopalae and Wahineomao reached the pit, which they descended, when they were immediately killed by Pele for leaving Hiiaka and Lohiau behind.

Hiiaka and Lohiau then came up to within the borders of Kahoalii, on the edge of the pit of Kilauea. Here Hiiaka suddenly sprang up and embraced and kissed Lohiau, when immediately loud cries were heard from the other sisters who were in the pit, saying: "Look at Hiiaka kissing your husband; look at her embracing him." While they were applauding their sister's actions, Pele remarked: "The nose is liable to be kissed by anyone," but turning to Lonomakua, the fireman of the pit, she ordered him to start the fires, which order was obeyed. Pele then directed the Hiiakas: "Say, all of you go up and scorch your sister's lover." They arose and went forth in their flaming bodies.

Ascending about half way up the cliffs the elder said to her sisters: "Say, when we reach there, if our sister's lover is a good looking man, let us only touch him with the sparks of fire, while the larger portion (the flames) we will retain." To this all were agreed. so they resumed the ascent and when they reached the top they saw that Lohiau was indeed handsome. They therefore threw only the sparks and returned to the pit below.

"Pele, aware of their course, bade them go back, saying: "Pshaw! You ascended and saw your sister's paramour a handsome man, so threw only the sparks at him and the greater portion of the fire you retained!" She then ordered them up again, but going back they did as before and returned to where Pele was waiting. She then said to them: "You are unaccountably strange; you simply went up, but why is it that man who is babbling is not dead?" She again ordered them to go back, but still they did as before.

At last Hiiaka said to Lohiau: "Say, pray thou!" to which Lohiau replied: "What man is there who has the power to fight with fire as his opponent? If this was at my place I could present a pig, the red fish, and coconut, and pacify the anger of the god, but it must not be. As this is your place, my wife, I am powerless."

After this conversation, the sisters again appeared and performed their work as before. As on former occasions, Lohiau chanted a mele in which he intimated his ignorance of Pele being superhuman. When Pele, down in pit, heard it she answered by saying: "Of course, I am superhuman. Did you suppose otherwise? You are human, and right there you will babble until you die." She then again ordered the sisters back up the cliffs to complete their work.

Before Lohiau expired, Hiiaka in loving words said: "Do not go to windward lest I may not find you, but go to the leeward that I may meet you again." The body of Lohiau then turned into stone and laid there where he had been scorched, at the borders of Kahoalii.

Soon after this Hiiaka, thinking that Lohiau was gone into the earth in fear of the winds of the upper regions, broke through the first stratum, but finding no one there she broke through the second stratum but still found no one, so she broke through the third stratum, and here she found the god Makaawa, with his tongue hanging out. She broke through a fourth stratum which was the floor of Wakea, where she rested.

Meanwhile Pele's anger cooled and her affection for her sister returned, for she missed her from among the rest of the Hiiakas. She therefore called them all together and asked: "How may our sister be induced to return?" They replied: "There are none among us who can persuade her. If you desire her return there are only two persons who could appease her anger and quiet her. They are her own attendants, Pauopalae and Wahineomao, the companions who endured the rain, the heat, and adversities with her." Whereupon Pele revived them. She then asked Pauopalae: "Say! which of you two can persuade Hiiaka to return?" She answered, "Wahineomao, her friend." Pele then endowed her with supernatural powers with which to seek Hiiaka and sent her away.

Wahineomao then broke through the first, second and third stratas, but found no one, so resting awhile in this latter sphere she chanted an endearing mele. Hiiaka heard the chant and said: "If this be my sisters I will not return, nor even if it were my brothers." Wahineomao chanted again, a mele in which Hiiaka plainly recognized the voice of her friend, so she turned back, and after meeting together returned to the surface, but remained away at some distance, Hiiaka not desiring to see Pele.

When Kauakahi heard of the death of his friend Lohiau, he bemoaned the loss of his chief, saying: "I am going to be avenged on Pele." He then journeyed from Kauai and came to Kilauea, where he saw the body of Lohiau turned to stone. He sat down and wept, after which he chanted a mele in which he revealed himself to the Hiiakas and to Pele. Furthermore, he spoke vile words to humiliate Pele in the presence of others, as he had vowed, thinking that by tantalizing her he would be killed, as was Lohiau, that he might join him. However, the anger of the goddess was too greatly mollified.

Pele thereafter sent Kauakahi to Mauliola, one of her brothers, to partake of food. When he reached the place Pele's brothers had already assembled together, and as they saw him they turned their faces to the wall. He entered the house and there lying before him was food and fish. He sat down and chanted prayers. At the close of his prayers the brothers turned about and asked, "Is that your deity you was praying to?" He assented, saying: "That is our deity from my grandfathers down to myself, from the greatest to the smallest of our land, Kauai," adding, "Were this my country edibles would be in abundance, but not so, I am in a strange land." Immediately the prepared meal was removed, as it was a meal of death, and good food and fish was given instead, of which he ate and was satisfied. He remained there some time, having won the affections of the entire Pele family, and on his return to Kauai, Hiiaka, Pauopalae and Wahineomao escorted him.

Kanemilohai, one of the brothers of Pele, set sail one day from Kahiki, and when in mid-channel of Kaieiewaho he discerned the spirit of Lohiau returning on the crest of the waves. He guided his canoe, a leho shell, in the direction that the spirit was coming. When near to each other he grabbed and secured it, and took it with him to Hawaii. Going up to the pit of Pele, he noticed the form of a man lying on the ground, which resembled the spirit that was in his possession. By his supernatural power he changed it into a natural human body, and after preparing it placed the spirit that he had secured in it, reviving Lohiau who became as his former self. Lohiau looked about him, and gazing down into the pit he saw Pele, the Hiiaka sisters and all those whom he knew, so he chanted a mele setting forth his revival by Kanemilohai.

Lohiau shortly afterwards set out for Kauai, touching at Oahu on the way, where he arrived on the night of a kilu entertainment given by the chief Peleula. Hiiaka and her companions were among those invited, and, as before, they occupied the place allotted to strangers. The game opened in the usual way, and when it came to Hiiaka's turn to throw the kilu she first chanted a mele, and as she ceased she heard the voice of a man from without chanting its continuance. She said within her, "Why, the voice of this person chanting is similar to that of my husband, but it cannot be since he is dead!"

At the time that Hiiaka seized the kilu, Lohiau arrived on the outside of the house and asked a man wearing a large mantle to conceal him and not tell anyone. The mele Hiiaka sang was known by heart to Lohiau, who knew well where to resume when she ceased.

After reflection she again sang a mele which, when she ended, Lohiau chanted in the very same manner. It was now clearly evident to Hiiaka that this person was no other than her husband, twice resuscitated, so she arose and went through the assembly in search of him but failed to find him. She then went outside the halau on her quest and discovered Lohiau under the mantle of the man. Loud was the joy-wailing that possessed them all at this reunion--hoped for by her husband, but so unlooked for by Hiiaka--that the kilu entertainment of Peleula came abruptly to an end, and gave place to the new pleasures of those reunited hearts.

In the morning the voyage to Kauai was resumed, and there they resided for some time, but afterwards the allurements of Pele and her goddess power drew Hiiaka and her companion back to Hawaii.

APPENDIX C.

Extracts from VANCOUVER'S JOURNAL, 1801*

...the king and queen, who had been present the whole time of their dressing, were obliged to withdraw, greatly to the mortification of the latter, who would gladly have taken her part as a performer, in which she was reputed to excel very highly. But the royal pair were compelled to retire, even from the exhibition, as they are prohibited by law from attending such amusements, excepting on the festival of the new year. Indeed, the performance of this day was contrary to the established rules of the island, but being intended as a compliment to us, the innovation was admitted.

As their majesties withdrew, the ladies of rank, and the principal chiefs, began to make their appearance. The reception of the former by the multitude was marked by a degree of respect that I had not before seen amongst any inhabitants of the countries in the Pacific Ocean. The audience assembled at this time were standing in rows, from fifteen to twenty feet deep, so close as to touch each other; but these ladies no sooner approached their rear, in any accidental direction, than a passage was instantly made for them and their attendants to pass through in the most commodious manner to their respective stations, where they seated themselves on the ground, which was covered with mats, in the most advantageous situation for seeing and hearing the performers. Most of these ladies were of a corpulent form, which, assisted by their stately gait, the dignity with which they moved, and the number of their pages, who followed with fans to court the refreshing breeze, or with fly flaps to disperse the offending insects, announced their consequence as the wives, daughters, sisters, or other near relations of the principal chiefs, who however experienced no such marks of respect or attention themselves; being obliged to make their way through the spectators in the best manner they were able.

The time devoted to the decoration of the actresses extended beyond the limits of the quiet patience of the audience, who exclaimed two or three times from all quarters, "*Hoorah, hoorah, poaliealee,*" signifying that it would be dark and black night before the performance would begin. But the audience here, like similar ones in other countries, attending with a predisposition to be pleased, was in good humour, and was easily appeased, by the address of our faithful and devoted friend *Trywhookee,* who was the conductor of the ceremonies, and sole manager on this occasion. He came forward, and apologized by a speech that produced a general laugh, and causing the music to begin, we heard no further murmurs.

The band consisted of five men, all standing up, each with a highly-polished wooden spear in the left, and a small piece of the same material, equally well finished, in the right hand; with this they beat on the spear, as an accompaniment to their voices in songs, that varied both as to time and measure, especially the latter; yet their voices, and the sounds produced from their rude instruments, which differed according to the place on which the tapering spear was struck, appeared to accord very well. Having engaged us a short time in this vocal performance, the court ladies made their appearance, and were received with shouts of the greatest applause. The musicians retired a few paces, and the actresses took their station before them.

The heroine of the piece, which consisted of four parts or acts, had once shared the affections and embraces of *Tamaahmaah,* but was now married to an inferior chief, whose occupation in the household was that of the charge of the king's apparel. This lady was distinguished by a green wreath round the crown of the head; next to her was the captive daughter of *Titeeree*; the third a younger sister to the queen, the wife of *Crymamahoo,* who being of the most exalted rank stood in the middle. On each side of these were two of inferior quality, making in all seven actresses. They drew themselves up in a line fronting that side of the square that was occupied by the ladies of quality and the chiefs. These were completely detached from the populace, not by any partition, but, as it were, by the respectful consent of the lower orders of the assembly; not one of which trespasses or produced the least inconvenience.

This representation, like that before attempted to be described, was a compound of speaking and singing; the subject of which was enforced by appropriate gestures and actions. The piece was in honor of a captive princess, whose name was *Crycowculleneaow;* and on her name being

---

*Vancouver, George, 1801. *A Voyage of Discovery to the North Pacific Ocean....* Vol. 5, pp. 70-75. London: Stockdale.

pronounced, every one present, men as well as women, who wore any ornaments above their waist, were obliged to take them off, though the captive lady was at least sixty miles distant. This mark of respect was unobserved by the actresses whilst engaged in the performance; but the instant any one sat down, or at the close of the act, they were also obliged to comply with this mysterious ceremony.

The variety of attitudes into which these women threw themselves, with the rapidity of their action, resembled no amusement in any other part of the world within my knowledge, by a comparison with which I might be enabled to convey some idea of the stage effect this produced, particularly in the three first parts, in which there appeared much correspondence and harmony between the tone of their voices, and the display of their limbs. One or two of the performers being not quite so perfect as the rest, afforded us an opportunity of exercising our judgement by comparison; and it must be confessed, that the ladies who most excelled, exhibited a degree of graceful action, for the attainment of which it is difficult to account.

In each of these first parts the songs, attitudes, and actions, appeared to me of greater variety than I had before noticed amongst the people of the great South Sea nation, on any former occasion. The whole, though I am unequal to its description, was supported with a wonderful degree of spirit and vivacity; so much indeed that some of their exertions were made with such a degree of agitating violence, as seemed to carry the performers beyond what their strength was able to sustain; and had the performance finished with the third act, we should have retired from their theatre with a much higher idea of the moral tendency of their drama, than was conveyed by the offensive, libidinous scene, exhibited by the ladies in the concluding part. The language of the song, no doubt, corresponded with the obscenity of their actions; which were carried to a degree of extravagance that was calculated to produce nothing but disgust even in the most licentious.

This *hooarah* occupied about an hour, and concluded with the descending fun, it being contrary to law that such representations should continue after that time of day. The spectators instantly retired in the most orderly manner, and dispersed in the greatest good humour; apparently highly delighted with the entertainment they had received.

APPENDIX D.

LIST OF HULA AT THE CORONATION OF KING KALĀKAUA*

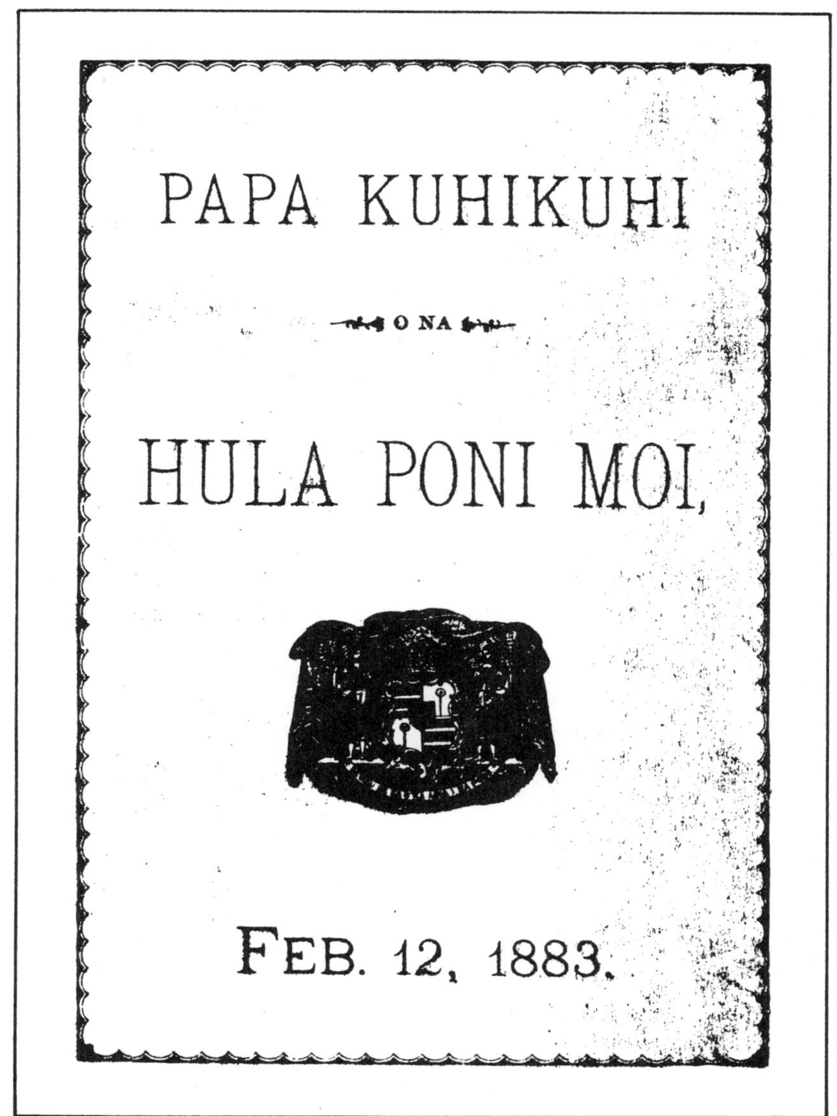

PAPA KUHIKUHI

O NA

HULA PONI MOI,

FEB. 12, 1883.

---

*Reproduction of program in Bishop Museum Library.

S. Kalaimano.

He Mele he Inoa nou e Kalani..............Hula Ku'i
Akahi makou a ike.......................... " "
Ua piha hauoli makou...................... " "
Eia Davida o ka heke o na pua.............. " "
Ka hoku ka malama ike ia oe...............Hula Ulili
Hoomaikai oe e Hawaii..................... " "
Ua ike Haumea me Haunuu................ " "

KALUA.

O Keeelanihonua Kama i na moku.....Mele Koihonua
1. O Kalani i poniia i ka ua noe...........Hula Ku'i
2. O Kalani i poniia i Waiolama........... " "
3. O Kalani i poniia i ka Waihau.......... " "
Moku leleahana Kanaloa i ka ino...........Koihonua
1. O Kalani i poniia i ka wai Iliahi.........Hula Ku'i
2. O Kalani i poniia i ka wai Aniani......... " "
3. O Kalani i poniia i ka wai Liula.......... " "
4. O Kalani i poniia i ka wai Kuauhoe....... " "
O mai o Kalani Kalakaua ke 'Lii nona ia Inoa. Koihonua
1. O Kalani i poniia i ka ua Kiowao.........Hula Ku'i
2. O Kalani i poniia i ka ua Paliloa......... " "
3. O Kalani i poniia e ka ua Paupili......... " "
O oe ka ia e Kalani Hoola o ka Lahui........Koihonua
O Kalani keia Pono ka Aina................. "

IOANE.

KOIHONUA—KAI WAWAE MAMUA.

1. Ike ia Haehae ... Hula Ku'i
2. Ike ia Kaukini ... " "
3. I aloha i ka lau Oliva ... " "
4. Hookahi pua e kau nei ... Hula Ukeke
5. Malama i ka Haku a he pua ... " "
6. Auhea wale oe e ke Kona ... " "
7. Nani wale no Maemae ... " "
8. Ia oe e ka La e alohi nei ... Hula Ulili
9. Anoai i ke Aloha ... " "
10. Kuupau lia mai ... " "
11. Ee aku o Kalani ... " "
12. A Kona Hema o Kalani ... " "
13. Aole i piliwi ia ... Hula Paipu
14. Auhea wale ana oe ... " "

EHU KEOHOHINA.

E poni ia ana o Kalani ... Hula Alaapapa
No Waipio o Kalani ... " "
O Kalakaua he Inoa ... " "
Ka Moi hoeueu ... " "
Hanohano Davida ... Hula Paiumauma
O Kalakaua he Inoa, Pua oi o ka hik. " "
O Kalakaua he Inoa, Pua nani o ke Kalaunu ... " "
Ko mai kiliopu ... " "
Poni ia ana o Kalani ... Hula Paipu
Maui o Papa ... " "
Kalakaua he Inoa ... " "
Ko mai hoolala-hu ... " "
O Kalani i poni ia e ke onaona ... Hula Ulili
Ia oe e ka La e alohi nei ... " "
O Kalani kai alo aku ... " "
Ko mai Kikiliki ... " "
Poni ia oe e Kalani ... Hula Kalaau
Aiai Hawaii o Keawe ... " "
Aiai Haupu ka Iwa makani ... " "
Inu aku o Halala Wai o Likemona ... " "
O Kalani i poni ia e ka wai loku ... Hula Puili
A Kona Hema o Kalani ... " "
I aloha i ka mapuna leo ... " "
Aia ko mai ka nuku i Nuuanu ... " "
O Kalani ke ala ... Hula Ku'i
O Kalakaua he Inoa ... " "
Eia no Davida ka Heke o na Pua ... " "
Nani Kalalaa, Holu Kalalaa ... " "
He poni hanohano nou e Kalani ... Hula Kii
Eia Wewehi hi-keke ... " "
Eleele Kaukau ... " "
A ka uka au i Halemano e ... " "

I.

Eia ko poni e Kalani	Hula Ku'i
Eia ko Lei Alii Poni	" "
Noho mai Davida i ke Kalaunu	" "
Eia ko Kahili Poni	" "
Noho ia ko Poni Kapu	" "
Eia ae e Kalani	" "
O ka Pua Kalaunu i Halealii	Hula Ulili
Eia ko la e Poni ai	" "
He Hiapo he Aloha na Hawaii	" "
O ka Pua Kaimana i Kinau Hale	" "
O ka maka no ia o ka onohi	" "
Poni Kapulani a Hawaii	" "
Nawai e Poni o Kalani	" "
Kau oe i ka Poni Hanohano	" "
Noho oe i ka Poni Ihiihi	" "

KAONOWAI.

Li mai Kalani Li Kalapana	Mele Oli
Kaulilua i ke anu Waialeale	" Ku'i
Anoai ke Aloha na Lai a Ehu	" "
Loe Kuaiwa o Laa ke Alii	" Oli
Ua poniia o Davida i ka la umi-kumalua	" Ku'i
Ua poniia o Davida imua o ke Akua Mana Loa	" "
Ke ai la Kalani i ka paka	Kielei
Hanalei aina kukele i ka ua	"
O Mana aina kumuwai i Kalani	"
Poniu Kona i ka la	Aihaa
A la, wela Kona	"
Kupilikii Hanalei he ua la	"
Holo ana Kalakaua imi i ka Pono o na Moku	"
Aloha mai ka hoa mai pelekane	"
Na Kane i hee ka nalu o Oahu	"
Kaulilua i ke anu Waialeale	"
Ulili walaau ka manu i ka wai	Mele Oli
Ua poni ia o Davida i ka la umi kumalua	Ulili
Ua poni ia o Davida imua o ke Akua Mana Loa	"
O ka wana halula	Mele Oli
Ua poni ia o Davida i ka la umi kumalua	Paiumauma
Ua poni ia o Davida imua o ke Akua Mana Loa	"

Hoehoene pua wai hoene i ka laau	Mele Oli
Ua poni ia Davida i ka Aila Mura Oliva	Ulili
Ua poni ia Davida i ke Ala Kupaoa	"
Ua poni ia Davida i ka Lauae o na pali	"
Nowelo ka manu ai pua manu i ke kula	Mele Oli
Ua poni ia Davida me ke Ala o ka Mokihana	Ulili
Ua poni ia Davida me ke Ala o ka Iliahi	"
Ua poni ia Davida me ke Ala o ke Kupukupu	"
O Kahiki kai malolo ka moku	Mele Oli
Ku mai o Kalanikumoku	Ulili
Nani wale ke kino o ia pua	"
Ai'e o Kaahupahau	"
Ai'e o Mauna Aniani	"
Ai'e o Mauna Kalaika	"
Nowelo ke anu i Mahiki	"
Nowelo ke anu i Manoa	"
Nowelo ke anu i Waimea	"
He mai	Aihaa
Ke kumu o ke kapu ka mole o ke'lii	Mele Oli
Auhea la Lose Lani	Ulili
Auhea la o Anoi	"

HULA PELE—AIHAA.

Wahi Umi i ka pali paa	Hula Pele
O Kalani o Keokinapau o Kalani	" "
Hulihia ka mauna wela i ke ahi	" "
He lua i ka hikina	" "
O Pele ke kumu o Kahiki	" "
He kai moe nei no Pele	" "
Kaiehu ko Kohala loa	" "
O Puuonioni	" "
E *o* e Mauna i ka Ohu	" "
O Molokai Nui a Hina	" "
O Lanai Kaulahea	" "
Aloha wale Puna i ka lehua	" "

NA KILU A LOHIAU.

Ke hele la Kaauhula ana o Kalalau	Kilu 1
He Makani pahele hala ko Mailehuna	" 2
A Kalalau a Ke-e	" 3
Mapu i Nualolo ke ahi a ka Lawakua	" 4
I Makua i Makua i Hoolulu	" 5
Aia no ke ahi i ka Mauna	" 6
Aia no ke ahi i ka Maile	" 7
Aia no ka makani ke hoala la iluna	" 8
E uwe mai ana ia'u	" 9
O Puna nahele uluhala	" 10

NA KILU A HIIAKA.

Lili Lehua pu-a ia lalo moe koa kahuhu iloko	Kilu 1
O Puna kai nehe i ka uluhala	" 2
O Puna ua pau i ke 'kua	" 3
He lalo ka lua he pali ka hako	" 4
Ke ano wale mai la no ka lua ia'u	" 5
O Hilo nahele paoa i ke alo	" 6
Ke kau aloha wale mai la no Hamakua ia'u	" 7

Hamakua aina pali loloa........................ " 8
O Hilo kai mu kai wa.......................... " 9
Mehameha kanaka ole ka hoi puu o Moeawa—e.. " 10

NA AMI HONUA A LOHIAU.

Ke lei mai la o Kaula i ke kai—e....................
Kuu hoa i ke kawelu o Malailua.................. 1
Kuu hoa i ka ili au o Mana....................... 2
Moe no i Wailua ke Koolau....................... 3
Aloha ka Nikiniki ke kanaenae pua Mailehuna...... 4
O Haupu mauna Kilohana.......................... 5
Nahaha i ka ua ka hale o Hanalei................. 6
A Kalihi au i Hanalei............................ 7
Aia la i Kawaihoa o kuu kane makani............. 8
Aia la o kuu kane Waikini........................ 9
Kuu hoa i ke anu o Alakai........................10
A pa mai ka makani o Kalelewaa—e............... 1
O Malaehaakoa lawaia o ka pueo.................. 2
O Malaehaakoa lawaia o ka pali................... 3
O oe ia e Keahiku na pua i ka wekiu.............. 4
Hana ke aho o ka maunu o ka ia e loaa'i. Hula Nemanema
Naue—he moe ulei—e............... " "
Naue—he moe ulei—e............... " "
Manamana ia Kaluae.................Hula Muumuu
Ka Ia iki maka inoino................. " "
Aauwaalalua ka ale i ka moana........ " "
O Puna kai kua i ka hala..............Hula Olepelepe
Ke haa la Puna i ka makani........... " "
O Ku o Ka o Wahineomao.................Hula Ami
Lau Lehua Punoniula......................Hula Paipu
Kahuaku Kalani iloli ka moku.................Aihaa

S. Ua.

Oi oe o ka mole uaua o ke'lii................Mele Oli
A luna wau o Kaimuki...................Hula Paipu
Ia oe e ka La e alohi nei................. " "
E ala e Hawaii o Keawe......................Aihaa

O aua ia e Kama ko na moku.................Mele Oli
Ka nalu nui e ku, ka nalu mai Kona.......Hula Paipu
Noho aku o Kalani i ka olu............... " "
Aole i manao ia, kahi wai o Alekoki............Aihaa

Ka nalu nui e ku, ka nalu mai Kona..........Mele Oli
Hulihia Kilauea po i ka uahi.............Hula Paipu
Ke amo la ke koi, ke kua la iuka......Aihaa (2 pauku)

Kaulilua i ke anu Waialeale..................Mele Oli
A ke poo o Puna i Puna ka makani........Hula Paipu
He lua i Kahiki ua aina e Pele........Aihaa (6 pauku)
Ko mai kiliopu, ke papani aku la.........Hula Paipu

A Koholalele pau ka ino a ka makani.........Mele Oli
Aia i Haili ko lei nani......... { Hula Paipu (7 pauku) (Elua Aihaa) }

Kiekie Kau hanohano i ka makani............Mele Oli
Aia i ka hikina ko kapa..........Hula Paipu (2 pauku)
Aia i ka hoku ko kapa.......................Aihaa

O Ulihiwa i ka lani na Uli....................Mele Oli
Ke hele mai nei ke Kuini................Hula Paipu
Auhea wale oe e ka ua.........................Aihaa

Nani wale ka liko o ia pua...............Hula Paipu
Kaulana ke anu i kanahele...................Aihaa
Kahiko ka nani i Iolani..................Hula Paipu
Kahiko ka nani i Lauhulu....................Aihaa

Hoouna ka Elele, kii e ka La................Mele Oli
O Kalauohua ka manu alii...............Hula Paipu
Hookumu ka Lani, kumu ka Honua............Aihaa

He Inoa nou e Kapili................................
Pualei a Makue..........................Hula Paipu
Pali mai Waipio i ka noe......................Aihaa

Koauli, Koakea la lani......................Mele Oli
E lei ana o Kalani i na lehua o Hilo. Hula Paipu (3 pauku)
E lei ana o Kalani i na lehua o Ohiaokalani......Aihaa

Ike ia Kaukini he lawaia manu..............Mele Oli
O Kalanikupu a pa i ka lani nui..Hula Paipu (2 pauku)
Puao Lihue me Malamanui....................Aihaa

Kukaipaoa Kalani ke'lii.....................Mele Oli
E Kalani e, he Koa oe..........Hula Paipu (e pauku)
Eia Kalani ka une pa pohaku..................Aihaa

O ke kui lei ula oe o ke'lii..................Mele Oli
Hanau mai Kalani, hanau Kalani..Hula Paipu (2 pauku)
Kalanikapu Keliikailimoku....................Aihaa

Hiki kaulia ka malama.....................Mele Oli
Lau lehua punoni i ke kai e Kona. Hula Paipu (4 pauku)
Kahuaku Kalani iloli ka moku.................Aihaa

Na Mano Kalani na Keawe ke 'Lii...........Mele Oli
E noho oe e naue au............Hula Paipu (7 pauku)
O lula oe o ka holo ana o ka moana............Aihaa

Ikeia Hawaii he aina nui....................Mele Oli
Ewa aina kai ula i ka lepo......Hula Paipu (6 pauku)
Nani ka makemake i ke Kalukalu..............Aihaa

O ka manu ke koae hulu melemele...........Mele Oli
Kapu ka moku hano ka leo ia Kalani......Hula Paipu
O Kawaiopua...............................Aihaa

Wela i ka la ka pua ilima o Mana...........Mele Oli
O Hilo muliwai a ka ua i Kalani..Hula Paipu (6 pauku)
Ke ku'i Kalani naue pu ka honua..............Aihaa

Hoinainau mea ipo ka nahele................Mele Oli
O Kaula-ke manu o hiki hanalea...........Hula Paipu
Kalani ka pohaku huli kaa-honua...............Aihaa

Pua mala lua Kawaihoa.....................Mele Oli
Kulia mai ana hoolono ia mai............Hula Paipu
E ala e Kalaninui, e Keanookalani.............Aihaa

Puaehu Kamalena ka uka o Kapaa............Mele Oli
Kalalaupali e pu i ka makani..............Hula Paipu
O Kalani o Kahoano o Kalani...................Aihaa
Waiho kahelahela ka mai o Kalani........Hula Paipu

HULA PELE.

O Lelepinaonao....................................
Me he nalo la i kuu maka...................Mele Oli
O Pele ke kumu o Kahiki.........Hula Pele (6 pauku)

Na Kahiko ka nalu na Wakea i hanau........Mele Oli
O ka nalu nui e ku }
Ka nalu mai Kona } ....Hula Pele

HULA LAAUPILI.

Ke hele la Kaauhulaana.....................Mele Oli
Aia no la ke ahi i ka mauna.................Laaupili

HULA PALANI.

O Kahiki lauena a ka makani..Hula Palani Paiumauma
O Kalauae ka Mai..................................

APPENDIX E

1. THE RUINS AT KĒ'Ē, HĀ'ENA
Report to the Kaua'i Historical Society

by
Kenneth P. Emory
Ethnologist

Bernice P. Bishop Museum
1928

It was my privilege on September 19, 20, and 21, 1927, to visit the ruins at Kē'ē, Hā'ena, on behalf of the Bishop Museum and the Kaua'i Historical Society, for the purpose of recording what is there and of seeing what might be done in the way of clearing, preserving, restoring, and opening them to the public. Through the generosity of Mr. C. A. Brown, the Kaua'i Historical Society has been provided with a fund of $500 for the preservation and restoration of the ruins, and this has served twice to clear the *heiau* and dancing platform, once about a year ago and again during my visit. In addition to this fund, Mr. Brown has granted the placing of a six-foot public right-of-way through his land to the *heiau*.

The ruins comprise (1) a *heiau* of the first or second rank, below which is a stone where Hawaiians placed the excised umbilici of their children; (2) a large terrace where dances were performed and where Lohi'au is attributed to have had his dance hall and shrine to the goddess of the *hula*, Laka (here the remains of offerings to Laka are still to be seen); and (3) an imposing house site where Lohi'au is said to have dwelt. About Lohi'au is woven one of the best-known and picturesque legends of the islands, the love stories of Pele and Hi'iaka. Dr. N. B. Emerson in his *Pele and Hiiaka, a myth from Hawaii* (Honolulu, 1915), has rendered this tale in much of its original beauty. William H. Rice in his *Hawaiian Legends* gives an interesting version, probably a Kaua'i version. A.Fornander has an outline of the legend (Bishop Museum Memoirs vol. 6, pp. 343-45, 1919).

According to Fornander, the Pele family were not known in the Hawaiian Islands until the last period of active intercourse between Hawai'i and the southern islands, about 28 generations ago (*Polynesian Race*, vol. 1, p. 163), or about 1200 A.D. (allowing 25 years to a generation, probably too much). Fornander shows clearly (Bishop Mus. Mem. vol. 6, p. 252) that the legends known to us were composed about the time of Kamalalawalu, King of Maui, who lived seven generations before Kamehameha, or about 1575. Lohi'au probably lived, therefore, about the 13th century. The technique of the facing of his traditional house site is Tahitian in style rather than Hawaiian, in fact I have seen no Hawaiian workmanship of this sort except something approaching it on Nihoa. This would tend to corroborate the traditional date, as during that period there was undoubtedly a direct Tahitian influence, probably more strongly focused on Kaua'i than elsewhere. The terrace of the dance hall is constructed like an ordinary house terrace in Hawai'i or Tahiti; its dimension--length 10 fathoms, width one third the length--are reminiscent of standard dimensions of Tahitian sacred and public structures. The *heiau* is not at all of Tahitian form, its masonry is distinct from that of Lohi'au's house site. Temple ruins of this sort are to be seen on all the larger Hawaiian islands and several are known to have been erected during the hundred years prior to the arrival of the whites. Though it is altogether likely that a temple has stood on this site from the time of Lohi'au, the present structures may not date back to his time. If it were contemporaneous, we would expect the same kind of stone construction as is to be seen in the house terrace.

The ruins of Hā'ena represent three kinds of Hawaiian structures. They have not yet been greatly disturbed by the inroads of our civilization which has obliterated the majority of the Kaua'i sites that meant so much to the native. Situated in a spot of scenic grandeur, which has changed comparatively little since the days of old Hawai'i, this group of ruins is worthy of all effort directed to their preservation, and, when practical, their restoration. Particularly is this true because two of the ruins are linked with one of the most famous and delightful of Hawaiian traditions. Being just at the end of the road, the ruins are easily accessible and furnish an interesting objective for tourists and those who live on the island.

The *heiau* and dancing platform are at present cleared, and the facing of Lohi'au's house site is cleared (as is to be seen in the photograph). This is all the clearing necessary to expose the ruins to view. If once in three months a man were to work two days clearing ($24.00

a year), I think the ruins could be kept in this open condition, particularly if each time more guava and lantana roots were extracted. The slope on which stands the *heiau* and dancing platform could be made attractive if entirely cleared, and planted with *kukui*, pandanus, and native *mokihana* trees, but this would entail quite an expense if properly done--perhaps $150 to $200.

As for the preservation of the ruins, the *heiau* and dancing platform are perfectly safe, providing cattle are not allowed over them. The Lohi'au house terrace is also safe if more stones are not taken for cattle walls. The owner of the land on which this ruin stands should be approached and the structure classed as a monument to be conserved.

I had a trail cut in to the Lohi'au dwelling site from the first bend in the Kalalau trail, and also a preliminary trail from several minutes' walk along the Kalalau trail, cut in to the dancing platform. A trail has been cleared from the latter to the *heiau*. This *mauka* trail to the platform offers an excellent view of the neighborhood and the *heiau*, and it is shaded. However, the new trail is rough. Should it be thought worthwhile, it could be smoothed and widened for perhaps $40.00. I do not know if this trail is on Mr. Brown's land; the owner should be looked up, of course, before establishing any permanent trail.

The land about Mr. Brown's new house is at present freshly cleared. To designate a way through it to the *heiau* would necessitate a flag-stone path, a lane between freshly planted hedges, or some such device, marked at the start with a sign. Such a trail might well branch off from the road to Mr. Brown's house and follow the upper margin of the beach. For the time being the way could be marked out by cairns in which are placed sticks with white arrows:

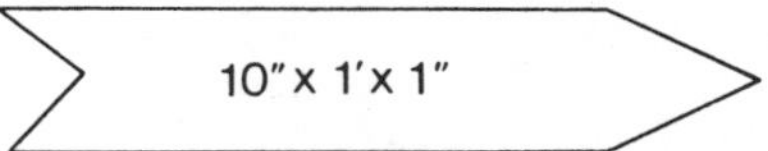

A dozen such arrows would be very helpful in marking the trails to the ruins. In the same way a trail could be pointed out from the northeast corner of the *heiau* to the stone where navel cords were placed. The first arrow should then be marked

Pōhaku Kilioi

Just beyond the stone is a level spot deeply shaded by a pandanus grove through which runs a cool rill. This is a delightful spot for a picnic lunch or supper. To my mind, the most pleasing way of visiting the ruins is to start at the Kalalau trail where a sign would be screwed to the single *lauhala* tree:

18" square, painted in black on white background. Screwed with 2" brass screws.
Cost: perhaps $10.

KALALAU TRAIL

Lohiau House Site	*2 minutes*
Dancing Platform	*5 minutes*
Heiau	*7 minutes*

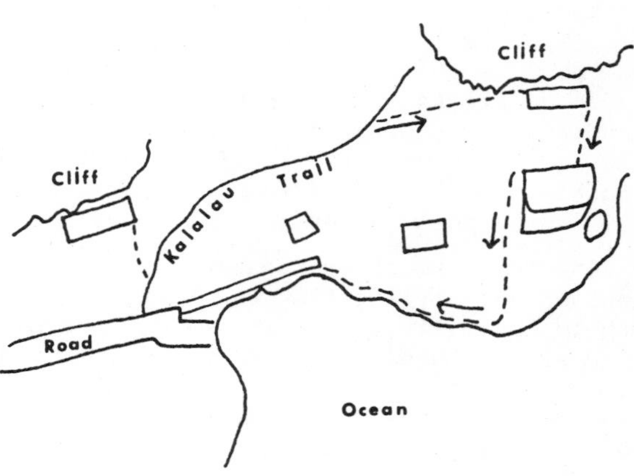

Then to follow the trail to an arrow marked *House Site*. Lohi'au's house site would then be looked over. Next, following the Kalalau trail and branching off at the arrow reading *Dancing Platform*. From the place of offerings to Laka and the dancing platform a sign on the *lauhala* tree at the northwest corner of the latter, would point out the trail to the *heiau*. From the *heiau*, if desired, the *Pōhaku Kilioi* would be visited and then a rest taken in the *hala* grove beyond, returning to the road by way of the beach.

The ruins in themselves are of no especial merit--the *heiau* foundations illustrate only a great sacrifice of human muscular strength, the dancing terrace neither care nor strength. The Lohi'au house terrace alone shows skill for primitive work, but we are so used to perfect walls as to fail to appreciate the advance in early culture which such workmanship represents. It is, of course, the associations with the past that bring these ruins to life and make them interesting.

The material associations would be brought to the spectator quickly and most pleasingly by reconstructions which would restore the superstructures (dwellings, dancing pavilion, images and buildings on the *heiau*). Such restorations, unfortunately, are extremely costly and are not practical at present for a more serious reason: in the absence of any records of them, the construction and placing of the original buildings would be 80 percent guess-work even after exhaustive researches through the data bearing on like structures. To produce this illusion would cost in the neighborhood of $5,000, and about $500 a year to keep up. A model of the ruins together with possible and probable superstructures would be more practical and equally satisfactory.

A restoration of the stone terraces and platforms (i.e., a renewing of the facings, a repaving, and relevelling) would not add so greatly to their appearance as might be thought, since Hawaiian stone structures are of the roughest sort--straight lines, perpendiculars, right angles, perfect levels, orientation to the cardinal points, seem not to have concerned the native mason. Restorations, even with meticulous care, are certain to introduce features which may never have been present and therefore to irreparably injure the archaeological value of the ruin (the Hōnaunau restorations are an example).

A retouching of the Hā'ena ruins, that is, a replacing of that which is practically certain to any archaeologist familiar with Hawaiian structures, would add a well-kept appearance to them which is not undesirable. Nevertheless, I would advise that this not be attempted until after the Bishop Museum has made a survey of the Kaua'i ruins.

I heartily agree with Mr. Thrum that "a deeper interest ever prevails over well kept ruins than can be maintained on false restorations" (*Hawaiian Annual for 1906*, p. 122).

I believe that the Kaua'i Historical Society will have done all it ought to do for the present, if it keeps the ruins cleared, preserved, and opened to the public, and the public supplied with interesting information concerning the sites. The little information I have been able to gather in a limited time I here give and also a description of the ruins. I suggest that some member of the Kaua'i Historical Society prepare a leaflet or pamphlet appropriate for the public from all the material available. A detailed record of the ruins, for the archaeologist and the student of Hawaiian history, would be included in any survey of the Kaua'i ruins published by the Bishop Museum.

HEIAU AT KĒ'Ē, HĀ'ENA, KAUA'I

Location

The *heiau* ruin stands on the end of a short spur which is the first low land east of the cliffs of Nāpali. It dominates the neighborhood in the manner typical of *heiau* of high rank. About fifty feet above the ocean and the coastal plain of Hā'ena, it commands a sweeping view over the plain, far out to sea, and westward along the lofty Nāpali cliffs, to the purple islet of Lehua. From the *heiau* the land slopes up to Lohi'au's dancing platform at the base of a cliff, some five hundred feet distant.

Description

The structure is an unenclosed stone terrace one hundred feet long and sixty feet wide. It appears to have been built up twenty feet at the highest corner. However, in characteristic fashion, the terrace was erected over the end of the spur, producing the illusion of a much greater expenditure of labor than was actually the case. In reality the end of the ridge has been little more than faced with large, unworked, field and beach stones, on the front and on the most conspicuous side. The other side is bounded by a bluff.

The retaining wall towards the sea is almost verticle, but that towards Hā'ena village to the east slopes so gradually as to allow one almost to walk up it. Although much of the retaining wall has been dislodged, a great part of the lower facing of the seaward wall is intact, and a portion of the east wall. It is quite possible that the east retaining wall rose originally in two or three narrow terraces. A common method of supporting a high *heiau* terrace was to add in front several narrow terraces, each faced from the ground. Then, if the outer facing fell away letting the stone behind pour forth, the facing of the next terrace would be revealed and this terrace would continue to support the structure. Several such supporting terraces appear traceable at the east end of the *heiau*. Particularly about the middle, an inner terrace facing seems to have been revealed by the collapsing of an outer terrace. Or was the outer terrace built up only about to this height to allow for a passageway up this face of the foundation? The stones of the facing are of rather uniform size. They average a foot in diameter and are laid up with ordinary care.

The top of the *heiau* ruin is divided off by different levels, different pavements, and by two disconnected short walls. The first section to be considered is the front part of the terrace, bounded on the east by a rough wall not more than three feet thick and three feet high, and bounded on the west by the bluff, and at the back by a terrace a foot higher. The area is paved with large stones. The eastern half is much more evenly paved than the western, and is rather sharply marked off from the latter by being a foot higher. Flat stones, as large as 2 by 3 by 1 feet are conspicuous in the pavement of the eastern division. There, also, are indications of holes in which house posts or the bases of images were probably set. The low wall may not be of ancient origin; at least the several uppermost courses have been added or replaced very laterly, as evidenced by the fresh unweathered surfaces exposed in them. This corner is now used by native fishermen as an observation station.

On the outer side of the wall is a large pit, 12 by 15 feet and 2 to 5 feet deep. This pit is a rough, unlined depression, undoubtedly the refuse pit for the decomposed remains of offerings.

The low stone terrace extending across the rear of the front terrace, is itself divided into three parts. The eastern end is a step six inches above the main floor and six inches below the rest of the terrace. The middle pavement is the most even and fine of the *heiau*. It is natural to suppose the temple tower of scaffolding, the *lana-nu'u-mamao*, stood here. This tower was at one end of the *heiau*, and near if not over the refuse pit. It occupied a square about the size of this pavement.

A third terrace rises back of the second and extends from one end to the other of the structure. It is nowhere more than a foot higher than the second, in fact the middle section of the last is flush with it. This upper terrace is divided nearly equally by a wall which is 3 feet high in front and a foot high at the rear end. The wall appears to have been built on the terrace at the time of its erection, as the terrace fill overlaps the wall. The western half of the upper terrace is unpaved. About midway between the ends against the back of it is a solid stone platform 10 by 12 feet and 18 inches high. The stones with which the top is dressed average a foot in diameter. The eastern half of the upper terrace is also divided by having its eastern half a foot lower. A loose, low, shapeless wall at present lies partly along this division, but it looks as if it had been heaped up with stones taken from the original pavement, which is hereabouts much disrupted.

Concerning the *Heiau*

Thomas G. Thrum, in the *Hawaiian Annual for 1907*, p. 43, mentions two *heiau* for Hā'ena, in his list of Kaua'i *heiau:*

> Kilioi...Haena.--A *heiau* consisting of two platforms, highly terraced; very famous, very sacred, and an immense structure.
> Lohiau...Ke'e, Haena point.--A walled *heiau* dedicated to Laka, goddess of the hula.

In the 32nd Annual Report of the Hawaiian Historical Society, 1924, Thrum says in speaking of the *heiau* of Kaua'i:

> A reported very famous, very sacred and large heiau of two terraced platforms was that of Kilioi, at Haena, which was not visited, nor that of the famous Lohiau temple at Ke-e, Haena point, dedicated to Laka, goddess of the hula. This is described as a walled heiau 77 by 85 feet in size.

I believe the *heiau* I have described is that which Thrum calls Kilioi, and not the one he calls Lohi'au, even though the six Hā'ena and Kalalau natives who cleared the ruins while I was there, pointed out the *heiau* as simply the place where Lohi'au performed religious ceremonies and did not know what the *heiau* was named. The oldest of them from Hā'ena, one Kapae, age 68, said Kilioi was the name of the great rock on the beach below the *heiau* and also of the beach by there. These natives were able to direct me to only one other *heiau* at Hā'ena: a low stone-walled enclosure, 33 by 41 feet, back of Kapae's house in the village. What could Thrum be referring to by Kilioi *heiau* if not the one we have been describing? Could this be the Lohi'au *heiau* dedicated to Laka and could the Kilioi *heiau* have disappeared since 1907?

The measurements given by Thrum for the temple to Laka are certainly of the *heiau* on the end of the point and I do not doubt that the one who took them believed this [was] the Lohi'au temple to Laka. But it is clear from Emerson's *Unwritten Literature of Hawaii* that Laka's shrines were rude, perishable altars, erected at one end of the dancing hall. The site of the dancing hall of Lohi'au is pointed out as the great level, artificial terrace against the cliff five hundred feet inland from the *heiau*, and along the ledges at the base of this cliff are the offerings to Laka. Is not this therefore the *heiau* Lohi'au, listed by Thrum? I certainly can not believe the massive ruin on the point with the great refuse pit at one end was dedicated to the mild goddess of the *hula*, therefore I provisionally locate the Lohi'au *heiau* to Laka at the site of the dancing hall and the place of offerings to her, and the Kilioi *heiau*, as that on the end of the spur. More extensive enquiries than I made would clear up the matter of the name of the *heiau*, and this should be done at once before it is too late.

The Lohi'au *heiau* is reported as walled. If by this is meant an enclosing wall of stone, which is Thrum's usual meaning of the term "walled," then it is an error, as neither the *heiau* on the point or the terrace against the bluff are walled.

However famous the *heiau* of Kilioi may have been, I can find no shred of reference to it except that of Thrum's, though I have searched through Fornander's and N. B. Emerson's works, through the *Hawaiian Annual* and the publications of the Hawaiian Historical Society. Therefore it is not known to what class this *heiau* belonged, but the size, the location, and the presence of numerous divisions and the large pit make it certain that it was one of high class if not of the highest. To have summoned the labor to erect such a *heiau*, to my knowledge the largest in the vicinity, must have required the controlling power of the high chief of that region.

The *heiau* of the highest rank were erected only by the king and on them alone were offered human sacrifices. On such *heiau*, called *luakini*, the king had services conducted to gain the favor and help of the gods during very important events in the life of the royal family and during national crises such as war, famine, and pestilence. Once dedicated, the *luakini* did not stand open and in repair from year to year, ready for the occasions when it was desired to approach the greater gods on serious errands. Each occasion required an elaborate and arduous rededication. The *luakini* was renovated, or completely made over even to features of its foundations, and sometimes abandoned as a site unfavorable to the gods, and another site chosen for the coming ceremony. It was the practice, then, to erect a new *heiau* on the site of some ancient *heiau*, particularly one at which worship had brought success.

The *heiau* next lowest in rank to those upon which human beings were offered in sacrifice, were built by the king and also by chiefs. In outward appearance these were probably not distinct from the *heiau* of the first class. They were smaller, and the timbers, thatchings, and decorations of the buildings were of different material but the kinds of buildings, their shapes and relative positions must have been much the same.

To be able to visualize a *heiau* with all its superstructures and decorations and to see with the mind's eye the usual and principal services enacted upon them--so often by torchlight on a cloudless, windless, tabu night, in awful stillness save for the chanting and the occasional drum beating--is the wish of every visitor to a *heiau* ruin. A model of the *heiau* of Waha'ula on the island of Hawai'i, is on exhibition in Bishop Museum. Descriptions of *heiau* and their ceremonies are available through the writings of David Malo and the historian Kamakau, and others. Each writer, in his description, agrees in the main with the others, but differs radically in such details as the number of buildings and their positions on the *heiau*. This is not to be wondered at as no two Hawaiian temples were alike. For this reason, reconstruction of a ruin and the placing of its superstructures is practically impossible in the absence of historical data. When a great many plans of *heiau* ruins on all the islands have been brought together and thoroughly studied, some order may become apparent enabling us to restore destroyed parts of some sites and to interpret more *heiau* features through analogy. In this connection it is interesting to note that the thirty-four temple ruins on Necker Island, 400 miles to the west of Kaua'i, are all alike, a condition which reappears in the interior of the island of Tahiti together with much the same type of structure.

With all their diversity, most of the Hawaiian *heiau* of the first and second rank probably had the following features in common: most conspicuous of all, a ten-to twenty-foot, square, tapering, frame-work tower of heavy poles 15 to 30 ft high. This was decorated with fringed, white tapa streamers or with cocoanut or banana leaves, and placed at one end of the court. The high priest and king here offered up prayers while all prostrated themselves. Under the tower, or close by, was a pit into which the remains of offerings were finally thrown. The large offerings (burnt) were laid upon a frame-work altar in front of the tower and before a row of male images. At the opposite end from the tower, or at about the middle of the court, stood the *mana* house and a small, thatched house called the drum house, where the large and small drums were kept and where at times the image bearers cried "continuously all night in prayer, from evening till morning dawn." Set at intervals of a few feet around the margin of the *heiau* were grotesque male and female images facing outward. These were purely for adornment--they were not worshipped. (See Thrum, T. G.)

I will not attempt here to give even the briefest summary of the *heiau* ceremonies as they are set forth rather fully by Malo in his *Hawaiian Antiquities* and by Thrum in the *Hawaiian Annual for 1910*, and as from these sources may be drawn as brief or as full an account as may be desirable, both of the ceremonies and of the appearance of the *heiau*.

Pōhaku Kilioi

Below the *heiau*, on the beach, is a great stone honey-combed by weathering. Here the umbilical cords of the children of the neighborhood were deposited, and the remains of one tiny package, wedged into a crevice by three small sticks, is still to be seen. Rocks and caves where umbilical cords were supposed to be safe from desecration are numerous in the Hawaiian Islands. The naval cord was one of the most sacred parts of the human body, as it was the material link with the past, along which was communicated the spiritual power of ancestors. To have the cord destroyed was, in a measure to cut the child off from his spiritual heritage. It is current belief of many Hawaiians that if a rat should eat the cord, the child will become a thief.

The rock was called *pōhaku kilioi*, by Mr. Kapae, age 68, born at Hā'ena. The name should be confirmed.

Dancing Platform

Site of dancing pavilion and shrine of Lohi'au, dedicated to Laka. At the upper end of the slope above the *heiau* at Kē'ē, Hā'ena, and against the base of the cliff are two successive, wide and low terraces (see plan). The first is almost entirely natural, the front being a line of boulders and the top the natural, rocky slope, except for some stone filling along the front. The upper terrace, however, is artificial. It is faced with a single course of large stones (averaging 1 by 2.5 by 3 feet) and leveled with earth. On this presumably stood the *hālau*--or long building open at least at both ends--in which dances are performed before the *kuahu* or altar to Laka, a simple frame decorated with leaves.

The eastern end of the earth-filled terrace is a little lower and slopes down as if forming a separate division. This end is faced with a wall four feet high which curves outward towards the back, forming the face of a short wing constructed entirely of stone. A few feet back to the level terrace rises the bluff. A small, rough platform stands against it, possibly a grave. On the lower ledges of the bluff lie numerous stones placed on bits of grass skirts, and anklets, and on remains of fern and *hala* wreaths: offerings to Laka. Wedged in a crevice with a small stone, I discovered a lock of human hair five inches long and loosely braided. There can be no doubt that this practice of placing offerings here has kept up until the last few years and probably to the present. Mr. Walter McBryde tells me he has known natives, after a *hula* performance, to make a pilgrimage to this site to offer some trinket. When the workmen were clearing the terrace during my visit, one of them picked up a tortoise-shell ring which happened to fall from the ledges above at that moment. This was regarded as a supernatural occurrence, as there was not the slightest breeze or disturbance to dislodge the ring. The natives showed some reluctance to clear on this site as well as the *heiau* and especially at the Lohi'au house site. On the second day of clearing, while at the dancing platform, they complained of a dizzy sensation. One of the men quit work on this account. They did not think my explanation of the sun being too hot was the whole explanation.

The House Site of Lohi'au

The house site of Lohi'au is a stone faced, earth and stone filled, unpaved terrace 80 feet long and 8.5 feet high at its highest part. It is built across a shallow swale at the base of a bluff. From the front of the terrace to the bluff, a distance of 54 feet, is level ground. The facing wall is unusually even for a Hawaiian wall. It is almost perpendicular in addition to being quite straight. In 8.5 feet the wall slopes in one foot from the perpendicular. The construction is characterized by the selection of large stones, with a flat smooth face which is exposed in the wall and supported in some instances by the comparatively small stones placed in the interstices. None of the stones show indications of having been artificially shaped. I had not seen this type of work in Hawai'i before, except an approach to it in some of the house foundations of Nihoa. The work is, however, common in the Society Islands.

2. EMORY'S PLAN MAP OF KA-ULU-A-PĀ'OA HEIAU, 1927*

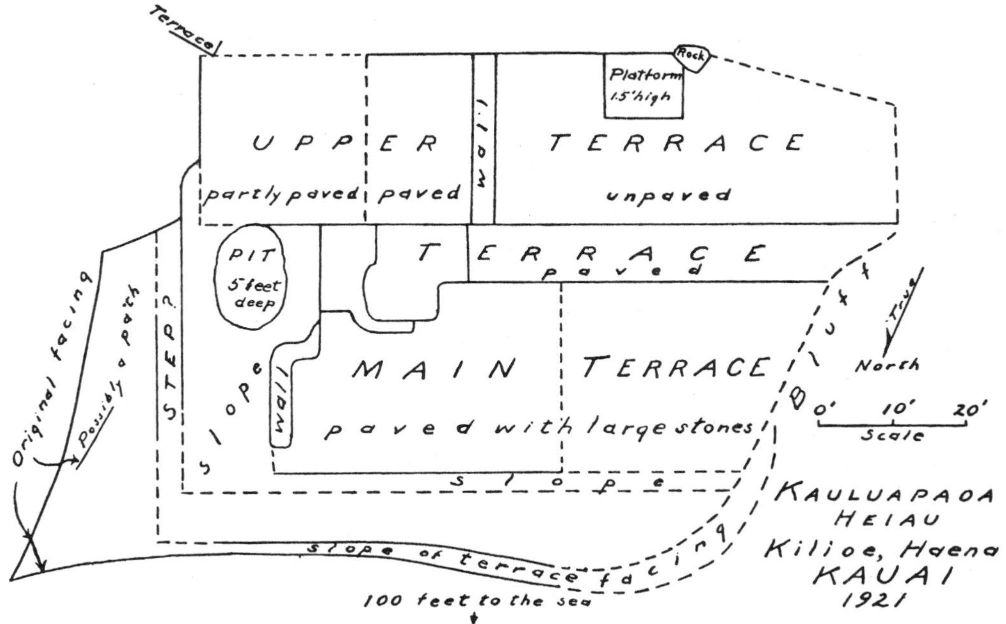

*From Kenneth P. Emory, "Ruins at Kee, Haena, Kauai." *Hawaiian Annual for 1929*. pp. 88-94. 1929. The date shown on the map is an error; Emory's survey was done in 1927.

3. BENNETT'S PLAN MAP OF KA-ULU-A-PĀ'OA HEIAU, 1931*

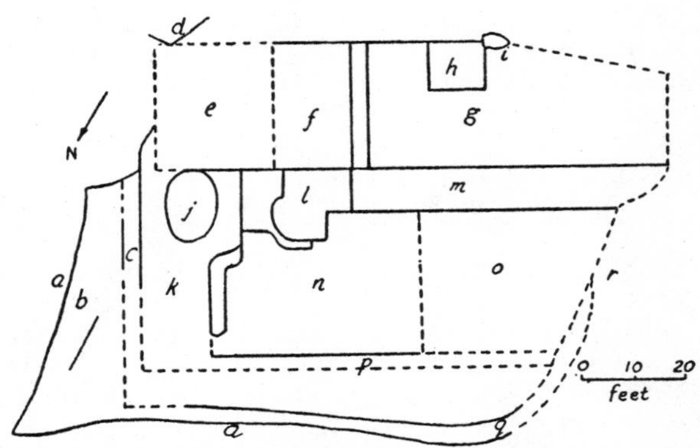

FIGURE 44.—Plan of Kaulaupaoa heiau, Kee, Haena, Site 154 (after Emory): *a*, original facing; *b*, path (?); *c*, step; *d*, terrace; *e*, *f*, and *g*, sections of the upper terrace; *h*, platform 1.5 feet high; *i*, rock in place; *j*, pit 5 feet deep; *k*, sloping ground; *l* and *m*, sections of a paved terrace; *n* and *o*, sections of main terrace paved with large stones; *p*, slope; *q*, slope of terrace facing; *r*, bluff.

---

*From Wendell C. Bennett, *Archaeology of Kauai*. B. P. Bishop Mus. Bull. 80. 1931.

GLOSSARY OF HAWAIIAN WORDS*

'aha	Sennit; cord braided of coconut husk, human hair, intestines of animals; cord stretched for the outline of a house so that the posts may be properly spaced.
ahu	A cairn of stones.
'ailolo	Ceremony marking the end of training, so called because the students ate (*'ai*) a portion of the head, and especially the brains (*lolo*) of a fish, dog, or hog offered to the gods.
'āla'apapa	Type of ancient dramatic *hula* (see Emerson 1909:57-59).
'alalā	Style of chanting with vibration and tremor.
ali'i	Chief, chiefly; possessed of some degree of social rank.
'ami	A *hula* step with hip revolutions; to do this step.
'anu'u	Scaffold-type of sacrificial offering stand on a *heiau*.
'auana ('auwana)	To wander, drift, go from place to place; modern or informal *hula*.
'aumakua	Ancestral god, of family or craft.
'ēkaha	The bird's-nest fern *(Asplenium nidus)*.
hala-pepe	A native tree *(Dracaena [Pleomele] aurea)* in the lily family; used on the *hula* altar to Laka.
hālau	Long rectangular house or shed, open at one or both ends for storage of canoes, or closed as a hall for *hula* instruction.
hānau	See *one*.
haole	Foreigner.
hau	A tree *(Hibiscus tiliaceus)* with a soft inner core.
heiau	Sacred structure or complex for offerings and rites for various gods.
hinahina-kuahiwi	A native Hawaiian aromatic shrub *(Artemesia australis)*.
ho'onānā	Informal *hula* (Emerson 1909:244).
ho'opa'a	Drummer and *hula* chanter; i.e., the memorizer.
hula	Dance; *mele hula* refer to the chants and songs used for its performance. Cf. *mele*.
hula 'ai ha'a	*Hula* step danced with bended knees; the chanting for this dance is usually bombastic and emphatic. (See Emerson 1909:58).
hula kāla'au	Dance to the rhythmic beating of sticks (Emerson 1909:116).
hula ki'i	*Hula* in which dancers postured stiffly like images. A dance of puppets (Emerson 1909:91).
hula kuolo	To kneel and beat a gourd to a chant, with gestures appropriate to the story. (See Emerson 1909:72).
hula 'ōlapa	Now, dance accompanied by chanting and drumming on a gourd.
hula pā ipu	Dance performed with gourd drums, also called *hula kuolo*.
'ie'ie	An endemic woody, branching climber *(Freycinetia arborea)*; one of five plants used on the *hula* altar.
'ilima	Small to large native shrubs (all species of *Sida*, esp. *S. fallax*), bearing yellow, orange, greenish, or dull-red flowers.

*Definitions are confined to contexts used in this volume; spelling and definition are according to Pukui & Elbert 1971, unless otherwise noted.

ipu	The bottle gourd *(Lagenaria siceraria)*; drum consisting of a single gourd, or made of two large gourds of unequal size joined together *(ipu hula)*.
kā'eke'eke	Bamboo pipes, varying in length, used to produce sounds by holding the bamboo upright and dropping one end on a mat or on the ground.
kahe	To cut or slit longitudinally.
kahiko	Ancient.
kahu	Honored attendant, guardian, keeper.
kahuna	Priest, minister, sorcerer.
kama'āina	Native born.
kaona	Hidden meaning in Hawaiian poetry; concealed reference, as to a person, thing, or place; words with double meanings.
kapa	Tapa, barkcloth.
kapu	Restriction, taboo, prohibition.
kauna'oa	A native plant *(Cuscuta sandwichiana)*, a parasitic vine, with slender orange stems used for *lei*. Grows densely on other plants.
kilu	Gourd or coconut shell cut lengthwise and used as quoit in game of same name.
kuahu	Altar of wood or stone upon which offerings were laid.
kukui	Candlenut tree *(Aleurites moluccana)*; oily kernels of the *kukui* nut were burned for light.
kumu hula	*Hula* teacher.
kūpe'e	Bracelet, anklet.
kupuna	Grandparent; grandparent generation.
lale	Legendary bird mentioned in old tales and songs as a sweet singer.
lama	All endemic kinds of ebony *(Diospyros,* syn. *Maha)*, hardwood trees with small flowers and fruits.
lehua	See *'ōhi'a lehua*.
lei	Garland, wreath.
luakini	Ruling chiefs' "state" *heiau*, where human sacrifices were offered.
lū'au	Hawaiian feast, named for the taro tops always served at one; this name is not ancient, but goes back at least to 1856, when so used by the *Pacific Commercial Advertiser*.
maile	A native twining shrub *(Alyxia olivaeformis)* with shiny fragrant leaves, used on the altar to Laka.
makahiki	Year; annual, yearly; ancient festival beginning about the middle of October and lasting about four months, with sports and religious festivities.
makai	Toward the sea.
makua	Parent, parent generation.
malo	Male's loincloth; chant in praise of chief's loincloth.
mana	In context, the main building on a *luakini heiau*.
mauka	Toward the uplands.
mele	Song, chant of any kind, poem, suitable for dancing. Cf. *oli*.
mele inoa	Name chant composed for a particular person, and belonging only to that person. Inheritable.
mōhai makana	Free-will offering.
mo'o	A female water spirit, or guardian of a pond.
na'au	Intestines, mind, heart, affections; of the heart or mind.

noa	Freed of taboo, released from restrictions.
'ōahi	Firebrand hurled from a cliff. *Na pali 'ōahi o Makana:* the cliffs of Makana, where firebrands were hurled forth.
'ohana	Family, relative, kin group.
'ōhi'a-'ai	The mountain apple *(Eugenia malaccensis)*.
'ōhi'a-lehua	A native tree *(Metrosideros macropus)* of hard wood used for images, house timbers, etc.
'ōlapa	Dancer, as contrasted with the chanter. See also *hula 'ōlapa*.
oli	Chant that was not danced to (cf. *mele*).
oli kāhea	Greeting chant; *kāhea*, recital of the first lines of a stanza by the dancer as a cue to the chanter.
oli kau	A sacred chant.
oli komo	A welcoming chant.
one	Sand; poetic name for land; *one hānau*, birthplace.
paepae	Assistant to the *po'opua'a*.
pahu	Large drum with one end covered with sharkskin; in context, a *hula* danced to the rhythm of this drum.
pala'ā	Lace fern, *Stenomeris chusana*.
palai	A fern, *Microlepia setosa*.
palapala	Formerly the arts of reading and writing; also, the Scriptures.
palapalai	Also *palai*, a fern.
pali	Cliff, precipice.
papa hehi	Resonant footboard sometimes used in *hula kāla'au*.
pāpala	A soft-wooded tree *(Charpentiera)* with a pithy center; firebrand.
pā'ū	Woman's skirt. In context, *hula* skirts worn by both men and women (see Emerson 1909:49).
piko	Navel, navel string, umbilical cord; crown of the head; fig., blood relative; genitals.
pi'o	Originally, marriage of a high chief with his full sister; child of such a marriage. Later, a child of half-sibling high chiefs was also called a *pi'o* chief. (Barrère, see p. 33).
po'e hula	Persons involved in the *hula* arts as dancers, chanters, drummers. Literally, *hula* people.
pōhaku piko	A sacred stone in which umbilical cords of babies were placed.
pule	Prayer, to pray; grace, blessing.
po'opua'a	Head pupil in a *hula* school.
pū'olo	Bundle, bag, container.
ti	A woody plant *(Cordyline terminalis)*, the leaves of which were used for many things, and the roots for famine food.
ulu	To grow, increase; inspire, possessed by a spirit.
'ulī'ulī	A gourd rattle containing seeds, with feathers at the top, used for *hula 'ulī'ulī*
'ūniki	Graduation exercises for *hula* and other ancient arts.

LITERATURE CITED

Advertiser
See *Pacific Commercial Advertiser.*

Andrews, Lorrin
1865 *A Dictionary of the Hawaiian Language....* Honolulu: H. M. Whitney. (Reprinted in 1974 by Charles E. Tuttle Co.)

Barrot, Theodore-Adolphe
1978 *Unless Haste is Made.* Rev. Daniel Dole, trans. Kailua, Hawai'i: Press Pacifica.

[Bates, G. W.]
1854 *Sandwich Island Notes by a Haole.* New York: Harper.

Beaglehole, John (ed.)
1967 *The Voyage of the* Resolution *and* Discovery...*1776-1780.* 2 vols. Cambridge: for the Hakluyt Society.

Beckwith, Martha Warren
1940 *Hawaiian Mythology.* (Reprinted 1970.) New Haven: Yale Univ. Press.
Ms. Hawaiian Ethnographic Notes, pp. 393-395. In Bishop Mus. Library.

Beechey, R. W.
1831 *Narrative of a Voyage...Performed in the Years 1825, 26, 27, 28.* 2 vols. London: Colburn & Bentley.

Bell, Edward
1929-30 "The Log of the Chatham." *Honolulu Mercury* 1(4):7-26;1(5):55-69;1(6):76-90; 2(1):80-91; 2(2):119-129. Honolulu.

Bennett, Wendell C.
1931 *Archaeology of Kauai.* B. P. Bishop Mus. Bull. 80.

Bingham, Hiram
1847 *A Residence of Twenty-One Years in the Sandwich Islands.* Hartford: Huntington.

Bloxam, Andrew
1925 *Diary of Andrew Bloxam.* B. P. Bishop Mus. Spec. Publ. 10.

[Byron, Lord]
1925 *Voyage of the H.M.S.* Blonde *to the Sandwich Islands, in the Years 1824-1825.* Capt. Lord Byron, Commander. Compiled by Martha Graham. London: John Murray.

Campbell, Archibald
1967 *A Voyage Round the World from 1806 to 1812.* Honolulu: Univ. Hawaii Press.

Chamisso, Adelbert von
1862 "Remarks and Opinions Respecting the Sandwich Islands." *The Friend* 2(3):9, 10, 11, 14, 15. (February 1.) Honolulu.

Civil Code of the Hawaiian Islands, Passed in...1859.
1859 Honolulu: printed for the government.

Cook, James, and James King
1784 *A Voyage to the Pacific Ocean...1776...1780.* 3 vols. London: W. and A. Strahan.

Corney, Peter
1965 *Early Voyages in the North Pacific.* Glen Adams, ed. Fairfield, Wash.: Ye Galleon Press.

Davies, Theo. H.
n.d. "Early Recollections of Honolulu, Written in 1885." Mimeographed. In Bishop Mus. Library.

Day, A. Grove (ed.)
1975 *Mark Twain's Letters from Hawaii.* Honolulu: Univ. Hawaii Press.

Degener, Otto
1945 *Plants of Hawaii National Parks.* Ann Arbor: Edwards Bros.

Dickey, Lyle
Ms. Notes on Heiau of Kauai. In Kaua'i Historical Society Library.

Ellis, William
1917 *A Narrative of a Tour through Hawaii....* Advertiser Historical Series No. 2. Honolulu: Hawaiian Gazette. (Reprinted 1963: Honolulu Advertiser.)

Emerson, Nathaniel B.
1909 *Unwritten Literature of Hawaii: The Sacred Songs of the Hula.* Smithsonian Inst. Bureau of American Ethnology Bull. 38. Washington, D. C.

1915 *Pele and Hiiaka: A Myth from Hawaii.* Honolulu: Honolulu Star-Bulletin Press.

Emory, Kenneth P.
1921 *An Archaeological Survey of Haleakala.* Bishop Mus. Occasional Papers 7(11).

1928 "The Ruins at Kē'ē, Hā'ena." Report to the Kaua'i Historical Society (Reproduced here as Appendix E.)

1929 "Ruins at Kee, Haena, Kauai." *Hawaiian Annual for 1929.* pp. 88-94. Honolulu.

Ms. Field Notes, Kē'ē, Hā'ena, Kaua'i (1921). In Bishop Mus.

Emory, Kenneth P., Edward J. Ladd, and Lloyd J. Soehren
1965 "The Archaeological Resources of Hawaii Volcanoes National Park, Hawaii. Part II, Additional Sites, Test Excavations, and Petroglyphs." Mimeographed. Honolulu: Dept. Anthropology, B. P. Bishop Mus.

Emory, T.
Ms. "Hawaiian Life in Kalalau Valley, Kauai." An interview with John Hanohano Pā and his mother, Wahine-i-Keouli Pā (1949). Typescript in Dept. Anthropology, B. P. Bishop Mus.

Fornander, Abraham
1880 *An Account of the Polynesian Race....* Vol. 2. London: Trubner & Co. (Reprinted by Tuttle, 1969.)

1916-20 *Fornander Collection of Hawaiian Antiquities and Folklore.* B. P. Bishop Mus. Memoirs. Vols. 4, 5, & 6.

Friend, The
1913 Letter of Samuel Ruggles, dated July 4, 1820. October, p. 235.

1925 Journal of Samuel Whitney. September, p. 208.

Gast, R. H., and Agnes C. Conrad
1973 *Don Francisco de Paula Marin.* Honolulu: U. Hawaii Press for Hawaiian Historical Society.

Gay, Francis
Ms. Notebook. Bishop Mus. Coll., Case 4, H84. 1873:69.

Gill, Lorin Tarr
1923 "Hawaiians Are Not to Blame for the Degradation of the Hula." *Paradise of the Pacific.* March, pp. 7-8.

Gilman, Gorham

1908 "An Extract from a Journal Written by Hon. Gorham D. Gilman, in His Youth, Entitled, 'Rustications on Kauai and Niihau, in the Summer of 1845.'" *Hawaiian Historical Society Annual Report for 1907.* pp. 52-55. Honolulu.

Ms. Rustications on Kauai and Niihau in the Summer of 1845. Manuscript in Hawaiian Historical Society Library.

Handy, E. S. Craighill, and Mary Kawena Pukui

1958 *The Polynesian Family System in Ka-u, Hawai'i.* Wellington: Polynesian Society.

Houston, Victor S. K. (trans.)

1940 "Chamisso in Hawaii." *Forty-Eighth Annual Report of the Hawaiian Historical Society for the Year 1939.* pp. 55-82. Honolulu.

Ii, John

1959 *Fragments of Hawaiian History.* Mary K. Pukui, trans.; Dorothy B. Barrère, ed. Honolulu: Bishop Mus. Press. (Reprinted 1963, 1973.)

Kamakau, Samuel M.

1961 *Ruling Chiefs of Hawaii.* Honolulu: Kamehameha Schools Press.

1964 *Ka Po̱'e Kahiko (The People of Old).* Mary K. Pukui, trans.; Dorothy B. Barrère, ed. B. P. Bishop Mus. Spec. Publ. 51.

1976 *The Works of the People of Old: Na Hana a Ka Po'e Kahiko.* Mary K. Pukui, trans.; Dorothy B. Barrère, ed. B. P. Bishop Mus. Spec. Publ. 61.

Kekahuna, Henry E. P.

1959 Ka-ulu-a-Paoa Heiau, Kē-ē, Ha'ena, Kaua'i. Brief descriptive notes, ground plan, and elevation. Oct. 4, 1959.

Knudsen, V.

n.d. *Teller of Hawaiian Tales.* Honolulu: Coca-Cola Bottling Co. of Honolulu, Ltd. (Originated and produced by W. H. Male, Advertising & Public Relation Counsel. Honolulu, 1945.)

Kuokoa See *Nupepa Kuokoa, Ka*

Laws, Session

1851 *Laws of His Majesty Kamehameha III...passed by the Nobles and Representatives... 1851.* Honolulu: printed by order of the government.

1864-65 *Laws of His Majesty Kamehameha V...passed by the Legislative Assembly*...1864-65. Honolulu: printed by order of the government.

1870 *Laws of His Majesty Kamehameha V...passed by the Legislative Assembly...1870.* Honolulu: printed by order of the government.

Loomis, Elisha

Ms. "The Journal of E. Loomis, Hawaii, 1824-1826." Mimeographed. Compiled by William D. Westervelt in 1937. Honolulu.

Luomala, Katharine

1955 *Voices on the Wind.* Honolulu: Bishop Mus. Press.

Malo, David

1951 *Hawaiian Antiquities.* N. B. Emerson, trans. B. P. Bishop Mus. Spec. Publ. 2 (2nd ed.) (Reprinted 1971.)

Manu, Moses

1899 & Ms. "A Hawaiian Legend of a Terrible War between Pele...and Waka...." *Ka Loea Kalaiaina,* May 13-Dec. 30, 1899. Mary K. Pukui, trans. Manuscript copy in Bishop Museum Library.

Menzies, Archibald
1920 *Hawaii Nei 128 Years Ago.* W. F. Wilson, ed. Honolulu.

Missionary Register, The
1823 *The Missionary Register for MDCCCXXIII....* London: L. B. Seeley & Son.

Neal, Marie C.
1965 *In Gardens of Hawaii.* B. P. Bishop Mus. Spec. Publ. 50.

Nupepa Kuokoa, Ka
1864-80 Weekly in Hawaiian language. Honolulu. Letters, as cited. Mary K. Pukui, trans.

1883 "Ka Lapuwale o ka Poaono nei." March 3, p. 2, col. 1.

1886 "Ka Iubile La Hanau." Nov. 27, p. 2, col. 6; Dec. 4, p. 2, c. 4.

Pacific Commercial Advertiser, The
1883 "The Coronation Luau at the Palace." Feb. 27, p. 2, cols. 3, 4.

1883a "Local and General." Feb. 28, p. 3, col. 1.

1886 "Saturday's Parade." Nov. 22, p. 2, col. 3.

1886a "The Royal Luau." Nov. 24, p. 2, col. 3.

Papa Kuhikuhi o na Hula Poni Moi, Feb. 12, 1883.
1883 List of *hula* at the Coronation of King Kalākaua. In Bishop Mus. Library. (Reprinted here as Appendix D.)

Pukui, Mary K.
1936 "Ancient Hulas of Kauai." *The Garden Island*, Feb. 18, 25; March 3, 10, 17, 24.

1942 "The Hula, Hawaii's Own Dance." *Thrum's Hawaiian Annual and...All About Hawaii.* pp. 107-112. Honolulu.

1943 "Games of My Hawaiian Childhood." *California Folklore Quarterly* 2(3):205-220.

Ms. Notes, interviews on Kaua'i. (n.d.) In Dept. Anthropology, B. P. Bishop Mus. Honolulu.

Pukui, Mary K., and Samuel H. Elbert
1971 *Hawaiian-English Dictionary.* 4th ed. Honolulu: Univ. Hawaii Press.

Pukui, M. K., Samuel H. Elbert, and Esther T. Mookini
1974 *Place Names of Hawaii.* Honolulu: Univ. Hawaii Press.

Pukui, Mary Kawena, E. W. Haertig, and C. A. Lee
1972 *Nānā I Ke Kumu (Look to the Source).* Honolulu: Hui Hānai, Queen Liliuokalani Children's Center.

Rice, William Hyde
1923 *Hawaiian Legends.* Bishop Mus. Bull. 3. Honolulu. Reprinted 1977, Bishop Mus. Spec. Publ. 63.

Roberts, Helen
1926 *Ancient Hawaiian Music.* B. P. Bishop Mus. Bull. 29.

Schmitt, Robert C.
1968 *Demographic Statistics of Hawaii: 1778-1965.* Honolulu: Univ. Hawaii Press.

Stauder, Catherine
1979 Extracts from Kaua'i Museum notes; in letter to D. Barrère, May 9.

Stewart, C. S.
1839 *A Residence in the Sandwich Islands.* Boston: Weeks, Jordan & Co.

Stokes, John F. G.
1933 "New Bases for Hawaiian Chronology." *Hawaiian Historical Society Forty-First Annual Report for the Year 1932.* pp. 23-65. Honolulu.

Thrum, Thomas G.
1875 "The Hawaiian Hula." *The Islander* 1(22):146. July 23. Honolulu.

1907 "Heiaus and Heiau Sites throughout the Hawaiian Islands." *Hawaiian Annual for 1907,* pp. 36-48. Honolulu.

1918 "Must We Countenance the Hula." *Hawaiian Annual for 1918,* pp. 120-125.

1924 "Heiaus (Temples) of Hawaii Nei: A Brief Sketch of the More Notable Heiaus throughout the Hawaiian Islands." *Hawaiian Historical Society Report for the Year 1923.* pp. 14-36. Honolulu.

1929 "Hiiaka and Lohiau." *Hawaiian Annual for 1929,* pp. 95-103.

Vancouver, George
1801 *A Voyage of Discovery to the North Pacific Ocean....* 6 vols. London: Stockdale.

Westervelt, W. D.
1915 *Legends of Gods and Ghosts.* Boston: George Ellis.

Wilcox, Elsie H.
Ms. "Hanalei in History." A Paper read before the Kaua'i Historical Society, April 26, 1917. Typescript, in Kaua'i Historical Society. 20 pp.

Wilkes, Charles
1845 *Narrative of the United States Exploring Expedition during the Years 1838, 1839, 1840, 1842.* 5 vols. Philadelphia: Lea & Blanchard.

PACIFIC ANTHROPOLOGICAL RECORDS

No.

1 *Studies in a Hawaiian Community: Na Makamaka o Nanakuli.* Ronald Gallimore and Alan Howard, Editors. 1968. 147 pp; 23 tables; 7 figs. (Out of Print)*

2 *Pinao Bay Site (H24): A Small Prehistoric Fishing Settlement Near South Point (Ka Lae), Hawaii.* William J. Wallace and Edith Taylor Wallace. 1969. 34 pp; 4 tables; 14 figs; 10 plates. (Out of Print)*

3 *The Kumuhonua Legends: A Study of Late 19th Century Hawaiian Stories of Creation and Origins.* Dorothy B. Barrère. 1969. 47 pp; 2 tables. $ 2.50

4 *Makaha Valley Historical Project: Interim Rept. No. 1.* Roger C. Green, Editor. 1969. 101 pp; 3 tables; 32 figs; glossary. (Out of Print)*

5 *Behavior Modification of the Underachieving Rural Hawaiian: An Experimental Classroom.* Barbara B. Sloggett. 1969. 14 pp. (Out of Print)*

6, 7, 8, and 9, bound together. 1969. $ 5.00

6 *Historical Background of the South Point Area, Ka'u, Hawaii.* Marion Kelly. 73 pp; 5 tables; 28 figs.

7 *Waiahukini Shelter, Site H8, Ka'u, Hawaii.* Kenneth P. Emory, William J. Bonk, and Yosihiko H. Sinoto. 12 pp; 4 tables; 9 figs.

8 *Age of the Sites in the South Point Area, Ka'u, Hawaii.* Kenneth P. Emory and Yosihiko H. Sinoto. 17 pp; 5 tables; 6 figs.

9 *Human Skeletal Remains from Sand Dune Site (H1), South Point (Ka Lae), Hawaii: A Preliminary Examination.* Jane Hainline Underwood. 24 pp; 5 tables; 5 figs.

10 *Makaha Valley Historical Project: Interim Rept. No. 2.* Roger C. Green, Editor. 1970. 139 pp; 3 tables; 46 figs; glossary. $ 6.50

11 *Studies in Oceanic Culture History, Vol. 1.* R. C. Green and M. Kelly, Editors. 1970. Papers presented at Wenner-Gren Symposium on Oceanic Culture History. Sigatoka, Fiji. August, 1969. 206 pp; 13 tables; 60 figs. (Out of Print)*

12 *Studies in Oceanic Culture History, Vol. 2.* R. C. Green and M. Kelly, Editors. 1971. Papers presented at Wenner-Gren Symposium on Oceanic Culture History. Sigatoka, Fiji. August, 1969. 120 pp; 5 graphs; 25 figs. (Out of Print)*

13 *Studies in Oceanic Culture History, Vol. 3.* R. C. Green and M. Kelly, Editors. 1972. Papers presented at Wenner-Gren Symposium on Oceanic Culture History. Sigatoka, Fiji. August,1969. 160 pp; 10 tables; 8 figs. $ 4.00

14 *Molokai: A Site Survey.* Catherine C. Summers. 1971. 241 pp; 3 tables; 85 figs; foldout map; glossary. (Out of Print)*

15 *Anaehoomalu: A Hawaiian Oasis. Preliminary Rept. of Salvage Research in South Kohala, Hawaii.* William Barrera, Jr. 1971. 179 pp; 2 tables; 101 figs. (Out of Print)*

*Available through University Microfilms International, 300 North Zeeb Road, Ann Arbor, Michigan 48106.

Prices subject to change without notice.

PACIFIC ANTHROPOLOGICAL RECORDS (continued)

No.

16 and 17, bound together. 1972. $ 4.50

16 *Excavation of a Habitation Cave, Hanapete'o Valley, Hiva Oa, Marquesas Islands.* Arne Skjølsvold. 41 pp; 4 tables; 31 figs.

17 *A Settlement Pattern Survey, Hanatekua Valley, Hiva Oa, Marquesas Islands.* Peter S. Bellwood. 49 pp; 5 tables; 19 figs.

18 *Makaha Valley Historical Project: Interim Rept. No. 3.* Edmund J. Ladd and D. E. Yen, Editors. 1972. 113 pp; 5 tables; 47 figs. $ 6.50

19 *Makaha Valley Historical Project: Interim Rept. No. 4.* Edmund J. Ladd, Editor. 1973. 64 pp; 33 figs. $ 5.00

20 *The Missionary Censuses of Hawaii.* Robert C. Schmitt. 1973. 50 pp; 5 tables; 7 appendices. $ 3.00

21 *Anuta: A Polynesian Outlier in the Solomon Islands.* D. E. Yen and Janet Gordon, Editors. 1973. 155 pp; 40 tables; 41 figs. $ 6.00

22 *Material Culture of the Tuamotu Archipelago.* Kenneth P. Emory. 1975. 253 pp; 6 tables; 191 figs. Clothbound. $16.50

23 *Kamehameha in Kona: Two Documentary Studies.* "Kamakahonu: Kamehameha's Last Residence" and "'The Morning Star Alone Knows...': A Documentary Search for the Bones of Kamehameha." Dorothy B. Barrère. 1975. 108 pp; 19 figs. $ 6.00

24 *Prehistory and Ecology in a Windward Hawaiian Valley: Halawa Valley, Molokai.* Patrick Vinton Kirch and Marion Kelly, Editors. 1975. 207 pp; 45 tables; 79 figs. (Out of Print)*

25 *Excavations on Upolu, Western Samoa.* Jesse D. Jennings, Richard N. Holmer, Joel C. Janetski, and Howard L. Smith. Appendix by W. R. Dickinson. 1976. 115 pp; 5 tables; 23 figs. $ 6.00

26 *Hawai'i in 1819: A Narrative Account by Louis Claude de Saulses de Freycinet.* Notes and Comments by Marion Kelly. Ella Wiswell, Translator. 1978. 138 pp; 30 figs. $ 6.00

27 *Archaeological Research in the Cook Islands.* Peter Bellwood. 1978. 214 pp; 9 tables; 98 figs. $10.00

28 *Symbols of Sovereignty: Feather Girdles of Tahiti and Hawai'i.* Roger G. Rose. 1978. 69 pp; 33 figs. $ 6.00

29 *Marine Exploitation in Prehistoric Hawai'i: Archaeological Investigations at Kalahuipua'a, Hawai'i Island.* Patrick Vinton Kirch. 1979. 235 pp; 64 tables; 105 figs. $11.00

30 *Hula: Historical Perspectives.* Dorothy B. Barrère, Mary Kawena Pukui, and Marion Kelly. 1980. Reprinted. 168 pp; 29 figs. $15.00

31 *Mākaha Before 1880 A. D. Makaha Valley Historical Project--Summary. Report No. 5.* Roger C. Green. 1980. 90 pp; 11 tables; 17 figs. $ 7.00

PACIFIC ANTHROPOLOGICAL RECORDS (continued)

No.

32 *Archaeological Excavations in Western Samoa.* Jesse D. Jennings and Richard N. Holmer. 1980. 155 pp; 19 tables; 50 figs. $ 8.00

33 *Nineteenth Century Hawaiian Chant.* Elizabeth Tatar. 1982. 176 pp; 33 tables; photographs of chanters; spectrogram transcriptions; soundsheet. $15.00

34 *The Prehistoric Archaeology of Norfolk Island.* Jim Specht. 1984. 76 pp; 15 figs; 3 tables; 3 appendices. $ 6.00

35 *Caroline Islands Archaeology: Investigations on Fefan, Faraulep, Woleai, and Lamotrek.* Yosihiko H. Sinoto, Editor. 1984. 149 pp; 18 tables; 51 figs. $14.00

36 *Social Relations in Ancient Tongareva.* Andrew R. T. Campbell. 1985. 112 pp; 7 tables; 30 figs. $14.00

C-328

CAREER EXAMINATION SERIES

THIS IS YOUR **PASSBOOK**® FOR ...

HOSPITAL CLERK

NLC®
NATIONAL LEARNING CORPORATION®
passbooks.com

NLC®

National Learning Corporation

212 Michael Drive, Syosset, NY 11791
(516) 921-8888 • www.passbooks.com
E-mail: info@passbooks.com

PUBLISHED IN THE UNITED STATES OF AMERICA

PASSBOOK® SERIES

THE *PASSBOOK® SERIES* has been created to prepare applicants and candidates for the ultimate academic battlefield – the examination room.

At some time in our lives, each and every one of us may be required to take an examination – for validation, matriculation, admission, qualification, registration, certification, or licensure.

Based on the assumption that every applicant or candidate has met the basic formal educational standards, has taken the required number of courses, and read the necessary texts, the *PASSBOOK® SERIES* furnishes the one special preparation which may assure passing with confidence, instead of failing with insecurity. Examination questions – together with answers – are furnished as the basic vehicle for study so that the mysteries of the examination and its compounding difficulties may be eliminated or diminished by a sure method.

This book is meant to help you pass your examination provided that you qualify and are serious in your objective.

The entire field is reviewed through the huge store of content information which is succinctly presented through a provocative and challenging approach – the question-and-answer method.

A climate of success is established by furnishing the correct answers at the end of each test.

You soon learn to recognize types of questions, forms of questions, and patterns of questioning. You may even begin to anticipate expected outcomes.

You perceive that many questions are repeated or adapted so that you can gain acute insights, which may enable you to score many sure points.

You learn how to confront new questions, or types of questions, and to attack them confidently and work out the correct answers.

You note objectives and emphases, and recognize pitfalls and dangers, so that you may make positive educational adjustments.

Moreover, you are kept fully informed in relation to new concepts, methods, practices, and directions in the field.

You discover that you arre actually taking the examination all the time: you are preparing for the examination by "taking" an examination, not by reading extraneous and/or supererogatory textbooks.

In short, this PASSBOOK®, used directedly, should be an important factor in helping you to pass your test.

HOSPITAL CLERK

DUTIES

This is routine clerical work involving responsibility for assisting staff nurses and other hospital personnel in various clerical duties associated with patient care in a hospital. The work is performed under the immediate supervision of a nurse or other professional hospital staff. The incumbent does related work as required.

SCOPE OF THE EXAMINATION

The written test will cover knowledge, skills and/or abilities in such areas as:

1. Clerical operations with letters and numbers;
2. Medical terminology;
3. Name and number checking;
4. Office record keeping; and
5. Understanding and interpreting written material.

HOW TO TAKE A TEST

I. YOU MUST PASS AN EXAMINATION

A. WHAT EVERY CANDIDATE SHOULD KNOW

Examination applicants often ask us for help in preparing for the written test. What can I study in advance? What kinds of questions will be asked? How will the test be given? How will the papers be graded?

As an applicant for a civil service examination, you may be wondering about some of these things. Our purpose here is to suggest effective methods of advance study and to describe civil service examinations.

Your chances for success on this examination can be increased if you know how to prepare. Those "pre-examination jitters" can be reduced if you know what to expect. You can even experience an adventure in good citizenship if you know why civil service exams are given.

B. WHY ARE CIVIL SERVICE EXAMINATIONS GIVEN?

Civil service examinations are important to you in two ways. As a citizen, you want public jobs filled by employees who know how to do their work. As a job seeker, you want a fair chance to compete for that job on an equal footing with other candidates. The best-known means of accomplishing this two-fold goal is the competitive examination.

Exams are widely publicized throughout the nation. They may be administered for jobs in federal, state, city, municipal, town or village governments or agencies.

Any citizen may apply, with some limitations, such as the age or residence of applicants. Your experience and education may be reviewed to see whether you meet the requirements for the particular examination. When these requirements exist, they are reasonable and applied consistently to all applicants. Thus, a competitive examination may cause you some uneasiness now, but it is your privilege and safeguard.

C. HOW ARE CIVIL SERVICE EXAMS DEVELOPED?

Examinations are carefully written by trained technicians who are specialists in the field known as "psychological measurement," in consultation with recognized authorities in the field of work that the test will cover. These experts recommend the subject matter areas or skills to be tested; only those knowledges or skills important to your success on the job are included. The most reliable books and source materials available are used as references. Together, the experts and technicians judge the difficulty level of the questions.

Test technicians know how to phrase questions so that the problem is clearly stated. Their ethics do not permit "trick" or "catch" questions. Questions may have been tried out on sample groups, or subjected to statistical analysis, to determine their usefulness.

Written tests are often used in combination with performance tests, ratings of training and experience, and oral interviews. All of these measures combine to form the best-known means of finding the right person for the right job.

II. HOW TO PASS THE WRITTEN TEST

A. NATURE OF THE EXAMINATION

To prepare intelligently for civil service examinations, you should know how they differ from school examinations you have taken. In school you were assigned certain definite pages to read or subjects to cover. The examination questions were quite detailed and usually emphasized memory. Civil service exams, on the other hand, try to discover your present ability to perform the duties of a position, plus your potentiality to learn these duties. In other words, a civil service exam attempts to predict how successful you will be. Questions cover such a broad area that they cannot be as minute and detailed as school exam questions.

In the public service similar kinds of work, or positions, are grouped together in one "class." This process is known as *position-classification*. All the positions in a class are paid according to the salary range for that class. One class title covers all of these positions, and they are all tested by the same examination.

B. FOUR BASIC STEPS

1) Study the announcement

How, then, can you know what subjects to study? Our best answer is: "Learn as much as possible about the class of positions for which you've applied." The exam will test the knowledge, skills and abilities needed to do the work.

Your most valuable source of information about the position you want is the official exam announcement. This announcement lists the training and experience qualifications. Check these standards and apply only if you come reasonably close to meeting them.

The brief description of the position in the examination announcement offers some clues to the subjects which will be tested. Think about the job itself. Review the duties in your mind. Can you perform them, or are there some in which you are rusty? Fill in the blank spots in your preparation.

Many jurisdictions preview the written test in the exam announcement by including a section called "Knowledge and Abilities Required," "Scope of the Examination," or some similar heading. Here you will find out specifically what fields will be tested.

2) Review your own background

Once you learn in general what the position is all about, and what you need to know to do the work, ask yourself which subjects you already know fairly well and which need improvement. You may wonder whether to concentrate on improving your strong areas or on building some background in your fields of weakness. When the announcement has specified "some knowledge" or "considerable knowledge," or has used adjectives like "beginning principles of..." or "advanced ... methods," you can get a clue as to the number and difficulty of questions to be asked in any given field. More questions, and hence broader coverage, would be included for those subjects which are more important in the work. Now weigh your strengths and weaknesses against the job requirements and prepare accordingly.

3) Determine the level of the position

Another way to tell how intensively you should prepare is to understand the level of the job for which you are applying. Is it the entering level? In other words, is this the position in which beginners in a field of work are hired? Or is it an intermediate or advanced level? Sometimes this is indicated by such words as "Junior" or "Senior" in the class title. Other jurisdictions use Roman numerals to designate the level – Clerk I, Clerk II, for example. The word "Supervisor" sometimes appears in the title. If the level is not indicated by the title, check the description of duties. Will you be working under very close supervision, or will you have responsibility for independent decisions in this work?

4) Choose appropriate study materials

Now that you know the subjects to be examined and the relative amount of each subject to be covered, you can choose suitable study materials. For beginning level jobs, or even advanced ones, if you have a pronounced weakness in some aspect of your training, read a modern, standard textbook in that field. Be sure it is up to date and has general coverage. Such books are normally available at your library, and the librarian will be glad to help you locate one. For entry-level positions, questions of appropriate difficulty are chosen – neither highly advanced questions, nor those too simple. Such questions require careful thought but not advanced training.

If the position for which you are applying is technical or advanced, you will read more advanced, specialized material. If you are already familiar with the basic principles of your field, elementary textbooks would waste your time. Concentrate on advanced textbooks and technical periodicals. Think through the concepts and review difficult problems in your field.

These are all general sources. You can get more ideas on your own initiative, following these leads. For example, training manuals and publications of the government agency which employs workers in your field can be useful, particularly for technical and professional positions. A letter or visit to the government department involved may result in more specific study suggestions, and certainly will provide you with a more definite idea of the exact nature of the position you are seeking.

III. KINDS OF TESTS

Tests are used for purposes other than measuring knowledge and ability to perform specified duties. For some positions, it is equally important to test ability to make adjustments to new situations or to profit from training. In others, basic mental abilities not dependent on information are essential. Questions which test these things may not appear as pertinent to the duties of the position as those which test for knowledge and information. Yet they are often highly important parts of a fair examination. For very general questions, it is almost impossible to help you direct your study efforts. What we can do is to point out some of the more common of these general abilities needed in public service positions and describe some typical questions.

1) General information

Broad, general information has been found useful for predicting job success in some kinds of work. This is tested in a variety of ways, from vocabulary lists to questions about current events. Basic background in some field of work, such as sociology or economics, may be sampled in a group of questions. Often these are principles which have become familiar to most persons through exposure rather than through formal training. It is difficult to advise you how to study for these questions; being alert to the world around you is our best suggestion.

2) Verbal ability

An example of an ability needed in many positions is verbal or language ability. Verbal ability is, in brief, the ability to use and understand words. Vocabulary and grammar tests are typical measures of this ability. Reading comprehension or paragraph interpretation questions are common in many kinds of civil service tests. You are given a paragraph of written material and asked to find its central meaning.

3) Numerical ability

Number skills can be tested by the familiar arithmetic problem, by checking paired lists of numbers to see which are alike and which are different, or by interpreting charts and graphs. In the latter test, a graph may be printed in the test booklet which you are asked to use as the basis for answering questions.

4) Observation

A popular test for law-enforcement positions is the observation test. A picture is shown to you for several minutes, then taken away. Questions about the picture test your ability to observe both details and larger elements.

5) Following directions

In many positions in the public service, the employee must be able to carry out written instructions dependably and accurately. You may be given a chart with several columns, each column listing a variety of information. The questions require you to carry out directions involving the information given in the chart.

6) Skills and aptitudes

Performance tests effectively measure some manual skills and aptitudes. When the skill is one in which you are trained, such as typing or shorthand, you can practice. These tests are often very much like those given in business school or high school courses. For many of the other skills and aptitudes, however, no short-time preparation can be made. Skills and abilities natural to you or that you have developed throughout your lifetime are being tested.

Many of the general questions just described provide all the data needed to answer the questions and ask you to use your reasoning ability to find the answers. Your best preparation for these tests, as well as for tests of facts and ideas, is to be at your physical and mental best. You, no doubt, have your own methods of getting into an exam-taking mood and keeping “in shape.” The next section lists some ideas on this subject.

IV. KINDS OF QUESTIONS

Only rarely is the “essay” question, which you answer in narrative form, used in civil service tests. Civil service tests are usually of the short-answer type. Full instructions for answering these questions will be given to you at the examination. But in case this is your first experience with short-answer questions and separate answer sheets, here is what you need to know:

1) Multiple-choice Questions

Most popular of the short-answer questions is the "multiple choice" or "best answer" question. It can be used, for example, to test for factual knowledge, ability to solve problems or judgment in meeting situations found at work.

A multiple-choice question is normally one of three types—

- It can begin with an incomplete statement followed by several possible endings. You are to find the one ending which *best* completes the statement, although some of the others may not be entirely wrong.
- It can also be a complete statement in the form of a question which is answered by choosing one of the statements listed.
- It can be in the form of a problem – again you select the best answer.

Here is an example of a multiple-choice question with a discussion which should give you some clues as to the method for choosing the right answer:

When an employee has a complaint about his assignment, the action which will *best* help him overcome his difficulty is to

A. discuss his difficulty with his coworkers
B. take the problem to the head of the organization
C. take the problem to the person who gave him the assignment
D. say nothing to anyone about his complaint

In answering this question, you should study each of the choices to find which is best. Consider choice "A" – Certainly an employee may discuss his complaint with fellow employees, but no change or improvement can result, and the complaint remains unresolved. Choice "B" is a poor choice since the head of the organization probably does not know what assignment you have been given, and taking your problem to him is known as "going over the head" of the supervisor. The supervisor, or person who made the assignment, is the person who can clarify it or correct any injustice. Choice "C" is, therefore, correct. To say nothing, as in choice "D," is unwise. Supervisors have and interest in knowing the problems employees are facing, and the employee is seeking a solution to his problem.

2) True/False Questions

The "true/false" or "right/wrong" form of question is sometimes used. Here a complete statement is given. Your job is to decide whether the statement is right or wrong.

SAMPLE: A roaming cell-phone call to a nearby city costs less than a non-roaming call to a distant city.

This statement is wrong, or false, since roaming calls are more expensive.

This is not a complete list of all possible question forms, although most of the others are variations of these common types. You will always get complete directions for answering questions. Be sure you understand *how* to mark your answers – ask questions until you do.

V. RECORDING YOUR ANSWERS

Computer terminals are used more and more today for many different kinds of exams.

For an examination with very few applicants, you may be told to record your answers in the test booklet itself. Separate answer sheets are much more common. If this separate answer sheet is to be scored by machine – and this is often the case – it is highly important that you mark your answers correctly in order to get credit.

An electronic scoring machine is often used in civil service offices because of the speed with which papers can be scored. Machine-scored answer sheets must be marked with a pencil, which will be given to you. This pencil has a high graphite content which responds to the electronic scoring machine. As a matter of fact, stray dots may register as answers, so do not let your pencil rest on the answer sheet while you are pondering the correct answer. Also, if your pencil lead breaks or is otherwise defective, ask for another.

Since the answer sheet will be dropped in a slot in the scoring machine, be careful not to bend the corners or get the paper crumpled.

The answer sheet normally has five vertical columns of numbers, with 30 numbers to a column. These numbers correspond to the question numbers in your test booklet. After each number, going across the page are four or five pairs of dotted lines. These short dotted lines have small letters or numbers above them. The first two pairs may also have a "T" or "F" above the letters. This indicates that the first two pairs only are to be used if the questions are of the true-false type. If the questions are multiple choice, disregard the "T" and "F" and pay attention only to the small letters or numbers.

Answer your questions in the manner of the sample that follows:

32. The largest city in the United States is
    - A. Washington, D.C.
    - B. New York City
    - C. Chicago
    - D. Detroit
    - E. San Francisco

1) Choose the answer you think is best. (New York City is the largest, so "B" is correct.)
2) Find the row of dotted lines numbered the same as the question you are answering. (Find row number 32)
3) Find the pair of dotted lines corresponding to the answer. (Find the pair of lines under the mark "B.")
4) Make a solid black mark between the dotted lines.

VI. BEFORE THE TEST

Common sense will help you find procedures to follow to get ready for an examination. Too many of us, however, overlook these sensible measures. Indeed, nervousness and fatigue have been found to be the most serious reasons why applicants fail to do their best on civil service tests. Here is a list of reminders:

- Begin your preparation early – Don't wait until the last minute to go scurrying around for books and materials or to find out what the position is all about.
- Prepare continuously – An hour a night for a week is better than an all-night cram session. This has been definitely established. What is more, a night a week for a month will return better dividends than crowding your study into a shorter period of time.
- Locate the place of the exam – You have been sent a notice telling you when and where to report for the examination. If the location is in a different town or otherwise unfamiliar to you, it would be well to inquire the best route and learn something about the building.
- Relax the night before the test – Allow your mind to rest. Do not study at all that night. Plan some mild recreation or diversion; then go to bed early and get a good night's sleep.
- Get up early enough to make a leisurely trip to the place for the test – This way unforeseen events, traffic snarls, unfamiliar buildings, etc. will not upset you.
- Dress comfortably – A written test is not a fashion show. You will be known by number and not by name, so wear something comfortable.
- Leave excess paraphernalia at home – Shopping bags and odd bundles will get in your way. You need bring only the items mentioned in the official notice you received; usually everything you need is provided. Do not bring reference books to the exam. They will only confuse those last minutes and be taken away from you when in the test room.
- Arrive somewhat ahead of time – If because of transportation schedules you must get there very early, bring a newspaper or magazine to take your mind off yourself while waiting.
- Locate the examination room – When you have found the proper room, you will be directed to the seat or part of the room where you will sit. Sometimes you are given a sheet of instructions to read while you are waiting. Do not fill out any forms until you are told to do so; just read them and be prepared.
- Relax and prepare to listen to the instructions
- If you have any physical problem that may keep you from doing your best, be sure to tell the test administrator. If you are sick or in poor health, you really cannot do your best on the exam. You can come back and take the test some other time.

VII. AT THE TEST

The day of the test is here and you have the test booklet in your hand. The temptation to get going is very strong. Caution! There is more to success than knowing the right answers. You must know how to identify your papers and understand variations in the type of short-answer question used in this particular examination. Follow these suggestions for maximum results from your efforts:

1) Cooperate with the monitor

The test administrator has a duty to create a situation in which you can be as much at ease as possible. He will give instructions, tell you when to begin, check to see that you are marking your answer sheet correctly, and so on. He is not there to guard you, although he will see that your competitors do not take unfair advantage. He wants to help you do your best.

2) Listen to all instructions

Don't jump the gun! Wait until you understand all directions. In most civil service tests you get more time than you need to answer the questions. So don't be in a hurry. Read each word of instructions until you clearly understand the meaning. Study the examples, listen to all announcements and follow directions. Ask questions if you do not understand what to do.

3) Identify your papers

Civil service exams are usually identified by number only. You will be assigned a number; you must not put your name on your test papers. Be sure to copy your number correctly. Since more than one exam may be given, copy your exact examination title.

4) Plan your time

Unless you are told that a test is a "speed" or "rate of work" test, speed itself is usually not important. Time enough to answer all the questions will be provided, but this does not mean that you have all day. An overall time limit has been set. Divide the total time (in minutes) by the number of questions to determine the approximate time you have for each question.

5) Do not linger over difficult questions

If you come across a difficult question, mark it with a paper clip (useful to have along) and come back to it when you have been through the booklet. One caution if you do this – be sure to skip a number on your answer sheet as well. Check often to be sure that you have not lost your place and that you are marking in the row numbered the same as the question you are answering.

6) Read the questions

Be sure you know what the question asks! Many capable people are unsuccessful because they failed to *read* the questions correctly.

7) Answer all questions

Unless you have been instructed that a penalty will be deducted for incorrect answers, it is better to guess than to omit a question.

8) Speed tests

It is often better NOT to guess on speed tests. It has been found that on timed tests people are tempted to spend the last few seconds before time is called in marking answers at random – without even reading them – in the hope of picking up a few extra points. To discourage this practice, the instructions may warn you that your score will be "corrected" for guessing. That is, a penalty will be applied. The incorrect answers will be deducted from the correct ones, or some other penalty formula will be used.

9) Review your answers

If you finish before time is called, go back to the questions you guessed or omitted to give them further thought. Review other answers if you have time.

10) Return your test materials

If you are ready to leave before others have finished or time is called, take ALL your materials to the monitor and leave quietly. Never take any test material with you. The monitor can discover whose papers are not complete, and taking a test booklet may be grounds for disqualification.

VIII. EXAMINATION TECHNIQUES

1) Read the general instructions carefully. These are usually printed on the first page of the exam booklet. As a rule, these instructions refer to the timing of the examination; the fact that you should not start work until the signal and must stop work at a signal, etc. If there are any *special* instructions, such as a choice of questions to be answered, make sure that you note this instruction carefully.

2) When you are ready to start work on the examination, that is as soon as the signal has been given, read the instructions to each question booklet, underline any key words or phrases, such as *least, best, outline, describe* and the like. In this way you will tend to answer as requested rather than discover on reviewing your paper that you *listed without describing*, that you selected the *worst* choice rather than the *best* choice, etc.

3) If the examination is of the objective or multiple-choice type – that is, each question will also give a series of possible answers: A, B, C or D, and you are called upon to select the best answer and write the letter next to that answer on your answer paper – it is advisable to start answering each question in turn. There may be anywhere from 50 to 100 such questions in the three or four hours allotted and you can see how much time would be taken if you read through all the questions before beginning to answer any. Furthermore, if you come across a question or group of questions which you know would be difficult to answer, it would undoubtedly affect your handling of all the other questions.

4) If the examination is of the essay type and contains but a few questions, it is a moot point as to whether you should read all the questions before starting to answer any one. Of course, if you are given a choice – say five out of seven and the like – then it is essential to read all the questions so you can eliminate the two that are most difficult. If, however, you are asked to answer all the questions, there may be danger in trying to answer the easiest one first because you may find that you will spend too much time on it. The best technique is to answer the first question, then proceed to the second, etc.

5) Time your answers. Before the exam begins, write down the time it started, then add the time allowed for the examination and write down the time it must be completed, then divide the time available somewhat as follows:

- If 3-1/2 hours are allowed, that would be 210 minutes. If you have 80 objective-type questions, that would be an average of 2-1/2 minutes per question. Allow yourself no more than 2 minutes per question, or a total of 160 minutes, which will permit about 50 minutes to review.
- If for the time allotment of 210 minutes there are 7 essay questions to answer, that would average about 30 minutes a question. Give yourself only 25 minutes per question so that you have about 35 minutes to review.

6) The most important instruction is to *read each question* and make sure you know what is wanted. The second most important instruction is to *time yourself properly* so that you answer every question. The third most important instruction is to *answer every question.* Guess if you have to but include something for each question. Remember that you will receive no credit for a blank and will probably receive some credit if you write something in answer to an essay question. If you guess a letter – say "B" for a multiple-choice question – you may have guessed right. If you leave a blank as an answer to a multiple-choice question, the examiners may respect your feelings but it will not add a point to your score. Some exams may penalize you for wrong answers, so in such cases *only*, you may not want to guess unless you have some basis for your answer.

7) Suggestions
   a. Objective-type questions
      1. Examine the question booklet for proper sequence of pages and questions
      2. Read all instructions carefully
      3. Skip any question which seems too difficult; return to it after all other questions have been answered
      4. Apportion your time properly; do not spend too much time on any single question or group of questions
      5. Note and underline key words – *all, most, fewest, least, best, worst, same, opposite,* etc.
      6. Pay particular attention to negatives
      7. Note unusual option, e.g., unduly long, short, complex, different or similar in content to the body of the question
      8. Observe the use of "hedging" words – *probably, may, most likely,* etc.
      9. Make sure that your answer is put next to the same number as the question
      10. Do not second-guess unless you have good reason to believe the second answer is definitely more correct
      11. Cross out original answer if you decide another answer is more accurate; do not erase until you are ready to hand your paper in
      12. Answer all questions; guess unless instructed otherwise
      13. Leave time for review

   b. Essay questions
      1. Read each question carefully
      2. Determine exactly what is wanted. Underline key words or phrases.
      3. Decide on outline or paragraph answer

4. Include many different points and elements unless asked to develop any one or two points or elements
5. Show impartiality by giving pros and cons unless directed to select one side only
6. Make and write down any assumptions you find necessary to answer the questions
7. Watch your English, grammar, punctuation and choice of words
8. Time your answers; don't crowd material

8) Answering the essay question

Most essay questions can be answered by framing the specific response around several key words or ideas. Here are a few such key words or ideas:

M's: manpower, materials, methods, money, management
P's: purpose, program, policy, plan, procedure, practice, problems, pitfalls, personnel, public relations

a. Six basic steps in handling problems:
   1. Preliminary plan and background development
   2. Collect information, data and facts
   3. Analyze and interpret information, data and facts
   4. Analyze and develop solutions as well as make recommendations
   5. Prepare report and sell recommendations
   6. Install recommendations and follow up effectiveness

b. Pitfalls to avoid
   1. *Taking things for granted* – A statement of the situation does not necessarily imply that each of the elements is necessarily true; for example, a complaint may be invalid and biased so that all that can be taken for granted is that a complaint has been registered
   2. *Considering only one side of a situation* – Wherever possible, indicate several alternatives and then point out the reasons you selected the best one
   3. *Failing to indicate follow up* – Whenever your answer indicates action on your part, make certain that you will take proper follow-up action to see how successful your recommendations, procedures or actions turn out to be
   4. *Taking too long in answering any single question* – Remember to time your answers properly

IX. AFTER THE TEST

Scoring procedures differ in detail among civil service jurisdictions although the general principles are the same. Whether the papers are hand-scored or graded by machine we have described, they are nearly always graded by number. That is, the person who marks the paper knows only the number – never the name – of the applicant. Not until all the papers have been graded will they be matched with names. If other tests, such as training and experience or oral interview ratings have been given, scores will be combined. Different parts of the examination usually have different weights. For example, the written test might count 60 percent of the final grade, and a rating of training and experience 40 percent. In many jurisdictions, veterans will have a certain number of points added to their grades.

After the final grade has been determined, the names are placed in grade order and an eligible list is established. There are various methods for resolving ties between those who get the same final grade – probably the most common is to place first the name of the person whose application was received first. Job offers are made from the eligible list in the order the names appear on it. You will be notified of your grade and your rank as soon as all these computations have been made. This will be done as rapidly as possible.

People who are found to meet the requirements in the announcement are called "eligibles." Their names are put on a list of eligible candidates. An eligible's chances of getting a job depend on how high he stands on this list and how fast agencies are filling jobs from the list.

When a job is to be filled from a list of eligibles, the agency asks for the names of people on the list of eligibles for that job. When the civil service commission receives this request, it sends to the agency the names of the three people highest on this list. Or, if the job to be filled has specialized requirements, the office sends the agency the names of the top three persons who meet these requirements from the general list.

The appointing officer makes a choice from among the three people whose names were sent to him. If the selected person accepts the appointment, the names of the others are put back on the list to be considered for future openings.

That is the rule in hiring from all kinds of eligible lists, whether they are for typist, carpenter, chemist, or something else. For every vacancy, the appointing officer has his choice of any one of the top three eligibles on the list. This explains why the person whose name is on top of the list sometimes does not get an appointment when some of the persons lower on the list do. If the appointing officer chooses the second or third eligible, the No. 1 eligible does not get a job at once, but stays on the list until he is appointed or the list is terminated.

X. HOW TO PASS THE INTERVIEW TEST

The examination for which you applied requires an oral interview test. You have already taken the written test and you are now being called for the interview test – the final part of the formal examination.

You may think that it is not possible to prepare for an interview test and that there are no procedures to follow during an interview. Our purpose is to point out some things you can do in advance that will help you and some good rules to follow and pitfalls to avoid while you are being interviewed.

What is an interview supposed to test?

The written examination is designed to test the technical knowledge and competence of the candidate; the oral is designed to evaluate intangible qualities, not readily measured otherwise, and to establish a list showing the relative fitness of each candidate – as measured against his competitors – for the position sought. Scoring is not on the basis of "right" and "wrong," but on a sliding scale of values ranging from "not passable" to "outstanding." As a matter of fact, it is possible to achieve a relatively low score without a single "incorrect" answer because of evident weakness in the qualities being measured.

Occasionally, an examination may consist entirely of an oral test – either an individual or a group oral. In such cases, information is sought concerning the technical knowledges and abilities of the candidate, since there has been no written examination for this purpose. More commonly, however, an oral test is used to supplement a written examination.

Who conducts interviews?

The composition of oral boards varies among different jurisdictions. In nearly all, a representative of the personnel department serves as chairman. One of the members of the board may be a representative of the department in which the candidate would work. In some cases, "outside experts" are used, and, frequently, a businessman or some other representative of the general public is asked to serve. Labor and management or other special groups may be represented. The aim is to secure the services of experts in the appropriate field.

However the board is composed, it is a good idea (and not at all improper or unethical) to ascertain in advance of the interview who the members are and what groups they represent. When you are introduced to them, you will have some idea of their backgrounds and interests, and at least you will not stutter and stammer over their names.

What should be done before the interview?

While knowledge about the board members is useful and takes some of the surprise element out of the interview, there is other preparation which is more substantive. It *is* possible to prepare for an oral interview – in several ways:

1) Keep a copy of your application and review it carefully before the interview

This may be the only document before the oral board, and the starting point of the interview. Know what education and experience you have listed there, and the sequence and dates of all of it. Sometimes the board will ask you to review the highlights of your experience for them; you should not have to hem and haw doing it.

2) Study the class specification and the examination announcement

Usually, the oral board has one or both of these to guide them. The qualities, characteristics or knowledges required by the position sought are stated in these documents. They offer valuable clues as to the nature of the oral interview. For example, if the job involves supervisory responsibilities, the announcement will usually indicate that knowledge of modern supervisory methods and the qualifications of the candidate as a supervisor will be tested. If so, you can expect such questions, frequently in the form of a hypothetical situation which you are expected to solve. NEVER go into an oral without knowledge of the duties and responsibilities of the job you seek.

3) Think through each qualification required

Try to visualize the kind of questions you would ask if you were a board member. How well could you answer them? Try especially to appraise your own knowledge and background in each area, *measured against the job sought*, and identify any areas in which you are weak. Be critical and realistic – do not flatter yourself.

4) Do some general reading in areas in which you feel you may be weak

For example, if the job involves supervision and your past experience has NOT, some general reading in supervisory methods and practices, particularly in the field of human relations, might be useful. Do NOT study agency procedures or detailed manuals. The oral board will be testing your understanding and capacity, not your memory.

5) Get a good night's sleep and watch your general health and mental attitude

You will want a clear head at the interview. Take care of a cold or any other minor ailment, and of course, no hangovers.

What should be done on the day of the interview?

Now comes the day of the interview itself. Give yourself plenty of time to get there. Plan to arrive somewhat ahead of the scheduled time, particularly if your appointment is in the fore part of the day. If a previous candidate fails to appear, the board might be ready for you a bit early. By early afternoon an oral board is almost invariably behind schedule if there are many candidates, and you may have to wait. Take along a book or magazine to read, or your application to review, but leave any extraneous material in the waiting room when you go in for your interview. In any event, relax and compose yourself.

The matter of dress is important. The board is forming impressions about you – from your experience, your manners, your attitude, and your appearance. Give your personal appearance careful attention. Dress your best, but not your flashiest. Choose conservative, appropriate clothing, and be sure it is immaculate. This is a business interview, and your appearance should indicate that you regard it as such. Besides, being well groomed and properly dressed will help boost your confidence.

Sooner or later, someone will call your name and escort you into the interview room. *This is it.* From here on you are on your own. It is too late for any more preparation. But remember, you asked for this opportunity to prove your fitness, and you are here because your request was granted.

What happens when you go in?

The usual sequence of events will be as follows: The clerk (who is often the board stenographer) will introduce you to the chairman of the oral board, who will introduce you to the other members of the board. Acknowledge the introductions before you sit down. Do not be surprised if you find a microphone facing you or a stenotypist sitting by. Oral interviews are usually recorded in the event of an appeal or other review.

Usually the chairman of the board will open the interview by reviewing the highlights of your education and work experience from your application – primarily for the benefit of the other members of the board, as well as to get the material into the record. Do not interrupt or comment unless there is an error or significant misinterpretation; if that is the case, do not hesitate. But do not quibble about insignificant matters. Also, he will usually ask you some question about your education, experience or your present job – partly to get you to start talking and to establish the interviewing "rapport." He may start the actual questioning, or turn it over to one of the other members. Frequently, each member undertakes the questioning on a particular area, one in which he is perhaps most competent, so you can expect each member to participate in the examination. Because time is limited, you may also expect some rather abrupt switches in the direction the questioning takes, so do not be upset by it. Normally, a board member will not pursue a single line of questioning unless he discovers a particular strength or weakness.

After each member has participated, the chairman will usually ask whether any member has any further questions, then will ask you if you have anything you wish to add. Unless you are expecting this question, it may floor you. Worse, it may start you off on an extended, extemporaneous speech. The board is not usually seeking more information. The question is principally to offer you a last opportunity to present further qualifications or to indicate that you have nothing to add. So, if you feel that a significant qualification or characteristic has been overlooked, it is proper to point it out in a sentence or so. Do not compliment the board on the thoroughness of their examination – they have been sketchy, and you know it. If you wish, merely say, "No thank you, I have nothing further to add." This is a point where you can "talk yourself out" of a good impression or fail to present an important bit of information. Remember, *you close the interview yourself.*

The chairman will then say, "That is all, Mr. _______, thank you." Do not be startled; the interview is over, and quicker than you think. Thank him, gather your belongings and take your leave. Save your sigh of relief for the other side of the door.

How to put your best foot forward

Throughout this entire process, you may feel that the board individually and collectively is trying to pierce your defenses, seek out your hidden weaknesses and embarrass and confuse you. Actually, this is not true. They are obliged to make an appraisal of your qualifications for the job you are seeking, and they want to see you in your best light. Remember, they must interview all candidates and a non-cooperative candidate may become a failure in spite of their best efforts to bring out his qualifications. Here are 15 suggestions that will help you:

1) Be natural – Keep your attitude confident, not cocky

If you are not confident that you can do the job, do not expect the board to be. Do not apologize for your weaknesses, try to bring out your strong points. The board is interested in a positive, not negative, presentation. Cockiness will antagonize any board member and make him wonder if you are covering up a weakness by a false show of strength.

2) Get comfortable, but don't lounge or sprawl

Sit erectly but not stiffly. A careless posture may lead the board to conclude that you are careless in other things, or at least that you are not impressed by the importance of the occasion. Either conclusion is natural, even if incorrect. Do not fuss with your clothing, a pencil or an ashtray. Your hands may occasionally be useful to emphasize a point; do not let them become a point of distraction.

3) Do not wisecrack or make small talk

This is a serious situation, and your attitude should show that you consider it as such. Further, the time of the board is limited – they do not want to waste it, and neither should you.

4) Do not exaggerate your experience or abilities

In the first place, from information in the application or other interviews and sources, the board may know more about you than you think. Secondly, you probably will not get away with it. An experienced board is rather adept at spotting such a situation, so do not take the chance.

5) If you know a board member, do not make a point of it, yet do not hide it

Certainly you are not fooling him, and probably not the other members of the board. Do not try to take advantage of your acquaintanceship – it will probably do you little good.

6) Do not dominate the interview

Let the board do that. They will give you the clues – do not assume that you have to do all the talking. Realize that the board has a number of questions to ask you, and do not try to take up all the interview time by showing off your extensive knowledge of the answer to the first one.

7) Be attentive

You only have 20 minutes or so, and you should keep your attention at its sharpest throughout. When a member is addressing a problem or question to you, give him your undivided attention. Address your reply principally to him, but do not exclude the other board members.

8) Do not interrupt

A board member may be stating a problem for you to analyze. He will ask you a question when the time comes. Let him state the problem, and wait for the question.

9) Make sure you understand the question

Do not try to answer until you are sure what the question is. If it is not clear, restate it in your own words or ask the board member to clarify it for you. However, do not haggle about minor elements.

10) Reply promptly but not hastily

A common entry on oral board rating sheets is "candidate responded readily," or "candidate hesitated in replies." Respond as promptly and quickly as you can, but do not jump to a hasty, ill-considered answer.

11) Do not be peremptory in your answers

A brief answer is proper – but do not fire your answer back. That is a losing game from your point of view. The board member can probably ask questions much faster than you can answer them.

12) Do not try to create the answer you think the board member wants

He is interested in what kind of mind you have and how it works – not in playing games. Furthermore, he can usually spot this practice and will actually grade you down on it.

13) Do not switch sides in your reply merely to agree with a board member

Frequently, a member will take a contrary position merely to draw you out and to see if you are willing and able to defend your point of view. Do not start a debate, yet do not surrender a good position. If a position is worth taking, it is worth defending.

14) Do not be afraid to admit an error in judgment if you are shown to be wrong

The board knows that you are forced to reply without any opportunity for careful consideration. Your answer may be demonstrably wrong. If so, admit it and get on with the interview.

15) Do not dwell at length on your present job

The opening question may relate to your present assignment. Answer the question but do not go into an extended discussion. You are being examined for a *new* job, not your present one. As a matter of fact, try to phrase ALL your answers in terms of the job for which you are being examined.

Basis of Rating

Probably you will forget most of these "do's" and "don'ts" when you walk into the oral interview room. Even remembering them all will not ensure you a passing grade. Perhaps you did not have the qualifications in the first place. But remembering them will help you to put your best foot forward, without treading on the toes of the board members.

Rumor and popular opinion to the contrary notwithstanding, an oral board wants you to make the best appearance possible. They know you are under pressure – but they also want to see how you respond to it as a guide to what your reaction would be under the pressures of the job you seek. They will be influenced by the degree of poise you display, the personal traits you show and the manner in which you respond.

ABOUT THIS BOOK

This book contains tests divided into Examination Sections. Go through each test, answering every question in the margin. At the end of each test look at the answer key and check your answers. On the ones you got wrong, look at the right answer choice and learn. Do not fill in the answers first. Do not memorize the questions and answers, but understand the answer and principles involved. On your test, the questions will likely be different from the samples. Questions are changed and new ones added. If you understand these past questions you should have success with any changes that arise. Tests may consist of several types of questions. We have additional books on each subject should more study be advisable or necessary for you. Finally, the more you study, the better prepared you will be. This book is intended to be the last thing you study before you walk into the examination room. Prior study of relevant texts is also recommended. NLC publishes some of these in our Fundamental Series. Knowledge and good sense are important factors in passing your exam. Good luck also helps. So now study this Passbook, absorb the material contained within and take that knowledge into the examination. Then do your best to pass that exam.

EXAMINATION SECTION

EXAMINATION SECTION
TEST 1

Questions 1-30.

DIRECTIONS: Questions 1 through 30 consist of statements. You are to decide whether the statement is true or false. Then, in the answer space on the right, PRINT the letter "T" if the statement is true, or PRINT the letter "F" if the statement is false. In order to help you understand the procedure, the following sample items are given:

SAMPLE ITEM: Albany is the capital of New York State.
Since this statement is correct, your answer should be written as follows:
SAMPLE ANSWER: T
SAMPLE ITEM: Buffalo is the largest city in New York State.
Since the statement is wrong, your answer should be written as follows:
SAMPLE ANSWER: F

1. It is worse for the hospital clerk to give a visitor incorrect information than for the clerk to say that he is unable to furnish the information. 1.____

2. If a visitor speaks to a hospital clerk in a loud and impertinent manner, the clerk is justified in then replying in the same manner 2.____

3. If a hospital clerk must deny a visitor's request for information, it is better for him to be firm than to explain tactfully the reason for the denial. 3.____

4. The manner in which a hospital clerk deals with visitors tends to affect the visitors' opinion of the hospital. 4.____

5. A hospital clerk who does not understand his instructions regarding an assignment should ask to have the instructions explained again before he begins to work on the assignment. 5.____

6. A hospital clerk is justified in reporting late for work if his immediate superior also reports late for work. 6.____

7. A hospital clerk should permit visitors to inspect patients' medical records. 7.____

8. The generally approved method of answering a telephone in a hospital is for the hospital clerk to say "Hello." 8.____

9. A proper method of obtaining a telephone number which cannot be located in the telephone directory is to dial 411. 9.____

10. The Classified Telephone Directory is also known as the "Yellow Pages." 10.____

11. Person-to-Person long distance telephone calls are more expensive than station-to-station long distance calls. 11.____

12. A clerk should usually wait until he is out of stock in certain items before reordering these items. 12.____

13. A semi-annual report is one that is issued every six months. 13.____

14. Letters filed in chronological order are those filed according to their dates. 14.____

15. "Out" cards are usually placed in a file when a useless record has been removed from the file and destroyed. 15.____

16. A clerk who notices that a letter has been misfiled should destroy the letter if he believes it is unimportant. 16.____

17. In alphabetic filing, Mary Brown is generally filed before Anna Browne. 17.____

18. In alphabetical filing, John Dewey is generally filed after Joan Dewey. 18.____

19. In alphabetical filing, Frank T. Mill is generally filed after Donald Millard. 19.____

20. If certain records must be attached together before being placed in the files, it is generally better to staple them together than to attach them together by a paper clip. 20.____

21. An exact copy of a letter or record can be made by means of a photostatic machine. 21.____

22. The symbol "c/o" appearing on an envelope as part of the address stands for the phrase "official correspondence." 22.____

23. Before starting to deliver mail addressed to patients in different wards of a hospital, the clerk should first sort the mail according to the wards in which the patients are located. 23.____

24. A mimeograph stencil cannot be used again if it has been removed from the machine. 24.____

25. A clerk who notices that the signature has been omitted from an outgoing letter should ignore the omission and mail the letter. 25.____

26. A hospital clerk should allow patients' visitors to remain after visiting hours are over as long as the other patients in the ward are not disturbed. 26.____

27. The domestic postage rate for ordinary post cards is now five cents. 27.____

28. When a mail clerk opens an envelope containing both a letter and an enclosure, it is ordinarily desirable for him to attach the enclosure to the letter. 28.____

29. The Dictaphone is a machine which stamps and seals envelopes. 29.____

30. Aid to the blind and old age assistance are of no concern to the hospital clerk. 30.____

KEY (CORRECT ANSWERS)

1. T	11. T	21. T
2. F	12. F	22. F
3. F	13. T	23. T
4. T	14. T	24. F
5. T	15. F	25. F
6. F	16. F	26. F
7. F	17. T	27. F
8. F	18. T	28. T
9. T	19. F	29. F
10. T	20. T	30. F

TEST 2

DIRECTIONS: Questions 1 through 13 consist of statements. You are to decide whether the statement is true or false. Then, in the answer space on the right, PRINT the letter "T" if the statement is true, or PRINT the letter "F" if the statement is false. In order to help you understand the procedure, the following sample items are given:

SAMPLE ITEM: Albany is the capital of New York State.
Since this statement is correct, your answer should be written as follows:
SAMPLE ANSWER: T
SAMPLE ITEM: Buffalo is the largest city in New York State.
Since the statement is wrong, your answer should be written as follows:
SAMPLE ANSWER: F

Questions 1-6.

DIRECTIONS: Questions 1 through 6 inclusive are to be answered *SOLELY* on the basis of the information contained in the following statement and *NOT* upon any other information you may have.

Blood transfusions are given to patients at the hospital upon recommendation of the physicians attending such cases. The physician fills out a "Request for Blood Transfusion" form in duplicate and sends both copies to the Medical Director's office where a list is maintained of persons called "donors" who desire to sell their blood for transfusions. A suitable donor is selected and the transfusion is given. Donors are in many instances medical students and employees of the hospital. Donors receive twenty-five dollars for each transfusion.

1. According to the above paragraph, a blood donor is paid twenty-five dollars for each transfusion. 1.___

2. According to the above paragraph, only medical students and employees of the hospital are selected as blood donors. 2.___

3. According to the above paragraph, the "Request for Blood Transfusion" form is filled out by the patient and sent to the Medical Director's Office. 3.___

4. According to the above paragraph, a list of blood donors is maintained in the Medical Director's office. 4.___

5. According to the above paragraph, cases for which the attending physicians recommend blood transfusions are usually emergency cases. 5.___

6. According to the above paragraph, one copy of the "Request for Blood Transfusion" form is kept by the patient and one copy is sent to the Medical Director's office. 6.___

Questions 7-13.

DIRECTIONS: Questions numbered 7 to 13 inclusive are to be answered *SOLELY* on the basis of the information contained in the following statement and *NOT* upon any other information you may have.

Before being admitted to a hospital ward, a patient is first interviewed by the Admitting Clerk who records the patient's name, age, sex, race, birthplace, and mother's maiden name. This clerk takes all of the money and valuables that the patient has on his person. A list of the valuables is written on the back of the envelope in which the valuables are afterwards placed. Cash is counted and placed in a separate envelope, and the amount of money and the name of the patient are written on the outside of the envelope. Both envelopes are sealed, fastened together, and placed in a compartment of a safe.

An orderly then escorts the patient to a dressing room where the patient's clothes are removed and placed in a bundle. A tag bearing the patient's name is fastened to the bundle. A list of the contents of the bundle is written on property slips which are made out in triplicate. The information contained on the outside of the envelopes containing the cash and valuables belonging to the patient is also copied on the property slips.

7. According to the above paragraph, patients are escorted to the dressing room by the Admitting Clerk. 7.____

8. According to the above paragraph, the patient's cash and valuables are placed together in one envelope. 8.____

9. According to the above paragraph, the number of identical property slips that are made out when a patient is being admitted to a hospital ward is three. 9.____

10. According to the above paragraph, the full names of both parents of a patient are recorded by the Admitting Clerk before a patient is admitted to a hospital ward. 10.____

11. According to the above paragraph, the amount of money that a patient has on his person when admitted to the hospital is entered on the patient's property slips. 11.____

12. According to the above paragraph, an orderly takes all the money and valuables that a patient has on his person. 12.____

13. According to the above paragraph, the patient's name is placed on the tag that is attached to the bundle containing the patient's clothing. 13.____

Questions 14-28.

DIRECTIONS: Each of Questions numbered 14 to 28 inclusive consists of a sentence. Some of these sentences contain errors in grammar or word usage; others are correct as they stand. If a sentence is correct as it stands, you are to print the letter "C" (Correct) in your answer space on the right; if a sentence contains an error in grammar or word usage, you are to print the letter "W" (Wrong).

14. The supervisor learned the new clerks their duties. 14.____

15. This report is the better of the two. 15.____

16. He wants you and me to distribute the mail. 16.____

17. She performs her work very careless. 17.____

18. Each of the four patients is talking to a visitor. 18.____

19. The new clerk don't know where to obtain the supplies. 19.____

20. The clerk would not of made the mistake if he had been trained properly. 20.____

21. Please give the report to either the nurse or I. 21.____

22. He begun to work immediately. 22.____

23. The clerk was asked to lay the charts on the nurse's desk. 23.____

24. The visitor was told whom to see regarding his request. 24.____

25. He suggested a more faster method of preparing the reports . 25.____

26. The clerk seen the charts last week. 26.____

27. He can hardly raise his head. 27.____

28. Most of the patients was eating their breakfast. 28.____

Questions 29-45.

DIRECTIONS: Each of Questions numbered 29 to 45 inclusive consists of a single word which is spelled either correctly or incorrectly. If the word is spelled correctly, you are to print the letter "C" (Correct) in your answer space on the right; if the word is spelled incorrectly, you are to print the letter "W "(Wrong).

29. pospone 29.____

30. diffrent 30.____

31. height 31.____

32. carefully 32.____

33. ability 33.____

34. temper 34.____

35. deslike 35.____

36. seldem 36.____

37. alcohol 37.____

38. expense 38.____

39. vegatable 39.____

40. dispensary 40.____

41. specemin 41.____

42. allowance 42.____

43. exersise 43.____

44. artifical 44.____

45. disagreeable 45.____

Questions 46-50.

DIRECTIONS: Each of Questions numbered 46 to 50 inclusive consists of a problem in arithmetic and the answer to the problem. If the answer given is correct, you are to print the letter "C" for Correct in the answer space at the right; if the answer given is incorrect, you are to print the letter "W" for Wrong.

46. If a temperature of 98.6 degrees is normal, then a temperature of 103.2 degrees is 4.6 degrees above normal. 46.____

47. If a hospital with a bed capacity of 2100 beds reports that 87% of its beds are occupied, then the number of beds not occupied is 373. 47.____

48. It takes a hospital clerk 8 minutes to prepare an admission report on one patient. At this rate, it will take the hospital clerk 5 hours and 36 minutes to prepare the admission reports on 42 patients. 48.____

49. Three-fifths of the patients in Hospital X are males. If the total number of patients in Hospital X is 1550, then the number of male patients is 930. 49.____

50. In a certain hospital, requests for laboratory examinations are made out in duplicate on a special laboratory request form. The laboratory request forms are bound in pads, each pad containing 80 forms. If 480 laboratory examinations were requested during the month of November, the number of pads used in November was 6 pads. 50.____

KEY (CORRECT ANSWERS)

1.	T	11.	T	21.	W	31.	C	41.	W
2.	F	12.	F	22.	W	32.	W	42.	C
3.	F	13.	T	23.	C	33.	C	43.	W
4.	T	14.	W	24.	C	34.	C	44.	W
5.	T	15.	C	25.	W	35.	W	45.	C
6.	F	16.	C	26.	W	36.	W	46.	C
7.	F	17.	W	27.	C	37.	C	47.	W
8.	F	18.	C	28.	W	38.	C	48.	C
9.	T	19.	W	29.	W	39.	W	49.	C
10.	F	20.	W	30.	W	40.	C	50.	W

TEST 3

Questions 1-12.

DIRECTIONS: Questions numbered 1 to 12 inclusive are to be answered *SOLELY* on the basis of the information which is given on the Weekly Patient Action Record shown on the following pages.

This record lists the names of fifty (50) patients who were newly admitted to, transferred into, transferred out of, discharged from, or who died, in four hospital wards during the week of May 4-10.

A key to the abbreviations for these types of actions is shown below the list of patients.

Each of Questions 1 through 12 consists of a statement relating to the information given on the Weekly Patient Action Record shown on the following pages.

You are to decide whether the statement is true or false. Then, in the answer space to the right of the question, you are to print the letter "T" if the statement is true or corect; or print the letter "F" if the statement is false or wrong.

WEEKLY PATIENT ACTION RECORD

Week of: May 4-10

Wards: Gyneoology (Gyn.)
Medical (Med.)
Obstetrical (Obs.)
Surgical (Sur.)

DATE	WARD	PATIENT	ACTION *
May 4	Gyn.	Niles, J.	D
4	Med.	Lewis, N.	N
4	Med.	Wiley, C.	N
4	Med.	Crump, D.	N
4	Sur.	Klein, B.	T I
4	Sur.	Okun , N .	D
May 5	Med.	Braun, M.	TO
5	Med.	Speer, S.	TO
5	Med.	Anson, R.	D
5	Med.	Darby, J.	D
5	Obs.	Pack, W.	N
5	Obs.	Heide, K.	N
5	Sur.	Wills, H.	N
5	Sur.	Amato , D.	N
May 6	Gyn.	Marks, H.	N
6	Med.	Hall, A.	N
6	Med.	Tracy, W.	N
6	Med.	Michel, F.	T I
6	Sur.	Crone, P.	D
May 7	Gyn.	Reid, W.	D
7	Med.	Usher, S.	T I
7	Med.	Dion, C.	T I
7	Med.	Kidd, O.	TO
7	Med.	Bryan, W.	E
7	Sur.	Vance, P.	D

*KEY TO ABBREVIATION OF ACTIONS

N - Newly admitted

T I - Transferred into the ward (from another ward)

TO - Transferred out of ward (to another ward)
D - Discharged from ward (to go home)
E - Died

	7	Sur.	Elder, K.	D
May	8	Gyn.	Lyons, B.	N
	8	Gyn.	Gong , S .	D
	8	Gyn.	Kahn, J.	D
	8	Med.	Pearl, E.	N
	8	Obs.	Bandor, N.	TO
	8	Sur.	Jason, A.	N
	8	Sur.	Sawyer, V.	N
	8	Sur.	Perez, G.	TO
May	9	Gyn.	Gutman, R.	T I
	9	Gyn.	Klein, I.	TO
	9	Med.	Welsh, H.	D
	9	Med.	Cole, F.	D
	9	Med.	Jacobs, K.	E
	9	Obs.	Madden , W.	N
	9	Sur.	Endler, L.	N
	9	Sur.	Lieber , R.	N
	9	Sur.	Ross, T.	D
May	10	Gyn.	Zayas, I.	N
	10	Med.	Smith, A.	N
	10	Med.	Pagan , C .	TO
	10	Obs.	Casey , M .	D
	10	Obs.	Taylor, R.	D
	10	Sur.	Knopf, F.	T I
	10	Sur.	Olsen, O.	E

*KEY TO ABBREVIATION OF ACTIONS
N - Newly admitted
T I - Transferred into the ward (from another ward)
TO - Transferred out of ward (to another ward)
D - Discharged from ward (to go home)
E - Died

1. On May 5, M. Braun was transferred out of the Medical ward. 1._____

2. On May 7, K. Elder was discharged from the Surgical ward. 2._____

3. Three patients were newly admitted to the Medical ward on May 4. 3._____

4. R. Lieber was transferred into the Surgical ward on May 9. 4._____

5. The number of patients who died during this seven-day period was two. 5._____

6. No patients were transferred into the Obstetrical ward during this seven-day period. 6._____

7. There are five (5) patients whose last names begin with the letter K. 7._____

8. More patients were transferred into these four wards than were transferred out of these wards during this week. 8.____

9. During this week, more patients were newly admitted to the Gynecology ward than were discharged from this ward. 9.____

10. More patients were discharged from the four wards on May 5 than were discharged on May 7. 10.____

11. The total number of patients newly admitted to the four wards during this week was nineteen. 11.____

12. During this week, the number of patients transferred out of the Medical ward was the same as the number discharged from this ward. 12.____

Questions 13-30.

DIRECTIONS: Each of questions numbered 13 to 30 inclusive consists of a pair of words which are either the same or opposite in meaning. If the two words of a pair are the same or nearly the same in meaning, you are to print the letter "S" (Same) in the answer space alongside the number of the question; if he words of a pair are opposite or nearly opposite in meaning, you are to print the letter "O" (Opposite).

13. stimulant–sedative 13.____

14. flexible–rigid 14.____

15. detrimental–harmful 15.____

16. incision–cut 16.____

17. antidote–poison 17.____

18. dilute–strengthen 18.____

19. immune–susceptible 19.____

20. expensive–costly 20.____

21. probe–search 21.____

22. retard–delay 22.____

23. relapse–recovery 23.____

24. stagger–totter 24.____

25. exaggerate–minimize 25.____

26. induce–persuade 26.____

27. remuneration–compensation 27.____

28. ominous–favorable 28.____

29. adept–skillful 29.____

30. dissipate–waste 30.____

KEY (CORRECT ANSWERS)

1. T	11. T	21. S
2. T	12. T	22. S
3. T	13. O	23. O
4. F	14. O	24. S
5. F	15. S	25. O
6. T	16. S	26. S
7. T	17. O	27. S
8. F	18. O	28. O
9. F	19. O	29. S
10. F	20. S	30. S

EXAMINATION SECTION
TEST 1

DIRECTIONS: Each question or incomplete statement is followed by several suggested answers or completions. Select the one that BEST answers the question or completes the statement. *PRINT THE LETTER OF THE CORRECT ANSWER IN THE SPACE AT THE RIGHT.*

Questions 1-10.

DIRECTIONS: Questions 1 through 10 consist of four names each. In the space at the right, print the letter of the name which should be filed FIRST according to generally accepted alphabetic filing rules.

1. A. George St. John B. Thomas Santos C. Frances Starks D. Mary S. Stranum 1.____

2. A. Franklin Carrol B. Timothy Carrol C. Timothy S. Carol D. Timothy S. Carol 2.____

3. A. Christie-Barry Storage
B. John Christie-Barry
C. The Christie-Barry Company
D. Anne Christie-Barrie 3.____

4. A. Inter State Travel Co. B. Interstate Car Rental C. Inter State Trucking D. Interstate Lending Inst. 4.____

5. A. The Los Angeles Tile Co.
B. Anita F. Los
C. The Lost & Found Detective Agency
D. Jason Los-Brio 5.____

6. A. Prince Charles B. Prince Charles Coiffures C. Chas. F. Prince D. Thomas A. Charles 6.____

7. A. U.S. Dept. of Agriculture B. United States Aircraft Co. C. U.S. Air Transport, Inc. D. The United Union 7.____

8. A. Meyer's Art Shop B. Frank B. Meyer C. Meyers' Paint Store D. Meyer and Goldberg 8.____

9. A. David Des Laurier B. Des Moines Flower Shop C. Henry Desanto D. Mary L. Desta 9.____

10. A. Jeffrey Van Der Meer B. Jeffrey M. Vander C. Jeffrey Van D. Wallace Meer 10.____

Questions 11-20.

DIRECTIONS: Questions 11 through 20 are to be answered on the basis of the following instructions: For each such numbered set of names, addresses, and numbers listed in Columns I and II, select your answer from the following options:

A. The names in Columns I and II are different.
B. The addresses in Columns I and II are different.
C. The numbers in Columns I and II are different.
D. The names, addresses, and numbers in Columns I and II are identical.

	COLUMN I	COLUMN II	
11.	Francis Jones 62 Stately Avenue 96-12446	Francis Jones 62 Stately Avenue 96-21446	11.___
12.	Julio Montez 19 Ponderosa Road 56-73161	Julio Montez 19 Ponderosa Road 56-71361	12.___
13.	Mary Mitchell 2314 Melbourne Drive 68-92172	Mary Mitchell 2314 Melbourne Drive 68-92172	13.___
14.	Harry Patterson 25 Dunne Street 14-33430	Harry Patterson 25 Dunne Street 14-34330	14.___
15.	Patrick Murphy 171 West Hosmer Street 93-81214	Patrick Murphy 171 West Hosmer Street 93-18214	15.___
16.	August Schultz 816 St. Clair Avenue 53-40149	August Schultz 816 St. Claire Avenue 53-40149	16.___
17.	George Taft 72 Runnymede Street 47-04033	George Taft 72 Runnymede Street 47-04023	17.___
18.	Angus Henderson 1418 Madison Street 81-76375	Angus Henderson 1418 Madison Street 81-76375	18.___
19.	Carolyn Mazur 12 Riverview Road 38-99615	Carolyn Mazur 12 Rivervane Road 38-99615	19.___
20.	Adele Russell 1725 Lansing Lane 72-91962	Adela Russell 1725 Lansing Lane 72-91962	20.___

21. The reason why the analysis of mortality statistics is an IMPORTANT tool of modern public health administration is that it 21.____

  A. provides a measure of the state of health of the people of the city
  B. provides for personal records of births and deaths
  C. indicates need for methods of disposition of human remains
  D. provides a method of uncovering changes in birth or death certificates

22. When a fetal death occurs in a hospital, it should be reported to the Health Department PRIMARILY by the 22.____

  A. person in charge at the hospital
  B. attending nurse
  C. person in charge of the maternity clinic with which the attending physician or midwife is associated
  D. chief medical examiner

23. When a nurse midwife attends at or after a fetal death in a location other than a hospital, she SHOULD 23.____

  A. sign the certificate of fetal death after it has been prepared by the physician, and forward it
  B. prepare the certificate of fetal death and confidential medical report and have it examined and countersigned by a physician before forwarding it
  C. prepare the certificate of fetal death and forward it thereafter to the nearest hospital
  D. prepare the certificate of fetal death and forward it thereafter to the commissioner of health

24. According to the Health Code, which of the following next-of-kin should be notified of an adult death FIRST? 24.____

  A. Parents of deceased
  B. Spouse of deceased
  C. Children of deceased who are over 21
  D. Attorney of record

25. A registry of deaths shall be maintained and permanently preserved in each hospital. When a death occurs in a hospital, the person RESPONSIBLE for entering the death in the registry shall be 25.____

  A. the floor nursing supervisor
  B. the medical superintendent on duty
  C. any licensed physician
  D. the person who prepares the death certificate

26. The name below that would MOST likely need to be cross-referenced in an alphabetic filing system is 26.____

  A. Dr. George G. D'Arcy
  B. Mrs. Dorothy C. Crown
  C. Mr. David E. Forbes-Watkins
  D. Prof. Harry D. Van Tassell

Questions 27-30.

DIRECTIONS: Questions 27 through 30 refer to the following Certificate of Death index number: 156-74-200863.

27. The numerical component that indicates the CITY in which death occurred is 27.____

A. 200 B. 156 C. 863 D. 74

28. The numerical component that indicates the CASE NUMBER is 28.____

A. 00863 B. 200863 C. 156-74 D. 74-200863

29. The numerical component that indicates the BOROUGH in which death occurred is 29.____

A. 1 B. 2 C. 3 D. 4

30. This Certificate of Death INDEX NUMBER refers to a death that occurred in 30.____

A. the Bronx
B. Queens
C. Brooklyn
D. Staten Island

KEY (CORRECT ANSWERS)

1. A
2. C
3. D
4. B
5. B

6. D
7. C
8. A
9. C
10. D

11. C
12. C
13. D
14. C
15. C

16. B
17. C
18. A
19. B
20. A

21. A
22. A
23. B
24. B
25. D

26. C
27. B
28. A
29. B
30. A

EXAMINATION SECTION
TEST 1

DIRECTIONS: Each question or incomplete statement is followed by several suggested answers or completions. Select the one that BEST answers the question or completes the statement. *PRINT THE LETTER OF THE CORRECT ANSWER IN THE SPACE AT THE RIGHT.*

QUESTIONS 1-25.

Questions 1-25 contain often used medical terms. Choose the lettered choice that is CLOSEST in meaning to the numbered items.

1. BIOPSY: 1.____

   A. routine physical
   B. exploratory surgery
   C. examination of living tissues
   D. excision of a tumor

2. CARDIOVASCULAR: relating to 2.____

   A. heart and blood vessels
   B. stress tests
   C. circulation in one's extremities
   D. blood supply to the muscles

3. CHOLECYSTECTOMY: excision of the 3.____

   A. kidneys
   B. gall bladder
   C. pancreas
   D. spleen

4. COAGULATION: 4.____

   A. thickening
   B. dispersion
   C. separation into categories
   D. suffocation

5. CONGENITAL: 5.____

   A. relating to the reproductive organs
   B. sexually reproductive
   C. normal
   D. from birth

6. DORSAL: relating to 6.____

   A. the sides
   B. aquatic animals
   C. the back
   D. sharks only

7. EDEMA: 7.____

   A. cleansing of the digestive tract
   B. fluid in the joints
   C. a skin condition
   D. a food-borne disease

8. EMBOLISM: 8.____

A. shortage of breath
B. reddening of the skin
C. deficiency of vitamin E
D. sudden blockage of a vessel

9. FETUS: 9.____

A. relating to foot disease
B. physiological reaction to hunger
C. unborn offspring
D. infant

10. HEMATURIA: 10.____

A. subdural blood clot
B. red blood cell count
C. blood cells in the urine
D. platelet count

11. HEPATIC: relating to the 11.____

A. liver
B. blood
C. skin
D. leg muscles

12. INCIPIENT: 12.____

A. in the final stages
B. beginning to become apparent
C. fatal
D. intermediary

13. INFRACOSTAL: 13.____

A. behind the lungs
B. near the spine
C. above the ribs
D. below the ribs

14. LAPAROTOMY: surgical section of the 14.____

A. lung
B. liver
C. abdominal wall
D. heart

15. NECROSIS: 15.____

A. obsession with corpses
B. localized death of living tissue
C. kidney disease
D. state of deep depression

16. NEONATAL: relating to 16.____

A. period before birth
B. gestation
C. infancy
D. childhood

17. POSTPARTUM: 17.____

A. after birth
B. after death
C. isolated during childhood
D. quarantined

18. RENAL: relating to the 18.____

A. kidneys
B. colon
C. adrenal gland
D. throat

19. SARCOID: disease characterized by 19.____

A. a sore throat
B. a red, itchy rash
C. growths on the heart
D. nodules under the skin

20. SEPTIC: relating to 20.____

A. poison
B. sewage
C. infection
D. contamination

21. SEQUELA: 21.____

A. aftereffect of a disease
B. follow-up examination
C. repeat of a surgical procedure
D. medication after surgery

22. TACHYCARDIA: 22.____

A. irregular pulse
B. infection of the heart
C. heart attack
D. rapid heartbeat

23. TOXEMIA: a condition associated with 23.____

A. lack of nutrients
B. toxins in the blood
C. loss of appetite
D. ingestion of human wastes

24. TRAUMATIC: 24.____

A. fatal
B. contagions
C. causing injury to tissue
D. chronic

25. VENTRAL: relating to the 25.____

A. respiratory system
B. circulatory system
C. belly
D. palms of the hands

QUESTIONS 26-35.

In questions 26-35, choose the word that is spelled INCORRECTLY.

26. A. angioma B. cereberum 26.____
C. dorsal D. embolism

27. A. urethra B. peritoneum 27.____
C. deficiency D. duodinum

28. A. deltoid B. cardiac 28.____
C. histerectomy D. colon

29. A. syringe B. ovarian 29.____
C. vitamin D. legament

30. A. mussle B. transfusion 30.____
C. rickets D. ulna

31. A. tendon B. subcutaneous 31.____
C. ocipital D. fracture

32. A. metacarpal B. podiatry 32.____
C. patela D. sprain

33. A. clavicle B. fallopian 33.____
C. calcium D. pancreis

34. A. hematocrit B. surgicle 34.____
C. tumor D. paroxysm

35. A. vertebri B. uterus 35.____
C. hemoglobin D. toxicity

QUESTIONS 36-55.

Questions 36-55 refer to the lists below. List I contains the names of 20 diseases or conditions. List II gives the 17 major subdivisions of the International Statistical Classification of Diseases, Injuries, and Causes of Death. For each of the diseases or conditions given in List I, write in the space provided at the right for the corresponding number, the letter preceding the major subdivision into which the disease or condition properly falls. (The same letter may be used more than once.)

EXAMPLE: x. acute appendicitis. Since this is a disease of the digestive system, the answer should be "i."

LIST I

36. abscess of scalp 36.____
37. acute poliomyelitis 37.____
38. adhesive peritonitis 38.____
39. aortic stenosis 39.____
40. arteriosclerosis 40.____
41. burns and trauma due to explosion of stove 41.____
42. cerebral hemorrhage 42.____
43. chronic glomerular nephritis 43.____
44. hypothyroidism 44.____
45. influenza 45.____
46. muscular dystrophy 46.____
47. multiple sclerosis 47.____
48. osteomyelitis 48.____
49. pernicious anemia 49.____
50. postnatal asphyxia 50.____
51. prolapse of umbilical cord 51.____
52. pulmonary congestion 52.____
53. rectal cancer 53.____
54. syphilis 54.____
55. ulcerative colitis 55.____

LIST II

A. infective and parasitic diseases
B. neoplasms
C. allergic, endocrine system, metabolic and nutritional diseases
D. diseases of the blood and blood-forming organs
E. mental, psychoneurotic and personality disorders
F. diseases of the nervous system and sense organs
G. diseases of the circulatory system
H. diseases of the respiratory system
I. diseases of the digestive system
J. diseases of the genitourinary system
K. deliveries and complications of pregnancy, childbirth and the puerperium
L. diseases of the skin and cellular tissue
M. diseases of the bones and organs of movement
N. congenital malformations
O. certain diseases of early infancy
P. symptoms, senility and ill-defined conditions
Q. accidents, poisonings and violence

KEY (CORRECT ANSWERS)

1. C	16. C	31. C	46. N
2. A	17. A	32. C	47. F
3. B	18. A	33. D	48. M
4. A	19. D	34. B	49. D
5. D	20. C	35. A	50. O
6. C	21. A	36. L	51. K
7. B	22. D	37. F	52. H
8. D	23. B	38. L	53. I
9. C	24. C	39. G	54. J
10. C	25. C	40. G	55. I
11. A	26. B	41. G	
12. B	27. D	42. F	
13. D	28. C	43. J	
14. C	29. D	44. C	
15. B	30. A	45. A	

TEST 2

DIRECTIONS: Each question or incomplete statement is followed by several suggested answers or completions. Select the one that BEST answers the question or completes the statement. *PRINT THE LETTER OF THE CORRECT ANSWER IN THE SPACE AT THE RIGHT.*

QUESTIONS 1-5.

Questions 1-5 are to be answered *solely* on the basis of the following paragraphs.

"No person shall disinter a coffin or casket containing human remains unless a disinterment permit has been issued by the Department of Health, except when the disinterment is ordered by the Office of the Chief Medical Examiner. Application for a disinterment permit shall be submitted at the office of the Department of Health in the borough in which the remains are buried. The application shall be accompanied by an affidavit from the next of kin or other authorized person."

No person shall remove human remains from the place of death unless a removal permit has been issued by the Department of Health or authorization to remove has been granted by telephone. A removal permit or telephone authorization to remove does not authorize burial or cremation. Human remains shall not be brought into the City unless a permit for their transportation or burial has been issued by the authorized agency of the municipality or -county within the United States within whose jurisdiction death occurred. A burial permit issued by such agency which specifies the cemetery in which burial is to take place shall be accepted for burial in New York City. If, however, such permit specifies no cemetery or a cemetery other than the one intended for burial then application for a permit must be made to the Department of Health. No permit to cremate shall be issued unless the application is accompanied by an affidavit from the next of kin or other authorized person, and unless the application is approved by the Office of the Chief Medical Examiner.

On the basis of the information given above, determine which of the following statements are TRUE and which are FALSE. Indicate your answer by using (T) for TRUE and (F) for FALSE.

1. A body now buried in Brooklyn is to be reburied in Queens. A permit to disinter must be obtained from the Queens office of the Department of Health. 1.____
2. The Office of the Chief Medical Examiner must approve an application to disinter a body. 2.____
3. A person who has died in Manhattan is to be buried in Staten Island. The Department of Health may give permission by telephone to have the body taken to Staten Island and buried there. 3.____
4. A permit is sought to cremate a dead body. Even though the Office of the Chief Medical Examiner agrees to the cremation, the next of kin or other authorized person must submit an affidavit. 4.____
5. A woman calls and tells the medical clerk that her cousin just died in Columbus, Ohio. She wants the body buried in Brooklyn, New York. The medical clerk should tell her that a burial permit must be obtained from the Brooklyn office of the Department of Health. 5.____

QUESTIONS 6-12.

Questions 6-12 refer to the following code tables which are to be used for classifying cases of death.

TABLE I

Code	Sex
X	Male
Y	Female

TABLE II

Code	Age
01	Under 1 year
02	1-10 years
03	11-20 years
04	21-30 years
05	31-40 years
06	41-50 years
07	51-60 years
08	Over 60 years

TABLE III

Code	Cause of Death
10	Heart Disease
20	Poliomyelitis
30	Cancer
40	Meningitis
50	Accident
60	Other

TABLE IV

Code	Borough Where Person Died
1	Manhattan
2	Brooklyn
3	Bronx
4	Queens
5	Richmond

TABLE V

Code	Present Occupation
101	Professional
102	Office Worker
103	Skilled Worker
104	Unskilled Worker
105	Housewife
106	Student
107	Other

TABLE VI

Code	Marital Status
a	Single
b	Married
c	Divorced
d	Widowed

Below are 7 cases of death which are to be classified. In accordance with the code tables given above, assign the proper code number to each case. The codes are to be arranged from left to right, in the order indicated by the numbers of the six code tables. EXAMPLE: A 3-year-old girl died in Richmond of meningitis. Her code number is: Y-02-40-5-107-a.

6. A 12-year-old high school boy died in the Bronx of injuries sustained in a traffic collision. 6.____
7. A 53-year-old clerk, divorced, died of a heart attack while shoveling snow in front of his home in Queens. 7.____
8. A 70-year-old widow, a housewife, died of cancer in a Queens hospital after a short stay. 8.____
9. A 37-year-old married porter died of pneumonia in his home in Brooklyn. 9.____
10. A 24-year-old lawyer, divorced from her husband, died in Manhattan of poliomyelitis. 10.____
11. A 4-month-old infant girl died in a Richmond hospital of a malformed kidney. 11.____
12. A 47-year-old machinist, married, died in the Bronx of injuries resulting from a fall at his place of employment. 12.____

QUESTIONS 13-22.

Questions 13-22 are to be answered based on the rules of filing. Column I containing the numbers 13-22, lists the names of 10 death certificates which are to be filed. Column II contains the heading of file drawers into which you are to file the certificates. For each number 13-22, choose the correct lettered file drawer and indicate said letter in the space at the right.

EXAMPLE: Eileen Sacks. The certificate of Eileen Sacks shouldbe filed in drawer headed Sa - Scl. The answer, therefore, would be A.

Column I	Column II	
13. Donald Spiller	A. Drawer 1. Sa - Scl	13.____
14. Stuart Simon	B. Drawer 2. Sco - Ses	14.____
15. Sidney Schofield	C. Drawer 3. Set - Sik	15.____
16. Mark Stetner	D. Drawer 4. Sil - Sni	E. 16.____
17. Nelson Sklar	E. Drawer 5. Sno - Suc	17.____
18. Daisy Saunders		18.____
19. Peter Sharpman		19.____
20. Arnold Snyder		20.____
21. Nathan Sentner		21.____
22. Marion Stoup		22.____

QUESTIONS 23-30.

In questions 23-30, choose the letter that corresponds to the correct answer.

23. Assume that total deaths in one year amounted to 80,000. If heart disease accounted for 44% of these deaths, how many people died of all other causes? 23.____

    A. 35,200 B. 79,000 C. 44,800 D. 80,000

24. Assume that, of 885 people who died of hepatitis during a given year, 1/3 died between January 1 and May 31. What was the average number of deaths per month between January and May? 24.____

    A. 59 B. 295 C. 147 D. 49

25. Of 1200 deaths from diabetes in one year, 1/4 were in Manhattan and 1/6 in the Bronx. Of the remaining number, 2/5 were in Brooklyn. How many deaths from diabetes occurred in Brooklyn? 25.____

    A. 200 B. 300 C. 280 D. 500

26. Assume that in one year there were 840 deaths from all causes among a given age group. If 247 people died as a result of accidents and 73 died as a result of homicides, what percentage of people in this group died as a result of accidents and homicides (taken together)? 26.____

A. 29 B. 38 C. 73 D. 84

27. Assume that in 2000, deaths from tuberculosis were 1400 and deaths from diabetes were 1260. If in 2001 deaths from tuberculosis declined to 1120, and deaths from diabetes declined at the same rate, how many deaths from diabetes occurred in 2001? 27.____

A. 1008 B. 1120 C. 1260 D. 1400

28. In a given year, the number of deaths from enteritis, duodenitis and colitis totalled 280. The following year, deaths from enteritis remained the same and deaths from duodenitis increased; total deaths from the 3 causes was 250. Did deaths from colitis increase, decrease, or remain the same? 28.____

A. Increased
B. Decreased
C. Remained the same
D. Cannot be determined

29. Assume that 200 men and 100 women died of influenza in one year. If the next year the total number of such deaths remained the same, but 25% fewer died of influenza, how many women died of influenza? 29.____

A. 100 B. 110 C. 125 D. 150

30. Assume that in one year, in the 45 to 64 year age group, 17,000 men and 10,000 women died. Of this number, 23% of the men and 35% of the women died of malignant neoplasms. In the 65 year and over age group, 25,000 men and 23,000 women died. Of this number, 19% of the men and 16% of the women died of malignant neoplasms. 30.____
Of these 4 groups of people, which had the largest number of deaths from malignant neoplasms?

A. Men, 45-64 years
B. Women, 45-64 years
C. Men, 65 and over
D. Women, 65 and over

KEY (CORRECT ANSWERS)

1. F
2. F
3. T
4. T
5. F
6. X-03-50-3-106-a
7. X-07-10-4-102-c
8. Y-08-30-4-105-d
9. X-05-60-2-104-b
10. Y-04-20-1-101-c
11. Y-01-60-5-107-a
12. X-06-50-3-103-b
13. E
14. D
15. A
16. E
17. D
18. A
19. C
20. E
21. B
22. E
23. C
24. A
25. C
26. B
27. A
28. B
29. D
30. C

EXAMINATION SECTION
TEST 1

DIRECTIONS: Each question or incomplete statement is followed by several suggested answers or completions. Select the one that BEST answers the question or completes the statement. *PRINT THE LETTER OF THE CORRECT ANSWER IN THE SPACE AT THE RIGHT.*

Questions 1-20.

DIRECTIONS: Column I below lists words used in medical practice. Column II lists phrases which describe the words in Column I. Opposite the number preceding each of the words in Column I, place the letter preceding the phrase in Column II which BEST describes the word in Column I.

COLUMN I

1. Abrasion 1.____
2. Aseptic 2.____
3. Cardiac 3.____
4. Catarrh 4.____
5. Contamination 5.____
6. Dermatology 6.____
7. Disinfectant 7.____
8. Dyspepsia 8.____
9. Epidemic 9.____
10. Epidermis 10.____
11. Incubation 11.____
12. Microscope 12.____
13. Pediatrics 13.____
14. Plasma 14.____
15. Prenatal 15.____
16. Retina 16.____
17. Syphilis 17.____
18. Syringe 18.____
19. Toxemia 19.____
20. Vaccine 20.____

COLUMN II

A. A disturbance of digestion
B. Destroying the germs of disease
C. A general poisoning of the blood
D. An instrument used for injecting fluids
E. A scraping off of the skin
F. Free from disease germs
G. An apparatus for viewing internal organs by means of x-rays
H. An instrument for assisting the eye in observing minute objects
I. An inoculable immunizing agent
J. The extensive prevalence in a community of a
K. Chemical product of an organ
L. Preceding birth
M. Fever
N. The branch of medical science that relates to the skin and its diseases
O. Fluid part of the blood
P. The science of the hygienic care of children
Q. Infection by contact
R. Relating to the heart
S. Inner structure of the eye
T. Outer portion of the skin
U. Pertaining to the ductless glands
V. An infectious venereal disease
W. The development of an infectious disease from the period of infection to that of the appearance of the first symptoms
X. Simple inflammation of a mucous membrane
Y. An instrument for measuring blood pressure

Questions 21-25.

DIRECTIONS: Each of Questions 21 through 25 consists of four words. Three of these words belong together. One word does NOT belong with the other three. For each group of words, you are to select the one word which does NOT belong with the other three words.

21. A. conclude B. terminate C. initiate D. end 21.____

22. A. deficient B. inadequate 22.____
C. excessive D. insufficient

23. A. rare B. unique C. unusual D. frequent 23.____

24. A. unquestionable B. uncertain 24.____
C. doubtful D. indefinite

25. A. stretch B. contract C. extend D. expand 25.____

KEY (CORRECT ANSWERS)

1. E
2. F
3. R
4. X
5. Q

6. N
7. B
8. A
9. J
10. T

11. W
12. H
13. P
14. O
15. L

16. S
17. V
18. D
19. C
20. I

21. C
22. C
23. D
24. A
25. B

TEST 2

DIRECTIONS: Each question or incomplete statement is followed by several suggested answers or completions. Select the one that BEST answers the question or completes the statement. *PRINT THE LETTER OF THE CORRECT ANSWER IN THE SPACE AT THE RIGHT.*

Questions 1-4.

DIRECTIONS: Questions 1 through 4 pertain to the meaning of terms which may be encountered in laboratory work. For each question, select the option whose meaning is MOST NEARLY the same as that of the numbered item.

1. Atrophied 1.____

   A. enlarged
   B. relaxed
   C. strengthened
   D. wasted

2. Leucocyte 2.____

   A. white cell
   B. red cell
   C. epithelial cell
   D. dermal cell

3. Permeable 3.____

   A. volatile
   B. variable
   C. flexible
   D. penetrable

4. Attenuate 4.____

   A. dilute
   B. infect
   C. oxidize
   D. strengthen

Questions 5-11.

DIRECTIONS: For Questions 5 through 11, select the letter preceding the word which means MOST NEARLY the same as the first word.

5. legible 5.____

   A. readable B. eligible C. learned D. lawful

6. observe 6.____

   A. assist B. watch C. correct D. oppose

7. habitual 7.____

   A. punctual
   B. occasional
   C. usual
   D. actual

8. chronological 8.____

   A. successive
   B. earlier
   C. later
   D. studious

9. arrest 9.____

A. punish B. run C. threaten D. stop

10. abstain 10.____

A. refrain B. indulge C. discolor D. spoil

11. toxic 11.____

A. poisonous
B. decaying
C. taxing
D. defective

12. The *initial* contact is of great importance in setting a pattern for future relations. 12.____
The word *initial,* as used in this sentence, means MOST NEARLY

A. first B. written C. direct D. hidden

13. The doctor prescribed a diet which was *adequate* for the patient's needs. 13.____
The word *adequate,* as used in this sentence, means MOST NEARLY

A. insufficient
B. unusual
C. required
D. enough

14. The child was reported to be suffering from a vitamin *deficiency.* 14.____
The word *deficiency,* as used in this sentence, means MOST NEARLY

A. surplus B. infection C. shortage D. injury

15. In obtaining medical case data, a medical record librarian should discourage the patient from giving *irrelevant* information. 15.____
The word *irrelevant,* as used in this sentence, means MOST NEARLY

A. too detailed
B. pertaining to relatives
C. insufficient
D. inappropriate

16. The doctor requested that a *tentative* appointment be made for the patient. 16.____
The word *tentative,* as used in this sentence, means MOST NEARLY

A. definite
B. subject to change
C. later
D. of short duration

17. The black plague resulted in an usually high *mortality rate* in the population of Europe. 17.____
The term *mortality rate,* as used in this sentence, means MOST NEARLY

A. future immunity of the people
B. death rate
C. general weakening of the health of the people
D. sickness rate

18. The public health assistant was asked to file a number of *identical* reports on the case. 18.____
The word *identical,* as used in this sentence, means MOST NEARLY

A. accurate B. detailed C. same D. different

19. The nurse assisted in *the biopsy* of the patient. 19.____
The word *biopsy,* as used in this sentence, means MOST NEARLY

A. autopsy
B. excision and diagnostic study of tissue
C. biography and health history
D. administering of anesthesia

20. The assistant noted that the swelling on the patient's face had *subsided.* 20.____
The word *subsided,* as used in this sentence, means MOST NEARLY

A. become aggravated
B. increased
C. vanished
D. abated

21. The patient was given food *intravenously.* 21.____
The word *intravenously,* as used in this sentence, means MOST NEARLY

A. orally
B. against his will
C. through the veins
D. without condiment

Questions 22-25.

DIRECTIONS: Each of Questions 22 through 25 consists of four words. Three of these words belong together. One word does NOT belong with the other three. For each group of words, you are to select the one word which does NOT belong with the other three words.

22. A. accelerate B. quicken C. accept D. hasten 22.____

23. A. sever B. rupture C. rectify D. tear 23.____

24. A. innocuous B. injurious C. dangerous D. harmful 24.____

25. A. adulterate B. contaminate C. taint D. disinfect 25.____

KEY (CORRECT ANSWERS)

1.	D	11.	A	21.	C
2.	A	12.	A	22.	C
3.	D	13.	D	23.	C
4.	A	14.	C	24.	A
5.	A	15.	D	25.	D
6.	B	16.	B		
7.	C	17.	B		
8.	A	18.	C		
9.	D	19.	B		
10.	A	20.	D		

TEST 3

DIRECTIONS: Each question or incomplete statement is followed by several suggested answers or completions. Select the one that BEST answers the question or completes the statement. *PRINT THE LETTER OF THE CORRECT ANSWER IN THE SPACE AT THE RIGHT.*

Questions 1-25.

DIRECTIONS: Each of Questions 1 through 25 consists of a word, in capitals, followed by four suggested meanings of the word. For each question, indicate in the space at the right the letter preceding the word which means MOST NEARLY the same as the word in capitals.

1. TEMPORARY 1.____
   - A. permanently
   - B. for a limited time
   - C. at the same time
   - D. frequently

2. INQUIRE 2.____
   - A. order
   - B. agree
   - C. ask
   - D. discharge

3. SUFFICIENT 3.____
   - A. enough
   - B. inadequate
   - C. thorough
   - D. capable

4. AMBULATORY 4.____
   - A. bedridden
   - B. left-handed
   - C. walking
   - D. laboratory

5. DILATE 5.____
   - A. enlarge
   - B. contract
   - C. revise
   - D. restrict

6. NUTRITIOUS 6.____
   - A. protective
   - B. healthful
   - C. fattening
   - D. nourishing

7. CONGENITAL 7.____
   - A. with pleasure
   - B. defective
   - C. likeable
   - D. existing from birth

8. ISOLATION 8.____
   - A. sanitation
   - B. quarantine
   - C. rudeness
   - D. exposure

9. SPASM 9.____
   - A. splash
   - B. twitch
   - C. space
   - D. blow

10. HEMORRHAGE 10.____

A. bleeding
B. ulcer
C. hereditary disease
D. lack of blood

11. NOXIOUS 11.____

A. gaseous B. harmful C. soothing D. repulsive

12. PYOGENIC 12.____

A. disease producing
B. fever producing
C. pus forming
D. water forming

13. RENAL 13.____

A. brain B. heart C. kidney D. stomach

14. ENDEMIC 14.____

A. epidemic
B. endermic
C. endoblast
D. peculiar to a particular people or locality, as a disease

15. MACULATION 15.____

A. reticulation
B. inoculation
C. maturation
D. defilement

16. TOLERATE 16.____

A. fear B. forgive C. allow D. despise

17. VENTILATE 17.____

A. vacate B. air C. extricate D. heat

18. SUPERIOR 18.____

A. perfect
B. subordinate
C. lower
D. higher

19. EXTREMITY 19.____

A. extent B. limb C. illness D. execution

20. DIVULGED 20.____

A. unrefined B. secreted C. revealed D. divided

21. SIPHON 21.____

A. drain B. drink C. compute D. discard

22. EXPIRATION 22.____

A. trip
B. demonstration
C. examination
D. end

23. AEROSOL 23.____

 A. a gas dispersed in a liquid
 B. a liquid dispersed in a gas
 C. a liquid dispersed in a solid
 D. a solid dispersed in a liquid

24. ETIOLOGY 24.____

 A. cause of a disease
 B. method of cure
 C. method of diagnosis
 D. study of insects

25. IN VITRO 25.____

 A. in alkali
 B. in the body
 C. in the test tube
 D. in vacuum

KEY (CORRECT ANSWERS)

1. B
2. C
3. A
4. C
5. A
6. D
7. D
8. B
9. B
10. A
11. B
12. C
13. C
14. D
15. D
16. C
17. B
18. D
19. B
20. C
21. A
22. D
23. B
24. A
25. C

EXAMINATION SECTION
TEST 1

DIRECTIONS: Each question or incomplete statement is followed by several suggested answers or completions. Select the one that BEST answers the question or completes the statement. *PRINT THE LETTER OF THE CORRECT ANSWER IN THE SPACE AT THE RIGHT.*

1. Assume that you are working in an admitting office near the main entrance of a hospital. Visitors often come into your office to ask questions about hospital procedures and your supervisor has told you to be as helpful as possible in these situations. 1.____
If a visitor comes in and asks you some questions about hospital procedures in a loud and emotional voice, the BEST course of action for you to take would be to

   A. ask him to leave the hospital and come back when he can control himself
   B. ask him to write the questions on a sheet of paper
   C. remain calm and try to answer his questions
   D. tell him to calm down or you will not answer any questions

2. A certain hospital office administers a community health program in which members of the public are enrolled. There has been a recent change of procedure in the program and the office expects to receive a large number of letters from those enrolled asking about the change. 2.____
Of the following, the MOST appropriate method of answering these letters is to

   A. invite each person who sends in a letter to come to the office so that the change can be explained in a personal interview
   B. prepare a form letter which explains the change of procedure and send a copy to each person who sends in a letter
   C. stamp the notation *Procedure Changed/Please Comply* on each letter and mail it back to the sender together with a description of the change of procedure
   D. telephone each person who sends in a letter and explain the change of procedure

3. Assume that you work in a business office of a hospital and your supervisor gives you an assignment to be completed in one week. Part of the assignment requires you to obtain information from the various departments of the hospital. All departments have cooperated in giving you the required information, except one. Despite your repeated attempts to secure the information, it is still missing the day before your assignment is scheduled for completion. Even if you received the missing information immediately, you could not complete the assignment on time. 3.____
Of the following, the FIRST action you should take in this situation is to

   A. advise your supervisor that you were not given enough time to complete the assignment
   B. contact the department which has the information you need and tell them that their failure to cooperate has made it impossible for you to complete your assignment on time
   C. explain to your supervisor why you cannot complete the assignment on time and ask him if he wishes to receive what you will be able to finish
   D. tell your supervisor that you will try to finish the assignment whenever the information is forthcoming

4. Suppose that you work in a hospital office and you are speaking on the telephone with another employee on hospital business. While you are speaking on the telephone, a co-worker enters the office and indicates that she would like to speak with you. 4.____
Of the following, the BEST course of action for you to take in this situation is to

A. excuse yourself on the telephone and ask your co-worker to wait until you are finished with the call
B. ignore your co-worker and continue your telephone conversation
C. immediately end your telephone conversation and tell your co-worker not to interrupt you again when you are speaking on the telephone
D. tell the employee on the telephone that you have to speak with someone else and will call back as soon as you are finished

5. Assume that you are in charge of the petty cash fund for your office. When an individual wants to be paid back for an expense, he must complete a receipt explaining the expense and sign the receipt when you give him the money. One day, a clerk in your office tells you that she has just returned after delivering a package and wants to be paid back immediately for the carfare she spent. The clerk says that she has a lot of work to do in the next few hours and will complete the receipt later in the day. The BEST course of action for you to take in this situation is to 5.____

A. explain to her that in order to receive the money she must complete and sign the receipt
B. give her the money and leave a note on her desk reminding her to complete and sign the receipt
C. give her the money and leave a note for yourself to make sure that she completes and signs the receipt
D. tell her that you will give her the money and that you will complete the receipt yourself

6. Suppose that you have recently been assigned to an office and that one of your tasks is to keep files in proper order. You observe that some of your co-workers remove folders from the files, with no indication of removal. These actions have made it difficult for you to locate the folders when you need them. 6.____
Of the following, the MOST desirable method of correcting this situation is to

A. make photocopies of the materials in all the folders and organize a duplicate set of files so that you will always have the folders readily available
B. make sure that there are enough out-guides available and that everyone in the office is instructed to use them whenever a folder is removed
C. tell your co-workers that they can use the files only after they tell you what folders they are going to remove
D. ask your co-workers to leave a note on your desk whenever anyone removes a folder from the files

7. Of the following, the LEAST desirable action to take when writing out a check to a person is to 7.____

A. fill out the check in pencil
B. date the check
C. number the check
D. write the person's full name

Questions 8-17.

DIRECTIONS: Questions 8 through 17 each show in Column I names written on four cards (lettered w, x, y, z) which have to be filed. You are to choose the option (lettered A, B, C, or D) in Column II which BEST represents the proper order of filing according to the rules and sample question given below. The cards are to filed according to the following Rules for Alphabetical Filing.

RULES FOR ALPHABETICAL FILING

1. The names of individuals are filed in strict alphabetical order, first according to the last name, then according to first name or initial, and finally according to middle name or initial. For example: George Allen precedes Edward Bell; Leonard Reston precedes Lucille Reston.

2. When last names are the same, for example, A. Green and Agnes Green, the one with the initial comes before the one with the name written out when the first initials are identical.

3. When first and last names are the same, a name without a middle initial comes before one with a middle initial. For example: Ralph Simon comes before both Ralph A. Simon and Ralph Adam Simon.

4. When first and last names are the same, a name with a middle initial comes before one with a middle name beginning with the same initial. For example: Sam P. Rogers comes before Sam Paul Rogers.

5. Prefixes such as De, O', Mac, Mc, and Van are filed as written and are treated as part of the names to which they are connected. For example: Gladys McTeaque is filed before Frances Meadows.

6. Titles and designations such as Dr., Mr., and Prof, are ignored in filing.

SAMPLE QUESTION

COLUMN I	COLUMN II	
w. Jane Earl	A. w, y, z, x	The correct way to file the cards is:
x. James A. Earle	B. y, w, z, x	y. James Earl
y. James Earl	C. x, y, w, z	w. Jane Earl
z. J. Earle	D. x, w, y, z	z. J. Earle
		x. James A. Earle

The correct filing order is shown by the letters y, w, z, x (in that order). Since, in Column II, B appears in front of the letters y, w, z, x (in that order), B is the correct answer to the sample question.

Now answer Questions 8 through 17 using the same procedure.

		COLUMN I	COLUMN II	
8.	w.	John Smith	A. w, x, y, z	8.____
	x.	Joan Smythe	B. y, z, x, w	
	y.	Gerald Schmidt	C. y, z, w, x	
	z.	Gary Schmitt	D. z, y, w, x	
9.	w.	A. Black	A. w, x, y, z	9.____
	x.	Alan S. Black	B. w, y, x, z	
	y.	Allan Black	C. w, y, z, x	
	z.	Allen A. Black	D. x, w, y, z	
10.	w.	Samuel Haynes	A. w, x, y, z	10.____
	x.	Sam C. Haynes	B. x, w, z, y	
	y.	David Haynes	C. y, z, w, x	
	z.	Dave L. Haynes	D. z, y, x, w	
11.	w.	Lisa B. McNeil	A. x, y, w, z	11.____
	x.	Tom MacNeal	B. x, z, y, w	
	y.	Lisa McNeil	C. y, w, z, x	
	z.	Lorainne McNeal	D. z, x, y, w	
12.	w.	Larry Richardson	A. w, y, x, z	12.____
	x.	Leroy Richards	B. y, x, z, w	
	y.	Larry S. Richards	C. y, z, x, w	
	z.	Leroy C. Richards	D. x, w, z, y	
13.	w.	Arlene Lane	A. w, z, y, x	13.____
	x.	Arlene Cora Lane	B. w, z, x, y	
	y.	Arlene Clair Lane	C. y, x, z, w	
	z.	Arlene C. Lane	D. z, y, w, x	
14.	w.	Betty Fish	A. w, x, z, y	14.____
	x.	Prof. Ann Fish	B. x, w, y, z	
	y.	Norma Fisch	C. y, z, x, w	
	z.	Dr. Richard Fisch	D. z, y, w, x	
15.	w.	Dr. Anthony David Lukak	A. w, y, z, x	15.____
	x.	Mr. Steven Charles Lucas	B. x, z, w, y	
	y.	Mr. Anthony J. Lukak	C. z, x, y, w	
	z.	Prof. Steven C. Lucas	D. z, x, w, y	
16.	w.	Martha Y. Lind	A. w, y, z, x	16.____
	x.	Mary Beth Linden	B. w, y, x, z	
	y.	Martha W. Lind	C. y, w, z, x	
	z.	Mary Bertha Linden	D. y, w, x, z	
17.	w.	Prof. Harry Michael MacPhelps	A. w, z, x, y	17.____
	x.	Mr. Horace M. MacPherson	B. w, y, z, x	
	y.	Mr. Harold M. McPhelps	C. z, x, w, y	
	z.	Prof. Henry Martin MacPherson	D. x, z, y, w	

18. Assume that one of your duties is to make sure that the office supply cabinet contains sufficient quantities of the forms used in your office. 18.____
Of the following, the BEST course of action for you to adopt in order to be able to perform this duty is to

A. ask your supervisor each day whether the office is low on any form and plan to order only those forms which are mentioned
B. decide what kind of duplicating equipment will be needed to produce copies of the forms when the current supply is exhausted
C. plan for your office's needs and order copies of the forms before the number of copies in the cabinet falls below a minimum amount
D. wait until one of your co-workers tells you that the office is running short of a form and then obtain copies of it as quickly as possible

19. The type of file in which reports are found under the heading *New York State-Queens* is MOST likely to be a ______ file. 19.____

A. chronological
B. geographic
C. numeric
D. tickler

20. Assume that you are working in the personnel office of a hospital. One day, you answer a telephone call and the caller asks to speak to one of your co-workers, Ms. Wilson, who is on sick leave. You explain this to the caller who then tells you that she is a friend of Ms. Wilson's and would like to invite her to a party but has lost Ms. Wilson's home address and telephone number. The caller then asks you if you can give her this information. 20.____
Of the following, the BEST course of action for you to take then is to

A. give the caller the information and then leave Ms. Wilson a message about the telephone call
B. decline to give the caller the information and ask the caller if she wants to leave a message for Ms. Wilson
C. tell the caller that all information about hospital employees is confidential and that you cannot spend any more time on a personal telephone call
D. tell the caller that you need some time to look up the information and ask her to call back later in the day

KEY (CORRECT ANSWERS)

1. C
2. B
3. C
4. A
5. A

6. B
7. A
8. C
9. A
10. D

11. B
12. B
13. A
14. C
15. D

16. C
17. A
18. C
19. B
20. B

TEST 2

DIRECTIONS: Each question or incomplete statement is followed by several suggested answers or completions. Select the one that BEST answers the question or completes the statement. *PRINT THE LETTER OF THE CORRECT ANSWER IN THE SPACE AT THE RIGHT.*

1. Suppose that you answer a telephone call and a woman asks to speak with your supervisor. Your supervisor, however, is speaking with someone on another telephone line. Of the following, the BEST course of action for you to take in this situation is to 1.____

   A. ask the caller for her name and telephone number and tell her that your supervisor will return the call as soon as possible
   B. ask the caller to call again later in the day because your supervisor is busy right now
   C. explain to the caller why your supervisor cannot answer the call and ask her to wait until your supervisor can speak with her
   D. tell the caller that your supervisor is speaking on another line and ask her if she wants to wait until that call is finished or wants to leave a message

2. One morning, you receive a telephone call and the caller requests an appointment with your supervisor. Your supervisor is out of the office for the day. You tell the caller that she can meet with your supervisor at 10 A.M. the next day and she agrees. After ending this telephone conversation, you discover that your supervisor already has scheduled an appointment with someone else for that time. Of the following, the BEST course of action for you to take in this situation is to 2.____

   A. contact your supervisor and find out which appointment he would rather keep
   B. decide which appointment is less important and cancel it
   C. try to change the appointment you made for the caller to another time
   D. wait until the next day and then tell your supervisor that he has a choice of two appointments scheduled at 10 A.M.

3. Assume that your supervisor has asked you to go to the stockroom to pick up supplies that your office has ordered. Of the following, the FIRST action you should take when you are given the supplies is to 3.____

   A. bring the supplies back to your office immediately
   B. call your supervisor to find out whether any other supplies are needed
   C. check to see whether you have received everything that was ordered
   D. sign a receipt for the supplies

Questions 4-8.

DIRECTIONS: In each of Questions 4 through 8, there is a sentence containing one underlined word. Choose the word (lettered A, B, C, or D) which means MOST NEARLY the same as the underlined word as it is used in the sentence.

4. The number of applicants exceeded the <u>anticipated</u> figure. 4.____

   A. expected B. required C. revised D. necessary

5. The clerk was told to <u>collate</u> the pages of the report. 5.____

   A. destroy B. edit C. correct D. assemble

6. Mr. Wells is not <u>authorized</u> to release the information. 6.____

   A. inclined B. pleased C. permitted D. trained

7. The secretary chose an <u>appropriate</u> office for the meeting. 7.____

   A. empty B. decorated C. nearby D. suitable

8. The employee performs a <u>complex</u> set of tasks each day. 8.____

   A. difficult B. important C. pleasant D. large

9. Of the following, the MOST important purpose of a filing system generally is to 9.____

   A. reduce the number of records which must be readily available
   B. make it possible to locate information quickly
   C. organize material under the fewest number of headings
   D. provide a secure storage place if an unexpected emergency occurs

10. Assume that you answer a telephone call and the caller wishes to speak to one of your co-workers, who is out of the office. 10.____
    Of the following, the LEAST appropriate information for you to indicate on a message which you leave for your co-worker is

    A. the caller's telephone number and extension
    B. the date and time the call was received
    C. the office telephone on which the call was received
    D. your name or initials

11. The notation *cc: Mr. Rogers* appearing at the bottom of a letter is MOST likely to indicate that Mr. Rogers 11.____

    A. typed the letter
    B. is the subject of the letter
    C. wrote the rough draft of the letter for his supervisor
    D. is to receive a copy of the letter

Questions 12-16.

DIRECTIONS: Questions 12 through 16 are to be answered ONLY on the basis of the information provided in the following passage.

For some office workers, it is useful to be familiar with the four main classes of domestic mail; for others, it is essential. Each class has a different rate of postage and some have requirements concerning wrapping, sealing or special information to be placed on the package. First class mail, the class which may not be opened for postal inspection, includes letters, postcards, business reply cards, and other kinds of written matter. There are different rates for some of the kinds of cards which can be sent by first class mail. The maximum weight for an item sent by first class mail is 70 pounds. An item which is not letter size should be marked *First Class* on all sides.

Although office workers most often come into contact with first class mail, they may find it helpful to know something about the other classes. Second class mail is generally used for mailing newspapers and magazines. Publishers of these articles must meet certain U.S. Postal Service requirements in order to obtain a permit to use second class mailing rates. Third class mail, which must weigh less than 1 pound, includes printed materials and merchandise parcels. There are two rate structures for this class, a single piece rate and a bulk rate. Fourth class mail, also known as parcel post, includes packages weighing from one to 40 pounds. For more information about these classes of mail and the actual mailing rates, contact your local post office.

12. According to this passage, first class mail is the only class which 12.____

A. has a limit on the maximum weight of an item
B. has different rates for items within the class
C. may not be opened for postal inspection
D. should be used by office workers

13. According to this passage, the one of the following items which may correctly be sent by fourth class mail is a 13.____

A. magazine weighing one-half pound
B. package weighing one-half pound
C. package weighing two pounds
D. postcard

14. According to this passage, there are different postage rates for 14.____

A. a newspaper sent by second class mail and a magazine sent by second class mail
B. each of the classes of mail
C. each pound of fourth class mail
D. printed material sent by third class mail and merchandise parcels sent by third class mail

15. In order to send a newspaper by second class mail, a publisher must 15.____

A. have met certain postal requirements and obtained a permit
B. indicate whether he wants to use the single piece or the bulk rate
C. make certain that the newspaper weighs less than one pound
D. mark the newspaper *Second Class* on the top and bottom of the wrapper

16. Of the following types of information, the one which is NOT mentioned in the passage is the 16.____

A. class of mail to which parcel post belongs
B. kinds of items which can be sent by each class of mail
C. maximum weight for an item sent by fourth class mail
D. postage rate for each of the four classes of mail

17. Assume that one of your tasks is to complete a form indicating which laboratory test a doctor is ordering. 17.____
A doctor has written an order for a laboratory test, but his writing is illegible, and you cannot tell which of two tests he is ordering.
Of the following, the BEST course of action for you to take in this situation is to

A. show the doctor his written order, ask the doctor which test he meant to order, and then fill out the form
B. indicate both tests on the form so that you will be certain that the correct test is performed
C. send the doctor's written order to the laboratory without indicating on the form which test is to be done, since the laboratory technician will know from experience which test the doctor meant to order
D. wait for the doctor to reorder the test when he finds out that it has not been done

18. Suppose that one of your tasks is to mail an application form and covering letter to each applicant for a program administered by your office. 18.____
Of the following, the MOST appropriate notation to use at the bottom of the letter to indicate that the form is included in the envelope is

A. Enc. B. etc. C. P.S. D. R.S.V.P.

19. Of the following, the LEAST appropriate practice involved in the proper use of a file cabinet and its contents is to 19.____

A. close a cabinet drawer immediately after using it
B. place active files in top drawers and less active files in bottom drawers
C. remove a file folder by holding the side of the folder, not the tab
D. store office supplies behind files in unfilled cabinet drawers

20. Assume that you are sending out a business letter and have to write *Attention: Mrs. Williams* on the envelope. Of the following, the PROPER place on the envelope for you to write this notation is the ______ of the envelope. 20.____

A. upper right corner of the back
B. upper right corner on the front
C. lower left corner of the back
D. lower left corner on the front

KEY (CORRECT ANSWERS)

1. D	11. D
2. C	12. C
3. C	13. C
4. A	14. B
5. D	15. A
6. C	16. D
7. D	17. A
8. A	18. A
9. B	19. D
10. C	20. D

TEST 3

DIRECTIONS: Each question or incomplete statement is followed by several suggested answers or completions. Select the one that BEST answers the question or completes the statement. *PRINT THE LETTER OF THE CORRECT ANSWER IN THE SPACE AT THE RIGHT.*

1. Which of the following is the MOST efficient method of reproducing 50 copies of a single-page form letter? 1.____

   A. Carbon copying
   B. Scanning and re-editing
   C. Word processing
   D. Photocopying

2. Removing inactive documents from the active files and transferring them to a records storage center is important for which of the following reasons? 2.____

   A. The active records can be filed and retrieved more quickly.
   B. The inactive files will no longer be needed.
   C. No control is necessary with respect to the inactive files.
   D. It allows you to know which documents must be filed and which need not be filed.

3. You are trying to obtain information from someone who is to be admitted to a hospital. The person tells you in an angry tone of voice that he will not give you a certain item of information. You need this information to complete the admission form. 3.____
   Of the following, the FIRST action which you should take in this situation is to

   A. tell him that he will not be admitted unless he gives you the information
   B. tell him to wait while you go asks your supervisor to get the information from the person
   C. leave out that item of information but clearly show your anger so he will not act that way again
   D. tell him the reason why you need that item of information

4. Assume that you work in a hospital office which often receives telephone calls from people requesting information about patients in the hospital. One day, you receive a telephone call from a person who says that he is the brother of a patient. The caller asks you what is wrong with the patient and how long he will remain in the hospital. 4.____
   Of the following, the BEST course of action for you to take in this situation is to

   A. check the patient's hospital records to make sure the patient has a brother and then give the caller the information he requested
   B. contact the patient's doctor to get the information and then give it to the caller
   C. inform the caller that you are not permitted to give out that information and refer him to the patient's doctor
   D. tell the caller that you will have to check the hospital records to get the information and ask the caller for his telephone number so that you can call him back

Questions 5-14.

DIRECTIONS: Questions 5 through 14 are based on the following table, which shows the number of persons admitted to and discharged from each of five hospitals for each of the first six months of 2005. Admissions are shown under the columns labeled *ADM* and discharges under the columns labeled *DIS.*

ADMISSIONS AND DISCHARGES
January-June, 2005

MONTH	HOSPITAL L		HOSPITAL M		HOSPITAL N		HOSPITAL O		HOSPITAL P	
	ADM	DIS	ADM	DIS	ADM	DIS	ADM	DIS	ADM	DIS
JAN.	367	291	389	372	738	694	1101	942	1567	1373
FEB.	447	473	411	376	874	841	1353	1296	1754	1687
MAR.	426	437	403	436	831	813	1297	1358	1690	1740
APR.	403	390	370	385	794	850	1057	1190	1389	1650
MAY	370	411	361	390	680	692	984	1039	1195	1210
JUNE	334	355	377	384	630	619	1121	1043	1125	1065

5. The TOTAL number of admissions to the five hospitals for the month of April was 5.____

A. 3,833 B. 3,952 C. 3,983 D. 4,013

6. The TOTAL number of discharges from Hospital N for the months of April, May, and June was 6.____

A. 1,159 B. 2,104 C. 2,161 D. 2,251

7. The TOTAL number of admissions to Hospitals L, M, and O for the month of February was 7.____

A. 1,732 B. 2,101 C. 2,145 D. 2,211

8. The TOTAL number of discharges from the five hospitals for the month of January was 8.____

A. 3,542 B. 3,672 C. 3,832 D. 4,162

9. For which month were there MORE discharges at each of the five hospitals than there were admissions? 9.____

A. January B. March C. May D. June

10. The average number of admissions each month at Hospital O for the first six months of 2005 was MOST NEARLY 10.____

A. 1,097 B. 1,152 C. 1,163 D. 1,196

11. Of the total number of admissions at the five hospitals for the month of March, what percentage, to the nearest whole percent, was admitted to Hospital P? 11.____

A. 29% B. 32% C. 34% D. 36%

12. The average number of discharges from each of the five hospitals for the month of May was MOST NEARLY 12.____

A. 748 B. 754 C. 762 D. 764

13. Of the total number of admissions to the five hospitals for the month of June, what percentage, to the nearest whole percent, was admitted to Hospital M? 13.____

A. 7% B. 9% C. 11% D. 13%

14. On the basis of the information given in the table, which one of the following statements is CORRECT? 14.____
The number of
   A. admissions to each hospital for the month of April was less than the number of admissions for the month of March
   B. admissions to Hospital L increased each month from January through April and decreased each month from May through June
   C. discharges from each hospital for the month of June was less than the number of discharges for the month of May
   D. discharges from Hospital O increased each month from January through March and decreased each month from April through June

Questions 15-20.

DIRECTIONS: Questions 15 through 20 consist of three lines of code letters and numbers. The numbers on each line should correspond with the code letters on the same line in accordance with the table below.

Code Letter	F	X	L	M	R	W	T	S	B	H
Corresponding Number	0	1	2	3	4	5	6	7	8	9

On some of the lines, an error exists in the coding. Compare the letters and numbers in each question carefully. If you find an error or errors on
only one of the lines in the question, mark your answer A;
any two lines in the question, mark your answer B;
all three lines in the question, mark your answer C;
none of the lines in the question, mark your answer D.

<u>SAMPLE QUESTION</u>:
LTSXHMF 2671930
TBRWHLM 6845913
SXLBFMR 5128034

In the above sample, the first line is correct since each code letter listed has the correct corresponding number. On the second line, an error exists because code letter L should have the number 2 instead of the number 1. On the third line, an error exists because the code letter S should have the number 7 instead of the number 5. Since there are errors on two of the three lines, the correct answer is B.

15. XMWBHLR 1358924 15.____
FWSLRHX 0572491
MTXBLTS 3618267

16. XTLSMRF 1627340 16.____
BMHRFLT 8394026
HLTSWRX 9267451

17.	LMBSFXS	2387016	17.____
	RWLHBSX	4532871	
	SMFXBHW	7301894	
18.	RSTWTSML	47657632	18.____
	LXRMHFBS	21439087	
	FTLBMRWX	06273451	
19.	XSRSBWFM	17478603	19.____
	BRMXRMXT	84314216	
	XSTFBWRL	17609542	
20.	TMSBXHLS	63781927	20.____
	RBSFLFWM	48702053	
	MHFXWTRS	39015647	

KEY (CORRECT ANSWERS)

1.	D	11.	D
2.	A	12.	A
3.	D	13.	C
4.	C	14.	A
5.	D	15.	D
6.	C	16.	A
7.	D	17.	C
8.	B	18.	B
9.	C	19.	C
10.	B	20.	D

EXAMINATION SECTION
TEST 1

DIRECTIONS: Each question or incomplete statement is followed by several suggested answers or completions. Select the one that BEST answers the question or completes the statement. *PRINT THE LETTER OF THE CORRECT ANSWER IN THE SPACE AT THE RIGHT.*

1. According to one suggested filing system, no more than 12 folders should be filed behind any one file guide and from 10 to 20 file guides should be used in each file drawer. Based on this filing system, the MAXIMUM number of folders that a four-drawer file cabinet can hold is 1.____

   A. 240 B. 480 C. 960 D. 1200

2. A certain office uses three different forms. Last year it used 3500 copies of Form L, 6700 copies of Form M, and 10,500 copies of Form P. This year, the office expects to decrease the use of each of these forms by 5%. 2.____
   The TOTAL number of these three forms which the office expects to use this year is

   A. 10,350 B. 16,560 C. 19,665 D. 21,735

3. The hourly rate of pay for a certain part-time employee is computed by dividing his yearly salary rate by the number of hours in the work year. The employee's yearly salary rate is $18,928, and there are 1,820 hours in the work year. 3.____
   If this employee works 18 hours during one week, his TOTAL earnings for these 18 hours are

   A. $180.00 B. $183.60 C. $187.20 D. $190.80

4. Assume that the regular work week of an employee is 35 hours and that the employee is paid for any extra hours worked according to the following schedule. For hours worked in excess of 35 hours, up to and including 40 hours, the employee receives his regular hourly rate of pay. For hours worked in excess of 40 hours, the employee receives 1 1/2 times his hourly rate of pay. 4.____
   If the employee's hourly rate of pay is $11.20 and he works 43 hours during a certain week, his TOTAL pay for the week would be

   A. $481.60 B. $498.40 C. $556.00 D. $722.40

5. The following table shows the total amount of money owed on the bills sent to each of four different accounts and the total amount of money which has been received from each of these accounts. 5.____

Name of Account	Amount Owed	Amount Received
Arnold	$55,989	$37,898
Barry	$97,276	$79,457
Carter	$62,736	$47,769
Daley	$77,463	$59,534

   The balance of an account is determined by subtracting the amount received from the amount owed. Based on this method of determining a balance, the account with the LARGEST balance is

   A. Arnold B. Barry C. Carter D. Daley

6. Suppose that you are transferring the charges of a number of hospital patients from each patient's individual records to one form. 6.____
To make sure that the amounts are transferred accurately, it would be BEST for you to

   A. check each amount copies against the appropriate patient's records after completing the transfers
   B. have someone read the amounts from the patient records while you write them on the form
   C. copy the amounts slowly and carefully so that you will not make a mistake
   D. write each amount lightly in pencil and then go over each number heavily with a pen

7. Assume that your office ordered supplies from a vendor on December 1. These supplies are to be used starting on February 2 of the following year, and it is essential that they arrive by that date. 7.____
Of the following, which is the BEST way to assure that the supplies arrive on time?

   A. Contact the post office before February 2 and inquire about the vendor's record in shipping supplies
   B. Keep in contact with the vendor until the supplies arrive, and follow up on any problems which arise
   C. Mail a duplicate copy of the order to the vendor sometime in January to serve as a reminder
   D. Telephone the vendor a week before February 2, and ask whether the supplies were shipped

8. Assume that you are working in an admissions area of a hospital and you are completing an admissions form for a new patient. In order to complete the form, you have to obtain certain information from the patient, such as his name, address, and age, and write it on the form. 8.____
Of the following, the FIRST action you should take after the patient tells you his name is to

   A. ask the patient for a copy of his birth certificate in order to verify his name
   B. ask the patient whether he has been a patient in your hospital before
   C. tell the patient to write his name on the form
   D. write his name in the appropriate place on the admissions form

9. Of the following, the BEST reason for a clerical division to have its own photocopying machine is that the division 9.____

   A. frequently needs copies of incoming correspondence
   B. frequently receives photographic negatives in the mail
   C. must enter the receipt date on all incoming mail
   D. uses 5,000 copies of a form each month

10. In your assignment to a hospital admitting office, you will be required to personally fill out an admissions form for each person before he is admitted to the hospital. Of the following, the MOST accurate way for you to obtain the information you need from a person is to 10.____

   A. ask him one question at a time based on the information you need
   B. ask him only those questions which can be answered by the words *yes* or *no*

C. give him the form and tell him to fill it out correctly
D. have him complete the entire form and then sign it yourself

Questions 11-20.

DIRECTIONS: Each of Questions 11 through 20 gives the identification number and name of aperson who has received treatment at a certain hospital. You are to choose the option (A, B, C, or D) which has EXACTLY the same identification number and name as those given in the question.

SAMPLE QUESTION

123765 Frank Y. Jones

A. 123675 Frank Y. Jones
B. 123765 Frank T. Jones
C. 123765 Frank Y. Johns
D. 123765 Frank Y. Jones

The correct answer is D. Only option D shows the identification number and name exactly as they are in the sample question. Option A has a mistake in the identification number. Option B has a mistake in the middle initial of the name. Option C has a mistake in the last name.

Now answer Questions 11 through 20 in the same manner.

11. 754898 Diane Malloy 11.____

A. 745898 Diane Malloy
B. 754898 Dion Malloy
C. 754898 Diane Malloy
D. 754898 Diane Maloy

12. 661018 Ferdinand Figueroa 12.____

A. 661818 Ferdinand Figeuroa
B. 661618 Ferdinand Figueroa
C. 661818 Ferdnand Figueroa
D. 661818 Ferdinand Figueroa

13. 100101 Norman D. Braustein 13.____

A. 100101 Norman D. Braustein
B. 101001 Norman D. Braustein
C. 100101 Norman P. Braustien
D. 100101 Norman D. Bruastein

14. 838696 Robert Kittredge 14.____

A. 838969 Robert Kittredge
B. 838696 Robert Kittredge
C. 388696 Robert Kittredge
D. 838696 Robert Kittridge

15. 243716 Abraham Soletsky 15.____

A. 243716 Abrahm Soletsky
B. 243716 Abraham Solestky
C. 243176 Abraham Soletsky
D. 243716 Abraham Soletsky

16. 981121 Phillip M. Maas 16.____

A. 981121 Phillip M. Mass
B. 981211 Phillip M. Maas
C. 981121 Phillip M. Maas
D. 981121 Phillip N. Maas

17. 786556 George Macalusso 17.____

A. 785656 George Macalusso
B. 786556 George Macalusso
C. 786556 George Maculasso
D. 786556 George Macluasso

18. 639472 Eugene Weber 18.____

A. 639472 Eugene Weber
B. 639472 Eugene Webre
C. 693472 Eugene Weber
D. 639742 Eugene Weber

19. 724936 John J. Lomonaco 19.____

A. 724936 John J. Lomanoco
B. 724396 John J. Lomonaco
C. 724936 John J. Lomonaco
D. 724936 John J. Lamonaco

20. 899868 Michael Schnitzer 20.____

A. 899868 Micheal Schnitzer
B. 898968 Michael Schnizter
C. 899688 Michael Schnitzer
D. 899868 Michael Schnitzer

KEY (CORRECT ANSWERS)

1. C
2. C
3. C
4. B
5. A
6. A
7. A
8. D
9. A
10. A
11. C
12. D
13. A
14. B
15. D
16. C
17. B
18. A
19. C
20. D

TEST 2

DIRECTIONS: Each question or incomplete statement is followed by several suggested answers or completions. Select the one that BEST answers the question or completes the statement. *PRINT THE LETTER OF TEE CORRECT ANSWER IN THE SPACE AT THE RIGHT.*

Questions 1-10.

DIRECTIONS: Questions 1 through 10 are to be answered on the basis of the information and the form given below.

The form below is a Daily Summary of Clinic Visits and lists ten persons who used a clinic in Washington Hospital on September 4.

The form includes the following information about each patient: Name, identification number, date of birth, case number, fee, and bill number.

SEPTEMBER 4
WASHINGTON HOSPITAL - DAILY SUMMARY OF CLINIC VISITS

Name of Patient Last, First	Identification Number	Date of Birth Mo.	Day	Yr.	Case Number	Fee	Bill Number
Enders, John	89-4143-67	08	01	71	434317	$ 90.00	129631
Dawes, Mary	71-6142-69	11	17	66	187963	$ 47.50	129632
Lang, Donald	54-1213-73	10	07	75	897436	$ 180.00	129633
Eiger, Alan	18-7649-63	06	19	51	134003	$ 110.00	129634
Ramirez, Jose	61-4319-69	03	30	96	379030	$ 130.00	129635
Ilono, Frank	13-9161-57	08	19	83	565645	$ 66.00	129636
Sloan, Irene	55-8643-66	05	13	57	799732	$ 112.50	129637
Long , Thomas	41-3963-74	12	03	76	009784	$ 37.50	129638
McKay, Cathy	14-9633-44	05	09	66	000162	$ 96.00	129639
Dale, Sarah	86-1113-69	11	13	59	543211	$ 138.00	129640

1. The fee for Cathy McKay is LESS than the fee for 1.____

   A. John Enders
   B. Alan Eiger
   C. Frank Ilono
   D. Thomas Long

2. The two patients who were born in the same year are 2.____

   A. John Enders and Frank Ilono
   B. Mary Dawes and Sarah Dale
   C. Donald Lang and Thomas Long
   D. Cathy McKay and Mary Dawes

3. The case number of Irene Sloan is 3.____

   A. 979732
   B. 799372
   C. 799732
   D. 797732

4. Cathy McKay's identification number is 4.____

   A. 44-9633-14
   B. 14-9633-44
   C. 000162
   D. 129639

5. Frank Ilono's case number is 5.____

A. 556645 B. 565465 C. 565645 D. 565654

6. The bill numbers for Jose Ramirez and Thomas Long are 6.____

A. 129635 and 129638
B. 129635 and 129683
C. 129634 and 129638
D. 129634 and 129637

7. The fees for Donald Lang, Sarah Dale, and Mary Dawes are 7.____

A. $47.50, $180.00, and $96.00
B. $110.00, $138.00, and $90.00
C. $180.00, $130.00, and $47.50
D. $180.00, $138.00, and $47.50

8. The case numbers for Thomas Long and Mary Dawes are 8.____

A. 009784 and 187963
B. 090784 and 187963
C. 009784 and 187693
D. 009874 and 187963

9. The identification numbers for Frank Ilono and Donald Lang are 9.____

A. 13-9161-57 and 54-1312-73
B. 54-1213-73 and 13-6191-57
C. 13-9161-57 and 54-1213-73
D. 54-1213-37 and 13-9161-57

10. The birth dates of Irene Sloan, John Enders, and Sarah Dale are 10.____

A. 05/31/57, 01/08/71, and 11/13/69
B. 05/13/67, 08/01/71, and 11/13/69
C. 05/31/57, 01/08/71, and 11/13/59
D. 05/13/57, 08/01/71, and 11/13/59

Questions 11-15.

DIRECTIONS: Questions 11 through 15 consist of sets of names and addresses. In each question, the name and address in Column II should be an EXACT copy of the name and address in Column I. Compare the name and address in Column II with the name and address in Column I.

If there is an error in the name only, mark your answer A;
If there is an error in the address only, mark your answer B;
If there is an error in both the name and address, mark your answer C;
If there is NO error in either the name or address, mark your answer D.

SAMPLE QUESTION

COLUMN I	COLUMN II
Mildred Bonilla 511 West 186 Street New York, N.Y. 10033	Mildred Bonila 511 West 186 Street New York, N.Y. 10032

Compare the name and address in Column II with the name and address in Column I. The name Bonila in Column II is spelled Bonilla in Column I. The zip code 10032 in Column II is given as 10033 in Column I. Since there is an error in both the name and address, the answer to the sample question is C.

Now answer Questions 11 through 15 in the same manner.

	COLUMN I	COLUMN II	
11.	Mr. & Mrs. George Petersson 87-11 91st Avenue Woodhaven, New York 11421	Mr. & Mrs. George Peterson 87-11 91st Avenue Woodhaven, New York 11421	11.____
12.	Mr. Ivan Klebnikov 1848 Newkirk Avenue Brooklyn, New York 11226	Mr. Ivan Klebikov 1848 Newkirk Avenue Brooklyn, New York 11622	12.____
13.	Samuel Rothfleisch 71 Pine Street New York, New York 10005	Samuel Rothfleisch 71 Pine Street New York, New York 10005	13.____
14.	Mrs. Isabel Tonnessen 198 East 185th Street Bronx, New York 10458	Mrs. Isabel Tonnessen 189 East 185th Street Bronx, New York 10458	14.____
15.	Esteban Perez 173 Eighth Street Staten Island, N.Y. 10306	Estaban Perez 173 Eighth Street Staten Island, N.Y. 10306	15.____

16. The MAIN purpose of an invoice is to 16.____

    A. confirm receipt of an order
    B. list items being sent to a buyer
    C. order items from a company
    D. provide written proof that a shipment has been received

17. You have been told to add various amounts listed on a billing form by operating a calculating machine. The machine prints on a roll of paper tape all amounts added and the answer to the computation. 17.____
    Of the following, the LEAST appropriate use for this tape is to

    A. check that no amounts were left out during the computation
    B. check that the amounts were entered correctly into the machine
    C. keep a record of the computation
    D. prove that the amounts on the original document are correct

18. Assume that you are working in a storehouse of a hospital system. One of your tasks is to fill requisitions from hospitals for office supplies. When a requisition is received, you much check inventory cards to determine whether an item is available. One day, you receive a requisition for office supplies; and upon checking the inventory cards, you find that one of the items ordered, a particular kind of paper, is not available. However, the other items are ready for shipment to the hospital. Of the following, the BEST course of action for you to take in this situation is to 18.____

A. have those items which are available sent to the hospital with an indication of which items were sent
B. purchase the missing paper yourself and then have the complete order sent to the hospital
C. substitute any other paper which is available and then have the order sent to the hospital
D. wait until the missing paper is available and then have the complete order sent to the hospital

19. One of your duties is to get certain information from people who are being treated at a hospital clinic. One day, you are trying to get this information from a person who begins to talk about matters unrelated to the information you are trying to obtain. 19.____
Of the following, the BEST course of action for you to take in this situation is to

A. allow the individual to continue talking about the unrelated matters since he will probably return to the information you need in a short time
B. ask the individual a question that may lead him back to the information you need
C. end the interview and obtain the information from other sources
D. tell the individual to give you the information you need and not discuss the unrelated matters

20. You have just asked a patient a question about the kind of hospitalization insurance he has. 20.____
The BEST way for you to make sure that you understand his answer to the question is to

A. ask the question again in a slightly different way and see if you get approximately the same answer
B. ask the same question again and listen carefully to see if the answer is the same
C. repeat the answer in your own words and ask the patient if that is what he meant
D. write the answer down on a piece of paper and read it back to the patient

---

KEY (CORRECT ANSWERS)

1.	B	11.	A
2.	D	12.	C
3.	C	13.	D
4.	B	14.	B
5.	C	15.	A
6.	A	16.	B
7.	D	17.	D
8.	A	18.	A
9.	C	19.	B
10.	D	20.	C

READING COMPREHENSION
UNDERSTANDING AND INTERPRETING WRITTEN MATERIAL
EXAMINATION SECTION
TEST 1

Questions 1-8.

DIRECTIONS: Each question or incomplete statement is followed by several suggested answers or completions. Select the one that BEST answers the question or completes the statement. *PRINT THE LETTER OF THE CORRECT ANSWER IN THE SPACE AT THE RIGHT.*

Questions 1 and 2.

DIRECTIONS: Your answers to Questions 1 and 2 must be based ONLY on the information given in the following paragraph.

Hospitals maintained wholly by public taxation may treat only those compensation cases which are emergencies and may not treat such emergency cases longer than the emergency exists; provided, however, that these restrictions shall not be applicable where there is not available a hospital other than a hospital maintained wholly by taxation.

1. According to the above paragraph, compensation cases 1.____

   A. are regarded as emergency cases by hospitals maintained wholly by public taxation
   B. are seldom treated by hospitals maintained wholly by public taxation
   C. are treated mainly by privately endowed hospitals
   D. may be treated by hospitals maintained wholly by public taxation if they are emergencies

2. According to the above paragraph, it is MOST reasonable to conclude that where a privately endowed hospital is available, 2.____

   A. a hospital supported wholly by public taxation may treat emergency compensation cases only so long as the emergency exists
   B. a hospital supported wholly by public taxation may treat any compensation cases
   C. a hospital supported wholly by public taxation must refer emergency compensation cases to such a hospital
   D. the restrictions regarding the treatment of compensation cases by a tax-supported hospital are not wholly applicable

Questions 3-7.

DIRECTIONS: Answer Questions 3 through 7 ONLY according to the information given in the following passage.

THE MANUFACTURE OF LAUNDRY SOAP

The manufacture of soap is not a complicated process. Soap is a fat or an oil, plus an alkali, water and salt. The alkali used in making commercial laundry soap is caustic soda. The salt used is the same as common table salt. A fat is generally an animal product that is not a liquid at room temperature. If heated, it becomes a liquid. An oil is generally liquid at room temperature. If the temperature is lowered, the oil becomes a solid just like ordinary fat.

At the soap plant, a huge tank five stories high, called a *kettle,* is first filled part way with fats and then the alkali and water are added. These ingredients are then heated and boiled together. Salt is then poured into the top of the boiling solution; and as the salt slowly sinks down through the mixture, it takes with it the glycerine which comes from the melted fats. The product which finally comes from the kettle is a clear soap which has a moisture content of about 34%. This clear soap is then chilled so that more moisture is driven out. As a result, the manufacturer finally ends up with a commercial laundry soap consisting of 88% clear soap and only 12% moisture.

3. An ingredient used in making laundry soap is 3.____

   A. table sugar
   B. potash
   C. glycerine
   D. caustic soda

4. According to the above passage, a difference between fats and oils is that fats 4.____

   A. cost more than oils
   B. are solid at room temperature
   C. have less water than oils
   D. are a liquid animal product

5. According to the above passage, the MAIN reason for using salt in the manufacture of soap is to 5.____

   A. make the ingredients boil together
   B. keep the fats in the kettle melted
   C. remove the glycerine
   D. prevent the loss of water from the soap

6. According to the passage, the purpose of chilling the clear soap is to 6.____

   A. stop the glycerine from melting
   B. separate the alkali from the fats
   C. make the oil become solid
   D. get rid of more moisture

7. According to the passage, the percentage of moisture in commercial laundry soap is 7.____

   A. 12%
   B. 34%
   C. 66%
   D. 88%

8. The x-ray has gone into business. Developed primarily to aid in diagnosing human ills, the machine now works in packing plants, in foundries, in service stations, and in a dozen ways to contribute to precision and accuracy in industry. 8.____
The above statement means *most nearly* that the x-ray

A. was first developed to aid business
B. is of more help to business than it is to medicine
C. is being used to improve the functioning of business
D. is more accurate for packing plants than it is for foundries

Questions 9-25.

DIRECTIONS: Each question consists of a statement. You are to indicate whether the statement is TRUE (T) or FALSE (F). *PRINT THE LETTER OF THE CORRECT ANSWER IN THE SPACE AT THE RIGHT.*

Questions 9-12.

DIRECTIONS: Read the paragraph below about *shock* and then answer Questions 9 through 12 according to the information given in the paragraph.

SHOCK

While not found in all injuries, shock is present in all serious injuries caused by accidents. During shock, the normal activities of the body slow down. This partly explains why one of the signs of shock is a pale, cold skin, since insufficient blood goes to the body parts during shock.

9. If the injury caused by an accident is serious, shock is sure to be present. 9.____

10. In shock, the heart beats faster than normal. 10.____

11. The face of a person suffering from shock is usually red and flushed. 11.____

12. Not enough blood goes to different parts of the body during shock. 12.____

Questions 13-18.

DIRECTIONS: Questions 13 through 18, inclusive, are to be answered SOLELY on the basis of the information contained in the following statement and NOT upon any other information you may have.

Blood transfusions are given to patients at the hospital upon recommendation of the physicians attending such cases. The physician fills out a *Request for Blood Transfusion* form in duplicate and sends both copies to the Medical Director's office, where a list is maintained of persons called *donors* who desire to sell their blood for transfusions. A suitable donor is selected, and the transfusion is given. Donors are, in many instances, medical students and employees of the hospital. Donors receive twenty-five dollars for each transfusion.

13. According to the above paragraph, a blood donor is paid twenty-five dollars for each transfusion. 13.____

14. According to the above paragraph, only medical students and employees of the hospital are selected as blood donors. 14.____

15. According to the above paragraph, the *Request for Blood Transfusion* form is filled out by the patient and sent to the Medical Director's office. 15.____

16. According to the above paragraph, a list of blood donors is maintained in the Medical Director's office. 16.____

17. According to the above paragraph, cases for which the attending physicians recommend blood transfusions are usually emergency cases. 17.____

18. According to the above paragraph, one copy of the *Request for Blood Transfusion* form is kept by the patient and one copy is sent to the Medical Director's office. 18.____

Questions 19-25.

DIRECTIONS: Questions 19 through 25, inclusive, are to be answered SOLELY on the basis of the information contained in the following passage and NOT upon any other information you may have.

Before being admitted to a hospital ward, a patient is first interviewed by the Admitting Clerk, who records the patient's name, age, sex, race, birthplace, and mother's maiden name. This clerk takes all of the money and valuables that the patient has on his person. A list of the valuables is written on the back of the envelope in which the valuables are afterwards placed. Cash is counted and placed in a separate envelope, and the amount of money and the name of the patient are written on the outside of the envelope. Both envelopes are sealed, fastened together, and placed in a compartment of a safe.

An orderly then escorts the patient to a dressing room where the patient's clothes are removed and placed in a bundle. A tag bearing the patient's name is fastened to the bundle. A list of the contents of the bundle is written on property slips, which are made out in triplicate. The information contained on the outside of the envelopes containing the cash and valuables belonging to the patient is also copied on the property slips.

According to the above passage,

19. patients are escorted to the dressing room by the Admitting Clerk. 19.____

20. the patient's cash and valuables are placed together in one envelope. 20.____

21. the number of identical property slips that are made out when a patient is being admitted to a hospital ward is three. 21.____

22. the full names of both parents of a patient are recorded by the Admitting Clerk before a patient is admitted to a hospital ward. 22.____

23. the amount of money that a patient has on his person when admitted to the hospital is entered on the patient's property slips. 23.____

24. an orderly takes all the money and valuables that a patient has on his person. 24.____

25. the patient's name is placed on the tag that is attached to the bundle containing the patient's clothing. 25.____

KEY (CORRECT ANSWERS)

1. D
2. A
3. D
4. B
5. C

6. D
7. A
8. C
9. T
10. F

11. F
12. T
13. T
14. F
15. F

16. T
17. T
18. F
19. F
20. F

21. T
22. F
23. T
24. F
25. T

TEST 2

DIRECTIONS: Each question or incomplete statement is followed by several suggested answers or completions. Select the one that BEST answers the question or completes the statement. *PRINT THE LETTER OF THE CORRECT ANSWER IN THE SPACE AT THE RIGHT.*

Questions 1-4.

DIRECTIONS: Questions 1 through 4 are to be answered in accordance with the following paragraphs.

One fundamental difference between the United States health care system and the health care systems of some European countries is the way that hospital charges for long-term illnesses affect their citizens.

In European countries such as England, Sweden, and Germany, citizens can face, without fear, hospital charges due to prolonged illness, no matter how substantial they may be. Citizens of these nations are required to pay nothing when they are hospitalized, for they have prepaid their treatment as taxpayers when they were well and were earning incomes.

On the other hand, the United States citizen, in spite of the growth of payments by third parties which include private insurance carriers as well as public resources, has still to shoulder 40 percent of hospital care costs, while his private insurance contributes only 25 percent and public resources the remaining 35 percent.

Despite expansion of private health insurance and social legislation in the United States, out-of-pocket payments for hospital care by individuals have steadily increased. Such payments, currently totalling $23 billion, are nearly twice as high as ten years ago.

Reform is inevitable and, when it comes, will have to reconcile sharply conflicting interests. Hospital staffs are demanding higher and higher wages. Hospitals are under pressure by citizens, who as patients demand more and better services but who as taxpayers or as subscribers to hospital insurance plans, are reluctant to pay the higher cost of improved care. An acceptable reconciliation of these interests has so far eluded legislators and health administrators in the United States.

1. According to the above passage, the one of the following which is an ADVANTAGE that citizens of England, Sweden, and Germany have over United States citizens is that, when faced with long-term illness, 1.____

   A. the amount of out-of-pocket payments made by these European citizens is small when compared to out-of-pocket payments made by United States citizens
   B. European citizens have no fear of hospital costs no matter how great they may be
   C. more efficient and reliable hospitals are available to the European citizen than is available to the United States citizens
   D. a greater range of specialized hospital care is available to the European citizens than is available to the United States citizens

2. According to the above passage, reform of the United States system of health care must reconcile all of the following EXCEPT 2.____

   A. attempts by health administrators to provide improved hospital care
   B. taxpayers' reluctance to pay for the cost of more and better hospital services
   C. demands by hospital personnel for higher wages
   D. insurance subscribers' reluctance to pay the higher costs of improved hospital care

3. According to the above passage, the out-of-pocket payments for hospital care that individuals made ten years ago was APPROXIMATELY ______ billion. 3.____

   A. $32 B. $23 C. $12 D. $3

4. According to the above passage, the GREATEST share of the costs of hospital care in the United States is paid by 4.____

   A. United States citizens
   B. private insurance carriers
   C. public resources
   D. third parties

Questions 5-8.

DIRECTIONS: Questions 5 through 8 are to be answered SOLELY on the basis of the information contained in the following passage.

Effective cost controls have been difficult to establish in most hospitals in the United States. Ways must be found to operate hospitals with reasonable efficiency without sacrificing quality and in a manner that will reduce the amount of personal income now being spent on health care and the enormous drain on national resources. We must adopt a new public objective of providing higher quality health care at significantly lower cost. One step that can be taken to achieve this goal is to carefully control capital expenditures for hospital construction and expansion. Perhaps the way to start is to declare a moratorium on all hospital construction and to determine the factors that should be considered in deciding whether a hospital should be built. Such factors might include population growth, distance to the nearest hospital, availability of medical personnel, and hospital bed shortage.

A second step to achieve the new objective is to increase the ratio of out-of-hospital patient to in-hospital patient care. This can be done by using separate health care facilities other than hospitals to attract patients who have increasingly been going to hospital clinics and overcrowding them. Patients should instead identify with a separate health care facility to keep them out of hospitals.

A third step is to require better hospital operating rules and controls. This step might include the review of a doctor's performance by other doctors, outside professional evaluations of medical practice, and required refresher courses and re-examinations for doctors. Other measures might include obtaining mandatory second opinions on the need for surgery in order to avoid unnecessary surgery, and outside review of work rules and procedures to eliminate unnecessary testing of patients.

A fourth step is to halt the construction and public subsidizing of new medical schools and to fill whatever needs exist in professional coverage by emphasizing the medical training of physicians with specialities that are in short supply and by providing a better geographic distribution of physicians and surgeons.

5. According to the above passage, providing higher quality health care at lower cost can be achieved by the 5.____

   A. greater use of out-of-hospital facilities
   B. application of more effective cost controls on doctors' fees
   C. expansion of improved in-hospital patient care services at hospital clinics
   D. development of more effective training programs in hospital administration

6. According to the above passage, the one of the following which should be taken into account in determining if a hospital should be constructed is the 6.____

   A. number of out-of-hospital health care facilities
   B. availability of public funds to subsidize construction
   C. number of hospitals under construction
   D. availability of medical personnel

7. According to the above passage, it is IMPORTANT to operate hospitals efficiently because 7.____

   A. they are currently in serious financial difficulties
   B. of the need to reduce the amount of personal income going to health care
   C. the quality of health care services has deteriorated
   D. of the need to increase productivity goals to take care of the growing population in the United States

8. According to the above passage, which one of the following approaches is MOST LIKELY to result in better operating rules and controls in hospitals? 8.____

   A. Allocating doctors to health care facilities on the basis of patient population
   B. Equalizing the workloads of doctors
   C. Establishing a physician review board to evaluate the performance of other physicians
   D. Eliminating unnecessary outside review of patient testing

Questions 9-14.

DIRECTIONS: Questions 9 through 14 are to be answered SOLELY on the basis of the information contained in the following passage.

The United States today is the only major industrial nation in the world without a system of national health insurance or a national health service. Instead, we have placed our prime reliance on private enterprise and private health insurance to meet the need. Yet, in a recent year, of the 180 million Americans under 65 years of age, 34 million had no hospital insurance, 38 million had no surgical insurance, 63 million had no out-patient x-ray and laboratory insurance, 94 million had no insurance for prescription drugs, and 103 million had no insurance for physician office visits or home visits. Some 35 million Americans under the age of 65 had no health insurance whatsoever. Some 64 million additional Americans under age 65 had health insurance coverage that was less than that provided to the aged under Medicare.

Despite more than three decades of enormous growth, the private health insurance industry today pays benefits equal to only one-third of the total cost of private health care, leaving the rest to be borne by the patient–essentially the same ratio which held true a decade ago. Moreover, nearly all private health insurance is limited; it provides partial benefits, not comprehensive benefits; acute care, not preventive care; it siphons off the young and healthy, and ignores the poor and medically indigent. The typical private carrier usually pays only the cost of hospital care, forcing physicians and patients alike to resort to wasteful and inefficient use of hospital facilities, thereby giving further impetus to the already soaring costs of hospital care. Valuable hospital beds are used for routine tests and examinations. Unnecessary hospitalization, unnecessary surgery, and unnecessarily extended hospital stays are encouraged. These problems are exacerbated by the fact that administrative costs of commercial carriers are substantially higher than they are for Blue Shield, Blue Cross, or Medicare.

9. According to the above passage, the PROPORTION of total private health care costs paid by private health insurance companies today as compared to ten years ago has 9.____

   A. *increased* by approximately one-third
   B. *remained* practically the same
   C. *increased* by approximately two-thirds
   D. *decreased* by approximately one-third

10. According to the above passage, the one of the following which has contributed MOST to wasteful use of hospital facilities is the 10.____

   A. increased emphasis on preventive health care
   B. practice of private carriers of providing comprehensive health care benefits
   C. increased hospitalization of the elderly and the poor
   D. practice of a number of private carriers of paying only for hospital care costs

11. Based on the information in the above passage, which one of the following patients would be LEAST likely to receive benefits from a typical private health insurance plan? A 11.____

   A. young patient who must undergo an emergency appendectomy
   B. middle-aged patient who needs a costly series of x-ray and laboratory tests for diagnosis of gastrointestinal complaints
   C. young patient who must visit his physician weekly for treatment of a chronic skin disease
   D. middle-aged patient who requires extensive cancer surgery

12. Which one of the following is the MOST accurate inference that can be drawn from the above passage? 12.____

   A. Private health insurance has failed to fully meet the health care needs of Americans.
   B. Most Americans under age 65 have health insurance coverage better than that provided to the elderly under Medicare.
   C. Countries with a national health service are likely to provide poorer health care for their citizens than do countries that rely primarily on private health insurance.
   D. Hospital facilities in the United States are inadequate to meet the nation's health care needs.

13. Of the total number of Americans under age 65, what percentage belonged in the combined category of persons with NO health insurance or health insurance less than that provided to the aged under Medicare? 13.____

A. 19% B. 36% C. 55% D. 65%

14. According to the above passage, the one of the following types of health insurance which covered the SMALLEST number of Americans under age 65 was 14.____

A. hospital insurance
B. surgical insurance
C. insurance for prescription drugs
D. insurance for physician office or home visits

Questions 15-17.

DIRECTIONS: Questions 15 through 17 are to be answered SOLELY on the basis of the information contained in the following passage.

Statistical studies have demonstrated that disease and mortality rates are higher among the poor than among the more affluent members of our society. Periodic surveys conducted by the United States Public Health Service continue to document a higher prevalence of infectious and chronic diseases within low income families. While the basic life style and living conditions of the poor are to a considerable extent responsible for this less favorable health status, there are indications that the kind of health care received by the poor also plays a significant role. The poor are less likely to be aware of the concepts and practices of scientific medicine and less likely to seek health care when they need it. Moreover, they are discouraged from seeking adequate health care by the depersonalization, disorganization, and inadequate emphasis on preventive care which characterize the health care most often provided for them.

To achieve the objective of better health care for the poor, the following approaches have been suggested: encouraging the poor to seek preventive care as well as care for acute illness and to establish a lasting one-to-one relationship with a single physician who can treat the poor patient as a whole individual; sufficient financial subsidy to put the poor on an equal footing with *paying patients,* thereby giving them the opportunity to choose from among available health services providers; inducements to health services providers to establish public clinics in poverty areas; and legislation to provide for health education, earlier detection of disease, and coordinated health care.

15. According to the above passage, the one of the following which is a function of the United States Public Health Service is 15.____

A. gathering data on the incidence of infectious diseases
B. operating public health clinics in poverty areas lacking private physicians
C. recommending legislation for the improvement of health care in the United States
D. encouraging the poor to participate in programs aimed at the prevention of illness

16. According to the above passage, the one of the following which is MOST characteristic of the health care currently provided for the poor is that it 16.____

    A. aims at establishing clinics in poverty areas
    B. enables the poor to select the health care they want through the use of financial subsidies
    C. places insufficient stress on preventive health care
    D. over-emphasizes the establishment of a one-to-one relationship between physician and patient

17. The above passage IMPLIES that the poor lack the financial resources to 17.____

    A. obtain adequate health insurance coverage
    B. select from among existing health services
    C. participate in health education programs
    D. lobby for legislation aimed at improving their health care

Questions 18-20.

DIRECTIONS: Questions 18 through 20 are to be answered SOLELY on the basis of the information contained in the following passage.

The concept of *affiliation,* developed more than ten years ago, grew out of a series of studies which found evidence of faulty care, surgery of *questionable* value and other undesirable conditions in the city's municipal hospitals. The affiliation agreements signed shortly thereafter were designed to correct these deficiencies by assuring high quality medical care. In general, the agreements provided the staff and expertise of a voluntary hospital–sometimes connected with a medical school–to operate various services or, in some cases, all of the professional divisions of a specific municipal hospital. The municipal hospitals have paid for these services, which last year cost the city $200 million, the largest single expenditure of the Health and Hospitals Corporation. In addition, the municipal hospitals have provided to the voluntary hospitals such facilities as free space for laboratories and research. While some experts agree that affiliation has resulted in improvements in some hospital care, they contend that many conditions that affiliation was meant to correct still exist. In addition, accountability procedures between the Corporation and voluntary hospitals are said to be so inadequate that audits of affiliation contracts of the past five years revealed that there may be more than $200 million in charges for services by the voluntary hospitals which have not been fully substantiated. Consequently, the Corporation has proposed that future agreements provide accountability in terms of funds, services supplied, and use of facilities by the voluntary hospitals.

18. According to the above passage, *affiliation* may BEST be defined as an agreement whereby 18.____

    A. voluntary hospitals pay for the use of municipal hospital facilities
    B. voluntary and municipal hospitals work to eliminate duplication of services
    C. municipal hospitals pay voluntary hospitals for services performed
    D. voluntary and municipal hospitals transfer patients to take advantage of specialized services

19. According to the above passage, the MAIN purpose for setting up the *affiliation* agreement was to 19.____

 A. supplement the revenues of municipal hospitals
 B. improve the quality of medical care in municipal hospitals
 C. reduce operating costs in municipal hospitals
 D. increase the amount of space available to municipal hospitals

20. According to the above passage, inadequate accountability procedures have resulted in 20.____

 A. unsubstantiated charges for services by the voluntary hospitals
 B. emphasis on research rather than on patient care in municipal hospitals
 C. unsubstantiated charges for services by the municipal hospitals
 D. economic losses to voluntary hospitals

Questions 21-25.

DIRECTIONS: Questions 21 through 25 are to be answered SOLELY on the basis of the information contained in the following passage.

The payment for medical services covered under the Outpatient Medical Insurance Plan (OMI) may be made, by OMI, directly to a physician or to the OMI patient. If the physician and the patient agree that the physician is to receive payment directly from OMI, the payment will be officially assigned to the physician; this is the assignment method. If payment is not assigned, the patient receives payment directly from OMI based on an itemized bill he submits, regardless of whether or not he has already paid his physician.

When a physician accepts assignment of the payment for medical services, he agrees that total charges will not be more than the allowed charge determined by the OMI carrier administering the program. In such cases, the OMI patient pays any unmet part of the $85 annual deductible, plus 10 percent of the remaining charges to the physician. In unassigned claims, the patient is responsible for the total amount charged by the physician. The patient will then be reimbursed by the program 90 percent of the allowed charges in excess of the annual deductible.

The rates of acceptance of assignments provide a measure of how many OMI patients are spared *administrative participation* in the program. Because physicians are free to accept or reject assignments, the rate in which assignments are made provide a general indication of the medical community's satisfaction with the OMI program, especially with the level of amounts paid by the program for specific services and the promptness of payment.

21. According to the above passage, in order for a physician to receive payment directly from OMI for medical services to an OMI patient, the physician would have to accept the assignment of payment, to have the consent of the patient, AND to 21.____

 A. submit to OMI a paid itemized bill
 B. collect from the patient 90% of the total bill
 C. collect from the patient the total amount of the charges for his services, a portion of which he will later reimburse the patient
 D. agree that his charges for services to the patient will not exceed the amount allowed by the program

22. According to the above passage, if a physician accepts assignment of payment, the patient pays 22.____

A. the total amount charged by the physician and is reimbursed by the program for 90 percent of the allowed charges in excess of the applicable deductible
B. any unmet part of the $85 annual deductible, plus 90 percent of the remaining charges
C. the total amount charged by the physician and is reimbursed by the program for 10 percent of the allowed charges in excess of the $85 annual deductible
D. any unmet part of the $85 annual deductible, plus 10 percent of the remaining charges

23. A physician has accepted the assignment of payment for charges to an OMI patient. The physician's charges, all of which are allowed under OMI, amount to $115. This is the first time the patient has been eligible for OMI benefits and the first time the patient has received services from this physician. 23.____
According to the above passage, the patient must pay the physician

A. $27 B. $76.50 C. $88 D. $103.50

24. In an unassigned claim, a physician's charges, all of which are allowed under OMI, amount to $165. The patient paid the physician the full amount of the bill. 24.____
If this is the FIRST time the patient has been eligible for OMI benefits, he will receive from OMI a reimbursement of

A. $72 B. $80 C. $85 D. $93

25. According to the above passage, if the rate of acceptance of assignments by physicians is high, it is LEAST appropriate to conclude that the medical community is generally satisfied with the 25.____

A. supplementary medical insurance program
B. levels of amounts paid to physicians by the program
C. number of OMI patients being spared administrative participation in the program
D. promptness of the program in making payment for services

KEY (CORRECT ANSWERS)

1. B	11. C	21. D
2. A	12. A	22. D
3. C	13. C	23. C
4. D	14. D	24. A
5. A	15. A	25. C
6. D	16. C	
7. B	17. B	
8. C	18. C	
9. B	19. B	
10. D	20. A	

RECORD KEEPING
EXAMINATION SECTION
TEST 1

DIRECTIONS: Each question or incomplete statement is followed by several suggested answers or completions. Select the one that BEST answers the question or completes the statement. *PRINT THE LETTER OF THE CORRECT ANSWER IN THE SPACE AT THE RIGHT.*

Questions 1-15.

DIRECTIONS: Questions 1 through 15 are to be answered on the basis of the following list of company names below. Arrange a file alphabetically, word-by-word, disregarding punctuation, conjunctions, and apostrophes. Then answer the questions.

A Bee C Reading Materials
ABCO Parts
A Better Course for Test Preparation
AAA Auto Parts Co.
A-Z Auto Parts, Inc.
Aabar Books
Abbey, Joanne
Boman-Sylvan Law Firm
BMW Autowerks
C Q Service Company
Chappell-Murray, Inc.
E&E Life Insurance
Emcrisco
Gigi Arts
Gordon, Jon & Associates
SOS Plumbing
Schmidt, J.B. Co.

1. Which of these files should appear FIRST? 1.____

   A. ABCO Parts
   B. A Bee C Reading Materials
   C. A Better Course for Test Preparation
   D. AAA Auto Parts Co.

2. Which of these files should appear SECOND? 2.____

   A. A-Z Auto Parts, Inc.
   B. A Bee C Reading Materials
   C. A Better Course for Test Preparation
   D. AAA Auto Parts Co.

3. Which of these files should appear THIRD? 3.____

   A. ABCO Parts
   B. A Bee C Reading Materials
   C. Aabar Books
   D. AAA Auto Parts Co.

4. Which of these files should appear FOURTH? 4.____

   A. Aabar Books
   B. ABCO Parts
   C. Abbey, Joanne
   D. AAA Auto Parts Co.

5. Which of these files should appear LAST? 5.____

   A. Gordon, Jon & Associates
   B. Gigi Arts
   C. Schmidt, J.B. Co.
   D. SOS Plumbing

6. Which of these files should appear between A-Z Auto Parts, Inc. and Abbey, Joanne? 6.____

   A. A Bee C Reading Materials
   B. AAA Auto Parts Co.
   C. ABCO Parts
   D. A Better Course for Test Preparation

7. Which of these files should appear between ABCO Parts and Aabar Books? 7.____

   A. A Bee C Reading Materials
   B. Abbey, Joanne
   C. Aabar Books
   D. A-Z Auto Parts

8. Which of these files should appear between Abbey, Joanne and Boman-Sylvan Law Firm? 8.____

   A. A Better Course for Test Preparation
   B. BMW Autowerks
   C. Chappell-Murray, Inc.
   D. Aabar Books

9. Which of these files should appear between Abbey, Joanne and C Q Service? 9.____

   A. A-Z Auto Parts,Inc.
   B. BMW Autowerks
   C. Choices A and B
   D. Chappell-Murray, Inc.

10. Which of these files should appear between C Q Service Company and Emcrisco? 10.____

   A. Chappell-Murray, Inc.
   B. E&E Life Insurance
   C. Gigi Arts
   D. Choices A and B

11. Which of these files should NOT appear between C Q Service Company and E&E Life Insurance? 11.____

   A. Gordon, Jon & Associates
   B. Emcrisco
   C. Gigi Arts
   D. All of the above

12. Which of these files should appear between Chappell-Murray Inc., and Gigi Arts? 12.____

    A. CQ Service Inc. E&E Life Insurance, and Emcrisco
    B. Emcrisco, E&E Life Insurance, and Gordon, Jon & Associates
    C. E&E Life Insurance and Emcrisco
    D. Emcrisco and Gordon, Jon & Associates

13. Which of these files should appear between Gordon, Jon & Associates and SOS Plumbing? 13.____

    A. Gigi Arts
    B. Schmidt, J.B. Co.
    C. Choices A and B
    D. None of the above

14. Each of the choices lists the four files in their proper alphabetical order except 14.____

    A. E&E Life Insurance; Gigi Arts; Gordon, Jon & Associates; SOS Plumbing
    B. E&E Life Insurance; Emcrisco; Gigi Arts; SOS Plumbing
    C. Emcrisco; Gordon, Jon & Associates; SOS Plumbing; Schmidt, J.B. Co.
    D. Emcrisco; Gigi Arts; Gordon, Jon & Associates; SOS Plumbing

15. Which of the choices lists the four files in their proper alphabetical order? 15.____

    A. Gigi Arts; Gordon, Jon & Associates; SOS Plumbing; Schmidt, J.B. Co.
    B. Gordon, Jon & Associates; Gigi Arts; Schmidt, J.B. Co.; SOS Plumbing
    C. Gordon, Jon & Associates; Gigi Arts; SOS Plumbing; Schmidt, J.B. Co.
    D. Gigi Arts; Gordon, Jon & Associates; Schmidt, J.B. Co.; SOS Plumbing

16. The alphabetical filing order of two businesses with identical names is determined by the 16.____

    A. length of time each business has been operating
    B. addresses of the businesses
    C. last name of the company president
    D. none of the above

17. In an alphabetical filing system, if a business name includes a number, it should be 17.____

    A. disregarded
    B. considered a number and placed at the end of an alphabetical section
    C. treated as though it were written in words and alphabetized accordingly
    D. considered a number and placed at the beginning of an alphabetical section

18. If a business name includes a contraction (such as *don't* or *it's*), how should that word be treated in an alphabetical filing system? 18.____

    A. Divide the word into its separate parts and treat it as two words.
    B. Ignore the letters that come after the apostrophe.
    C. Ignore the word that contains the contraction.
    D. Ignore the apostrophe and consider all letters in the contraction.

19. In what order should the parts of an address be considered when using an alphabetical filing system? 19.____

    A. City or town; state; street name; house or building number
    B. State; city or town; street name; house or building number
    C. House or building number; street name; city or town; state
    D. Street name; city or town; state

20. A business record should be cross-referenced when a(n) 20.____

A. organization is known by an abbreviated name
B. business has a name change because of a sale, incorporation, or other reason
C. business is known by a *coined* or common name which differs from a dictionary spelling
D. all of the above

21. A geographical filing system is MOST effective when 21.____

A. location is more important than name
B. many names or titles sound alike
C. dealing with companies who have offices all over the world
D. filing personal and business files

Questions 22-25.

DIRECTIONS: Questions 22 through 25 are to be answered on the basis of the list of items below, which are to be filed geographically. Organize the items geographically and then answer the questions.

1. University Press at Berkeley, U.S.
2. Maria Sanchez, Mexico City, Mexico
3. Great Expectations Ltd. in London, England
4. Justice League, Cape Town, South Africa, Africa
5. Crown Pearls Ltd. in London, England
6. Joseph Prasad in London, England

22. Which of the following arrangements of the items is composed according to the policy of: *Continent, Country, City, Firm or Individual Name?* 22.____

A. 5, 3, 4, 6, 2, 1
B. 4, 5, 3, 6, 2, 1
C. 1, 4, 5, 3, 6, 2
D. 4, 5, 3, 6, 1, 2

23. Which of the following files is arranged according to the policy of: *Continent, Country, City, Firm or Individual Name?* 23.____

A. South Africa. Africa. Cape Town. Justice League
B. Mexico. Mexico City, Maria Sanchez
C. North America. United States. Berkeley. University Press
D. England. Europe. London. Prasad, Joseph

24. Which of the following arrangements of the items is composed according to the policy of: *Country, City, Firm or Individual Name*? 24.____

A. 5, 6, 3, 2, 4, 1
B. 1, 5, 6, 3, 2, 4
C. 6, 5, 3, 2, 4, 1
D. 5, 3, 6, 2, 4, 1

25. Which of the following files is arranged according to a policy of: *Country, City, Firm or Individual Name*? 25.____

A. England. London. Crown Pearls Ltd.
B. North America. United States. Berkeley. University Press
C. Africa. Cape Town. Justice League
D. Mexico City. Mexico. Maria Sanchez

26. Under which of the following circumstances would a phonetic filing system be MOST effective? 26.____

A. When the person in charge of filing can't spell very well
B. With large files with names that sound alike
C. With large files with names that are spelled alike
D. All of the above

Questions 27-29.

DIRECTIONS: Questions 27 through 29 are to be answered on the basis of the following list of numerical files.

1. 391-023-100
2. 361-132-170
3. 385-732-200
4. 381-432-150
5. 391-632-387
6. 361-423-303
7. 391-123-271

27. Which of the following arrangements of the files follows a consecutive-digit system? 27.____

A. 2, 3, 4, 1
B. 1, 5, 7, 3
C. 2, 4, 3, 1
D. 3, 1, 5, 7

28. Which of the following arrangements follows a terminal-digit system? 28.____

A. 1, 7, 2, 4, 3
B. 2, 1, 4, 5, 7
C. 7, 6, 5, 4, 3
D. 1, 4, 2, 3, 7

29. Which of the following lists follows a middle-digit system? 29.____

A. 1, 7, 2, 6, 4, 5, 3
B. 1, 2, 7, 4, 6, 5, 3
C. 7, 2, 1, 3, 5, 6, 4
D. 7, 1, 2, 4, 6, 5, 3

Questions 30-31.

DIRECTIONS: Questions 30 and 31 are to be answered on the basis of the following information.

1. Reconfirm Laura Bates appointment with James Caldecort on December 12 at 9:30 A.M.
2. Laurence Kinder contact Julia Lucas on August 3 and set up a meeting for week of September 23 at 4 P.M.
3. John Lutz contact Larry Waverly on August 3 and set up appointment for September 23 at 9:30 A.M.
4. Call for tickets for Gerry Stanton August 21 for New Jersey on September 23, flight 143 at 4:43 P.M.

30. A chronological file for the above information would be 30.____

A. 4, 3, 2, 1
B. 3, 2, 4, 1
C. 4, 2, 3, 1
D. 3, 1, 2, 4

31. Using the above information, a chronological file for the date of September 23 would be 31.____

A. 2, 3, 4
B. 3, 1, 4
C. 3, 2, 4
D. 4, 3, 2

Questions 32-34.

DIRECTIONS: Questions 32 through 34 are to be answered on the basis of the following information.

1. Call Roger Epstein, Ashoke Naipaul, Jon Anderson, and Sarah Washington on April 19 at 1:00 P.M. to set up meeting with Alika D'Ornay for June 6 in New York.
2. Call Martin Ames before noon on April 19 to confirm afternoon meeting with Bob Greenwood on April 20th
3. Set up meeting room at noon for 2:30 P.M. meeting on April 19th;
4. Ashley Stanton contact Bob Greenwood at 9:00 A.M. on April 20 and set up meeting for June 6 at 8:30 A.M.
5. Carol Guiland contact Shelby Van Ness during afternoon of April 20 and set up meeting for June 6 at 10:00 A.M.
6. Call airline and reserve tickets on June 6 for Roger Epstein trip *to* Denver on July 8
7. Meeting at 2:30 P.M. on April 19th

32. A chronological file for all of the above information would be 32.____

A. 2, 1, 3, 7, 5, 4, 6
B. 3, 7, 2, 1, 4, 5, 6
C. 3, 7, 1, 2, 5, 4, 6
D. 2, 3, 1, 7, 4, 5, 6

33. A chronological file for the date of April 19th would be 33.____

A. 2, 3, 7, 1
B. 2, 3, 1, 7
C. 7, 1, 3, 2
D. 3, 7, 1, 2

34. Add the following information to the file, and then create a chronological file for April 20th: 34.____
8. April 20: 3:00 P.M. meeting between Bob Greenwood and Martin Ames.

A. 4, 5, 8
B. 4, 8, 5
C. 8, 5, 4
D. 5, 4, 8

35. The PRIMARY advantage of computer records filing over a manual system is 35.____

A. speed of retrieval
B. accuracy
C. cost
D. potential file loss

KEY (CORRECT ANSWERS)

1. B
2. C
3. D
4. A
5. D

6. C
7. B
8. B
9. C
10. D

11. D
12. C
13. B
14. C
15. D

16. B
17. C
18. D
19. A
20. D

21. A
22. B
23. C
24. D
25. A

26. B
27. C
28. D
29. A
30. B

31. C
32. D
33. B
34. A
35. A

CLERICAL ABILITIES

EXAMINATION SECTION
TEST 1

DIRECTIONS: Each question or incomplete statement is followed by several suggested answers or completions. Select the one that BEST answers the question or completes the statement. *PRINT THE LETTER OF THE CORRECT ANSWER IN THE SPACE AT THE RIGHT.*

Questions 1-4.

DIRECTIONS: Questions 1 through 4 are to be answered on the basis of the information given below.

The most commonly used filing system and the one that is easiest to learn is alphabetical filing. This involves putting records in an A to Z order, according to the letters of the alphabet. The name of a person is filed by using the following order: first, the surname or last name; second, the first name; third, the middle name or middle initial. For example, *Henry C. Young* is filed under *Y* and thereafter under *Young, Henry C.* The name of a company is filed in the same way. For example, *Long Cabinet Co.* is filed under *L,* while *John T. Long Cabinet Co.* is filed under *L* and thereafter under *Long., John T. Cabinet Co.*

1. The one of the following which lists the names of persons in the CORRECT alphabetical order is: 1.____

   A. Mary Carrie, Helen Carrol, James Carson, John Carter
   B. James Carson, Mary Carrie, John Carter, Helen Carrol
   C. Helen Carrol, James Carson, John Carter, Mary Carrie
   D. John Carter, Helen Carrol, Mary Carrie, James Carson

2. The one of the following which lists the names of persons in the CORRECT alphabetical order is: 2.____

   A. Jones, John C.; Jones, John A.; Jones, John P.; Jones, John K.
   B. Jones, John P.; Jones, John K.; Jones, John C.; Jones, John A.
   C. Jones, John A.; Jones, John C.; Jones, John K.; Jones, John P.
   D. Jones, John K.; Jones, John C.; Jones, John A.; Jones, John P.

3. The one of the following which lists the names of the companies in the CORRECT alphabetical order is: 3.____

   A. Blane Co., Blake Co., Block Co., Blear Co.
   B. Blake Co., Blane Co., Blear Co., Block Co.
   C. Block Co., Blear Co., Blane Co., Blake Co.
   D. Blear Co., Blake Co., Blane Co., Block Co.

4. You are to return to the file an index card on *Barry C. Wayne Materials and Supplies Co.* Of the following, the CORRECT alphabetical group that you should return the index card to is 4.____

   A. A to G B. H to M C. N to S D. T to Z

Questions 5-10.

DIRECTIONS: In each of Questions 5 through 10, the names of four people are given. For each question, choose as your answer the one of the four names given which should be filed FIRST according to the usual system of alphabetical filing of names, as described in the following paragraph.

In filing names, you must start with the last name. Names are filed in order of the first letter of the last name, then the second letter, etc. Therefore, BAILY would be filed before BROWN, which would be filed before COLT. A name with fewer letters of the same type comes first; i.e., Smith before Smithe. If the last names are the same, the names are filed alphabetically by the first name. If the first name is an initial, a name with an initial would come before a first name that starts with the same letter as the initial. Therefore, I. BROWN would come before IRA BROWN. Finally, if both last name and first name are the same, the name would be filed alphabetically by the middle name, once again an initial coming before a middle name which starts with the same letter as the initial. If there is no middle name at all, the name would come before those with middle initials or names.

<u>Sample Question:</u> A. Lester Daniels
B. William Dancer
C. Nathan Danzig
D. Dan Lester

The last names beginning with D are filed before the last name beginning with L. Since DANIELS, DANCER, and DANZIG all begin with the same three letters, you must look at the fourth letter of the last name to determine which name should be filed first. C comes before I or Z in the alphabet, so DANCER is filed before DANIELS or DANZIG. Therefore, the answer to the above sample question is B.

5. A. Scott Biala 5.____
B. Mary Byala
C. Martin Baylor
D. Francis Bauer

6. A. Howard J. Black 6.____
B. Howard Black
C. J. Howard Black
D. John H. Black

7. A. Theodora Garth Kingston 7.____
B. Theadore Barth Kingston
C. Thomas Kingston
D. Thomas T. Kingston

8. A. Paulette Mary Huerta 8.____
B. Paul M. Huerta
C. Paulette L. Huerta
D. Peter A. Huerta

9. A. Martha Hunt Morgan 9.____
   B. Martin Hunt Morgan
   C. Mary H. Morgan
   D. Martine H. Morgan

10. A. James T. Meerschaum 10.____
    B. James M. Mershum
    C. James F. Mearshaum
    D. James N. Meshum

Questions 11-14.

DIRECTIONS: Questions 11 through 14 are to be answered SOLELY on the basis of the following information.

You are required to file various documents in file drawers which are labeled according to the following pattern:

DOCUMENTS

MEMOS		LETTERS	
File	Subject	File	Subject
84PM1 -	(A-L)	84PC1 -	(A-L)
84PM2 -	(M-Z)	84PC2 -	(M-Z)

REPORTS		INQUIRIES	
File	Subject	File	Subject
84PR1 -	(A-L)	84PQ1 -	(A-L)
84PR2 -	(M-Z)	84PQ2 -	(M-Z)

11. A letter dealing with a burglary should be filed in the drawer labeled 11.____

    A. 84PM1 B. 84PC1 C. 84PR1 D. 84PQ2

12. A report on Statistics should be found in the drawer labeled 12.____

    A. 84PM1 B. 84PC2 C. 84PR2 D. 84PQ2

13. An inquiry is received about parade permit procedures. It should be filed in the drawer labeled 13.____

    A. 84PM2 B. 84PC1 C. 84PR1 D. 84PQ2

14. A police officer has a question about a robbery report you filed. You should pull this file from the drawer labeled 14.____

    A. 84PM1 B. 84PM2 C. 84PR1 D. 84PR2

Questions 15-22.

DIRECTIONS: Each of Questions 15 through 22 consists of four or six numbered names. For each question, choose the option (A, B, C, or D) which indicates the order in which the names should be filed in accordance with the following filing instructions:

- File alphabetically according to last name, then first name, then middle initial.
- File according to each successive letter within a name.

- When comparing two names in which, the letters in the longer name are identical to the corresponding letters in the shorter name, the shorter name is filed first.
- When the last names are the same, initials are always filed before names beginning with the same letter.

15. I. Ralph Robinson
II. Alfred Ross
III. Luis Robles
IV. James Roberts

The CORRECT filing sequence for the above names should be 15.____

A. IV, II, I, III
B. I, IV, III, II
C. III, IV, I, II
D. IV, I, III, II

16. I. Irwin Goodwin
II. Inez Gonzalez
III. Irene Goodman
IV. Ira S. Goodwin
V. Ruth I. Goldstein
VI. M.B. Goodman

The CORRECT filing sequence for the above names should be 16.____

A. V, II, I, IV, III, VI
B. V, II, VI, III, IV, I
C. V, II, III, VI, IV, I
D. V, II, III, VI, I, IV

17. I. George Allan
II. Gregory Allen
III. Gary Allen
IV. George Allen

The CORRECT filing sequence for the above names should be 17.____

A. IV, III, I, II
B. I, IV, II, III
C. III, IV, I, II
D. I, III, IV, II

18. I. Simon Kauffman
II. Leo Kaufman
III. Robert Kaufmann
IV. Paul Kauffmann

The CORRECT filing sequence for the above names should be 18.____

A. I, IV, II, III
B. II, IV, III, I
C. III, II, IV, I
D. I, II, III, IV

19. I. Roberta Williams
II. Robin Wilson
III. Roberta Wilson
IV. Robin Williams

The CORRECT filing sequence for the above names should be 19.____

A. III, II, IV, I
B. I, IV, III, II
C. I, II, III, IV
D. III, I, II, IV

20. I. Lawrence Shultz 20.____
II. Albert Schultz
III. Theodore Schwartz
IV. Thomas Schwarz
V. Alvin Schultz
VI. Leonard Shultz

The CORRECT filing sequence for the above names should be

A. II, V, III, IV, I, VI
B. IV, III, V, I, II, VI
C. II, V, I, VI, III, IV
D. I, VI, II, V, III, IV

21. I. McArdle 21.____
II. Mayer
III. Maletz
IV. McNiff
V. Meyer
VI. MacMahon

The CORRECT filing sequence for the above names should be

A. I, IV, VI, III, II, V
B. II, I, IV, VI, III, V
C. VI, III, II, I, IV, V
D. VI, III, II, V, I, IV

22. I. Jack E. Johnson 22.____
II. R.H. Jackson
III. Bertha Jackson
IV. J.T. Johnson
V. Ann Johns
VI. John Jacobs

The CORRECT filing sequence for the above names should be

A. II, III, VI, V, IV, I
B. III, II, VI, V, IV, I
C. VI, II, III, I, V, IV
D. III, II, VI, IV, V, I

Questions 23-30.

DIRECTIONS: The code table below shows 10 letters with matching numbers. For each question, there are three sets of letters. Each set of letters is followed by a set of numbers which may or may not match their correct letter according to the code table. For each question, check all three sets of letters and numbers and mark your answer:

A. if no pairs are correctly matched
B. if only one pair is correctly matched
C. if only two pairs are correctly matched
D. if all three pairs are correctly matched

CODE TABLE

T	M	V	D	S	P	R	G	B	H
1	2	3	4	5	6	7	8	9	0

Sample Question:
TMVDSP - 123456
RGBHTM - 789011
DSPRGB - 256789

In the sample question above, the first set of numbers correctly matches its set of letters. But the second and third pairs contain mistakes. In the second pair, M is incorrectly matched with number 1. According to the code table, letter M should be correctly matched with number 2. In the third pair, the letter D is incorrectly matched with number 2. According to the code table, letter D should be correctly matched with number 4. Since only one of the pairs is correctly matched, the answer to this sample question is B.

23. RSBMRM 759262
GDSRVH 845730
VDBRTM 349713
23.____

24. TGVSDR 183247
SMHRDP 520647
TRMHSR 172057
24.____

25. DSPRGM 456782
MVDBHT 234902
HPMDBT 062491
25.____

26. BVPTRD 936184
GDPHMB 807029
GMRHMV 827032
26.____

27. MGVRSH 283750
TRDMBS 174295
SPRMGV 567283
27.____

28. SGBSDM 489542
MGHPTM 290612
MPBMHT 269301
28.____

29. TDPBHM 146902
VPBMRS 369275
GDMBHM 842902
29.____

30. MVPTBV 236194
PDRTMB 647128
BGTMSM 981232
30.____

KEY (CORRECT ANSWERS)

1. A	11. B	21. C
2. C	12. C	22. B
3. B	13. D	23. B
4. D	14. D	24. B
5. D	15. D	25. C
6. B	16. C	26. A
7. B	17. D	27. D
8. B	18. A	28. A
9. A	19. B	29. D
10. C	20. A	30. A

TEST 2

DIRECTIONS: Each question or incomplete statement is followed by several suggested answers or completions. Select the one that BEST answers the question or completes the statement. *PRINT THE LETTER OF THE CORRECT ANSWER IN THE SPACE AT THE RIGHT.*

Questions 1-10.

DIRECTIONS: Questions 1 through 10 each consists of two columns, each containing four lines of names, numbers and/or addresses. For each question, compare the lines in Column I with the lines in Column II to see if they match exactly, and mark your answer A, B, C, or D, according to the following instructions:

A. all four lines match exactly
B. only three lines match exactly
C. only two lines match exactly
D. only one line matches exactly

		COLUMN I	COLUMN II	
1.	I.	Earl Hodgson	Earl Hodgson	1.____
	II.	1409870	1408970	
	III.	Shore Ave.	Schore Ave.	
	IV.	Macon Rd.	Macon Rd.	
2.	I.	9671485	9671485	2.____
	II.	470 Astor Court	470 Astor Court	
	III.	Halprin, Phillip	Halperin, Phillip	
	IV.	Frank D. Poliseo	Frank D. Poliseo	
3.	I.	Tandem Associates	Tandom Associates	3.____
	II.	144-17 Northern Blvd.	144-17 Northern Blvd.	
	III.	Alberta Forchi	Albert Forchi	
	IV.	Kings Park, NY 10751	Kings Point, NY 10751	
4.	I.	Bertha C. McCormack	Bertha C. McCormack	4.____
	II.	Clayton, MO.	Clayton, MO.	
	III.	976-4242	976-4242	
	IV.	New City, NY 10951	New City, NY 10951	
5.	I.	George C. Morill	George C. Morrill	5.____
	II.	Columbia, SC 29201	Columbia, SD 29201	
	III.	Louis Ingham	Louis Ingham	
	IV.	3406 Forest Ave.	3406 Forest Ave.	
6.	I.	506 S. Elliott Pl.	506 S. Elliott Pl.	6.____
	II.	Herbert Hall	Hurbert Hall	
	III.	4712 Rockaway Pkway	4712 Rockaway Pkway	
	IV.	169 E. 7 St.	169 E. 7 St.	

		COLUMN I	COLUMN II	
7.	I.	345 Park Ave.	345 Park Pl.	7.____
	II.	Colman Oven Corp.	Coleman Oven Corp.	
	III.	Robert Conte	Robert Conti	
	IV.	6179846	6179846	
8.	I.	Grigori Schierber	Grigori Schierber	8.____
	II.	Des Moines, Iowa	Des Moines, Iowa	
	III.	Gouverneur Hospital	Gouverneur Hospital	
	IV.	91-35 Cresskill Pl.	91-35 Cresskill Pl.	
9.	I.	Jeffery Janssen	Jeffrey Janssen	9.____
	II.	8041071	8041071	
	III.	40 Rockefeller Plaza	40 Rockafeller Plaza	
	IV.	407 6 St.	406 7 St.	
10.	I.	5971996	5871996	10.____
	II.	3113 Knickerbocker Ave.	3113 Knickerbocker Ave.	
	III.	8434 Boston Post Rd.	8424 Boston Post Rd.	
	IV.	Penn Station	Penn Station	

Questions 11-14.

DIRECTIONS: Questions 11 through 14 are to be answered by looking at the four groups of names and addresses listed below (I, II, III, and IV) and then finding out the number of groups that have their corresponding numbered lines exactly the same.

	GROUP I	GROUP II
Line 1.	Richmond General Hospital	Richman General Hospital
Line 2.	Geriatric Clinic	Geriatric Clinic
Line 3.	3975 Paerdegat St.	3975 Peardegat St.
Line 4	Loudonville, New York 11538	Londonville, New York 11538

	GROUP III	GROUP IV
Line 1.	Richmond General Hospital	Richmend General Hospital
Line 2.	Geriatric Clinic	Geriatric Clinic
Line 3.	3795 Paerdegat St.	3975 Paerdegat St.
Line 4.	Loudonville, New York 11358	Loudonville, New York 11538

11. In how many groups is line one exactly the same? 11.____

    A. Two B. Three C. Four D. None

12. In how many groups is line two exactly the same? 12.____

    A. Two B. Three C. Four D. None

13. In how many groups is line three exactly the same? 13.____

    A. Two B. Three C. Four D. None

14. In how many groups is line four exactly the same? 14.____

A. Two B. Three C. Four D. None

Questions 15-18.

DIRECTIONS: Each of Questions 15 through 18 has two lists of names and addresses. Each list contains three sets of names and addresses. Check each of the three sets in the list on the right to see if they are the same as the corresponding set in the list on the left. Mark your answers:

A. if none of the sets in the right list are the same as those in the left list
B. if only one of the sets in the right list is the same as those in the left list
C. if only two of the sets in the right list are the same as those in the left list
D. if all three sets in the right list are the same as those in the left list

15.	Mary T. Berlinger 2351 Hampton St. Monsey, N.Y. 20117	Mary T. Berlinger 2351 Hampton St. Monsey, N.Y. 20117	15.____
	Eduardo Benes 473 Kingston Avenue Central Islip, N.Y. 11734	Eduardo Benes 473 Kingston Avenue Central Islip, N.Y. 11734	
	Alan Carrington Fuchs 17 Gnarled Hollow Road Los Angeles, CA 91635	Alan Carrington Fuchs 17 Gnarled Hollow Road Los Angeles, CA 91685	
16.	David John Jacobson 178 35 St. Apt. 4C New York, N.Y. 00927	David John Jacobson 178 53 St. Apt. 4C New York, N.Y. 00927	16.____
	Ann-Marie Calonella 7243 South Ridge Blvd. Bakersfield, CA 96714	Ann-Marie Calonella 7243 South Ridge Blvd. Bakersfield, CA 96714	
	Pauline M. Thompson 872 Linden Ave. Houston, Texas 70321	Pauline M. Thomson 872 Linden Ave. Houston, Texas 70321	
17.	Chester LeRoy Masterton 152 Lacy Rd. Kankakee, Ill. 54532	Chester LeRoy Masterson 152 Lacy Rd. Kankakee, Ill. 54532	17.____
	William Maloney S. LaCrosse Pla. Wausau, Wisconsin 52146	William Maloney S. LaCross Pla. Wausau, Wisconsin 52146	
	Cynthia V. Barnes 16 Pines Rd. Greenpoint, Miss. 20376	Cynthia V. Barnes 16 Pines Rd. Greenpoint, Miss. 20376	

18.	Marcel Jean Frontenac 8 Burton On The Water Calender, Me. 01471	Marcel Jean Frontenac 6 Burton On The Water Calender, Me. 01471	18.____
	J. Scott Marsden 174 S. Tipton St. Cleveland, Ohio	J. Scott Marsden 174 Tipton St. Cleveland, Ohio	
	Lawrence T. Haney 171 McDonough St. Decatur, Ga. 31304	Lawrence T. Haney 171 McDonough St. Decatur, Ga. 31304	

Questions 19-26.

DIRECTIONS: Each of Questions 19 through 26 has two lists of numbers. Each list contains three sets of numbers. Check each of the three sets in the list on the right to see if they are the same as the corresponding set in the list on the left. Mark your answers:

A. if none of the sets in the right list are the same as those in the left list
B. if only one of the sets in the right list is the same as those in the left list
C. if only two of the sets in the right list are the same as those in the left list
D. if all three sets in the right list are the same as those in the left list

19.	7354183476 4474747744 57914302311	7354983476 4474747774 57914302311	19.____
20.	7143592185 8344517699 9178531263	7143892185 8344518699 9178531263	20.____
21.	2572114731 8806835476 8255831246	257214731 8806835476 8255831246	21.____
22.	331476853821 6976658532996 3766042113715	331476858621 6976655832996 3766042113745	22.____
23.	8806663315 74477138449 211756663666	8806663315 74477138449 211756663666	23.____
24.	990006966996 53022219743 4171171117717	99000696996 53022219843 4171171177717	24.____
25.	24400222433004 5300030055000355 20000075532002022	24400222433004 5300030055500355 20000075532002022	25.____

26. 611166640660001116 — 61116664066001116 — 26.____
7111300117001100733 — 7111300117001100733
26666446664476518 — 26666446664476518

Questions 27-30.

DIRECTIONS: Questions 27 through 30 are to be answered by picking the answer which is in the correct numerical order, from the lowest number to the highest number, in each question.

27. A. 44533, 44518, 44516, 44547 — 27.____
B. 44516, 44518, 44533, 44547
C. 44547, 44533, 44518, 44516
D. 44518, 44516, 44547, 44533

28. A. 95587, 95593, 95601, 95620 — 28.____
B. 95601, 95620, 95587, 95593
C. 95593, 95587, 95601, 95620
D. 95620, 95601, 95593, 95587

29. A. 232212, 232208, 232232, 232223 — 29.____
B. 232208, 232223, 232212, 232232
C. 232208, 232212, 232223, 232232
D. 232223, 232232, 232208, 232212

30. A. 113419, 113521, 113462, 113588 — 30.____
B. 113588, 113462, 113521, 113419
C. 113521, 113588, 113419, 113462
D. 113419, 113462, 113521, 113588

KEY (CORRECT ANSWERS)

1.	C	11.	A	21.	C
2.	B	12.	C	22.	A
3.	D	13.	A	23.	D
4.	A	14.	A	24.	A
5.	C	15.	C	25.	C
6.	B	16.	B	26.	C
7.	D	17.	B	27.	B
8.	A	18.	B	28.	A
9.	D	19.	B	29.	C
10.	C	20.	B	30.	D

BASIC FUNDAMENTALS OF FILING SCIENCE

TABLE OF CONTENTS

	Page
I. COMMENTARY	1
II. BASIS OF FILING	1
1. Types of Files	1
(1) Shannon File	1
(2) Spindle File	1
(3) Box File	1
(4) Flat File	1
(5) Bellows File	1
(6) Vertical File	1
(7) Clip File	1
(8) Visible File	1
(9) Rotary File	1
2. Aids in Filing	2
3. Variations of Filing Systems	2
4. Centralized Filing	2
5. Methods of Filing	2
(1) Alphabetic Filing	3
(2) Subject Filing	3
(3) Geographical File	3
(4) Chronological File	3
(5) Numerical File	3
6. Indexing	3
7. Alphabetizing	3
III. RULES FOR INDEXING AND ALPHABETIZING	3
IV. OFFICIAL EXAMINATION DIRECTIONS AND RULES	7
Official Directions	8
Official Rules for Alphabetical Filing	8
Names of Individuals	8
Names of Business Organizations	8
Sample Question	8

BASIC FUNDAMENTALS OF FILING SCIENCE

I. COMMENTARY

Filing is the systematic arrangement and storage of papers, cards, forms, catalogues, etc., so that they may be found easily and quickly. The importance of an efficient filing system cannot be emphasized too strongly. The filed materials form records which may be needed quickly to settle questions that may cause embarrassing situations if such evidence is not available. In addition to keeping papers in order so that they are readily available, the filing system must also be designed to keep papers in good condition. A filing system must be planned so that papers may be filed easily, withdrawn easily, and as quickly returned to their proper place. The cost of a filing system is also an important factor.

The need for a filing system arose when the business man began to carry on negotiations on a large scale. He could no longer be intimate with the details of his business. What was needed in the early era was a spindle or pigeon-hole desk. Filing in pigeon-hole desks is now almost completely extinct. It was an unsatisfactory practice since pigeon holes were not labeled, and the desk was an untidy mess.

II. BASIS OF FILING

The science of filing is an exact one and entails a thorough understanding of basic facts, materials, and methods. An overview of this important information now follows.

1. Types of files

(1) SHANNON FILE

This consists of a board, at one end of which are fastened two arches which may be opened laterally.

(2) SPINDLE FILE

This consists of a metal or wood base to which is attached a long, pointed spike. Papers are pushed down on the spike as received. This file is useful for temporary retention of papers.

(3) BOX FILE

This is a heavy cardboard or metal box, opening from the side like a book.

(4) FLAT FILE

This consists of a series of shallow drawers or trays, arranged like drawers in a cabinet.

(5) BELLOWS FILE

This is a heavy cardboard container with alphabetized or compartment sections, the ends of which are closed in such a manner that they resemble an accordion.

(6) VERTICAL FILE

This consists of one or more drawers in which the papers are stood on edge, usually in folders, and are indexed by guides. A series of two or more drawers in one unit is the usual file cabinet.

(7) CLIP FILE

This file has a large clip attached to a board and is very similar to the *SHANNON FILE.*

(8) VISIBLE FILE

Cards are filed flat in an overlapping arrangement which leaves a part of each card visible at all times.

(9) ROTARY FILE

The *ROTARY FILE* has a number of visible card files attached to a post around which they can be revolved. The wheel file has visible cards which rotate around a horizontal axle.

(10) TICKLER FILE

This consists of cards or folders marked with the days of the month, in which materials are filed and turned up on the appropriate day of the month.

2. Aids in filing

(1) GUIDES

Guides are heavy cardboard, pasteboard, or bristol-board sheets the same size as folders. At the top is a tab on which is marked or printed the distinguishing letter, words, or numbers indicating the material filed in a section of the drawer.

(2) SORTING TRAYS

Sorting trays are equipped with alphabetical guides to facilitate the sorting of papers preparatory to placing them in a file.

(3) CODING

Once the classification or indexing caption has been determined, it must be indicated on the letter for filing purposes.

(4) CROSS REFERENCE

Some letters or papers might easily be called for under two or more captions. For this purpose, a cross-reference card or sheet is placed in the folder or in the index.

3. Variations of filing systems

(1) VARIADEX ALPHABETIC INDEX

Provides for more effective expansion of the alphabetic system.

(2) TRIPLE-CHECK NUMERIC FILING

Entails a multiple cross-reference, as the name implies.

(3) VARIADEX FILING

Makes use of color as an aid in filing.

(4) DEWEY DECIMAL SYSTEM

The system is a numeric one used in libraries or for filing library materials in an office. This special type of filing system is used where material is grouped in finely divided categories, such as in libraries. With this method, all material to be filed is divided into ten major groups, from 000 to 900, and then subdivided into tens, units, and decimals.

4. Centralized filing

Centralized filing means keeping the files in one specific or central location. Decentralized filing means putting away papers in files of individual departments. The first step in the organization of a central filing department is to make a careful canvass of all desks in the offices. In this manner we can determine just what material needs to be filed, and what information each desk occupant requires from the central file. Only papers which may be used at some time by persons in the various offices should be placed in the central file. A paper that is to be used at some time by persons in the various offices should be placed in the central file. A paper that is to be used by one department only should never be filed in the central file.

5. Methods of filing

While there are various methods used for filing, actually there are only five basic systems: alphabetical, subject, numerical, geographic, and chronological. All other systems are derived from one of these or from a combination of two or more of them.

Since the purpose of a filing system is to store business records systemically so that any particular record can be found almost instantly when required, filing requires, in addition to the proper kinds of equipment and supplies, an effective method of indexing.

There are five basic systems of filing:

(1) ALPHABETIC FILING

Most filing is alphabetical. Other methods, as described below, require extensive alphabetization.

In alphabetic filing, lettered dividers or guides are arranged in alphabetic sequence. Material to be filed is placed behind the proper guide. All materials under each letter are also arranged alphabetically. Folders are used unless the file is a card index.

(2) SUBJECT FILING

This method is used when a single, complete file on a certain subject is desired. A subject file is often maintained to assemble all correspondence on a certain subject. Such files are valuable in connection with insurance claims, contract negotiations, personnel, and other investigations, special programs, and similar subjects.

(3) GEOGRAPHICAL FILE

Materials are filed according to location: states, cities, counties, or other subdivisions. Statistics and tax information are often filed in this manner.

(4) CHRONOLOGICAL FILE

Records are filed according to date. This method is used especially in "tickler" files that have guides numbered 1 to 31 for each day of the month. Each number indicates the day of the month when the filed item requires attention.

(5) NUMERICAL FILE

This method requires an alphabetic card index giving name and number. The card index is used to locate records numbered consecutively in the files according to date received or sequence in which issued, such as licenses, permits, etc.

6. Indexing

Determining the name or title under which an item is to be filed is known as indexing. For example, how would a letter from Robert E. Smith be filed? The name would be rearranged Smith,Robert E., so that the letter would be filed under the last name.

7. Alphabetizing

The arranging of names for filing is known as alphabetizing. For example, suppose you have four letters indexed under the names Johnson, Becker, Roe, and Stern. How should these letters be arranged in the files so that they may be found easily? You would arrange the four names alphabetically, thus, Becker, Johnson, Roe, and Stern.

III. RULES FOR INDEXING AND ALPHABETIZING

1. The names of persons are to be transposed. Write the surname first, then the given name, and, finally, the middle name or initial. Then arrange the various names according to the alphabetic order of letters throughout the entire name. If there is a title, consider that after the middle name or initial.

NAMES	*INDEXED AS*
Arthur L.Bright	Bright, Arthur L.
Arthur S.Bright	Bright, Arthur S.
P.E. Cole	Cole, P.E.

Dr. John C. Fox	Fox, John C. (Dr.)

2. If a surname includes the same letters of another surname, with one or more additional letters added to the end, the shorter surname is placed first regardless of the given name or the initial of the given name.

NAMES	*INDEXED AS*
Robert E. Brown	Brown, Robert E.
Gerald A. Browne	Browne, Gerald A.
William O. Brownell	Brownell, William O.

3. Firm names are alphabetized under the surnames. Words like the, an, a, of, and for, are not considered.

NAMES	*INDEXED AS*
Bank of America	Bank of America
Bank Discount Dept.	Bank Discount Dept.
The Cranford Press	Cranford Press, The
Nelson Dwyer & Co.	Dwyer, Nelson, & Co.
Sears, Roebuck & Co.	Sears, Roebuck & Co.
Montgomery Ward & Co.	Ward, Montgomery, & Co.

4. The order of filing is determined first of all by the first letter of the names to be filed. If the first letters are the same, the order is determined by the second letters, and so on. In the following pairs of names, the order is determined by the letters underlined:

Austen	Hayes	Hanson	Harvey	Heath	Green	Schwartz
Baker	Heath	Harper	Harwood	Heaton	Greene	Schwarz

5. When surnames are alike, those with initials only precede those with given names, unless the first initial comes alphabetically after the first letter of the name.

Gleason, S.	*but,*	Abbott, Mary
Gleason, S.W.		Abbott, W.B.
Gleason, Sidney		

6. Hyphenated names are treated as if spelled without the hyphen.

Lloyd, Paul N.	Lloyd, Robert
Lloyd-Jones, James	Lloyd-Thomas, A.S.

7. Company names composed of single letters which are not used as abbreviations precede the other names beginning with the same letter.

B & S Garage	E Z Duplicator Co.
B X Cable Co.	Eagle Typewriter Co.
Babbitt, R.N.	Edison Company

8. The ampersand (&)andthe apostrophe (') in firm names are disregarded in alphabetizing.

Nelson & Niller	M & C Amusement Corp.
Nelson, Walter J.	M C Art Assn.
Nelson's Bakery	

9. Names beginning with Mac, Mc, or M' are usually placed in regular order as spelled. Some filing systems file separately names beginning with Mc.

MacDonald, R.J.	Mazza, Anthony
Macdonald, S.B.	McAdam, Wm.
Mace, Wm.	McAndrews, Jerry

10. Names beginning with St. are listed as if the name Saint were spelled in full. Numbered street names and all abbreviated names are treated as if spelled out in full.

Saginaw	Fifth Avenue Hotel	Hart Mfg. Co.
St. Louis	42nd Street Dress Shop	Hart, Martin
St. Peter's Rectory	Hart, Chas.	Hart, Thos.

Sandford	Hart, Charlotte	Hart, Thomas A.
Smith, Wm.	Hart, Jas.	Hart, Thos. R.
Smith, Willis	Hart, Janice	

11. Federal, state, or city departments of government should be placed alphabetically under the governmental branch controlling them.
    Illinois, State of -- Departments and Commissions
        Banking Dept.
        Employment Bureau
    United States Government Departments
        Commerce
        Defense
        State
        Treasury
12. Alphabetic order
    Each word in a name is an indexing unit. Arrange the names in alphabetic order by comparing similar units in each name. Consider the second units only when the first units are identical. Consider the third units only when both the first and second units are identical.
13. Single surnames or initials
    A surname, when used alone, precedes the same surname with a first name or initial. A surname with a first initial only precedes a surname with a complete first name. This rule is sometimes stated, "nothing comes before something."
14. Surname prefixes
    A surname prefix is not a separate indexing unit, but it is considered part of the surname. These prefixes include: d', D', Da, de, De, Del, Des, Di, Du, Fitz., La, Le, Mc, Mac, 'c, O', St., Van, Van der, Von, Von der, and others. The prefixes M', Mac, and Mc are indexed and filed exactly as they are spelled.
15. Names of firms
    Names of firms and institutions are indexed and filed exactly as they are written when they do not contain the complete name of an individual.
16. Names of firms containing complete individual names
    When the firm or institution name includes the complete name of an individual, the units are transposed for indexing in the same way as the name of an individual.
17. Article "The"
    When the article <u>the</u> occurs at the beginning of a name, it is placed at the end in parentheses but it is not moved. In both cases, it is not an indexing unit and is disregarded in filing.
18. Hyphenated names
    Hyphenated firm names are considered as separate indexing units. Hyphenated surnames of individuals are considered as one indexing unit; this applies also to hyphenated names of individuals whose complete names are part of a firm name.
19. Abbreviations
    Abbreviations are considered as though the name were written in full; however, single letters other than abbreviations are considered as separate indexing units.
20. Conjunctions, prepositions and firm endings
    Conjunctions and prepositions, such as and, for, in, of, are disregarded in indexing and filing but are not omitted or their order changed when writing names on cards and folders. Firm endings, such as Ltd., Inc., Co., Son, Bros., Mfg., and Corp., are treated as a unit in indexing and filing and are considered as though spelled in full, such as Brothers and Incorporated.

21. One or two words

Names that may be spelled either as one or two words are indexed and filed as one word.

22. Compound geographic names

Compound geographic names are considered as separate indexing and filing units, except when the first part of the name is not an English word, such as the Los in Los Angeles.

23. Titles or degrees of individuals, whether preceding or following the name,are not considered in indexing or filing. They are placed in parentheses after the given name or initial. Terms that designate seniority, such as Jr., Sr., 2d, are also placed in parentheses and are considered for indexing and filing only when the names to be indexed are otherwise identical.

Exception A:

When the name of an individual consists of a title and one name only, such as Queen Elizabeth, it is not transposed and the title is considered for indexing and filing.

Exception B:

When a title or foreign article is the initial word of a firm or association name, it is considered for indexing and filing.

24. Possessives

When a word ends in apostrophe s, the s is not considered in indexing and filing. However, when a word ends in s apostrophe, because the s is part of the original word, it is considered. This rule is sometimes stated, "Consider everything up to the apostrophe. "

25. United States and foreign government names

Names pertaining to the federal government are indexed and filed under United States Government and then subdivided by title of the department, bureau, division, commission, or board. Names pertaining to foreign governments are indexed and filed under names of countries and then subdivided by title of the department, bureau, division, commission, or board. Phrases, such as department of, bureau of, division of, commission of, board of, when used in titles of governmental bodies, are placed in parentheses after the word they modify, but are disregarded in indexing and filing. Such phrases, however, are considered in indexing and filing nongovernmental names.

26. Other political subdivisions

Names pertaining to other political subdivisions, such as states, counties, cities, or towns, are indexed and filed under the name of the political subdivision and then subdivided by the title of the department, bureau, division, commission, or board.

27. Addresses

When the same name appears with different addresses, the names are indexed as usual and arranged alphabetically according to city or town. The State is considered only when there is duplication of both individual or company name and city name. If the same name is located at different addresses within the same city, then the names are arranged alphabetically by streets. If the same name is located at more than one address on the same street, then the names are arranged from the lower to the higher street number.

28. Numbers

Any number in a name is considered as though it were written in words, and it is indexed and filed as one unit.

29. Bank names

Because the names of many banking institutions are alike in several respects, as first National Bank, Second National Bank, etc., banks are indexed and filed first by city location, then by bank name, with the state location written in parentheses and considered only if necessary

30. Married women

The legal name of a married woman is the one used for filing purposes. Legally, a man's surname is the only part of a man's name a woman assumes when she marries. Her legal name, therefore, could be either:

(1) Her own first and middle names together with her husband's surname, or
(2) Her own first name and maiden surname, together with her husband's surname.

Mrs. is placed in parentheses at the end of the name. Her husband's first and middle names are given in parentheses below her legal name.

31. An alphabetically arranged list of names illustrating many difficult points of alphabetizing follows.

COLUMN I	COLUMN II
Abbot , W.B.	54th St. Tailor Shop
Abbott, Alice	Forstall, W.J.
Allen, Alexander B.	44th St. Garage
Allen, Alexander B., Inc.	M A Delivery Co.
Andersen, Hans	M & C Amusement Corp.
Andersen, Hans E.	M C Art Assn.
Andersen, Hans E., Jr.	MacAdam, Wm.
Anderson, Andrew Andrews,	Macaulay, James
George Brown Motor Co., Boston	MacAulay, Wilson
Brown Motor Co., Chicago	MacDonald, R.J.
Brown Motor Co., Philadelphia	Macdonald, S.B.
Brown Motor Co., San Francisco	Mace, Wm.
Dean, Anna	Mazza, Anthony
Dean, Anna F.	McAdam, Wm.
Dean, Anna Frances	McAndrews, Jerry
Dean & Co.	Meade & Clark Co.
Deane-Arnold Apartments	Meade, S.T.
Deane's Pharmacy	Meade, Solomon
Deans, Felix A.	Sackett Publishing Co.
Dean's Studio	Sacks, Robert
Deans, Wm.	St.Andrew Hotel
Deans & Williams	St.John, Homer W.
East Randolph	Saks, Isaac B.
East St.Louis	Stephens, Ira
Easton, Pa.	Stevens, Delevan
Eastport, Me.	Stevens, Delila

IV. OFFICIAL EXAMINATION DIRECTIONS AND RULES

To preclude the possibility of conflicting or varying methods of filing, explicit directions and express rules are given to the candidate before he answers the filing questions on an examination.

The most recent official directions and rules for the filing questions are given immediately hereafter.

OFFICIAL DIRECTIONS

Each of questions ... to ... consists of four(five)names. For each question, select the one of the four(five)names that should be first (second)(third)(last) if the four(five)names were arranged in alphabetical order in accordance with the rules for alphabetical filing given below. Read these rules carefully. Then, for each question, indicate in the correspondingly numbered row on the answer sheet the letter preceding the name that should be first(second)(third)(last) in alphabetical order.

OFFICIAL RULES FOR ALPHABETICAL FILING

Names of Individuals

1. The names of individuals are filed in strict alphabetical order, first according to the last name, then according to first name or initial, and, finally, according to middle name or initial. For example: William Jones precedes George Kirk and Arthur S. Blake precedes Charles M. Blake.
2. When the last names are identical, the one with an initial instead of a first name precedes the one "with a first name beginning with the same initial. For example: J.Green precedes Joseph Green.
3. When identical last names also have identical first names, the one without a middle name or initial precedes the one with a middle name or initial. For example:Robert Jackson precedes both Robert C.Jackson and Robert Chester Jackson.
4. When last names are identical and the first names are also identical, the one with a middle initial precedes the one with a middle name beginning with the same initial. For example: Peter A. Brown precedes Peter Alvin Brown.
5. Prefixes such as De, El, La, and Van are considered parts of the names they precede. For example:Wilfred DeWald precedes Alexander Duval.
6. Last names beginning with "Mac" or "Mc" are filed as spelled.
7. Abbreviated names are treated as if they were spelled out. For example: Jos. is filed as Joseph and Robt. is filed as Robert.
8. Titles and designations such as Dr. ,Mrs., Prof. are disregarded in filing.

Names of Business Organizations

1. The names of business organizations are filed exactly as written, except that an organization bearing the name of an individual is filed alphabetically according to the name of the individual in accordance with the rules for filing names of individuals given above. For example: Thomas Allison Machine Company precedes Northern Baking Company.
2. When numerals occur in a name, they are treated as if they were spelled out. For example: 6 stands for six and 4th stands for fourth.
3. When the following words occur in names, they are disregarded: the, of, and Sample: Choose the name that should be filed *third.*

   (A) Fred Town (2) (C) D. Town (1)
   (B) Jack Towne (3) (D) Jack S.Towne (4)

   The numbers in parentheses indicate the proper alphabetical order in which these names should be filed. Since the name that should be filed third is Jack Towne, the answer is (B).

FILING

EXAMINATION SECTION
TEST 1

DIRECTIONS: Questions 1 through 8 each show in Column I names written on four cards (lettered w, x, y, z) which have to be filed. You are to choose the option (lettered A, B, C, or D) in Column II which *BEST* represents the proper order of filing according to the Rules for Alphabetic Filing, given before, and the sample question given below. Print the letter of the correct answer in the space at the right.

SAMPLE QUESTION

	Column I		Column II
w.	Jane Earl	A.	w, y, z, x
x.	James A. Earle	B.	y, w, z, x
y.	James Earl	C.	x, y, w, z
z.	J. Earle	D.	x, w, y, z

The correct way to file the cards is:

y. James Earl
w. Jane Earl
z. J. Earle
x. James A. Earle

The correct filing order is shown by the letters, y, w, z, x (in that sequence). Since, in Column II, B appears in front of the letters, y, w, z, x (in that sequence), B is the correct answer to the sample question.

Now answer the following questions using that same procedure.

		Column I		Column II	
1.	w.	James Rothschild	A.	x, z, w, y	1.____
	x.	Julius B. Rothchild	B.	x, w, z, y	
	y.	B. Rothstein	C.	z, y, w, x	
	z.	Brian Joel Rothenstein	D.	z, w, x, y	
2.	w.	George S. Wise	A.	w, y, z, x	2.____
	x.	S. G. Wise	B.	x, w, y, z	
	y.	Geo. Stuart Wise	C.	y, x, w, z	
	z.	Prof. Diana Wise	D.	z, w, y, x	
3.	w.	10th Street Bus Terminal	A.	x, z, w, y	3.____
	x.	Buckingham Travel Agency	B.	y, x, w, z	
	y.	The Buckingham Theater	C.	w, z, y, x	
	z.	Burt Tompkins Studio	D.	x, w, y, z	
4.	w.	National Council of American Importers	A.	w, y, x, z	4.____
	x.	National Chain Co. of Providence	B.	x, z, w, y	
	y.	National Council on Alcoholism	C.	z, x, w, y	
	z.	National Chain Co.	D.	z, x, y, w	

5. w. Dr. Herbert Alvary
   x. Mr. Victor Alvarado
   y. Alvar Industries
   z. V. Alvarado

   A. w, y, x, z
   B. z, w, x, y
   C. y, z, x, w
   D. w, z, x, y

5.____

6. w. Joan MacBride
   x. Wm. Mackey
   y. Roslyn McKenzie
   z. Winifred Mackey

   A. w, x, z, y
   B. w, y, z, x
   C. w, z, x, y
   D. w, y, x, z

6.____

7. w. 3 Way Trucking Co.
   x. 3rd Street Bakery
   y. 380 Realty Corp.
   z. Three Lions Pub

   A. y, x, z, w
   B. y, z, w, x
   C. x, y, z, w
   D. x, y, w, z

7.____

8. w. Miss Rose Leonard
   x. Rev. Leonard Lucas
   y. Sylvia Leonard Linen Shop
   z. Rose S. Leonard

   A. z, w, x, y
   B. w, z, y, x
   C. w, x, z, y
   D. z, w, y, x

8.____

KEY (CORRECT ANSWERS)

1. A
2. D
3. B
4. D
5. C
6. A
7. C
8. B

TEST 2

DIRECTIONS: Questions 1 through 7 each show in Column I four names (lettered w, x, y, z) which have to be entered in an agency telephone directory. You are to choose the option (lettered A, B, C, or D) in Column II which *BEST* represents the proper order for entering them according to the Rules for Alphabetic Filing, given before, and the sample question given below.

SAMPLE QUESTION

	Column I		Column II
w.	Doris Jenkin	A.	w, y, z, x
x.	Donald F. Jenkins	B.	y, w, z, x
y.	Donald Jenkin	C.	x, y, w, z
z.	D. Jenkins	D.	x, w, y, z

The correct way to enter these names is:

y. Donald Jenkin
w. Doris Jenkin
z. D. Jenkins
x. Donald F. Jenkins

The correct order is shown by the letters y, w, z, x, in that sequence. Since, in Column II, B appears in front of the letters y, w, z, x, in that sequence, B is the correct answer to the sample question.

Now answer the following questions using the same procedure.

		Column I		Column II	
1.	w.	Lawrence Robertson	A.	x, y, w, z	1.____
	x.	Jack L. Robinson	B.	w, z, x, y	
	y.	John Robinson	C.	z, w, x, y	
	z.	William B. Roberson	D.	z, w, y, x	
2.	w.	P. N. Figueredo	A.	y, x, z, w	2.____
	x.	M. Alice Figueroa	B.	x, z, w, y	
	y.	Jose Figueredo	C.	x, w, z, y	
	z.	M. Alicia Figueroa	D.	y, w, x, z	
3.	w.	George Steven Keats	A.	y, x, w, z	3.____
	x.	George S. Keats	B.	z, y, x, w	
	y.	G. Samuel Keats	C.	x, z, w, y	
	z.	Dr. Samuel Keats	D.	w, z, x, y	
4.	w.	V. Merchant	A.	w, x, y, z	4.____
	x.	Dr. William Mercher	B.	w, y, z, x	
	y.	Prof. Victor Merchant	C.	z, y, w, x	
	z.	Dr. Walter Merchan	D.	z, w, y, x	
5.	w.	Brian McCoy	A.	z, x, y, w	5.____
	x.	William Coyne	B.	y, w, z, x	
	y.	Mr. William MacCoyle	C.	x, z, y, w	
	z.	Dr. D. V. Coyne	D.	w, y, z, x	

6. w. Ms. M. Rosie Buchanan
   x. Rosalyn M. Buchanan
   y. Rosie Maria Buchanan
   z. Rosa Marie Buchanan

   A. z, y, x, w
   B. w, z, x, y
   C. w, z, y, x
   D. z, x, y, w

   6.____

7. w. Prof. Jonathan Praga
   x. Dr. Joan Prager
   y. Alan VanPrague
   z. Alexander Prague

   A. w, z, y, x
   B. w, x, z, y
   C. x, w, z, y
   D. x, w, y, z

   7.____

KEY (CORRECT ANSWERS)

1. C
2. D
3. A
4. D
5. A
6. B
7. B

TEST 3

DIRECTIONS: Questions 1 through 10 each show in Column I names written on four cards (lettered w, x, y, z) which have to be filed. You are to choose the option (lettered A, B, C, or D) in Column II which *BEST* represents the proper order of filing according to the rules and sample question given below. The cards are to be filed according to the Rules for Alphabetical Filing, given before, and the sample question given below.

SAMPLE QUESTION

	Column I		Column II
w.	Jane Earl	A.	w, y, z, x
x.	James A. Earle	B.	y, w, z, x
y.	James Earl	C.	x, y, w, z
z.	J. Earle	D.	x, w, y, z

The correct way to file the cards is:

y. James Earl
w. Jane Earl
z. J. Earle
x. James A. Earle

The correct filing order is shown by the letters y, w, z, x (in that order). Since, in Column II, B appears in front of the letters y, w, z, x (in that order), B is the correct answer to the sample question.

Now answer Questions 1 through 10 using the same procedure.

		Column I		Column II	
1.	w.	John Smith	A.	w, x, y, z	1.____
	x.	Joan Smythe	B.	y, z, x, w	
	y.	Gerald Schmidt	C.	y, z, w, x	
	z.	Gary Schmitt	D.	z, y, w, x	
2.	w.	A. Black	A.	w, x, y, z	2.____
	x.	Alan S. Black	B.	w, y, x, z	
	y.	Allan Black	C.	w, y, z, x	
	z.	Allen A. Black	D.	x, w, y, z	
3.	w.	Samuel Haynes	A.	w, x, y, z	3.____
	x.	Sam C. Haynes	B.	x, w, z, y	
	y.	David Haynes	C.	y, z, w, x	
	z.	Dave L. Haynes	D.	z, y, x, w	
4.	w.	Lisa B. McNeil	A.	x, y, w, z	4.____
	x.	Tom MacNeal	B.	x, z, y, w	
	y.	Lisa McNeil	C.	y, w, z, x	
	z.	Lorainne McNeal	D.	z, x, y, w	
5.	w.	Larry Richardson	A.	w, y, x, z	5.____
	x.	Leroy Richards	B.	y, x, z, w	
	y.	Larry S. Richards	C.	y, z, x, w	
	z.	Leroy C. Richards	D.	x, w, z, y	

6. w. Arlene Lane
x. Arlene Cora Lane
y. Arlene Clair Lane
z. Arlene C. Lane

A. w, z, y, x
B. w, z, x, y
C. y, x, z, w
D. z, y, w, x

6.____

7. w. Betty Fish
x. Prof. Ann Fish
y. Norma Fisch
z. Dr. Richard Fisch

A. w, x, z, y
B. x, w, y, z
C. y, z, x, w
D. z, y, w, x

7.____

8. w. Dr. Anthony David Lukak
x. Mr. Steven Charles Lucas
y. Mr. Anthony J. Lukak
z. Prof. Steven C. Lucas

A. w, y, z, x
B. x, z, w, y
C. z, x, y, w
D. z, x, w, y

8.____

9. w. Martha Y. Lind
x. Mary Beth Linden
y. Martha W. Lind
z. Mary Bertha Linden

A. w, y, z, x
B. w, y, x, z
C. y, w, z, x
D. y, w, x, z

9.____

10. w. Prof. Harry Michael MacPhelps
x. Mr. Horace M. MacPherson
y. Mr. Harold M. McPhelps
z. Prof. Henry Martin MacPherson

A. w, z, x, y
B. w, y, z, x
C. z, x, w, y
D. x, z, y, w

10.____

KEY (CORRECT ANSWERS)

1.	C	6.	A
2.	A	7.	C
3.	D	8.	D
4.	B	9.	C
5.	B	10.	A

TEST 4

DIRECTIONS: Answer Questions 1 through 5 on the basis of the following information:

A certain shop keeps an informational card file on all suppliers and merchandise. On each card is the supplier's name, the contract number for the merchandise he supplies, and a delivery date for the merchandise. In this filing system, the supplier's name is filed alphabetically, the contract number for the merchandise is filed numerically, and the delivery date is filed chronologically.
In Questions 1 through 5 there are five notations numbered 1 through 5 shown in Column I. Each notation is made up of a supplier's name, a contract number, and a date which is to be filed according to the following rules:

First: File in alphabetical order;
Second: When two or more notations have the same supplier, file according to the contract number in numerical order beginning with the lowest number;
Third: When two or more notations have the same supplier and contract number, file according to the date beginning with the earliest date.

In Column II the numbers 1 through 5 are arranged in four ways to show four different orders in which the merchandise information might be filed. Pick the answer (A., B, C, or D) in Column II in which the notations are arranged according to the above filing rules.

SAMPLE QUESTION

Column I	Column II
1. Cluney (4865) 6/17/02	A. 2, 3, 4, 1, 5
2. Roster (2466) 5/10/01	B. 2, 5, 1, 3, 4
3. Altool (7114) 10/15/02	C. 3, 2, 1, 4, 5
4. Cluney (5296) 12/18/01	D. 3, 5, 1, 4, 2
5. Cluney (4865) 4/8/02	

The correct way to file the cards is:

3. Altool (7114) 10/15/02
5. Cluney (4865) 4/8/02
1. Cluney (4865) 6/17/02
4. Cluney (5276) 12/18/01
2. Roster (2466) 5/10/01

Since the correct filing order is 3, 5, 1, 4, 2, the answer to the sample question is D. Now answer Questions 1 through 5.

		Column I			Column II	
1.	1. warren	(96063)	3/30/03		A. 2, 4, 3, 5, 1	1.____
	2. moore	(21237)	9/4/04		B. 2, 3, 5, 4, 1	
	3. newman	(10050)	12/12/03		C. 4, 5, 2, 3, 1	
	4. downs	(81251)	1/2/03		D. 4, 2, 3, 5, 1	
	5. oliver	(60145)	6/30/04			

2.
1. Henry (40552) 7/6/04
2. Boyd (91251) 9/1/03
3. George (8196) 12/12/03
4. George (31096) 1/12/04
5. West (6109) 8/9/03

A. 5, 4, 3, 1, 2
B. 2, 3, 4, 1, 5
C. 2, 4, 3, 1, 5
D. 5, 2, 3, 1, 4

2._____

3.
1. Salba (4670) 9/7/03
2. Salba (51219) 3/1/03
3. Crete (81562) 7/1/04
4. Salba (51219) 1/11/04
5. Texi (31549) 1/25/03

A. 5, 3, 1, 2, 4
B. 3, 1, 2, 4, 5
C. 3, 5, 4, 2, 1
D. 5, 3, 4, 2, 1

3._____

4.
1. Crayone (87105) 6/10/04
2. Shamba (49210) 1/5/03
3. Valiant (3152) 5/1/04
4. Valiant (3152) 1/9/04
5. Poro (59613) 7/1/03

A. 1, 2, 5, 3, 4
B. 1, 5, 2, 3, 4
C. 1, 5, 3, 4, 2
D. 1, 5, 2, 4, 3

4._____

5.
1. Mackie (42169) 12/20/03
2. Lebo (5198) 9/12/02
3. Drummon (99631) 9/9/04
4. Lebo (15311) 1/25/02
5. Harvin (81765) 6/2/03

A. 3, 2, 1, 5, 4
B. 3, 2, 4, 5, 1
C. 3, 5, 2, 4, 1
D. 3, 5, 4, 2, 1

5._____

KEY (CORRECT ANSWERS)

1. D
2. B
3. B
4. D
5. C

TEST 5

DIRECTIONS: Each of Questions 1 through 8 represents five cards to be filed, numbered 1 through 5 in Column I. Each card is made up of the employee's name, the date of a work assignment, and the work assignment code number shown in parentheses. The cards are to be filed according to the following rules:

First: File in alphabetical order;
Second: When two or more cards have the same employee's name, file according to the assignment date beginning with the earliest date;
Third: When two or more cards have the same employee's name and the same date, file according to the work assignment number beginning with the lowest number.

Column II shows the cards arranged in four different orders. Pick the answer (A, B, C, or D) in Column II which shows the cards arranged correctly according to the above filing rules.

SAMPLE QUESTION

	Column I				Column II
1.	Cluney	4/8/02	(486503)	A.	2, 3, 4, 1, 5
2.	Roster	5/10/01	(246611)	B.	2, 5, 1, 3, 4
3.	Altool	10/15/02	(711433)	C.	3, 2, 1, 4, 5
4.	Cluney	12/18/02	(527610)	D.	3, 5, 1, 4, 2
5.	Cluney	4/8/02	(486500)		

The correct way to file the cards is:

3. Altool 10/15/02 (711433)
5. Cluney 4/8/02 (486500)
1. Cluney 4/8/02 (486503)
4. Cluney 12/18/02 (527610)
2. Roster 5/10/01 (246611)

The correct filing order is shown by the numbers in front of each name (3, 5, 1, 4, 2). The answer to the sample question is the letter in Column II in front of the numbers 3, 5, 1, 4, 2. This answer is D.

Now answer Questions 1 through 8 according to these rules.

1.

1.	Kohls	4/2/02	(125677)	A.	1, 2, 3, 4, 5	1.____
2.	Keller	3/21/02	(129698)	B.	3, 2, 1, 4, 5	
3.	Jackson	4/10/02	(213541)	C.	3, 1, 2, 4, 5	
4.	Richards	1/9/03	(347236)	D.	5, 2, 1, 3, 4	
5.	Richmond	12/11/01	(379321)			

2.

1.	Burroughs	5/27/02	(237896)	A.	1, 4, 3, 2, 5	2.____
2.	Charlson	1/16/02	(114537)	B.	4, 1, 5, 3, 2	
3.	Carlsen	12/2/02	(114377)	C.	1, 4, 3, 5, 2	
4.	Burton	5/1/02	(227096)	D.	4, 1, 3, 5, 2	
5.	Charlson	12/2/02	(114357)			

3. A. Ungerer 11/11/02 (537924)
B. Winters 1/10/02 (657834)
C. Ventura 12/1/02 (698694)
D. Winters 10/11/02 (675654)
E. Ungaro 1/10/02 (684325)

A. 1, 5, 3, 2, 4
B. 5, 1, 3, 4, 2
C. 3, 5, 1, 2, 4
D. 1, 5, 3, 4, 2

3.____

4. 1. Norton 3/12/03 (071605)
2. Morris 2/26/03 (068931)
3. Morse 5/12/03 (142358)
4. Morris 2/26/03 (068391)
5. Morse 2/26/03 (068391)

A. 1, 4, 2, 3, 5
B. 3, 5, 2, 4, 1
C. 2, 4, 3, 5, 1
D. 4, 2, 5, 3, 1

4.____

5. 1. Eger 4/19/02 (874129)
2. Eihler 5/19/03 (875329)
3. Ehrlich 11/19/02 (874839)
4. Eger 4/19/02 (876129)
5. Eihler 5/19/02 (874239)

A. 3, 4, 1, 2, 5
B. 1, 4, 5, 2, 3
C. 4, 1, 3, 2, 5
D. 1, 4, 3, 5, 2

5.____

6. 1. Johnson 12/21/02 (786814)
2. Johns 12/21/03 (801024)
3. Johnson 12/12/03 (762814)
4. Jackson 12/12/03 (862934)
5. Johnson 12/12/03 (762184)

A. 2, 4, 3, 5, 1
B. 4, 2, 5, 3, 1
C. 4, 5, 3, 1, 2
D. 5, 3, 1, 2, 4

6.____

7. 1. Fuller 7/12/02 (598310)
2. Fuller 7/2/02 (598301)
3. Fuller 7/22/02 (598410)
4. Fuller 7/17/03 (598710)
5. Fuller 7/17/03 (598701)

A. 2, 1, 5, 4, 3
B. 1, 2, 4, 5, 3
C. 1, 4, 5, 2, 3
D. 2, 1, 3, 5, 4

7.____

8. 1. Perrine 10/27/99 (637096)
2. Perrone 11/14/02 (767609)
3. Perrault 10/15/98 (629706)
4. Perrine 10/17/02 (373656)
5. Perine 10/17/01 (376356)

A. 3, 4, 5, 1, 2
B. 3, 2, 5, 4, 1
C. 5, 3, 4, 1, 2
D. 4, 5, 1, 2, 3

8.____

KEY (CORRECT ANSWERS)

1. B
2. A
3. B
4. D
5. D
6. B
7. D
8. C

TEST 6

DIRECTIONS: Each question or incomplete statement is followed by several suggested answers or completions. Select the one that *BEST* answers the question or completes the statement. *PRINT THE LETTER OF THE CORRECT ANSWER IN THE SPACE AT THE RIGHT.*

1. Which one of the following *BEST* describes the usual arrangement of a tickler file? 1._____

   A. Alphabetical
   B. Chronological
   C. Numerical
   D. Geographical

2. Which one of the following is the *LEAST* desirable filing practice? 2._____

   A. Using staples to keep papers together
   B. Filing all material without regard to date
   C. Keeping a record of all materials removed from the files
   D. Writing filing instructions on each paper prior to filing

3. The one of the following records which it would be *MOST* advisable to keep in alphabetical order is a 3._____

   A. continuous listing of phone messages, including time and caller, for your supervisor
   B. listing of individuals currently employed by your agency in a particular title
   C. record of purchases paid for by the petty cash fund
   D. dated record of employees who have borrowed material from the files in your office

4. Tickler systems are used in many legal offices for scheduling and calendar control. Of the following, the *LEAST* common use of a tickler system is to 4._____

   A. keep papers filed in such a way that they may easily be retrieved
   B. arrange for the appearance of witnesses when they will be needed
   C. remind lawyers when certain papers are due
   D. arrange for the gathering of certain types of evidence

5. A type of file which permits the operator to remain seated while the file can be moved backward and forward as required is *BEST* termed a 5._____

   A. lateral file
   B. movable file
   C. reciprocating file
   D. rotary file

6. In which of the following cases would it be *MOST* desirable to have two cards for one individual in a single alphabetic file? The individual has 6._____

   A. a hyphenated surname
   B. two middle names
   C. a first name with an unusual spelling
   D. a compound first name

KEY (CORRECT ANSWERS)

1. B
2. B
3. B
4. A
5. C
6. A

NAME AND NUMBER CHECKING

EXAMINATION SECTION
TEST 1

DIRECTIONS: This test is designed to measure your speed/and accuracy. You are urged to work both quickly and accurately and to do correctly as many lists as you can in the time allowed. The test consists of lists of pairs of names and numbers. Count the number of IDENTICAL pairs in each list. Then, select the correct number, 1,2, 3, 4, or 5, and indicate your choice by circling the corresponding number on your answer paper. Two sample questions are presented for your guidance, together with the correct solutions.

SAMPLE QUESTIONS — CIRCLE CORRECT ANSWER

SAMPLE LIST A

Adelphi College - Adelphia College — 1 2 3 4 5
Braxton Corp. - Braxeton Corp.
Wassaic State School - Wassaic State School
Central Islip State Hospital - Central Isllip State Hospital
Greenwich House - Greenwich House

NOTE that there are only two correct pairs - Wassaic State School and Greenwich House. Therefore, the CORRECT answer is 2.

SAMPLE LIST B

78453694	- 78453684	1 2 3 4 5
784530	- 784530	
533	- 534	
67845	- 67845	
2368745	- 2368755	

NOTE that there are only two correct pairs - 784530 and 67845. Therefore, the CORRECT answer is 2.

LIST 1

Diagnostic Clinic	- Diagnostic Clinic	1 2 3 4 5
Yorkville Health	- Yorkville Health	
Meinhard Clinic	- Meinhart Clinic	
Corlears Clinic	- Carlears Clinic	
Tremont Diagnostic	- Tremont Diagnostic	

LIST 2

73526	- 73526	1 2 3 4 5
7283627198	- 7283627198	
627	- 637	
728352617283	- 728352617282	
6281	- 6281	

CIRCLE CORRECT ANSWER

LIST 3

Jefferson Clinic	- Jeffersen Clinic	1 2 3 4 5
Mott Haven Center	- Mott Havan Center	
Bronx Hospital	- Bronx Hospital	
Montefiore Hospital	- Montifeore Hospital	
Beth Isreal Hospital	- Beth Israel Hospital	

LIST 4

936271826	- 936371826	1 2 3 4 5
5271	- 5291	
82637192037	- 82637192037	
527182	- 5271882	
726354256	- 72635456	

LIST 5

Trinity Hospital	- Trinity Hospital	1 2 3 4 5
Central Harlem	- Centrel Harlem	
St. Luke's Hospital	- St. Lukes' Hospital	
Mt.Sinai Hospital	- Mt.Sinia Hospital	
N.Y.Dispensery	- N.Y.Dispensary	

LIST 6

725361552637	- 725361555637	1 2 3 4 5
7526378	- 7526377	
6975	- 6975	
82637481028	- 82637481028	
3427	- 3429	

LIST 7

Misericordia Hospital	- Miseracordia Hospital	1 2 3 4 5
Lebonan Hospital	- Lebanon Hospital	
Gouverneur Hospital	- Gouverner Hospital	
German Polyclinic	- German Policlinic	
French Hospital	- French Hospital	

LIST 8

8277364933251	- 827364933351	1 2 3 4 5
63728	- 63728	
367281	- 367281	
62733846273	- 6273846293	
62836	- 6283	

LIST 9

King's County Hospital	- Kings County Hospital	1 2 3 4 5
St.Johns Long Island	- St.John's Long Island	
Bellevue Hospital	- Bellvue Hospital	
Beth David Hospital	- Beth David Hospital	
Samaritan Hospital	- Samariton Hospital	

		CIRCLE CORRECT ANSWER
LIST 10		
62836454	- 62836455	1 2 3 4 5
42738267	- 42738369	
573829	- 573829	
738291627874	- 738291627874	
725	- 735	
LIST 11		
Bloomingdal Clinic	- Bloomingdale Clinic	1 2 3 4 5
Communitty Hospital	- Community Hospital	
Metroplitan Hospital	- Metropoliton Hospital	
Lenox Hill Hospital	- Lonex Hill Hospital	
Lincoln Hospital	- Lincoln Hospital	
LIST 12		
6283364728	- 6283648	1 2 3 4 5
627385	- 627383	
54283902	- 54283602	
63354	- 63354	
7283562781	- 7283562781	
LIST 13		
Sydenham Hospital	- Sydanham Hospital	1 2 3 4 5
Roosevalt Hospital	- Roosevelt Hospital	
Vanderbilt Clinic	- Vanderbild Clinic	
Women's Hospital	- Woman's Hospital	
Flushing Hospital	- Flushing Hospital	
LIST 14		
62738	- 62738	1 2 3 4 5
727355542321	- 72735542321	
263849332	- 263849332	
262837	- 263837	
47382912	- 47382922	
LIST 15		
Episcopal Hospital	- Episcapal Hospital	1 2 3 4 5
Flower Hospital	- Flouer Hospital	
Stuyvesent Clinic	- Stuyvesant Clinic	
Jamaica Clinic	- Jamaica Clinic	
Ridgwood Clinic	- Ridgewood Clinic	
LIST 16		
628367299	- 628367399	1 2 3 4 5
111	- 111	
118293304829	- 1182839489	
4448	- 4448	
333693678	- 333693678	

CIRCLE
CORRECT ANSWER

LIST 17

Arietta Crane Farm	- Areitta Crane Farm	1 2 3 4 5
Bikur Chilim Home	- Bikur Chilom Home	
Burke Foundation	- Burke Foundation	
Blythedale Home	- Blythdale Home	
Campbell Cottages	- Cambell Cottages	

LIST 18

32123	- 32132	1 2 3 4 5
2738933326783	- 27389326783	
473829	- 473829	
7382937	- 7383937	
362890122332	- 36289012332	

LIST 19

Caraline Rest	- Caroline Rest	1 2 3 4 5
Loreto Rest	- Loretto Rest	
Edgewater Creche	- Edgwater Creche	
Holiday Farm	- Holiday Farm	
House of St. Giles	- House of st. Giles	

LIST 20

557286777	- 55728677	1 2 3 4 5
3678902	- 3678892	
1567839	- 1567839	
7865434712	- 7865344712	
9927382	- 9927382	

LIST 21

Isabella Home	- Isabela Home	1 2 3 4 5
James A. Moore Home	- James A. More Home	
The Robin's Nest	- The Roben's Nest	
Pelham Home	- Pelam Home	
St.Eleanora's Home	- St. Eleanora's Home	

LIST 22

273648293048	- 273648293048	1 2 3 4 5
334	- 334	
7362536478	- 7362536478	
7362819273	- 7362819273	
7362	- 7363	

LIST 23

St.Pheobe's Mission	- St.Phebe's Mission	1 2 3 4 5
Seaside Home	- Seaside Home	
Speedwell Society	- Speedwell Society	
Valeria Home	- Valera Home	
Wiltwyck	- Wildwyck	

		CIRCLE CORRECT ANSWER
LIST 24		
63728	- 63738	1 2 3 4 5
63728192736	- 63728192738	
428	- 458	
62738291527	- 62738291529	
63728192	- 63728192	
LIST 25		
McGaffin	- McGafin	1 2 3 4 5
David Ardslee	- David Ardslee	
Axton Supply	- Axeton Supply Co	
Alice Russell	- Alice Russell	
Dobson Mfg.Co.	- Dobsen Mfg. Co.	

KEY (CORRECT ANSWERS)

1. 3
2. 3
3. 1
4. 1
5. 1
6. 2
7. 1
8. 2
9. 1
10. 2
11. 1
12. 2
13. 1
14. 2
15. 1
16. 3
17. 1
18. 1
19. 1
20. 2
21. 1
22. 4
23. 2
24. 1
25. 2

TEST 2

DIRECTIONS: This test is designed to measure your speed and accuracy. You are urged to work both quickly and accurately and to do correctly as many lists as you can in the time allowed. The test consists of lists of pairs of names and numbers. Count the number of IDENTICAL pairs in each list. Then, select the correct number, 1, 2, 3, 4, or 5, and indicate your choice by circling the corresponding number on your answer paper. Two sample questions are presented for your guidance, together with the correct solutions.

CIRCLE CORRECT ANSWER

LIST 1

82637381028 - 82637281028 — 1 2 3 4 5
928 - 928
72937281028 - 72937281028
7362 - 7362
927382615 - 927382615

LIST 2

Albee Theatre - Albee Theatre — 1 2 3 4 5
Lapland Lumber Co. - Laplund Lumber Co.
Adelphi College - Adelphi College
Jones & Son Inc. - Jones & Sons Inc.
S.W.Ponds Co. - S.W. Ponds Co.

LIST 3

85345 - 85345 — 1 2 3 4 5
895643278 - 895643277
726352 - 726353
632685 - 632685
7263524 - 7236524

LIST 4

Eagle Library - Eagle Library — 1 2 3 4 5
Dodge Ltd. - Dodge Co.
Stromberg Carlson - Stromberg Carlsen
Clairice Ling - Clairice Linng
Mason Book Co. - Matson Book Co.

LIST 5

66273 - 66273 — 1 2 3 4 5
629 - 620
7382517283 - 7382517283
637281 - 639281
2738261 - 2788261

CIRCLE CORRECT ANSWER

LIST 6

Robert MacColl	- Robert McColl	1 2 3 4 5
Buick Motor	- Buck Motors	
Murray Bay & Co.Ltd.	- Murray Bay Co.Ltd.	
L.T. Ltyle	- L.T, Lyttle	
A.S. Landas	- A.S. Landas	

LIST 7

627152637490	- 627152637490	1 2 3 4 5
73526189	- 73526189	
5372	- 5392	
63728142	- 63728124	
4783946	- 4783046	

LIST 8

Tyndall Burke	- Tyndell Burke	1 2 3 4 5
W. Briehl	- W, Briehl	
Burritt Publishing Co.	- Buritt Publishing Co.	
Frederick Breyer & Co.	- Frederick Breyer Co.	
Bailey Buulard	- Bailey Bullard	

LIST 9

634	- 634	1 2 3 4 5
162837	- 163837	
273892223678	- 27389223678	
527182	- 527782	
3628901223	- 3629002223	

LIST 10

Ernest Boas	- Ernest Boas	1 2 3 4 5
Rankin Barne	- Rankin Barnes	
Edward Appley	- Edward Appely	
Camel	- Camel	
Caiger Food Co.	- Caiger Food Co.	

LIST 11

6273	- 6273	1 2 3 4 5
322	- 332	
15672839	- 15672839	
63728192637	- 63728192639	
738	- 738	

LIST 12

Wells Fargo Co.	- Wells Fargo Co.	1 2 3 4 5
W.D. Brett	- W.D. Britt	
Tassco Co.	- Tassko Co.	
Republic Mills	- Republic Mill	
R.W. Burnham	- R.W. Burhnam	

CIRCLE CORRECT ANSWER

LIST 13

7253529152	- 7283529152	1 2 3 4 5
6283	- 6383	
52839102738	- 5283910238	
308	- 398	
82637201927	- 8263720127	

LIST 14

Schumacker Co.	- Shumacker Co.	1 2 3 4 5
C.H. Caiger	- C.H. Caiger	
Abraham Strauss	- Abram Straus	
B.F. Boettjer	- B.F. Boettijer	
Cut-Rate Store	- Cut-Rate Stores	

LIST 15

15273826	- 15273826	1 2 3 4 5
72537	- 73537	
726391027384	- 72639107384	
637389	- 627399	
725382910	- 725382910	

LIST 16

Hixby Ltd.	- Hixby Lt'd.	1 2 3 4 5
S. Reiner	- S. Riener	
Reynard Co.	- Reynord Co.	
Esso Gassoline Co.	- Esso Gasolene Co.	
Belle Brock	- Belle Brock	

LIST 17

7245	- 7245	1 2 3 4 5
819263728192	- 819263728172	
682537289	- 682537298	
789	- 789	
82936542891	- 82936542891	

LIST 18

Joseph Cartwright	- Joseph Cartwrite	1 2 3 4 5
Foote Food Co.	- Foot Food Co.	
Weiman & Held	- Weiman & Held	
Sanderson Shoe Co.	- Sandersen Shoe Co.	
A.M. Byrne	- A.N. Byrne	

LIST 19

4738267	- 4738277	1 2 3 4 5
63728	- 63729	
6283628901	- 6283628991	
918264	- 918264	
263728192037	- 2637728192073	

		CIRCLE CORRECT ANSWER
LIST 20		
Exray Laboratories	- Exray Labratories	1 2 3 4 5
Curley Toy Co.	- Curly Toy Co.	
J. Lauer & Cross	- J. Laeur & Cross	
Mireco Brands	- Mireco Brands	
Sandor Lorand	- Sandor Larand	
LIST 21		
607	- 609	1 2 3 4 5
6405	- 6403	
976	- 996	
101267	- 101267	
2065432	- 20965432	
LIST 22		
John Macy & Sons	- John Macy & Son	1 2 3 4 5
Venus Pencil Co.	- Venus Pencil Co,	
Nell McGinnis	- Nell McGinnis	
McCutcheon & Co.	- McCutcheon & Co.	
Sun-Tan Oil	- Sun-Tan Oil	
LIST 23		
703345700	- 703345700	1 2 3 4 5
46754	- 466754	
3367490	- 3367490	
3379	- 3778	
47384	- 47394	
LIST 24		
arthritis	- athritis	1 2 3 4 5
asthma	- asthma	
endocrene	- endocrene	
gastro-enterological	- gastrol-enteralogical	
orthopedic	- orthopedic	
LIST 25		
743829432	- 743828432	1 2 3 4 5
998	- 998	
732816253902	- 732816252902	
46829	- 46830	
7439120249	- 7439210249	

KEY (CORRECT ANSWERS)

1. 4
2. 3
3. 2
4. 1
5. 2
6. 1
7. 2
8. 1
9. 1
10. 3
11. 3
12. 1
13. 1
14. 1
15. 2
16. 1
17. 3
18. 1
19. 1
20. 1
21. 1
22. 4
23. 2
24. 3
25. 1

GLOSSARY OF MEDICAL TERMS

Contents

	Page
ABCESS ...... BLOOD GROUPING	1
BLOOD CHEMISTRY ...... CYSTITIS	2
DIABETES (MELLITUS) ...... EPILEPSY	3
FURUNCLE (BOIL) ...... HEMATOMA	4
HEMORRHAGE (BLEEDING) ...... KIDNEY FAILURE (RENAL FAILURE)	5
LABORATORY PROCEDURES ...... METASTASIS	6
MULTIPLE SCLEROSIS ...... PARKINSONISM (PARALYSIS AGITANS)	7
PELLAGRA ...... PSORIASIS	8
PULMONARY EDEMA ...... SPASTIC PARALYSIS (CEREBRAL PALSY)	9
STROKE (CEREBRAL APOPLEXY) ...... VARICOSE VEINS	10

GLOSSARY OF MEDICAL TERMS

A

ABSCESS

Collection of pus in a tissue cavity resulting from a localized infection associated with cellular disintegration.

ALLERGY

Hypersensitive state stemming from exposure to a substance foreign to the body or to a physical agent (allergen) following a first contact. Subsequential exposure produces a reaction far more intense than the first one and entirely different.

ANEMIA

Decrease in the number of circulating red blood cells or in their hemoglobin (oxygen-carrying pigment) content. Can result from excessive bleeding or blood destruction (either inherited or disease caused) or from decreased blood formation (either nutritional deficiency or disease).

ANGINA

Choking pain. Angina pectoris: chest pain resulting from insufficient blood circulation through the hear vessels (coronaries), precipiated by exertion or emotion and usually relieved by a vasodilator drug.

ARTERIOSCLEROSIS

Generalized thickening, loss of elasticity, and hardening of the body's small and medium-size arteries.

ASTHMA

Disease characterized by repeated attacks of breath shortness, with wheezing, cough, and choking feeling due to a spasmodic narrowing of the small bronchi (small air tubes opening into the lung respiratory alveoli or cavities).

B

BIOPSY

Removal of a small piece of tissue or organ from the living body for microscopic or chemical examination to assist in disease diagnosis.

BRONCHITIS

Inflammation of the bronchi (tubular passages leading to lung cavities). It may be acute or chronic and caused by infection or the action of physical or chemical agents.

BLOOD COUNT

See: LABORATORY PROCEDURES

BLOOD GROUPING

See: LABORATORY PROCEDURES

2

BLOOD CHEMISTRY
See: LABORATORY PROCEDURES

BLOOD CULTURE
See: LABORATORY PROCEDURES

C

CANCER (NEOPLASM)
A cellular tumor (swelling) resulting from uncontrolled tissue growth. Its natural evolution is to spread locally and to other body locations through the blood and lymph stream.

CATARACT
Opacity of the normally transparent eye lens; this condition leads to impaired vision and stems from hereditary, nutritional, inflammatory, toxic, traumatic, or degenerative causes.

CATHETERIZATION
Introduction of a narrow tubular instrument called a catheter into a body cavity to withdraw liquids (usually into the bladder for urine withdrawal).

CEREBROSPINAL FLUID EXAMINATION
Chemical, microscopic, and bacteriological examination of a sample of the usually clear and colorless liquid bathing the brain and spinal cord. The sample is usually removed by needle puncture of the lumbar spine.

CIRRHOSIS
Chronic liver ailment, characterized by an increase in its fibrous support tissue that results in a progressive destruction of liver cells and impairment of the organ's function.

CONJUNCTIVITIS
Acute or chronic inflammation of the conjuctiva the delicate transparent membrane lining the eyelids and covering the exposed surface of the eyeball. It results from the action of bacteria, allergens, and physical or chemical irritants.

CYST
Any normal or abnormal sac in the body, especially one containing a liquid or semiliquid material.

CYSTIC FIBROSIS
An inherited disease of the glands of external secretion, affecting mostly the pancreas, respiratory tract, and sweat glands. It usually manifests itself in infancy.

CYSTITIS
Acute or chronic inflammation of the urinary bladder, caused by infection or irritation from foreign bodies (kidney stones) or chemicals. Its symptoms are frequent voiding accompanied by burning sensation

3

D

DIABETES (MELLITUS)

Hereditary or acquired disorder in which there is a sugar-utilization deficiency in the body, caused by an absolute or relative insufficiency of the normal internal secretion of the pancreas (insulin). Symptoms are thirst, hunger, itching, weakness, and increased frequency of urination. Diabetes can be controlled by diet drugs, or the administration of insulin. Lack of treatment leads to various complications, including death.

E

ECZEMA

Inflammatory skin disease that produces a great variety of lesions, such as vesicles, thickening of skin, watery discharge, and scales and crusts, with itching and burning sensations. Eczema is caused by allergy, infections, and nutritional, physical, and sometimes unknown factors.

EDEMA

Excessive accumulation of water and salt in the tissue spaces, caused by kidney or heart disease (generalized edema) or by local circulatory impairment stemming from inflammation, trauma, or neoplasm (localized edema).

ELECTROCARDIOGRAM (ECG or EKG)

Graphic tracing of the electric current that is produced by the rhythmic contraction of the heart muscle. Visually, a periodic wave pattern is produced. Changes in the wave pattern may appear in the course of various heart diseases; the tracing is obtained by applying electrodes on the skin of the chest and limbs.

ELECTROENCEPHALOGRAM (EEG)

Graphic recording of the electric current created by the activity of the brain. The electrodes are placed on the scalp. It is used in the diagnosis of organic brain disease.

EMBOLISM

Sudden blocking of an artery by a dislodged blood clot (after surgery), a fat globule (after a fracture), gas bubbles (after sudden decompression), bacterial clumps (bacterial endocarditis), or other foreign matter. The arteries most usually affected are those of the brain, heart, lungs, and extremities.

EMPHYSEMA

Lung disease characterized by overdistention of the chest and destruction of the walls separating the lung air sacs (alveoli). It results in a reduction of the respiratory surface, chronic shortness of breath, wheezing, and cough.

EPILEPSY

Disease characterized by sudden and brief attacks of convulsions, which are associated with impairment or loss of consciousness, psychic or sensory disturbances, and autonomic nervous system perturbations. Epilepsy causes the EEG to show characteristic brain wave alterations.

F

FURUNCLE (BOIL)

Acute and painful infection of the skin surrounding a hair root. Its center contains pus and dead tissue (core) that has to be discharged either spontaneously or surgically for proper cure.

G

GANGRENE

Localized tissue death, following interruption of the blood supply to the area; gangrene is associated with bacterial infection and putrefaction.

GASTRITIS

Acute or chronic inflammation of the lining of the stomach. It may be caused by the ingestion of alcohol, spices, medicines, chemicals, foods, as well as by infections or allergy.

GASTROSCOPY

Diret visualization of the stomach interior by means of an optical instrument called a gastroscope.

GASTROINTESTINAL SERIES (G.I. SERIES)

Serial X-ray examination of the stomach and intestines to detect, organic or functional alterations, enabling proper diagnosis and treatment of disease.

GLAUCOMA

Eye disease characterized by an increase in its internal pressure, caused by alteration of the intra-ocular fluid flow, and resulting in visual impairment, and if untreated, blindness.

GOITER

Enlargement of the thyroid gland that shows as a well-defined swelling at the base of the neck. Goiter is usually associated with iodine deficiency (endemic goiter), or with excessive secretion of thyroid hormones (exopthalmic goiter).

GOUT

A disturbance of body chemistry, manifested by elevated uric acid blood levels and excessive deposits in tissues, particularly joints and cartilages. It is characterized by repeated attacks of acute and very painful inflammation of joints, especially those of the big toe but also of ankles, knees, wrists, and elbows.

H

HEMATOMA

Swelling produced by a collection of blood escaping from a ruptured blood vessel, resulting from trauma or injury. It is generally located under the skin and subcutaneous tissue, or under the bony structure of the skull.

5

HEMORRHAGE (BLEEDING)

Any copious blood loss from the circulation. If sufficently severe or unchecked, it may lead to anemia or shock.

HEMORRHOIDS (PILES)

Abnormal dilation of the veins of the rectum and anus, causing local swelling, pain, itching, bleeding, and induration.

HEPATITIS

Liver inflammation, caused by infection or toxics. It is characterized by jaundice (yellow coloration of skin and membranes, especially of the eye) and is usually accompanied by fever and other disease manifestations.

HERNIA

Protrusion of a portion of an organ or tissue through an abnormal body opening. Inguinal hernia is one of the most common and consists of an intestinal loop protruding at the groin.

HYPERTENSION

Disease characterized by elevated blood pressure, resulting from the functional or pathological narrowing of the peripheral small arteries. Except in limited instances, its cause is generally unknown.

I

INFARCT

A circumscribed portion of tissue which has suddenly been deprived of its blood supply by embolism or thrombosis and which, as a result, is undergoing death (necrosis), to be replaced by scar tissue.

INFARCTION

The formation of an infarct; an infarct.

INTESTINAL OBSTRUCTION

Blocking of the normal flow of the intestinal contents, caused by twisting of a gut loop, benign tumor, cancer, or foreign body.

INTRADERMAL INJECTION

Injection into the skin proper. It is used less than hypodermic injection, which is done into the loose subcutaneous (under the skin) tissue.

K

KIDNEY FAILURE (RENAL FAILURE)

Severe reduction or impairment of the excretory function of the kidney. The acute form occurs most frequently after crushing injuries, transfusion of mismatched blood, severe burns or shock, generalized infections, obstetric accidents, and certain chemical poisoning.

6

L

LABORATORY PROCEDURES

Laboratory tests performed to assist in disease diagnosis and treatment, Usually these tests are carried out on samples of blood, urine, or other body fluids.

The MOST common are:

Blood Count

Determination of the number and percentage of red and white blood cells from a blood sample that is obtained by puncturing a vein or the skin. It consists of a red blood cell count (RBC), white blood count (WBC), and platelet count.

Blood Grouping

Blood typing for selecting and matching blood transfusion donors and for the diagnosis of various diseases.

Blood Chemistry

Determination of the content of various blood chemicals; the most usual are: sugar, for diabetes; urea nitrogen (BUN), for kidney or liver disease; uric acid, for gout; and cholesterol, for vascular and liver disease.

Blood Culture

Investigation to detect the presence of pathogenic germs by special culturing in artificial media.

Urinalysis (Urine Analysis)

Examination of urine constituents, both normal (urea, uric acid, total nitrogen, ammonia, chlorides, phosphate, and others) and abnormal (albumin, glucose, acetone, bile, blood, cells, and bacteria).

M

MENINGITIS

Inflammation of the enveloping membranes of the brain or spinal cord, caused by virus, bacteria, yeasts, fungi, or protozoa. It is a serious disease and may be a complication of another bodily infection.

METABOLISM

The total of the physical and chemical processes occuring in the living organism by which its substance is produced, maintained, and exchanged with transformation of energy; this energy itself provides fuel for all body functions and heat production.

METASTASIS

Transfer of a disease (usually cancer) from one part of the body to another that is not immediately connected with it.

MULTIPLE SCLEROSIS

A chronic and slowly progressive disease of unknown cause that is characterized by patches of fibrous tissue degeneration in brain and spinal cord, causing various nervous system symptoms; the disease's course is marked by occasional periods of worsening or improvement.

MUSCULAR DYSTROPHY

An inherited disease that involves the progressive weakness and degeneration of voluntary skeletal muscle fibers without nerve involvement.

MYOCARDITIS

Inflammation of the heart muscle that is associated with or caused by a number of infectious diseases, toxic chemicals, drugs and traumatic agents.

MYOCARDIUM

The muscular substance of the heart; adj., myocardial.

N

NEPHRITIS

Inflammatory, acute or chronic disease of the kidneys, which usually follows some form of infection or toxic chemical poisoning. It impairs renal function, causing headache, dropsy, elevated blood pressure, and appearance of albumin in urine.

NEURALGIA

Brief attach of acute and severe shooting pain along the course of one or more peripheral nerves, usually with clear cause.

NEURITIS

Inflammation or degeneration of one or more peripheral nerves, causing pain, tenderness, tingling, sensations, numbness, paralysis, muscle weakness, and wasting and disappearance of reflexes in the area involved. The cause may be infectious, toxic, nutritional (vitamin Bl deficiency), or unknown.

P

PANCREATITIS

Inflammation of the pancreas, either mild or acute, and fulminating. The chronic form is characterized by recurrent attacks of diverse severity. Symptoms are sudden abdominal pain, tenderness and distention, vomiting and, in severe cases, shock and circulatory collapse.

PAP SMEARS (PAPANICOLAU SMEARS)

Method of staining smears of various body secretions -- especially vaginal but also respiratory, digestive, or genitourinary -- to detect cancer by examining the normally shed cells in the smear. The procedure is named for its developer.

PARKINSONISM (PARALYSIS AGITANS)

A usually chronic condition, marked by muscular rigidity, immobile face, excessive salivation, and tremor. These symptoms characterize Parkinson's disease; however, they are also observed in the course of treatment with psycho-pharmaceutical drugs or following encephalitis or trauma.

PELLAGRA

A disease caused by a vitamin (niacin) deficiency and characterized by skin, alimentary tract, and nervous system disturbances.

PERICARDITIS

Acute or chronic inflammation of the pericardium (fibrous sac surrounding the heart), caused by infection, trauma, myocardial infarction, cancer, or complication from other diseases.

PERITONITIS

Acute or chronic inflammation of the serous membrane lining abdominal walls and covering the contained viscerae. Its symptoms are abdominal pain and tenderness, nausea, vomiting, moderate fever, and constipation. It is usually caused by infectious agents or foreign matter entering the abdominal cavity from the intestinal tract (perforation), female genital tract, blood dissemination, or the outside (wounds, surgery).

PERNICIOUS ANEMIA

A chronic anemia, characterized by gastrointestinal and neurological disturbances that usually occur in late adult life and are caused by a deficiency (Biz).

PHLEBITIS

Condition caused by inflammation of a vein wall, resulting in the formation of a blood clot inside its cavity. Phlebitis produces pain, swelling, and stiffness of the affected part, generally a limb.

PLEURISY

Acute or chronic inflammation of the pleura (serous membrane lining the thoracic cavity and lungs). It often accompanies inflammatory lung diseases and may be caused by infection (tuberculous, viral or other), cancer, or cardiac infarction. Symptoms are stabbing pain in the thorax, aggravated by respiratory movements and shortness of breath.

PNEUMONIA

An acute inflammation or infection of the lung, caused by bacteria or virus. Chills, sharp chest pain, shortness of breath, cough, rusty sputum, fever, and headache are primary symptoms.

PNEUMOTHORAX

Accumulation of air or gas in the pleural cavity (between the chest wall and the lung), resulting in lung collapse. It may be spontaneous, following a penetrating chest wound or some diseases, or may be deliberately induced for treatment of lung ailments (tuberculosis).

POLYP

A protruding excrescence or growth from a mucous membrane, usually of the nasal passages but also of the uterine cervix, alimentary tract, or vocal cords.

PSORIASIS

Chronic, occasionally acute, recurrent skin disease of unknown cause, characterized by thickened red skin patches that are covered with whitish shiny scales. Psoriasis usually affects the scalp, elbows, knees, back, and buttocks.

PULMONARY EDEMA

Usually an acute condition in which there is a waterlogging of the lung tissue, including its alveolar cavities. Respiration is impaired. If inadequately treated, it may lead to rapid death; it is often a complication of chronic heart disease.

R

RHEUMATIC FEVER

Disease characterized by initial sore throat, chills, high fever, and painful inflammation of large joints. Frequently cardiac complications follow, leading to permanent organic heart disease.

RICKETS

Generally a disease of infants and young children caused by a vitamin D deficiency. There is defective bone calcification that causes skeletal deformities, such as bow legs, knock knees, and pigeon chest.

S

SCIATICA

A severe pain along the sciatic nerve, which extends from the buttocks along the back of the thigh and leg to the ankle. It is caused by mechanical pressure on the nerve at its spinal origin (from injury, local disease, or tumors).

SCOLIOSIS

A marked lateral curvature of the normally straight vertical spine, which may be caused by disease or mechanical deviation of the bones or muscles of the spine, hips, or legs.

SEPTICEMIA

Presence of bacteria or bacterial toxins in the circulating blood. This condition results from breakdown of local defenses, permitting the spread of a circumscribed infection to the bloodstream and rest of the body.

SILICOSIS

Occupational disease, usually chronic, causing fibrosis of the lungs. It results from inhalation of the dust of stone, flint, or sand that contains silica (quartz). Called "grinders* disease," it is observed in workers who have breathed such dust over a period of five to 25 years.

SLIPPED DISK

An acute or chronic condition, caused by the traumatic or degenerative displacement and protrusion of the softened central core of an intervertebral disk (cartilagenous disk between the spine bones), especially of the lower back. Symptoms are low back pain, which frequently extends to the thigh; muscle spasm; and tenderness.

SPASTIC PARALYSIS (CEREBRAL PALSY)

A condition probably stemming from various causes present since birth. Associated with nonprogressive brain damage, cerebral palsy is characterized by spastic, jerky voluntary movements, or constant involuntary and irregular writhing motion.

STROKE (CEREBRAL APOPLEXY)

A sudden attack of paralysis, with disturbance of speech and thought. It is caused by the destruction of brain substance, as the result of brain hemorrhage, vascular damage, intravascular clotting, or local circulatory insufficiency.

T

THROMBOPHLEBITIS

Condition caused by the inflammation of a vein complicated by the formation of an intravascular blood clot (thrombus). Circulation is obstructed in the affected area, usually the legs.

THROMBOSIS

Formation, development, or presence of a blood clot inside an artery or vein. This condition can be serious, if it affects the blood vessels of vital organs, such as the brain, heart, or lungs.

TUMOR

A swelling or growth of new tissue; it develops independently of surrounding structures and serves no specific function of its own.

U

UREMIA

Toxic clinical condition, caused by renal insufficiency resulting in the retention of urinary waste products in the circulating blood.

URINANALYSIS

See: LABORATORY PROCEDURES

V

VARICOSE VEINS

Abnormally distended and lengthened superficial veins caused by slowing and obstruction of the normal blood backflow. Varicose veins are most commonly observed in the legs, anus and rectum (hemorrhoids), and scrotum (varicocele).

Made in the USA
Coppell, TX
06 March 2021